Bodies/Machines

Bodies/Machines

Edited by
Iwan Rhys Morus

Oxford • New York

First published in 2002 by
Berg
Editorial offices:
150 Cowley Road, Oxford, OX4 1JJ, UK
838 Broadway, Third Floor, New York, NY 10003-4812, USA

Berg is an imprint of Oxford International Publishers Ltd.

Library of Congress Cataloging-in-Publication Data
Bodies/machines / edited by Iwan Rhys Morus.
    p. cm.
Includes bibliographical references and index.
    ISBN 1-85973-690-4 – ISBN 1-85973-695-5
    1. Human-machine systems. 2. Artificial intelligence. 3. Technology–
History. I. Morus, Iwan Rhys, 1964-
    TA166 .B618 2002
    620.8′2—dc21

British Library Cataloguing-in-Publication Data
A catalogue record for this book is available from the British Library.

ISBN 1 85973 690 4 (Cloth)
      1 85973 695 5 (Paper)

Typeset by JS Typesetting Ltd, Wellingborough, Northants.
Printed in the United Kingdom by MPG Books, Cornwall.

Contents

Contents

Illustrations

Contributors

Jon Agar lives and writes in Dalston, London, and has taught at the Centre for History of Science, Technology and Medicine (CHSTM), Manchester University and the Department of Science and Technology Studies, University College London. His books include *Science and Spectacle* (1998), *Turing and the Universal Machine* (2001), and *The Government Machine* (forthcoming).

William J. Ashworth is a lecturer in history at the University of Liverpool. He has recently returned from leave as a senior research fellow at the Dibner Institute and Visiting Scholar in the History of Science Department at Harvard University. Whilst there he completed a book for the Oxford University Press on trade, production and the English customs and excise, 1640–1845.

Graeme Gooday is a senior lecturer in history and philosophy of science in the School of Philosophy, University of Leeds. His main area of specialization is the history of electrical science and technology in the late nineteenth century, and a monograph *The Morals of Measurement: Accuracy, Irony and Trust in Late Victorian Electrical Practice* will soon be published by Cambridge University Press.

Elizabeth Green Musselman is an assistant professor of history at Southwestern University, a liberal arts college in Georgetown, Texas. She recently completed a book manuscript on British natural philosophers' nervous disorders, their contexts and meanings. She is now researching European and African natural knowledge in the Cape Colony, 1652–1910.

Michael Hawkins is a PhD student at the Centre for the History of Science, Technology and Medicine at Imperial College. He is currently finishing his dissertation on Dr Thomas Willis's cerebral anatomy and his physiology of the passions.

Iwan Rhys Morus studied history and philosophy of science at the University of Cambridge. He was a research fellow of Clare Hall, Cambridge, and has held postdoctoral fellowships at Cambridge, the Smithsonian Institution and the University of California, San Diego. He now lectures in History of Science at Queen's University, Belfast. His research mainly focuses on the physical sciences, technology and popular culture in nineteenth-century Britain. His first book, *Frankenstein's Children: Electricity, Exhibition and Experiment in early Nineteenth-Century London* was published by Princeton University Press in 1998. He is presently completing a project, financed by the Wellcome Trust, on electricity and the body in the nineteenth century.

Richard Noakes is the British Academy/Royal Society Postdoctoral Fellow in the History of Science at the Department of History and Philosophy of Science, Cambridge. He has published on Victorian science and spiritualism and was part of the 'Science in the Nineteenth-Century Periodical' project, which is producing an electronic database and scholarly essays on the science, technology, and medicine in over thirty general periodicals published in Britain between 1800 and 1900. He is currently writing a monograph on nineteenth century British scientific investigations into evanescent phenomena.

Acknowledgements

Early versions of some of these chapters were presented at a two-day workshop, 'Bodies/Machines' at the School of Anthropological Studies, Queen's University, Belfast on 10–11 September 1999. The contributors and the editor would like to thank everyone who attended that workshop for their lively contributions. In particular we would like to thank Aileen Fyfe, Rob Iliffe, Simon Schaffer, Crosbie Smith, Steve Sturdy and Christian Talbot for their commentaries and contributions. The workshop was made possible by generous financial assistance from the British Academy, the Wellcome Trust and the School of Anthropological Studies at Queen's. We would like to thank them for their generosity. An earlier version of William Ashworth's chapter also appeared in the *Canadian Journal of History*.[1] I thank David E. Michael for his diligent and helpful copy-editing. Finally, I would like to thank all the editorial staff at Berg Publishers – and particularly Kathryn Earle and Samantha Jackson – for their forebearance during the long process of bringing this book to publication.

Notes

1. William Ashworth, 'England and the Machinery of Reason 1780 to 1830', *Canadian Journal of History*, 2000, 35: 1–36.

–1–

Introduction
Iwan Rhys Morus

We live in an age that is simultaneously fascinated by and terrified of the boundaries surrounding the human body and what happens (or might happen) there. Newspapers are filled with predictions of the promises and perils of genetic engineering. Even respected physicists like Stephen Hawking raise the spectre of machines more intelligent than us taking over from the human race. Cyberneticists predict the increasing breakdown of the distinction between machines and organic beings. One British researcher goes so far as to implant electronic gadgetry in his own body in an effort to demonstrate that the age of the cyborg is literally already here and proposes an 'anti-proliferation treaty' to save us from our own creations.[1] Movies like the *Terminator* series provide us with a graphic illustration of the horrors of intelligent machines. The *Star Trek* TV series gives us both ends of the spectrum, with Data, the hyper-intelligent android, yearning to make himself human in contrast with the swarmlike Borg, half-machine, half-organic and threatening to remake humanity in their own image. Back in the world of non-fiction, functioning electro-mechanical limbs and organs are already a reality. Most contemporary debates around these issues take it for granted that this is a uniquely contemporary matter. *Frankenstein* was fiction, what we face now is the reality. Concerns about understanding (and policing) the boundaries between machines and humans do nevertheless have a long history. Understanding that history seems an important first step towards understanding some of the currents of contemporary debate.

Talk about the possibility of understanding the human body as a complex machine has its origins in the early modern period. The best exemplar is Descartes with his separation of the mechanical body from the disembodied and supervisory soul. Descartes' man-machine was an element in a mechanical universe, with the immaterial soul governing the body's motions just as God governed the mechanism of the Cosmos. It was a philosophy that fitted well, as we shall see later, with a culture that increasingly viewed bodily restraint and self-management as the hallmarks of civility.[2] Following Elias, cultural historians have come to identify this culture of manners as a crucial feature in the emergence of modern sensibilities. Less well recognized, maybe, is early modern culture's fascination with clocks and automatic machinery. Clockwork mechanisms seemed to many in the sixteenth and seventeenth centuries to provide good models not only for the operations of the universe, but for the constitution of society and the actions of human beings too.[3] By the eighteenth century mechanical automata reproducing the movements and behaviour of animals and people were perennial objects of fascination. To many contemporaries they seemed to offer the real possibility of creating artificial life by mechanical means. They provided powerful political ammunition to absolutists and revolutionaries alike.[4]

Understanding the relationship between humans and machines stood at the heart of many Enlightenment projects. D'Alambert's and Diderot's *Encyclopédie* provided exhaustive accounts not only of the latest industrial machinery but of the ways in which the labour surrounding and operating it was organized. It was a given of their version of Enlightened rationality that imposing the disciplined regularity of machines not only on the bodies but also on the individual rationalities of workers was a prerequisite of social order and progress. As Darnton has argued, at the core of the *Encyclopédistes'* grand project was the aim of reorganizing the Tree of Knowledge in terms of new rational and socially pragmatic categories.[5] Enlightened knowledge was meant to be useful knowledge and understanding the relationship between individual human bodies, social order and machinery was supremely useful. This was a lesson learned by, amongst others, Adam Smith in the *Wealth of Nations*. As we shall see, later eighteenth- and early nineteenth-century students of the new factory system found much that they could adapt towards their own local preoccupations in these kinds of grand universalizing systems of ordered rationality. Cultural historians have also found them just as fruitful and suggestive as ways of understanding how the body was imagined within different eighteenth-century social orders. Unsurprisingly, therefore, the Enlightenment theme of machinery as a means of managing bodies runs through all the chapters in this book.

Historians and sociologists of science have approached the question of the boundary between machine and human from a somewhat different perspective. Sociological analyses of scientific practice in the wake of Michael Polanyi's articulation of the notion of tacit knowledge paid particular attention to the instrumentality of the scientist's own body.[6] The scientist's corporeality was regarded as an active participant in the making of knowledge – just like a piece of scientific apparatus. From this perspective the body itself was a scientific instrument, or at least part of a material and instrumental configuration. From a historian's point of view this raises two questions. How has the body been configured historically such that it can be regarded in this way? What has it meant for bodies to be treated instrumentally in this fashion? Cultural historians of science have become increasingly interested in the ways in which practitioners of science have dealt with their own and others' bodies as active elements in the knowledge-making process.[7]

One outcome of this concern has been a focus on the ways in which practitioners have in various ways tried to orient their bodies in relation to machines of various kinds – forcing their bodies to act mechanically; using machine-based surrogates for human senses and behaviours; extolling the body's tacit sensitivities at the expense of instrumental alternatives.[8] Increasingly, cultural historians and sociologists of science have focussed attention on the ways in which practitioners themselves manage the interface between bodies and machines.

The way in which historians of science have focussed attention on the bodily experience of scientific practice has close affinities with recent trends in other areas. Historians of labour have become increasingly concerned to understand the experience of work in constructing individuals' sense of selves and group solidarity. Being in possession of the 'property of skill', as the historian John Rule argues, was a crucial component of eighteenth- and early nineteenth-century artisans' sense of themselves.[9] Similarly, military historians now pay more attention to the experience of warfare, looking at the ways in which frontline soldiers respond bodily and emotionally to the 'face of battle'.[10] What these accounts have in common is the way in which they focus on bodies and bodily interactions with machines and material technologies of various kinds as sites for investigating the construction of cultural values. This is an important and growing area where histories of science and technology can interact fruitfully with other disciplinary perspectives. Schivelbusch has shown how looking at Victorians' bodily experiences of railway travel – a perfect example of novel interaction between bodies and machines – casts new light on their perceptions of their place within natural and social orders.[11] Others have looked at the ways in which mechanization affected individuals' bodily experiences and sense of cultural place in different contexts.[12]

Anthropologists have long been aware of the relationship between social organization and bodily demeanour and description.[13] Human cultures very often look to the body as a resource in trying to make sense of and organize both the natural and social worlds around them. The human body has provided the basis for cosmological models and the resources for social classificatory systems. The body has often been understood as existing simultaneously in the natural and cultural worlds being both innately and irreducibly biological and incorrigibly embedded in culture. This makes the body as machine a particularly interesting cultural artefact. It works both as a way of naturalizing machinery and of denaturalizing human beings. It provides a way of making technological society appear as a natural extension of the human body itself.[14] If there is a close relationship between the ways in which we typically think about our bodies and the ways in which we organize our social structures then the body-machine provides a bridge linking the ways in which we approach both nature and society. Particularly in the context of industrializing Western culture from the beginnings of the modern period there is clearly something significant about the way in which the human body was increasingly visualized and acted upon as if it were a machine.

Elias and others have noted the degree to which modernism coincided with an increasing emphasis on particular bodily disciplines.[15] Marxist historians and sociologists have similarly linked the rise of industrial society to the imposition of new forms of bodily disciplines explicitly enforced by machinery. Marx regarded industrial machinery as the ultimate disciplinary agent, obliging workers to adopt the rhythms and the pace of machinework. Ironically enough it was an analysis that Marx largely borrowed from early nineteenth-century advocates of the factory system. From this perspective, breaking down the distinction between human and machine was an integral part of the development of industrial capitalism. It also underlines how the body as machine has often been regarded as a product of alienation. Forcing labourers to adapt to the disciplines of the machine was a way of alienating them from their own labour and their own bodies.[16] This suggests too that the body as machine has acquired a certain class specificity. Where Elias and others have described the self-disciplined body as a feature of the middle and upper classes, analysts in the Marxist tradition have looked at the body-machine as a product of alienated labour. As we shall see, these kinds of tensions concerning the politics of the machinelike body have a long pedigree.

Both approaches acknowledge the importance of bodily discipline in this context. The machinelike body is usually regarded as a disciplined body, whether that discipline is internally or externally imposed. Given this, Michel Foucault's writings provide an obvious resource for discussions of the cultural and historical ramifications of bodies as machines. His account of the modern body as the product of constant discipline and surveillance dovetails neatly with the image of the man-machine. In *Discipline and Punish*, as in other writings, he articulates how emerging disciplinary regimes were used to inscribe power on the human body. The body according to Foucault was rendered docile and manageable by being re-made as part of all-pervasive networks of power.[17] He emphasizes in particular the crucial important of materiality and spatiality in the disciplinary matrix. Foucaldian bodies are unambiguously real things, acted upon in real space and time.[18] What the contributions to this collection make clear however is the sheer heterogeneity of disciplined machinelike bodies. There was more than just one way of solving the problem of making sense of the social place of the human body like this. What also becomes clear is that human bodies, messy and recalcitrant as they are, were not quite as easily integrated into the frameworks of discipline as Foucault sometimes leads us to believe.

Bodies as machines turn out to have been endlessly malleable products. In different contexts and locations they were continually being formed and reformed. Ranging from seventeenth to mid-twentieth century, this book's contributions look at the ways in which the body-machine was the outcome of particular and local cultural contexts. This has largely been a process of building (or demolishing) and managing boundaries between the mechanical and the organic, between the artificial and the natural, even between the dead and the alive. Treating bodies like machines, or treating machines as animated beings, could be productive of a whole new range of understandings of the cultural place of human beings within industrializing society. In this respect it is not coincidental that most of the chapters in this book focus on the nineteenth century. In many ways, this was a period when interest in understanding the body as a mechanized construct was particularly intense. The focus also reveals the relationship between the body as machine and the commodification of the human body.[19] Machinelike bodies, increasingly, were standardized bodies, treated like other components of mechanical systems. Standardization was a feature of commodification as well. The bodies that late-nineteenth century (and early twenty-first century for that matter) consumers were encouraged to buy for themselves were the products of systems of standardized mass production.[20]

Several of the chapters in this volume focussing on nineteenth-century perspectives pay particular attention to the role played by electricity in understanding the relationship between bodies and machines. Just as early moderns looked towards clockwork, hydraulics and the steam engine as they searched for examples of bodily machinery – and just as we now look to computer hardware and software Victorians looked to new electrical technologies. Marshall McLuhan has identified this juncture with the emergence of a new sense of continuity between inward bodily self and outward technology. As he expressed it: 'all previous technology (save speech, itself) had, in effect, extended some part of our bodies, electricity may be said to have outered the central nervous system itself, including the brain.'[21] This is a perspective with which, as we shall see, many Victorian commentators would have concurred. Analogies between the nervous system and telegraph networks were certainly commonplace. They also used those analogies to make new links between the ways in which minds interacted with bodies and the ways imperial networks of power operated. It is not entirely clear nevertheless whether the emergence of electricity as the dominant model for understanding the relationship between minds, bodies and machines (both material and social) was as unique or decisive a disjuncture as McLuhan suggests.

One of the fundamental preoccupations of early modern natural philosophers was to understand the relationship between mind and body, between soul and matter. As Michael Hawkins suggests in the opening chapter, there was far more to this than making the body mechanical and relegating the soul from the ambit of the new mechanical philosophy. On the contrary, concerns about the operations of the immaterial remained central to the mechanical worldview. The immaterial soul had a physical location within the material body and natural philosophers directed much of their attention towards understanding the complex interplay between immaterial and material.[22] This meant trying to draw careful boundaries between actions and behaviours resulting from the mechanical organization of the body and those emanating from the incorporeal soul. As Hawkins shows, the ambiguities of the early modern mechanical body made it fertile ground for appropriation by a variety of different groups from doctors to theologians. Different ways of drawing the boundaries allowed different groups to claim the body as their own intellectual domain. It is a point repeated elsewhere in the book. Morus and Noakes in their respective chapters pay particular attention to the continually contested nature of the body as machine as well. Hawkins also makes clear the ramifications for early modern commentators of seemingly arcane and technical discussions about the physical organization of the body. Such discussions were arguments about the nature of being human as well.

Ashworth's chapter, taking us to the Industrial Revolution, has similar concerns with the relationships between the technicalities of machine performance and the cultural place of human beings. What he looks at in particular is the ways in which accounts of machines' performance in the late eighteenth and early nineteenth century both informed and was informed by ideas about the operations of human intelligence.[23] As he reminds us, the introduction of new mechanized modes of production from the late eighteenth century onwards went along with an increasingly thoroughgoing reorganization of working practices. This meant redefining the social identity and cultural place of the skilled labourer. Paeans to the machine as the grand agent of economic growth were also often attacks on the 'mysteries' of craft skill and entailed alternative accounts of how human intelligence and skill might best be understood and harnessed. Ashworth shares with Hawkins an emphasis on the way the apparent technicalities of the mechanized body blended easily into issues carrying considerable moral and political weight. Like Green Musselman (and other contributors) he also draws out the increasing importance of machine culture in sustaining regimes of management. Machinelike bodies – or bodies that could be integrated into mechanical systems like the prison treadmill – were conveniently managed and made docile. What he emphasizes however is the way in which these kinds of concerns emerged out of the very particular local culture of (largely English) early nineteenth-century factory management.[24]

Green Musselman also looks to the early nineteenth century as the focus for her account of machines and management. Like Ashworth she emphasizes the role machinery played in schemes of bodily discipline and control during this period. What Green Musselman highlights in particular however is the limitations of such schemes and the explicit recognition of their proponents that ideals of bodily management would inevitably fall short of absolute realization. Indeed it was precisely because human bodies could not be trusted to behave with perfect, predictable regularity that enthusiasts for machinery called for their careful management.[25] Natural philosophers from the late eighteenth century were as concerned to identify the limitations of mechanization for both machines and humans as they were to stretch it to those limits. Like Hawkins, Green Musselman draws our attention to the ways in which the mind figured in regimes of bodily management, keeping the body under control just as mechanical devices like flywheels and governors kept machinery on an even keel.[26] Nineteenth-century commentators appropriated the grey boundary area between machines and humans as the domain of managerial expertise – it was, after all, just because bodies could not be made entirely machinelike that experts managers were needed. This reminds us forcefully of the local class (and gender) identity of the body configured as a machine. Morus, in his contribution, similarly draws attention to the limitations of the machinelike body and the efforts of specialist experts from a variety of domains to present themselves as managers of those limitations.

One of the central concerns of this collection is to explore the variety of ways in which the relationship between humans and machines has been articulated since the early modern period. It also suggests how, in terms of practice at least, distinctions between organic and mechanical representations quickly dissolved.[27] In contexts where bodies might provide models for understanding machinery as easily as machines provided models for understanding bodies, there was little to choose between two seemingly diametrically opposed categories. Morus emphasizes the way in which discussions and practices surrounding bodies and machines in mid-Victorian Britain crossed traditional disciplinary boundaries. Focussing in particular on the uses of electricity, Morus follows the fortunes of different constructions of the body as machine throughout the nineteenth century. He pays particular attention to the performative aspects of the electrical body. The electrical body was put together and made sense of in different ways through a variety of local performances. Just what it meant depended on who performed on and with it, how and where.[28] Noakes makes much the same point with regard to the spiritualist bodies he discusses in his contribution. The local context of performance and the identity of the performer were crucial elements in making sense of the electrical body. Morus draws attention too to the importance of material culture and management in this context. Like Gooday in his contribution he draws attention to the importance of relating the body to its material context to make sense of its cultural significance. According to Morus a key feature of the electrical body throughout the nineteenth century was its heterogeneity. It was precisely this heterogeneity and ambiguity that lent itself so well to a variety of uses. The electrical body was a good site for expressing hopes and fears about nature and culture precisely because of the multiple ways in which it was articulated and represented.[29]

Noakes's contribution likewise emphasizes the ways in which the human body provided a focus for Victorian debates about the possibilities, limitations and cultural place of science. As he shows, disputes between spiritualists and natural philosophical sympathizers and antagonists were disputes about how human bodies could be expected to act as much as they were disagreements about the reality of spiritualist phenomena. On Noakes's reading, completely opposed accounts of how the body performed under different circumstances – in other words, of what kind of thing the human body actually was – were at stake in the various protagonists' positions regarding the reality or otherwise of spiritualist phenomena. He emphasizes the importance of different bodily performances in establishing the ontological status of spiritualism.[30] In this respect he shares the same perspective as Gooday and Morus, who similarly emphasize the importance of bodily performances with respect to the body's place in material culture. As with Morus's discussion of the electrical body, Noakes emphasizes the heterogeneity of the spiritualist body as it and its performances were appropriated and reappropriated in a variety of contexts. He draws our attention to the ways in which his actors' constructions of the body as machine transgress what might be regarded as conventional disciplinary boundaries.

Gooday in his contribution draws our attention to the dynamic interface between machines and humans. In particular he looks at the ways in which human bodies need to be orchestrated in order to be accommodated into the process. Looking at the seemingly mundane and unproblematic process of observation he shows just how much effort is required to make such a process reliably secure. He shares with Green Musselman the perception that dealing with this interface between machine and human has typically been recognized by the actors themselves as something requiring careful management. As Gooday points out, a process like 'reading' an instrument has typically been regarded as a comparatively straightforward matter. In contrast to traditional accounts he points out that what goes on in the encounter between instruments and their readers is a thoroughgoingly bodily and cultural process rather than simply a mental process. Gooday draws attention to the ways in which nineteenth-century physicists and engineers themselves were aware of the bodily requirements of instrumental reading. There were good and bad instrument readers and such people could be produced by careful training regimes designed to inculcate the appropriate bodily gestures and postures.[31] Like Agar and others he points to the class and gender dimension of the body-machine matrix in this context as well. Particular kinds of bodies might turn out to be just better readers of instruments than others.

Agar's chapter surveys some of the ways in which articulations of the body as a machine could be used from the mid-nineteenth century onwards – and particularly during the first half of the twentieth century – to portray and propagandize for particular kinds of relationship between the individual and society.[32] Focussing on the activities of the middle-class and professional promoters of the Anti-Noise League from the mid-1930s he shows how their campaigns for noise abatement casts new light on such groups' concerns about industrialization, secularization and their bodily impacts. Agar charts efforts from the nineteenth century onwards to articulate the impact of industrial culture on human bodies. The Anti-Noise League's promoters were in some cases quite explicit that the problem of noise was a problem of social class as well, just as Charles Babbage in the previous century had regarded himself as hounded by working-class street musicians. They linked noise with crime, danger and the proletariat. Silence was a mark of civility. Like Green Musselman and Morus, Agar portrays his protagonists as experts aiming to establish themselves as managers able to contain the problems of bodily indiscipline. As he points out, one way of combating the noise produced by technological society was by bringing in more technology. Managing the interface between frail human bodies and all-pervasive industrial culture could itself be constructed as a problem needing a technological fix.

One of the most striking themes running through this book is that of management. From the early modern period onwards natural philosophers, doctors and other commentators concerned themselves with the problem of managing the body. This was clearly one reason why talk of bodies as machines seemed so attractive. Machines – so long as they were working properly – exhibited regularity. If Elias is right in suggesting that manners and bodily restraint were increasingly coming to be considered as the hallmarks of civility, then machines could well appear to be the epitomé of civilized behaviour. They acted as they were expected to act. Many Victorians certainly regarded machines as models of gentlemanly decorum – think of Phineas Fogg's clockwork regularity simultaneously admired and lampooned by Jules Verne.[33] At the same time machines seemed to promise an useful means of making sure that those apparently incapable of self-restraint like women and the working classes, had restraint thrust upon them.[34] In the practice of natural philosophy as well the ordered and predictable regularity promised by machinery seemed a good way of doing away with the vagaries of merely human observers. Treating bodies like machines, carefully redefining the boundaries separating humans from their artefacts and finding new ways of fitting human bodies into machine culture has turned out to be a promising strategy for maintaining political order, sustaining social boundaries and establishing managerial expertise. One lesson that this book suggests is that understanding such strategies means paying careful attention to particular experiences and particular local contexts.

What this book also points out however is that the strategy has rarely, if ever, been entirely successful. As Foucault acknowledges, there is always something beyond the Panopticon.[35] In the same way there always seems to be something beyond the body as machine. As nineteenth-century factory managers and political economists tried to impose machine disciplines on workers, or as proponents of scientific medicine tried to persuade doctors to depend on instruments rather than their own senses they met resistance from those who insisted that there was something ineffable about human capacity that eluded reduction to machinery. Michael Polanyi's analysis of tacit knowledge that drew many historians and sociologists of science to consider the boundary area between bodies and machines was itself an argument in favour of the notion that some level of knowledge and skill was simply irreducible to machinery.[36] Interestingly, however, the argument has often been made by way of defending the legitimacy of autonomous expertise, of demarcating certain areas of human activity from others. What this book suggests is that looking historically at the boundaries between machines and humans, at the variety of ways in which such boundaries have been constructed, managed, re-evaluated, resisted and sustained, we can learn a great deal not only about how and why that boundary has been continually refashioned in the past, but about why it remains such a focus for hopes and fears today.

Notes

1. K. Warwick, *In the Mind of the Machine* (London: Arrow Books, 1998).
2. P. Dear, 'A Mechanical Microcosm: Bodily Passions, Good Manners, and Cartesian Mechanism', C. Lawrence and S. Shapin (eds), *Science Incarnate: Historical Embodiments of Natural Knowledge* (Chicago IL: University of Chicago Press, 1998), pp. 51–82.
3. N. Elias, *The Civilizing Process* trans. E. Jephcott, 2 vols (Oxford: Blackwell, 1986); Otto Mayr, *Authority, Liberty and Automatic Machinery in Early Modern Europe* (Baltimore MD: Johns Hopkins University Press, 1986).
4. S. Schaffer, 'Enlightened Automata', W. Clark, J. Golinski and S. Schaffer (eds), *The Sciences in Enlightened Europe* (Chicago IL: University of Chicago Press, 1999), pp. 126–65; J.-C. Beaune, 'The Classical Age of Automata: An Impressionistic Survey from the Sixteenth to the Nineteenth Century', M. Feher, R. Naddaff and N. Tazi (eds), *Fragments for a History of the Human Body, Part One* (New York NY: Urzone Inc, 1989); A. Chapuis and E. Droz, *Automata: A Historical and Technological Study* (Neuchâtel: Éditions du Griffon, 1958).
5. R. Darnton, 'Philosophers Trim the Tree of Knowledge: The Epistemological Strategy of the *Encyclopédie*', *The Great Cat Massacre and other Episodes in French Cultural History* (Harmondsworth: Penguin, 1984), pp. 185–207.
6. M. Polanyi, *Personal Knowledge* (Chicago IL: University of Chicago Press, 1958).
7. A key collection in this respect is Lawrence and Shapin, *Science Incarnate*.

8. S. Schaffer, 'Experimenters' Techniques, Dyers' Hands and the Electric Planetarium', *Isis*, 1997, 88: 456–83; S. Schaffer, 'Astronomers Mark Time: Discipline and the Personal Equation', *Science in Context*, 1988, 2: 115–45; I. R. Morus, 'Different Experimental Lives: Michael Faraday and William Sturgeon', *History of Science*, 1992, 30: 1–28; H. O. Sibum, 'Reworking the Mechanical Equivalent of Heat: Instruments of Precision and Gestures of Accuracy in early Victorian England', *Studies in History and Philosophy of Science*,1995, 26: 73–106; C. Lawrence, 'Incommunicable Knowledge: Science, Technology and the Clinical Art in Britain 1850–1914', *Journal of Contemporary History*, 1985, 20: 503–20.

9. J. Rule, 'The Property of Skill in the Period of Manufacture', P. Joyce (ed.), *The Historical Meanings of Work* (Cambridge: Cambridge University Press, 1987), pp. 99–118.

10. J. Keegan, *The Face of Battle* (London: Pimlico, 1991).

11. W. Schivelbusch, *The Railway Journey: The Industrialization of Time and Space in the Nineteenth Century* (Berkeley and Los Angeles CA: University of California Press, 1986).

12. A. Rabinbach, *The Human Motor: Energy, Fatigue and the Origins of Modernity* (Berkeley and Los Angeles CA: University of California Press, 1992); D. Mindell, *War, Technology and Experience aboard the USS Monitor* (Baltimore MD: Johns Hopkins University Press, 2000).

13. M. Douglas, *Natural Symbols: Explorations in Cosmology* (London: Cresset Press, 1970).

14. M. Heidegger, *The Question Concerning Technology* (London: HarperCollins, 1977).

15. Elias, *Civilizing Process*.

16. H. Braverman, *Labor and Monopoly Capital: The Degradation of Work in the Twentieth Century* (New York NY: Monthly Review Press, 1974).

17. M. Foucault, *Discipline and Punish: The Birth of the Prison* (Harmondsworth: Penguin Books, 1977).

18. F. Driver, 'Bodies in Space: Foucault's Account of Disciplinary Power', C. Jones and R. Porter (eds), *Reassessing Foucault: Power, Medicine and the Body* (London: Routledge, 1994), pp. 113–31.

19. M. Featherstone, 'The Body in Consumer Culture', M. Featherstone, M. Hepworth and B. S. Turner (eds), *The Body: Social Process and Cultural Theory* (London: Sage Publications, 1991), pp. 170–96.

20. D. Porter, *Health, Civilization and the State* (London: Routledge, 1999), pp. 281–313.

21. M. McLuhan, *Understanding Media: The Extensions of Man* (New York NY: McGraw Hill, 1964), p. 247.

22. See for example S. Shapin, 'Descartes the Doctor: Rationalism and its Therapies', *British Journal for the History of Science*, 2000, 33: 131–54; Dear, 'Mechanical Microcosm.'

23. See also W. Ashworth, 'Memory, Efficiency and Symbolic Analysis: Charles Babbage, John Herschel and the Industrial Mind', *Isis*, 1996, 87: 629–53; W. Ashworth, 'The Calculating Eye: Baily, Herschel, Babbage and the Business of Astronomy', *British Journal for the History of Science*, 1994, 27: 409–41; E. P. Thompson, 'Time, Work-discipline and Industrial Capitalism', *Customs in Common* (Harmondsworth: Penguin, 1993), pp. 352–403.

24. S. Schaffer, 'Babbage's Dancer and the Impresarios of Mechanism', F. Spufford and J. Uglow (eds), *Cultural Babbage: Technology, Time and Invention* (London: Faber and Faber, 1996), pp. 53–80; S. Schaffer, 'Babbage's Intelligence: Calculating Engines and the Factory System', *Critical Inquiry*, 1994, 21: 203–27; M. Berg, *The Machinery Question and the Making of Political Economy* (Cambridge: Cambridge University Press, 1980).

25. R. Benschop and D. Draaisma, 'In Pursuit of Precision: The Calibration of Minds and Machines in Late Nineteenth-century Psychology', *Annals of Science*, 2000, 57: 1–25; S. de Chadarevian, 'Graphical Method and Discipline: Self-recording Instruments in Nineteenth-century Physiology', *Studies in History and Philosophy of Science*, 1993, 24: 267–91; S. Schaffer, 'Astronomers Mark Time: Discipline and the Personal Equation', *Science in Context*, 1988, 2: 115–45.

26. See also A. Winter, *Mesmerized: Powers of Mind in Victorian Britain* (Chicago IL: University of Chicago Press, 1998).

27. T. Lenoir, *The Strategy of Life: Teleology and Mechanics in Nineteenth Century German Biology* (Dordrecht: Reidel, 1982); T. Lenoir, 'Models and Instruments in the Development of Electrophysiology', *Historical Studies in the Physical Sciences*, 1986, 17: 1–54.

28. I. R. Morus, *Frankenstein's Children: Electricity, Exhibition and Experiment in Early Nineteenth-century London* (Princeton NJ: Princeton University Press, 1998).

29. C. Marvin, *When Old Technologies were New: Thinking about Electrical Communication in the Late Nineteenth Century* (Oxford: Oxford University Press, 1988).

30. A. Owen, *The Darkened Room: Women, Power and Spiritualism in Late Victorian England* (London: Virago, 1989); J. Oppenheim, *The Other World: Spiritualism and Psychical Research in England, 1850–1914* (Cambridge: Cambridge University Press, 1985); R. Noakes, 'Telegraphy is an Occult Art: Cromwell Fleetwood Varley and the Diffusion of Electricity to the Other World', *British Journal for the History of Science*, 1999, 32: 421–59.

31. For physics, bodies and precision see G. Gooday, 'The Morals of Energy Metering: Constructing and Deconstructing the Precision of the Victorian Electrical Engineer's Ammeter', M. N. Wise (ed.), *The Values of Precision* (Princeton NJ: Princeton University Press, 1995), pp. 239–82; G. Gooday, 'Teaching Telegraphy and Electrotechnics in the Physics Laboratory: William Ayrton and the Creation of an Academic Space for Electrical Engineering, 1873–84', *History of Technology*, 1991, 13: 73–111; S. Schaffer, 'Accurate Measurement is an English Science', Wise (ed.), *Values*, pp. 135–72; S. Schaffer, 'A Manufactory of Ohms: Late Victorian Metrology and its Instrumentation', R. Bud and S. Cozzens (eds), *Invisible Connections* (Bellingham: SPIE Optical Engineering Press, 1992), pp. 23–56; B. Hunt, 'The Ohm is where the Art is: British Telegraph Engineers and the Development of Electrical Standards', *Osiris*, 1993, 9: 48–63.
32. For the earlier period see Rabinbach, *The Human Motor*.
33. J. Verne, *Around the World in Eighty Days* (Harmondsworth: Penguin Books, 1996), first published 1873.
34. On the management of women's bodies see amongst others J. Oppenheim, *Shattered Nerves: Doctors, Patients and Depression in Victorian England* (Oxford: Oxford University Press, 1991); C. E. Russett, *Sexual Science: The Victorian Construction of Womanhood* (Cambridge MA: Harvard University Press, 1989), E. Showalter, *The Female Malady: Women, Madness and English Culture, 1830–1980* (London: Virago, 1987).
35. M. Foucault, 'La Poussière et la Nuage', M. Perrot (ed.), *L'impossible Prison* (Paris: Seuil, 1980), pp. 29–39, discussed in Driver, 'Bodies in Space', p. 121.
36. H. Collins, *Artificial Experts: Social Knowledge and Intelligent Machines* (Cambridge MA: MIT Press, 1990). More generally D. Bloor, *Wittgenstein: A Social Theory of Knowledge* (London: Macmillan, 1983).

'A Great and Difficult Thing': Understanding and Explaining the Human Machine in Restoration England

Michael Hawkins

One of the perennial topics concerning early modern conceptions of bodies and machines is the relationship between the mind and body. Historians have long focussed their attentions on explaining early modern understandings of their relations, in particular, exploring how the rise of mechanical philosophies during the latter half of the seventeenth century posed challenges for understanding the 'wiring' of an incorporeal immortal soul to a body that was increasingly depicted as a complex physical machine. These new philosophies may have explained all natural phenomena according to the motions of small particles of matter, but they did not eschew consideration of incorporeal substances. On the contrary, non-mechanical phenomena remained central concerns in the new mechanical philosophy.[1] The explication of physiological phenomena according to mechanical causes and operations did not remove the soul from its place of prominence within the human body; it only cast doubt on its precise role and location. The immortal soul was simply relocated as the mechanical actions of the body were granted increasing responsibility for operation of the physiological functions of animate life. Early modern philosophers and physicians faced the challenge of finding a place for the incorporeal soul within the changing physical landscape of the bodily machine.

René Descartes provided, in his *Treatise on Man*, what is now perhaps the most familiar account of the challenges associated with explaining the relations between the body and soul and his formulation of the problems has served as the starting point for most historical inquiries. The bodies of humans and brutes according to Descartes were complex machines whose many actions and physiological functions were caused by the mechanical motions of their parts following 'from the mere arrangement of the machine's organs every bit as naturally as the movements of a clock or other automaton follow from the arrangement of its counter-weights and wheels.'[2] Having only a corporeal existence, brute animals were just complex physical automata driven by the mechanical force of their passions. Humans, however, had both a corporeal and incorporeal existence. They had an incorporeal soul lodged within the body that was believed responsible for all acts of reason and that acted as the 'fountain keeper' directing mechanical forces according to its own dictates. Humans, therefore, were driven both by physical bodily forces and the incorporeal inclinations of their immortal soul. The body and soul are treated in Descartes' account as though they were two divinely created, yet contrarily inclined, contrivances. The body was a physical machine that generated the physiological processes of animate life and drove creatures towards the furtherance of their bodily needs. The incorporeal soul was a spiritual engine that generated reason and understanding impelling humans towards the aspirations of religion and morality over the lusts of the flesh. Historians' accounts have typically revolved around attempts to reconcile the seemingly contrary aims and functions of immaterial soul with those of the bodily machine.

This conception of the relationship between the body and soul obscures more than it reveals because it fails to take into account early modern conceptions of what it meant to be human. Being human was not believed to be dependent solely on any one specific aspect of human existence. It was not simply a matter of having an immortal rational soul nor was it having this incorporeal noble essence housed within a corruptible mechanical body. God had purposefully created humans as a synthesis of flesh and spirit; being human entailed being a union of base physical and divine incorporeal matter. Humans were complex corporo-spiritual contrivances; the body and soul were just their principal parts. Understanding early modern conceptions of their relations fully requires an appreciation of how, working in unison, they created all the functions and properties of human life.

When explaining the relations between the body and soul, early modern physicians, philosophers, theologians and moralists typically focussed their attentions on explaining the grey area where they seemingly overlapped and where their distinctions were least obvious. Their explanations typically revolved around the actions and significance of the passions. Early modern understandings of the word 'passion' bear little resemblance to modern conceptions. Broadly speaking, they referred to emotions and desires but their actions, influence and purposes were markedly different from modern notions. The passions were physical not mental phenomena. They were not impulses or feelings arising from the mind but the uncontrollable effects of bodily states that were experienced both in body and mind. They were an essential element of animate life common to both humans and animals. Though not *morally* good, the passions were innately beneficial to individual creatures because they urged the creature to the furtherance of its own condition by driving the instinctual desires for the four 'F's' (fighting, fleeing, feeding and reproduction).[3] The passions had a moral significance for humans. The passions were the only things that drove the brute animals, but humans had an incorporeal soul that was capable of directing them towards the higher aspirations of reason and of resisting the passions of their terrestrial flesh. The struggles between reason and the passions informed understandings of human behaviour explaining how and why humans' inclination to consider God's will and follow His precepts was so often defeated by the desires of their flesh and senses. In humans, therefore, the passions were both the driving forces behind both moral failings and the physiological functions of animate life.

Explaining the actions, operations and significance of the passions was fraught with difficulties during the early modern period. The passions had a multifaceted and nebulous existence as medical, physiological and moral phenomena. No single community of specialists held a monopoly on explicating them and knowledge of their actions touched on matters of natural philosophical, medical, theological, political and moral significance. Physicians, natural philosophers, priests and moral philosophers, could all boast specialized knowledge and expertise and they were not afraid to assert their rights. As Thomas Wright noted

> there be few estates or conditions of men, that haue not interest in the matter: the Diuine, the Philosopher, the curers of body and soule, I meane the Preacher & Physitian, the good Christian . . . & the prudent ciuill Gentleman . . . may reape some commodity touching their professions . . .[4]

Individuals' beliefs were often quite idiosyncratic and the distinctions between philosophical, medical and theological inquiries could be as flexible or rigid as one wanted. Dr Thomas Willis had good reason to begin his study of the physiology of the passions and the animal soul by noting that 'as many men there are, so many different opinions are produced.'[5] The intellectual and professional boundaries were subject to constant negotiation as individuals synthesized, reinterpreted and redefined the resources available to suit their own particular needs and contexts. Theology, moral philosophy and even personal experience contributed as much to individuals' understandings as natural philosophy and medicine.[6]

Not surprisingly, scholars found it difficult to map the functions of the passions onto the corporeal and incorporeal aspects of human existence and they had trouble determining exactly *where* the interconnected actions of the spiritual motions of the passions in the incorporeal soul ended and their mechanical actions within the corporeal body began. These difficulties were made all the more challenging because how one chose to map the passions had significant implications concerning conceptions of the nature of human and animal life. For example, if one granted too many of their functions to the incorporeal soul, it became difficult to explain their actions in brute animals because they were believed to lack such a soul. On the other hand, relegating their functions completely to the physical body was believed to denigrate the importance of the incorporeal soul and perhaps even to cast doubt on its immateriality or existence. Mappings of the passions also had ramifications for understandings of human behaviour and morality. For example, to what degree were moral failings to be attributed to the physical motions of the passions and to what extent were they to be considered the product of the faulty choices made by fallen man's deformed will? Were moral failings caused primarily by the irresistible physiological forces the passions exerted or were they caused by the misuse of reason? Theories of the passions had to provide the ability to understand both how the passions impelled individual creatures towards the fulfilment of their instinctual desires while also explaining how humans, the only creatures endowed with an incorporeal soul capable of directing them towards the aspirations of reason and morality, were so often inclined to follow the baser desires of their flesh just like brute animals. They had to explain simultaneously humans – corporo-spiritual contrivances – and animals – purely physical machines. They had to mark out a space and a role for the immortal soul within the human body while simultaneously providing the ability to understand and explain the functions of animate life without reference to it. Knowledge of the passions, therefore, was as much about ethics and morality as natural philosophy and medicine.

This chapter examines how two Restoration English physicians and natural philosophers understood and explained the operations of the passions. The differences between Thomas Willis and Walter Charleton's accounts provide a lens through which we can understand and explain the interconnected and often opaque boundaries between medical, natural philosophical, theological and ethical concerns. Although their dispute seemed to revolve around technical physiological and anatomical details concerning the structures of the brain and nerves, it had less to do with matters of physiology and anatomy than it did with their more generalized conceptions of the nature of human existence and the degree to which they believed individuals were able to govern and moderate their own behaviour. It was not simply that Willis and Charleton disagreed as to how and where the different capabilities of human beings were to be mapped onto the physical structures of the brain, but rather that they disagreed as to what those capabilities were and how they were to be best explained and understood. Underlying their dispute were fundamental differences concerning the degree to which the passions were to be best understood as physical or mental conditions and about where the line between ethics and medicine was to be best drawn. These conceptions informed their understandings of the degree to which they believed the excesses of human behaviour could be examined anatomically, explained physiologically and treated medically and about the extent to which individuals could be trusted to moderate their own passions. Willis believed the passions were primarily physical phenomena and his physiology stressed the physical forces they exerted within the body. Physic and the ministrations of a learned physician were, for

Willis, the best remedies for the problems they caused. Charleton, on the other hand, believed that the passions were to be best understood as diseases of the mind. His account stressed their ethical elements arguing that introspection and self-examination provided the surest ways to counter their influence. Each of their accounts reflected and promoted beliefs about the ways in which society and the people in it were to be best ordered. As we shall see, understanding the actions of the passions and the knitting together of the incorporeal soul and the bodily machine required coming to terms with the nature of human existence in the terrestrial world as both a corporo-spiritual contrivance and a social creature. Beliefs about the ordering of the body politic were built into their accounts about the body.

Willis's cerebral physiology emphasized the fragility of the rule of reason within the human body. His physiology stressed the importance of a highly rarefied and volatile substance distilled from the blood flowing through the minute blood vessels in the brain called animal spirits. They served many crucial functions within the animal oeconomy. The animal spirits distributed in the nerves were the chief means of communication within the body. They carried impressions from the sense organs to the brain and also transmitted the voluntary and involuntary forces of the sensitive functions between the body and the brain. They were also the actuating forces behind most vital physiological functions, such as nutrition and muscular motion. When the highly volatile spirituous particles contained within the animal spirits in the nerves interacted with the saline and sulphurous particles in the solid parts of the body, their naturally impetuous motions excited and drove the other kinds of particles to perform their own natural actions thereby causing the physical motions and chemical processes underling most physiological functions. Their motions and actions within the solid parts of the brain were also responsible for all the sensitive acts common to humans and the brutes, like memory, apprehension, imagination, sensation and appetite.

Unlike traditional accounts that portrayed the brain as a pump with the ventricles filling up and pumping spirituous liquor throughout the body, Willis emphasized the actions and motions of the animal spirits within the solid parts of the brain. He argued that the actions of the higher functions (imagination, memory and appetite) were dependent on the motions of the spirits in the *cerebrum* whereas the natural functions (the passions, sense and involuntary motion) depended primarily on their motions in the *cerebellum* and the *medulla oblongata*. It is easiest to explain Willis's cerebral physiology by providing an account of what he believed happened upon hearing a sound from behind. Animal spirits carrying the auditory impressions first came to the *protuberantia annularis* where their force and quantity were magnified by the addition of the spirits already present there before being dispatched to the *cerebellum*. Their motions in the *cerebellum* caused a rudimentary form of 'natural memory' that triggered involuntary physiological responses (like, the pricking of the ears to locate the origin of the sound). Some spirits were then diverted to the *medulla oblongata* for distribution throughout the body in the nerves to enact these responses. Others were dispatched to the *cerebrum* where their motions caused the acts of sensation, memory, imagination and appetite whereby awareness of the act of sensation takes place, the sensory data are remembered and compared with existing memories, its potential benefits and dangers are rudimentarily assessed by the imagination and finally desire or aversion to the object would be stirred in the appetite. The results of these motions were then transmitted back to the body through the *medulla oblongata* and nerves for the enactment of whatever physical acts seemed appropriate (perhaps turning around to see from where and from what the noise is coming). While this was the end of the process in brute animals, the spirits performed further actions in humans. The animal spirits were communicated through some unknown mechanism deep within the *cerebrum* to the rational soul where judgement and understanding took place and from whence spirits (now carrying the dictates of reason) would be distributed back outwards through the *cerebrum* to the nerves for physical enactment. The motions of the animal spirits within the brain either caused or facilitated both the sensitive functions common to man and the brutes and the rational functions unique to humans in the terrestrial world. The animal spirits, therefore, carried the forces of both reason and the passions.[7]

Willis contended that humans had the greatest need for an abundant supply of animal spirits compared to any of the brutes. Composed of both corporeal and incorporeal matter, human beings were the most complicated of God's terrestrial creations; they were capable of a greater variety and complexity of action than any other terrestrial creature. Animal spirits were the central driving force behind the functioning of the corporo-spiritual human contrivance that enabled or facilitated the functioning of all vital, sensitive and rational acts. Their supply, however, was variable and any deficiency in the concoction of nutriment, the circulation of the blood or in their extraction and purification could result in a shortage of spirits. Willis believed, therefore, that there needed to be a repository within the human brain to ensure that animal spirits would always be in ready supply. He located this repository in the *protuberantia annularis* because it was centrally located within the brain between the *cerebrum* and *cerebellum* nearby the origins of many of the sensory and pathetic nerves. It was, therefore, in a position to augment the supply of spirits within the brain quickly in the event of any shortage. Additionally, as Willis noted, the *protuberantia annularis* was larger in humans than in the other brutes which, he argued, provided anatomical proof of the function he had ascribed to it and of humans' greater abilities and need for animal spirits. The *protuberantia annularis*, he concluded, contained a ready supply of spirits to be dispatched to augment any deficiency of animal spirits in the brain thereby ensuring the continual functioning of the animal oeconomy.

Animal spirit, however, was a dangerous and volatile substance that could not be easily controlled. By concentrating them into such a centrally located structure as the *protuberantia annularis*, Willis had placed a potentially explosive magazine within the brain. A strong sensory experience or an immoderate influx of blood into the brain could easily disrupt the spirits' delicate tranquillity by introducing excited spirits into the *protuberantia annularis*, causing those already present to rush impetuously into the *cerebrum* and *cerebellum*. There they agitated more spirits and enkindled the passions, which, in turn, disrupted the flow of the blood and animal spirits in the animal oeconomy thereby introducing more excited spirits to the brain. If this process went unchecked, unruly spirits would overwhelm the brain, perhaps overthrowing the rule of reason in favour of the passions of the flesh and senses. According to Willis, the abundance of animal spirits needed to maintain human life made humans – the noblest of God's creatures in the terrestrial realm and the only ones endowed with incorporeal souls and, therefore, the only ones capable of reason and with the ability to restrain their passions – also the most passionate of His creations.

Although Charleton questioned some of Willis's claims, he did not seek to supplant Willis's cerebral physiology with one of his own. On the contrary, he generally accepted Willis's account apart from having a few reservations concerning the functions attributed to certain anatomical structures. He argued, for example, that the *protuberantia annularis* was not a storage house of spirits intended to augment the operations of the brain but rather that it was a filter that calmed the spirits conveying auditory sensations before entering the brain. The specific details of his anatomical objections, however, are of secondary importance as far as this chapter is concerned as his primary concern with Willis's physiology was the presupposition that humans were the most passionate creatures in God's creation. Charleton believed that the veracity of much of Willis's account depended upon this presumption. Not discounting the possibility, he nevertheless argued that it was unwise to construct an entire physiology based upon this presupposition because 'it was no small rashness to consign to any part of the Brain such an office and use as absolute presupposeth it.'[8]

The differences between Willis and Charleton's accounts primarily reflected their differing conceptions of the causes of the passions and of the potential for human beings to behave passionately. Willis believed the passions were best understood as physical rather than mental conditions. To him, humans were a powder keg of explosive spirits and passions ready to explode outwards at the slightest notice. Charleton, on the other hand, believed the passions could be best understood as diseases of the mind. Humans were not passionate because of the physiological power of animal spirits, they were passionate because they had misused their reason: 'When therefore we fall into Errors, occasioned by our Passions; the defect lieth in our own act, or in the use of our *liberty*, not in our nature.'[9]

Willis's account emphasized the physical aspects of the passions and the powerful physiological forces they exerted within the animal oeconomy more than their hidden actions within the incorporeal soul. He stressed the instability of animal spirits within the animal oeconomy. Constant vigilance and moderation were needed to prevent the spirits in the *protuberantia annularis* from exploding outwards and enkindling the passions. However, there was more to the promotion of mental, physical and moral health according to Willis's scheme than simply preventing the explosion of spirits within the brain. Animal spirits forged physical pathways through the solid structures of the brain when performing the functions of the sensitive and rational acts. Once these pathways were established, they were more likely to receive the further traffic of spirits; the more travelled the path, the larger it became and the more likely it would be travelled in the future. One moral failing or passionate act would, therefore, invariably lead to other more powerful ones as the flow of animal spirits associated with them quickly changed from being a small meandering creek to a raging river. According to Willis's physiology, the problem was not just that the animal spirit was a volatile and dangerous substance, but also that the structure of the brain was inclined to magnify their power especially if it had been conquered.

It can never be known for certain why Willis believed humans to be so passionate but it seems probable that his experiences in Oxford during the Civil Wars and Interregnum informed his conceptions of human behaviour and the ability of individuals to moderate its excesses. Willis lived most of his life in or around the university. He was educated in Christ Church (BA 1639, MA 1642) and his family home was located a couple of miles outside the university. Oxford University played a major role in the civil wars. It had served as the Royalist headquarters until 1646 and numerous battles were fought nearby. The events of that time demonstrated to Willis just how dangerously passionate humans could become. Immoderate and excessive behaviour had brought about the civil wars and the destruction of the established Church as well as the executions of a king and his archbishop.

For Willis, a staunch supporter of the established Church and royal cause, the late 1640s and early 1650s were a time of destruction and chaos in which he had seen *his* world forcibly destroyed and torn apart. On a more personal level, his parents had died in 1643 of the same epidemic fever that ravaged the royalist and parliamentary forces in the area and his family home had been subject to frequent parliamentary raids.[10] The social landscape of the university had also changed considerably with the defeat of the royalist cause and, with the expulsion of his old friends and patrons, like Henry Hammond, Gilbert Sheldon, John Fell and Richard Allestree, Willis found himself isolated from the 'official' academic and social life of the university. Willis found it difficult to adapt to the new social and political realities and he actively resisted these changes. He was one of a number of individuals in Oxford who tried to maintain the rites and ceremonies of the old Caroline church. Services were held according to the 'outlawed' Book of Common Prayer in his rooms opposite Merton College where, as Leoline Jenkins later recalled: 'the Church may be said to have retired . . . there with such Circumstances of Primitive Devotion and Solemnity as was hardly to be parallel'd otherwhere during the Storm of that Persecution.'[11]

Willis faced the challenges associated with having to forge new patronage relations to advance his career. Although he initially lacked the relations required to improve his standing within the local philosophical and medical community, he quickly found that his chemical, medical, and natural philosophical skills brought him to the attention of influential new members of the Oxford community, such as William Petty, John Wilkins and Robert Boyle. Willis capitalized on these skills and by 1656, he had established a significant reputation for himself as a chemist, physician and philosopher. He was acknowledged by Samuel Hartlib to be 'a leading and prime man in the Philosophical Club at Oxford.'[12] Willis's fortunes improved greatly with the Restoration of Charles II to the throne in 1660. He was granted his doctorate in medicine and made Sedleian Professor of Natural Philosophy largely through the influence of his old friend and patron, Gilbert Sheldon, then Bishop of London but soon to be Archbishop of Canterbury. He also went on to become the pre-eminent physician of his time establishing a thriving practice first in Oxford and later in London.

The restoration of the Crown and Church, however, did little to assuage the fears that Willis and his friends had about a return of the madness of the previous decades. Society seemed to be teetering on the brink of chaos just as it had two decades earlier. As Allestree noted '[we] are still as full of the same animosities as ever, and want nothing but opportunity to confound all again, *Religion* and *our selves*'.[13] For men like Sheldon, Allestree, Fell and Willis, lasting social order was predicated on unanimity of religious belief and worship and the acceptance of the undisputed authority of the episcopal Church. To them the newly restored Church seemed under attack from all sides. It was menaced by external threats like religious non-conformity and enthusiasm while simultaneously being eroded from the inside by the King's promises of indulgence and toleration to non-conformists.[14] Willis believed that civil society was on the brink of chaos as madness drove individuals from 'the union of saints and the society of men.'[15] He later conjectured that if all the fools and madmen were gathered in one place, 'I do not know whether or not they would divide the whole world equally with *sober* and prudent men.'[16] Dangerous passions and rebellious animal spirits threatened the practice of religion and the stability of civil society. These unruly passions and spirits needed to be vigilantly moderated and uncompromisingly governed lest they explode outwards destroying the body and the body politic.[17]

Willis's physiology encapsulated his concern with the political and social turmoil of the previous twenty years as events like the civil wars and the unpredictable actions of the New Model Army were played out within the human body. He described the maintenance of cerebral health in terms of siege warfare and he stressed that enemies, especially the passions, constantly besieged the brain. Although Willis believed humans were subject to the powerful forces of their passions, God had provided the means to temper and moderate their influence.[18] Most importantly, He had endowed humans with an incorporeal soul capable of potentially resisting their passions. God had also structured the brain to protect it from the rages of the passions: 'so the brain, like a Castle, divided into many citadels or ramparts, is the more fortified and harder to conquer.'[19] The vessels that supplied the brain with the blood from which the animal spirits were distilled, for example, were designed to temper and purify it. The branches of the vertebral and carotid arteries intermingled with each other to equalize the blood flow before reaching the brain and the twists and turns of the cerebral arteries slowed the blood while the increasingly smaller vessels ensured that only the most purified blood and spirits were carried into the brain. Furthermore, each hemisphere of the *cerebrum* was further divided into two lobes each supplied with blood from many different arteries thereby ensuring that the disruption of part of the *cerebrum* might not easily spread to the others. When these defences failed to temper the blood and spirits the governance of reason within the body was overthrown and the sensitive and rational appetites set against each other as they vied for control of the animal oeconomy. During these physiological conflicts, which Willis called civil wars, the incorporeal rational soul and corporeal animal soul (respectively responsible for the rational and sensitive functions) competed for control of the body until 'this or that combatant, becoming superior, leads away the other clearly captive.'[20] During these intestine civil wars individuals were ruled more by the whims of their passions than by the dictates of their reason. Their actions and judgements were driven more by their bodily desires than by the higher aspirations of their reason.

Animal spirits were the troops the souls arrayed and distributed throughout the body to carry out the orders of the two souls. When the souls were at peace they co-operated and physiological functions operated normally as each soul governed its own particular provinces through the actions of the spirits it directed. When the souls set against each other, the stability of the animal oeconomy was disrupted. The ordinary flow of spirits was interrupted as each soul dispatched, arrayed and directed spirits in its attempts to gain ascendancy within the body. Some spirits served the animal soul and the passions of the flesh and the senses, whereas others served the incorporeal soul and reason. Whenever and wherever these spirits met, they clashed and struggled to carry out the dictates of their own particular master.

The spirits were especially troublesome in the parts of the body distant from the brain, like the muscles of the extremities. According to Willis, these spirits were veteran soldiers in a border outpost stationed to respond promptly to the body's changing needs and circumstances.[21] During civil wars, however, these 'veterans' were unable to fulfil their offices for long because of the disruption to the regular flow of spirits that ordinarily sustained their vigour. Isolated from the ordered governance of the souls, they quickly became corrupt and defective. They became so defective that they remained dangerous even after the rule of the rational soul had been restored. For the body to operate effectively and for the governance of reason to be maintained, these defective spirits needed to be replaced with more tempered and less rebellious ones. Willis strikingly compared the replacement of these 'veterans' with the problems of disbanding a powerful and unpredictable standing army.[22] This had been a pressing concern during the negotiations concerning the restoration of the monarchy. After the death of Oliver Cromwell, the New Model Army became increasingly unpredictable as each general pursued his own particular agenda. Although the actions of one had facilitated the return of Charles II to the throne, it was feared others could remove him. One of the first orders of business was to disband the New Model Army and replace potentially troublesome troops.[23] This was easier said than done. Willis noted that if new 'troops' were supplied too quickly, the security and health of the body would suffer because by 'the excessively dense gathering of the *younger ones* . . . the previously instructed *army of the veterans* would be thrown into disorder, and so the order of all being disturbed.' Yet, if the 'veterans' were allowed to stand too long, they became 'excessively sharp, that, on that account as if excited with frenzy, they rush through the nervous system with tumult and impetuosity; thereupon a great disturbance and continual shaking of the limbs are wont to be excited, from which sometimes madness and insanity succeed.'[24]

During the early modern period, knowledge of the passions – whether overtly theological, medical or natural philosophical – was primarily to be practical in nature. It was to provide individuals with the ability to moderate their passions and promote virtuous behaviour. Willis and Charleton both believed they had provided their readers with the practical tools necessary to identify, understand and moderate the passions. The kinds of explanations they gave and the tools they supplied, however, were markedly different. The passions had long existed as both pathological and moral phenomena and Willis and Charleton differed as to where the line between the two was to be drawn. Their differences became more apparent in the decade following the publication of their cerebral anatomies as each author continued to publish works on human behaviour and the passions. Charleton stressed their ethical elements as phenomena of the rational soul, whereas Willis emphasized their physiological and pathological nature as a physical phenomenon.

Charleton did not believe that anatomical investigations would ever fully resolve the difficulties associated with explaining and moderating the passions. He started his anatomical examination of Willis's theories by noting that he could never think about the relations between the animal and rational souls 'without being dividing betwixt the contrary passions of Hope and Despair.'[25] He concluded his inquiry none the wiser, lamenting that despite all his efforts 'I am very neer relapsing into my former despair of ever being able to comprehend, How far that Noble Essence is tied to the laws of Matter, and how far exempt from them.'[26] He later advised the unknown recipient of his anonymously published letter entitled *Of the Different Wits of Men* (London, 1669) that:

> As for Your expectation of further discoveries from Anatomy, that may afford more light to direct the *Virtuosi* in their researches into this dark Argument; I cannot indeed divine what time may bring forth: but am of Opinion, that there is less reason for Your *Hope*, than for Your *Wish* for any such discovery; the nature of Mans *Mind* being such that it cannot understand it self. [27]

Charleton believed anatomy could not show how the passions influenced human behaviour because their actions largely lay beyond the reach of the anatomist's knife. The triumph of the passions over reason was caused by faulty reasoning and choices:

> Nature hath made Man subject to no other *real* Evil, but only *pain* of the *Body*; all *Grief* or pain of the *Mind*, though many times more sharp and intolerable, being created by our own false *Opinion* ... [M]ost commonly *false Opinions* are occasioned, and so exorbitant *Desires* suggested to us by our *Passions*.[28]

Anatomical investigations might offer a way to explain the physical actions of the passions and the physical pains they caused, but anatomy provided little insight into their actions and influence upon the incorporeal rational soul, which could not even be perceived by the physical human senses let alone physically anatomized.

Although Charleton was sceptical of the ability of anatomical investigations to provide the practical knowledge necessary for the moderation of the passions and promotion of virtuous behaviour, he did not eschew consideration of medical matters in his own investigation. The passions had long been a central aspect of the practice of learned medicine. They were one of the six non-naturals that physicians traditionally moderated to promote health and cure illness.[29] Charleton's intent 'was to write of this Argument, neither as an Orator, nor as a Moral Philosopher, but only as a *Natural* one conversant in *Pathology*, and that too more for his own private satisfaction, than the instruction of others.'[30] Anatomical and medical knowledge might provide useful insight into the actions of the passions, but Charleton believed the chief means to understand and moderate their influence was through the rigorous self-examination and government of one's feelings, thoughts and impulses: 'But what need I thus perplex my thoughts in searching for Medicins to mitigate the violence of Passions, when there is one singular Remedy infallibly sufficient to secure us from all the Evils they can possibly occasion, and that is the *constant exercise of Vertue?*'[31] Rather than anatomizing the corporeal and incorporeal souls, individuals were to examine 'the *Operations* of this Celestial guest in our frail and darksom Tabernacles of Flesh' and what was 'daily observed within the theatre of my own breast.'[32] The best aids for the promotion of virtue, he argued, were the Scriptures and the ethics of Epicurus (his anonymous translation of which was published in 1657 and again in 1670): 'in the *Morals* of that grave and profound Philosopher, you will find as good *Precepts* for the moderating your Passions, as *Human wisedom* can give.'[33]

Although Charleton's work was predicated on detailed anatomical knowledge derived from Willis's work, he presented a different account of how the passions were to be best moderated in his *Natural History of the Passions* (London, 1674). His goal was not to offer simple cures for every possible passion but rather to provide individuals with the knowledge necessary firstly to recognize their stirrings within themselves and secondly to moderate them. Charleton contended that individuals were capable of governing their own passions for 'by virtue of his Understanding, Man is capable of *Wisedom,* which is alone able to teach him how to subdue and govern his Affections.'[34] Although the passions exerted a powerful influence upon both the body and the mind, they could be resisted since they 'cannot carry us on to any actions whatsoever, but only by the *Desire* they excite in us.'[35] The misuse of reason, Charleton contended, was the cause of most, if not all, false opinions and excessive behaviour. The passions deceived the rational faculty regarding the good and evil of the objects presented to it. Charleton argued that the passions gained ascendancy in thought and behaviour through the adoption of quick and rash judgements. His account, not surprisingly, stressed the importance of allowing time for their moderation. Time gave individuals the opportunity to reflect upon the reasons underlying their beliefs and actions giving them the opportunity to ascertain if they were being driven more by the force of their passions than the dictates of reason. Time, however, was of little use if individuals lacked the knowledge and experience required to recognize their passions. To this end, Charleton presented his theories as a natural history with each passion being described in a temporal framework according to feelings of desire or aversion it aroused concerning events in the past, present or in the future. He believed this format allowed him to describe the simpler passions and demonstrate how they could be combined to produce more complex passions. This was a familiar and traditional framework in literature on the passions.[36] The most exceptional feature of Charleton's work was the degree to which it was informed by a detailed knowledge of Willis's contemporary neurological and physiological research.

Willis presented a different account of how the passions were to be best understood and moderated. He acknowledged the difficulties inherent in their anatomical investigation since 'nothing can be certainly affirmed or demonstrated,' but he believed that his probabilistic anatomy and physiology provided the soundest foundation upon which to build a pathology of cerebral and passionate illnesses.[37] Although Willis conducted many natural philosophical and anatomical investigations, he was primarily a practising physician. As a learned physician, he stressed the importance of treating the true causes rather than the most obvious manifestations of an illness. Any quack or empirical practitioner could focus their attentions on remedying the more apparent signs of an illness, but only a learned physician could identify their more hidden causes. A learned physician was able to focus his attentions on remedying the underlying physiological imbalances and disruptions for although the more outward signs might be more visible, they were typically only the by-products rather than the cause of some deep-seated physiological disturbance. For Willis an understanding of the physical actions and origins of the passions, rather than theories about their influence on the incorporeal soul, were crucial since they provided him with the ability to understand and explain 'the true and genuine Reasons . . . of the very many actions and passions that are accustomed to occur in our Body, which in other respects seem most difficult and inexplicable.'[38] Willis's cerebral anatomy marked the beginning of a larger project to promote a neurologically centred human physiology. He concluded his anatomy stating that 'a superstructure may indeed be promised to be laid upon this foundation' and he provided just such a superstructure in his following three works: his *Pathologiae Cerebri* (1667), his work on hysteria and hypochondria (1670) and his *De Anima Brutorum* (1672).[39] As he constructed his 'superstructure' Willis, with increasing frequency, blurred the distinctions between the passions as moral and pathological phenomena. His theories increasingly made the passions physiological and pathological concerns rather than moral issues.

The differences between Willis and Charleton's accounts reflect more than simply their views about the scope of the learned physician's professional interests and the degree to which the passions were capable of being explained and cured medically. They reflect a fundamental difference about the extent to which they believed individuals could be trusted to moderate their own passions. Their explanations of the passions simultaneously reflected and promoted competing forms of life that informed how one understood, explained and related to one's neighbours.[40] While self-knowledge and government were essential aspects in the promotion of virtue, they had their difficulties. One had to *trust* that an individual suffering from their passions would be capable of identifying and counteracting their effects. This raised a fundamental problem for Willis: how could one trust that an individual whose reason has been assaulted or overthrown by their passions would be able to identify – let alone moderate – them? How could individuals ruled by their passions act in a reasonable and understanding way to counteract them when passionate was the antithesis of reasonable? Would he not have already lost the capacity for reasonable self-knowledge because he was unable to ascertain truly whether the passions of his flesh *or* the aspirations of reason motivated his actions, thoughts and desires? How could such an individual be trusted to identify and moderate the passions until the extent of the disruption to his reason had been independently ascertained?

Charleton was willing to trust that his intended audience, namely civil gentlemen, would be able to moderate and control their passions under normal circumstances, but Willis appeared reluctant – perhaps even unable – to believe that individuals could be trusted to moderate their own passions without the assistance of the learned physician. His medicalization of the passions reflected and bolstered his views. Curing the influence of immoderate passions and restoring physiological balance was a long and complicated process that could take months or even years. Willis argued that only a learned physician had the specialized skills and abilities to recognize the passions' true underlying causes and actions and, therefore, moderate their excesses safely and successfully. Physicians' therapies, however, could not fully cure a patient. The lasting promotion of virtue and mental health required that the patient eventually be able to moderate his or her own passions. Unlike Charleton, who believed that individuals were able to do this without assistance, Willis believed that the advice and the skills of a learned physician played a crucial role in promoting the moderation of the passions. The physician did more than simply advocate cures; he taught his patients to recognize and govern their own passions. He offered them the ability to regain self-knowledge. He taught them to discern their passions from their reasons down to a physiological level and only then could individuals be trusted to be able to moderate their own passions safely.

Willis's and Charleton's theories highlight a fundamental problem facing the political nation after the Restoration of the Crown and Church, namely the lack of trust. After the events of the Civil Wars and Interregnum many found it difficult to trust that those who held dissenting religious beliefs or claimed different sorts of spiritual experiences would behave civilly and in an orderly manner. The proliferation of alternative   and mostly Protestant – forms of spirituality and worship during the middle decades of the seventeenth century were believed by many in the Restoration period to pose a particular challenge to the establishment of social and religious order. It was believed order was predicated on unanimity of religious belief and practice, so how could there be order when there was no unanimity? Some, like Willis and Sheldon, believed that legal compulsion was the surest way to promote order. Dissenters and non-conformists could not be trusted to behave in an orderly way; they needed to be forced back into the fold through the strict legal enforcement of the practices and liturgy of the episcopal English Church. Others, on the other hand, advocated varying degrees of religious toleration believing that some of the more moderate non-conforming Protestants could be trusted to behave in an orderly and civil manner.

Concerns about the dangers that the practice of alternative forms of spirituality posed were informed by contemporary beliefs regarding the nature of the relations between spiritual experiences and the passions. The relations between the passions, spiritual experiences and worship were complicated during the Restoration period. On the one hand, the excessively passionate practice of religion was considered a pathological condition. The chief manifestation of the passionate practice of religion was enthusiasm. Enthusiasts were individuals who claimed that they alone were privy to God's will and His truths through direct and personal revelation. They were believed to have been so deluded by their passions that they had mistaken the sensations caused by their physical motions for the incorporeal influence of God's divine Spirit.[41] On the other hand, the passions were an essential aspect of heartfelt devotion. Worship, prayer and contrition for one's sins all required the force of the passions to be sincere. A delicate balance of the passions needed to be maintained; enough passions had to be provided for the experience of devotion and worship to be heartfelt yet not so much as to overwhelm reason and cause pathological conditions. Maintaining this balance was easier said than done because the hidden motions of the passions in body and immortal soul during spiritual experiences could not be easily ascertained and evaluated.

A passage from Simon Patrick's *Friendly Debate between a Conformist and a Non-Conformist* (London, 1669) exemplifies the perceived difficulties concerning the inherently unverifiable claims of religious belief and experience. Patrick presented his argument in favour of religious conformity through a fictional dialogue between two neighbours: one a conformist, the other a non-conformist. After a lengthy argument with his neighbour on the validity and value of private conventicles, the conformist concluded:

> do not tell me any more of the good you have got by your private meetings, nor make it an Argument of their Lawfulness. For the Same argument will be used against our selves by the Quakers, who will tell you God is in private meetings, but only theirs, for otherwise they could never find him. Take your choice: And either let it alone your selves, or else allow it them. It will either serve both, or neither.[42]

This was the crucial problem concerning religious non-conformity in Restoration England: how could one accept the validity of one kind of private religious experience while disallowing others? Those that had been responsible for the political and legal re-establishment of the Church were reluctant to trust *any* claims made by individuals resulting from private religious experiences because they had already seen how passionate claims of personal revelation and divine inspiration had contributed to the chaos of the civil wars and Interregnum. Moreover, the validity of private spiritual experiences could not be evaluated or judged with any certainty. Heartfelt religious experiences required the presence and influence of the passions, yet how could one judge whether those experiences were valid if they were undertaken in private outside the established liturgy of the Church? How could one establish whether they were heartfelt or pathologically passionate experiences? Many in the political nation felt that the only safe solution to the problems of evaluating these experiences was to draw an uncompromising line between conformity and non-conformity by claiming that *no* private non-conforming practices and experiences were valid. The only experiences that were certainly safe were those expressed publicly within the established Church.

The tension between the acceptable and unacceptable use of the passions in the practice of religion is evident in Willis's work. He believed the passions – when moderated by reason – were an essential aspect of devotion; worship was literally heartless without them:

> the exercise of *sacred affections* are not accomplished merely by conceptions of the mind: moreover, their acts being related from the *rational soul* into the *sensitive*, first fall upon the *brain* through the *imagination*, then transmitted from the *brain* to the *breast*, since there they produce various motions in the heart and blood and receive their completion.[43]

The expression and performance of religious truths required the influence of the passions: 'wherefore always in reverence of God, *piety* and *devotion* are attributed very much to the *heart*: hence, *repentance, love of God* and hatred of *sin, hope of salvation, fear of divine vengeance* and many other acts of *religion*, are usually ascribed to the work and endeavour of the heart.'[44] The ebullition of the blood in the heart had to be 'offered as a sacrifice to God.'[45] However, the passions needed to be carefully moderated lest they run freely through the animal oeconomy and cause religious enthusiasm and other pathological conditions. The rational soul needed to order and moderate the passions for the exercise of true piety and devotion:

> while the *rational soul* orders the spirits native to the brain into sacred notions and thoughts; by the influence of the same spirits, the interior of the heart is also affected, that they cause to blood to concentrate and be more fully attracted to them and they retain it there longer, as if it were a holocaust offered to God.[46]

This union of passion and reason was central to Willis's conceptions of physiologically healthy, theologically sound and socially safe devotion. The passions needed to be judged, moderated and ruled by the rational soul. Proper and healthy spirituality – like healthy behaviour – was the result of the balanced relations between the rational and sensitive appetites.

Willis's cerebral physiology linked matters of pathology to morality; ethical behaviour and the successful practice of piety required the careful maintenance and calibration of the corporo-spiritual human contrivance to ensure that enough passions were provided for devotion to be heartfelt but not so much as to overwhelm reason. To him, religious non-conformity was only an outward man-ifestation of deep-seated disturbances in the actions of the animal spirits that 'proceed from an insufficient and unsound brain and have driven some from the union of saints and the society of men.'[47] Willis believed that *only* the learned physician armed with *his* physiology and pathology had the ability to promote and maintain the delicate balance and temperament of the animal spirits. Hence the learned physician was a soldier on the front line in the war against the passions and religious dissent and non-conformity.[48] He was to promote physical, mental, moral and spiritual health and, consequently, social and religious order. These conceptions of the power and duties of a healer were not new, as he himself noted: 'it is not new that there should be an entrance to the Church through the Hospital since it is known that our Saviour had used the same method himself, who, for the most part, wanted to obtain the health of the soul first from the restored health of the body.'[49] Like Christ, the learned physician using Willis's physiology and pathology was to bring the sick and mad back to their senses and the true Church. He had the ability and the duty to heal both individual patients and the body politic. Because of him, the sick 'saying good-bye to their errors and disease at the same time, become not only healthy and wise men but more virtuous.'[50]

Charleton presented a different account of how social order was to be best maintained. Order was not to be based on a rigidly enforced uniformity inspired by fear of dissenting beliefs but rather on the voluntary bonds of mutual association and assistance.[51] He claimed that the differences between individuals' beliefs and abilities should not be seen as the cause of social disorder but rather that these differences had been ordained by God's providence for beneficial ends; God had made the many varieties of men to

> accommodate Mankind to a *Civil life*: it being no more possible for a Society of Men, or Commonwealth, to be composed of Members all of the like endowments of Mind; than it is for an Animal to exercise various Functions with many Organs all of the same parts, shape and fabrick; or for Musical harmony to result from a multitude of Unisons.[52]

A certain amount of heterogeneity was required for the body politic to function. Unlike Willis who conceived of a sharp distinction between those who were and were not ruled by the passions, Charleton blurred the distinctions between the two.

Vice and virtue bordered on each other and he wanted his readers to appreciate the slenderness of their distinction. He claimed that by observing the different varieties of men 'every one might contemplate, as in a Mirrour, some part at least of his *own* Image, and know in what *Classis* to rank himself. Then, by observing what is *beautiful* or *deform* in the picture of another, he might the better judge of what himself either *desires* or *fears* to be.'[53] Studying one's own character in this manner promoted a more lasting tranquillity in the mind *and* the body politic for: 'by such general Characters, we might learn how to moderate our *Praises* of some Persons, and our causless *Aversation* from others.'[54] By observing the different varieties of men, one could better understand both one's neighbours and oneself.

Despite the differences between Charleton and Willis's conceptions of the manner in which society was to be ordered and the degree to which individuals were able to moderate their passions, they were not motivated by vastly different political, social or religious agendas. Charleton, like Willis, supported the Crown and established Church. He had fought for the Royalist cause in Oxford and his convictions never seemed to change. Unlike Willis, Charleton seemed better able to adjust to the new political and social realities of the Interregnum. He moved to London shortly after the Royalist defeat and there he attempted to attract the attention of high-profile patrons from a wide range of political affiliations, including Dr Francis Prujean (President of the Royal College of Physicians 1650 5), Elizabeth Villiers (the daughter of the regicide John Danvers) and William Brouncker (later Viscount of Castle Lyons). Charleton seemed unable, however, to maintain lasting patronage relations and his career was marked by alternating periods of public success with high profile patrons and periods of social invisibility and isolation.[55] Willis and Charleton's differences were subtle, perhaps reflecting the growing division between those who advocated a powerful *de iure divino* episcopacy that was uncompromising in regards to religious uniformity and those who advocated an episcopacy that would accept some religious toleration.[56] For all his talk of heterogeneity, Charleton also believed in religious uniformity – just one that was not as stark as Willis's or Sheldon's. Their major distinction concerned the degree to which they were willing to trust that others could behave in a civil manner. Whereas Charleton seemed able to accept that his intended gentle audience could generally be trusted to moderate its passions and behave in an orderly way, Willis seemed unable to extend this trust to those who failed to conform to his own standards.

At the start of this chapter I noted how historians have long focussed their attentions on explaining early modern understandings of the relationship between the incorporeal immortal soul and physical bodily machine. It has not been my intent to try the patience of my audience by contributing yet another article to the vast literature concerning early modern conceptions of the relations between the body and soul. While not discounting the value of such studies, I have tried to offer a different perspective on how their relations might be understood and explained by historians. Humans were believed to be more than simply complex physical machines that housed an incorporeal essence; they were complex corporo-spiritual contrivances created by God for specific purposes according to His great plan. Attempts to explain the construction, functions and actions of this human machine both reflected and were informed by fundamental beliefs about the nature of God's great creation and plan and man's role in it. Understanding historical conceptions of its functioning requires that we consider more than simply the actions of its many parts, we also need to examine the broader contexts in which the very existence and functioning of this human machine was understood. As this chapter has shown, beliefs about the functions of the incorporeal soul and the bodily machine were informed by a wide range of interests concerning the human nature and the ways in which human behaviour and society were to be best ordered. Willis believed that medicine and physiology provided the best ways to understand and explain these issues and he constructed an elaborate physiology that both reflected and proved his underlying presumption that human beings had the potential to be the most passionate of God's creations. Charleton, on the other hand, believed that ethics provided the best way to explain human behaviour and his *Natural History of the Passions* was predicated on the notion that humans had the natural ability to resist the rages of their passions given the right circumstances. Approaching the historical literature in this fashion, gives us the opportunity to explore the complex and often nebulous boundaries between natural philosophy, medicine, theology and moral philosophy. It highlights that underlying attempts to understand and explain the functioning of the corporo-spiritual human machine were often much broader questions like: 'What does it mean to be human?' 'For what purposes were human beings created?' 'How was one to be and understand what it means to be a well-ordered person living in a well-ordered society?' And finally, perhaps even 'Who am I?'[57]

Notes

1. On the importance of occult qualities and incorporeal phenomena in Restoration English philosophy, see J. Henry, 'Occult Qualities and the Experimental Philosophy: Active Principles in Pre-Newtonian Matter Theory', *History of Science*, 1986, 24: 335–81 and S. J. Schaffer, 'Godly Men and Mechanical Philosophers: Souls and Spirits in Restoration Natural Philosophy', *Science in Context*, 1987, 1: 55–86.

2. R. Descartes, *The Philosophical Writings of Rene Descartes*, vol. 1, tr. J. Cottingham, R. Stoothoff and D. Murdoch, (Cambridge: Cambridge University Press, 1985), p. 108.
3. E. Reynolds, *A Treatise of the Passions and faculties of the Soule of Man*, (London, 1640), pp. 31–2.
4. T. Wright, *The Passions of the Minde in Generall* (London, 1630), p. 2.
5. T. Willis, *De Anima Brutorum Quae Hominis Vitalis ac Sensitiva est exercitationes duae*. (Oxford, 1672), p. 1. Both a quarto and an octavo edition were published in Oxford in 1672. All citations in this paper refer to the quarto edition.
6. Robert Boyle's 'Aretology', for example, was based on a combination of divines, poets and the Scriptures. R. Boyle, *The Early Essays and Ethics of Robert Boyle*, J. Harwood (ed.) (Carbondale: Southern Illinois University Press, 1991), pp. xxii–xl; 3–141. On the many ways in which the passions were explained during the early modern period, see S. James, 'The Passions in Metaphysics and the Theory of Action', D. Garber and M. Ayers (eds), *The Cambridge History of Seventeenth-Century Philosophy*, (Cambridge: Cambridge University Press, 1998), pp. 913–49; S. James, 'Reason, the Passions and the Good Life', D. Garber and M. Ayers, pp. 1358–96; S. James, *Passion and action: The Emotions in 17th-century Philosophy* (Oxford: Oxford University Press, 1997); and A. Levi, *French Moralists* (Oxford: Clarendon Press, 1964).
7. On the functions of the animal spirits and their actions within the *cerebrum*, *cerebellum* and the *protuberantia annularis*, see T. Willis, *De Cerebri Anatome cui accessit Nervorum descriptio et usus* (London, 1664), *esp.* pp. 119–41; 196–34; 259–73. Both a quarto and an octavo edition were published in London in 1664. All citations in this paper refer to the quarto edition. See also W. Bynum, 'The Anatomical Method, Natural Theology, and the Functions of the Brain', *Isis*, 1973, 64: 445–68; R. Frank Jr., 'Thomas Willis and His Circle: Brain and Mind in 17th-Century Medicine', G. S. Rousseau (ed.), *Languages of Psyche: Mind and Body in Enlightenment Thought* (Berkeley and Los Angeles CA: University of California Press, 1990); R. Martensen, '"Habit of reason": Anatomy and Anglicanism in Restoration England', *Bulletin of the History of Medicine*, 1992, 66: 511–35; R. Martensen, *The Circles of Willis: Physiology, Culture, and the Formation of the 'Neurocentric' Body in England, 1640–1690*, PhD dissertation, University of California, 1993, 73–108; A. Meyer and R. Hierons, 'On Thomas Willis's Concepts of Neurophysiology: Part I', *Medical History*, 1965, 9: 1–15. My account differs slightly from that of Frank Jr and Martensen. Martensen and Frank Jr are correct to emphasize the degree to which Willis attempted to distance the operation of incorporeal rational soul from the body, but this separation is not as great as it first appears as Willis had also simultaneously magnified the influence that the sensitive

faculty and the passions were able to exert on the rational soul. This increased 'distance' seems designed to match a similar increase in the power of the sensitive faculty rather than to show that humans were less susceptible to their passions.

8. British Library, Sloane MS 698, fo. 79.

9. W. Charleton, *The Natural History of the Passions* (London, 1674), p. 171.

10. J. Fell 'Postscript' in T. Willis, *Pharmaceutice Rationalis, pars secunda* (Oxford, 1675), sig. A$_{3v}$.

11. L. Jenkins, *The Life of Francis Mansell, D.D. Principal of Jesus College, in Oxford* (London, 1854), pp. 22–3. On Oxford during the Civil Wars and Interregnum, see I. Roy and D. Reinhart, 'Oxford and the Civil Wars', N. Tyacke (ed.), *The History of the University of Oxford,* vol. IV, (Oxford: Oxford University Press, 1997), pp. 687–731 and B. Worden, 'Cromwellian Oxford', N. Tyacke, pp. 733–72.

12. Sheffield University Library, Hartlib Papers, *Ephemerides* (1656), 29/5/102A (quoted by the kind permission of their owner, Lord Delamere). On Willis's early life and career, see T. Willis, *Willis' Oxford Casebook (1650–52),* K. Dewhurst (ed.), Oxford and J.T. Hughes, *Thomas Willis, 1621–1675: His Life and Work* (London: Royal Society of Medicine, 1991). See also the works by R. Frank Jr. and R. Martensen cited in note 7.

13. R. Allestree, *Eighteen Sermons* (London, 1669), p. 316.

14. On the Restoration Church see R. Bosher, *The Making of the Restoration Settlement* (London: Dacre Press, 1951); J. Collins, 'The Restoration Bishops and the Royal Supremacy' *Church History,* 1999, 68: 549–80; I. M. Green, *The Re-establishment of the Church of England, 1660–1663* (Oxford: Oxford University Press, 1978); J. Spurr, *The Restoration Church of England, 1646–1689* (New Haven: Yale University Press, 1991).

15. T. Willis, *Pathologiae Cerebri et Nervosi Generis Specimen* (London, 1668), sig. *$_3$.

16. Willis, *De Anima Brutorum*, p. 502.

17. On the perceived dangers of religious non-conformity, see the works cited in note 14.

18. The extent to which humans were able to use their reason to resist their passions was a highly contentious issue throughout the seventeenth century. Claims about the ability to resist the passions were intimately connected with conceptions about the nature of Fallen man's deformed will and the extent of free will. For an example of some of the theological issues involved, see Spurr, *Restoration Church*, pp. 304; 311–29. On conceptions of the relations between the Fall and the passions, see P. Harrison, 'Reading the Passions: the Fall, the Passions, and Dominion over Nature', S. Gaukroger (ed.), *The Soft Underbelly of Reason: The Passions in the Seventeenth Century* (London: Routledge, 1998), pp. 49–78.

19. Willis, *Cerebri Anatome,* p. 122.
20. Willis, *De Anima Brutorum,* p. 123.
21. Willis, *Cerebri Anatome,* p. 249.
22. Willis, *Cerebri Anatome,* pp. 249–52.
23. On the final years of the Interregnum and the re-establishment of the monarchy, see R. Hutton, *The Restoration: A Political and Religious History of England and Wales, 1658–1667* (Oxford: Oxford University Press, 1985), *esp.* pp. 108–16; 138–9.
24. Willis, *Cerebri Anatome,* p. 252.
25. British Library, Sloane MS 698, fo. 74v.
26. *Ibid.,* fo. 87.
27. W. Charleton, *Two Discourses. I. Concerning the Different Wits of Man: II. Concerning the Mysteries of the Vintners* (London, 1669), p. 47.
28. W. Charleton, *The Natural History of the Passions* (London, 1674), sig. A₃.
29. On the six non-naturals see P. Nicbyl, 'The Non-Naturals', *Bulletin of the History of Medicine,* 1971, 45: 486–92 and L. J. Rather, 'The "Six Things Non-Natural": A Note on the Origins and Fate of a Doctrine and Phrase', *Clio Medica,* 1968, 3: 333–47. On the use of the passions for healing see S. Jackson, 'The Use of the Passions in Psychological Healing', *Journal of the History of Medicine and Allied Sciences,* 1990, 45: 150–75.
30. Charleton, *Natural History of the Passions,* sig. A₅.
31. *Ibid.,* p.185.
32. *Ibid.,* 3, sig. A₄ᵥ.
33. *Ibid.,* p. 187–8.
34. *Ibid.,* p. 172.
35. *Ibid.,* p. 173.
36. For a survey of the intellectual traditions and styles of the literature of the passions, see the works cited in note 6.
37. Willis, *Cerebri Anatome,* p. 226.
38. *Ibid.,* p. 235. On Willis's views concerning empirical practitioners and the treatment of the outward signs of illness rather than their underlying causes, see his *Diatribae duae Medico–philosophicae* (London, 1659), sigs. H₄*–H₄*v.
39. Willis, *Cerebri Anatome,* p. 456.
40. For a discussion of Ludwig Wittgenstein's conceptions of 'language games' and 'forms of life' see D. Bloor, *Wittgenstein: A Social Theory of Knowledge* (London: Macmillan, 1983), pp. 22–8.
41. On religious enthusiasm, see M. Heyd, *'Be Sober and Reasonable': The Critique of Enthusiasm in the Seventeenth and early Eighteenth Centuries* (Leiden: Brill, 1995); and A. Johns, 'The Physiology of Reading and the Anatomy of Enthusiasm', O. P. Grell and A. Cunningham (eds), *Religio Medici: Medicine and Religion in Seventeenth-Century England* (Aldershot: Scolar Press, 1996), pp. 136–70.

42. S. Patrick, *A Friendly Debate between a Conformist and a Non-conformist* (London, 1669), p. 131.
43. Willis, *De Anima Brutorum*, p. 131.
44. *Ibid.*
45. *Ibid.*, p. 132.
46. *Ibid.*
47. Willis, *Pathologiae Cerebri*, sig. $*_3$.
48. For a discussion of early modern conceptions of the contestable boundaries between medicine and religion, see D. Harley, 'James Hart of Northampton and the Calvinist Critique of Priest-physicians: An Unpublished Polemic of the early 1620s', *Medical History*, 1998, 42: 362–86.
49. Willis, *Pathologiae Cerebri*, sig. $*_3$.
50. *Ibid.*, sig. $*_{3v}$.
51. Charleton, *Two Discourses*, pp. 39–40.
52. *Ibid.*, p. 37.
53. *Ibid.*, p. 6.
54. *Ibid.*, p. 7.
55. For a brief account of Charleton's life and career see N. Gelbart, 'The Intellectual Development of Walter Charleton', *Ambix*, 1971, 18: 149–68; and L. Sharp, 'Walter Charleton's early Life, 1620–1659, and Relationship to Natural Philosophy in mid-17th Century England', *Annals of Science*, 1973, 30: 311–40.
56. On this, see Collins and the other works cited in note 14.
57. Interesting explorations of the relationships between internal cartographies and the construction of self-knowledge can be found in R. Iliffe, '"That Puzleing Problem": Isaac Newton and the Political Philosophy of Self', *Medical History,* 1995, 39: 433–58; R. Iliffe, 'Isaac Newton: Lucatello Professor of Mathematics', C. Lawrence and S. Shapin (eds), *Science Incarnate: Historical Embodiments of Natural Knowledge* (Chicago: University of Chicago Press, 1998), pp. 121–55; P. Dear, 'A mechanical microcosm: Bodily passions, good manners, and Cartesian mechanism', C. Lawrence and S. Shapin, pp. 51–82.

–3–

England and the Machinery of Reason
1780 to 1830

William J. Ashworth

Labour is, first of all, a process between man and nature, a process by which man, through his own actions, mediates, regulates and controls the metabolism between himself and nature. He confronts the materials of nature as a force of nature. He sets in motion the natural forces which belong to his own body, his arms, legs, head and hands, in order to appropriate the materials of nature in a form adapted to his own needs. Through this movement he acts upon external nature and changes it, and in this way he simultaneously changes his own nature.

Karl Marx, *Capital*

During the eighteenth century the increasingly sturdy optimism that nature could be understood and controlled both influenced and was equally strengthened by the growing development of manufactures and attempts to measure work productivity. Through this intensifying preoccupation, stemming generally from the increasing emphasis on commodity production, came a co-emerging view of both nature and man. In other words, an altered view of man's own nature simultaneously appeared along with his changed perception of nature. Within this reciprocal context the perceived relationship between the human body and machine preoccupied numerous men of science, engineers, and industrialists. Experiments were devised and conducted to discover comparative work measures between man, horse, and machine. In some instances metal and person were literally conflated into a mechanical contraption, as can be found in the early nineteenth-century invention of the prison treadmill, which, by the mid-century had been installed into over half of British prisons.

Within this turbulent transition the status of the machine and the application of an accompanying form of reason was an ambiguous subject. As Adrian Randall and Larry Stewart have recently shown, the meaning of machines was mutable, ambivalent and fiercely contested. Maxine Berg has demonstrated that it played an integral role in forging the new discipline of political economy during the first half of the following century.[1] Building on their work, this chapter attempts to illuminate further the impact of the machine on the English physical and social landscape. In particular, it seeks to reveal how the machine was informed by, and also helped form, a particular notion of intelligence; inspired the mechanization of social punishment; and, lastly, helped define work practices and arrangements at the vanguard of English industry. Within these areas a dominant set of objectives came to the fore, namely, visibility, economy, order and predictability. I use the phrase 'machinery of reason' to capture these imperatives.

The Coming of the Machine

The machine was greeted with enthusiasm by some as a potentially liberating development that embodied God's natural legislation and the workings of nature, but it was regarded equally by others as something despotic that would erode liberty, the organic nature of life and institutions, and traditional forms of employment. In addition, the specialization demanded by a mechanically inspired division of labour fed the fears of a classical civic tradition, which saw such an evolution as eclipsing virtue and fuelling widespread corruption. This critique, in turn, was effectively countered by the 'conjectural histories' stemming predominantly from Scotland in the latter half of the century. Here, it was argued, society went through a progression of stages that became more and more specialized until it became a commercial society. The machine, within this context, was marketed from about the 1770s on the basis it would fuel economic growth.[2]

Stewart has revealed, in some detail, how the commercialization of instruments, machines, and science in general, had carried these objects and forms of knowledge prominently into the public sphere over the course of the eighteenth century. This expansion had been fuelled less by the irresistible march of scientific developments and their inevitable application to technology, and far more by a rampant gambling spirit emanating from Exchange Alley. Here, shady projectors attempting to woo ignorant subscribers, promiscuously peddled mechanically based projects purporting to be based on Newtonian experimental philosophy. The ever-greater public appearance of the machine brought with it an increased urgency, enthusiasm and volatility over the impact it was having on the traditional fabric of society. It also made manifest a form of reasoning that, over the course of the following century, would eventually spread its tentacles deep within the sinews of society.[3]

Overcoming nature was often a much simpler challenge than changing embedded work practices and making workers amenable to new machines and tools. This was to prove vital in defining the future trajectory and political place of the machine in British history. Fundamental to its successful application within the workplace of traditional industries was the repeal of old legislation built upon mature protectionist policies. These restrictions were viewed as the last guard against the unimpeded march of a particular rationality; a form of reason predominantly defined by the possibilities mechanization offered to both material and intellectual production. In this sense the statutes operated in much the same way legislation controlling the marketplace for food did, namely, they restricted its march. This debate and controversial development symbolically came to a head with the final repeal of the regulatory laws in 1809. It was also during this period, as Berg has shown, that the machinery question became instrumental in shaping political economy.[4]

From an enlightened perspective, the social organization of work practices, no less than the method of making political decisions, should be visible and virtuous like the divine regularity of the heavens, or, indeed, the more earthbound movement of a machine. Corruption and waste were perceived as a product of secrecy as much in the workplace as they were in the body politic. The regularity of mechanization would discipline labour and act as a safeguard on dishonesty, mistakes and laziness. Indeed it would offer moral guidance – because consistency, efficiency, and predictability in an age plagued by attacks on Old Corruption – were increasingly associated with high moral standing. This was a view that fed wonderfully into nineteenth-century moral crusades. It also offered the master manufacturer a level of control over the workforce hitherto unparalleled. As Clive Behagg argues in his close study of the politics of production in early-nineteenth century Birmingham: 'As long as the workplace retained its enigmatic quality it could be controlled by those whose position within its broadly integrated culture made them privy to its internal complexity.' The privacy of many workers and their fierce defence of the 'mystery' of their skills, could potentially be prised apart by the revision of the system of production and/or the substitution of their skills by machines. In other words, under industrial capitalism people became subservient to the machine rather than emancipated by it. This view, of course, was most famously put by Karl Marx in 1867. Here the machine represented the material face of capital.[5]

However, it was the threatening presence of the machine rather than its initial impact that first fed the fears of particular communities. For example, as Adrian Randall has shown in the case of the west of England woollen workers, it was its potential 'to destroy established patterns of work' and thus erode values of 'status, customary social structures and concepts and feeling of community identity' that ignited both legal and hostile resistance to the machine and its closely aligned cohort, the factory. The reaction to the introduction of machinery was very much regionally based. To begin with, the west of England woollen workers were far more hostile to the introduction of machinery than their equivalents in West Riding and Yorkshire. This, as Randall demonstrates, can be understood when the different forms of production both communities worked under is examined. Reaction predominantly took two forms – either through legal channels or through violence. The 'craft consciousness and solidarity' of the West Country woollen workers was a major obstacle to mechanization. The woollen industry was not simply some economic system that could be overhauled but was an entrenched way of life. The machine innovators were frequently viewed in the same way the moral economy treated the forestaller and regrater in the marketplace.[6]

Like the food market, the woollen industry was regulated and protected by a number of old laws. In addition, the West England woollen workers were deeply proud of their status, craft specializations and skills. These customs were integral to their way of life and they were determined to defend them against the machine and factory – the fact that neither dominated the landscape at this time is not the issue. Those mighty machines and factories that had appeared sent a shiver through the community and represented a potential end to their independence, skills, and autonomy. The old legislation was regarded as the final safeguard to the new form of centralized production that they felt was fast breathing down their necks. The machine and factory were thus seen as the destruction of traditional relationships between the woollen masters and the workers in both the putting out and domestic systems.[7]

Just as the common law and customary practices in the market were being successfully challenged and eventually usurped in the early nineteenth century by dismantling protective and regulating legislation, the same form of reasoning was seeking to redefine and objectify the workplace and make it amenable to mechaniz-ation and mechanical organization. By the 1820s the machinery question and the machine economy was far starker, and the voice of supposed market forces had defined in a much clearer way where the machinery of reason fell.[8]

Meeting the Machinery of Reason

Although the Enlightenment has traditionally been predominantly associated with France, the French themselves viewed Britain as the place to actually view radical change. The result, as historians such as John R. Harris, Margaret Bradley and Margaret C. Jacob have shown, was a flood of French savants, industrial spies and curious politicians (frequently men straddling all three domains) during the late eighteenth and early nineteenth centuries into Britain.[9]

For the well-known early nineteenth-century French mathematician and engineer, Charles Dupin, to observe certain sites of English manufactures and state complexes was to witness the source of British power and to literally see the nation's reason in action. He claimed that it was due to the celebrated engineer and industrialist, James Watt, that England owed 'the immense increase of its wealth within the last fifty years.' It seems that Dupin was immersed in the propaganda surrounding men like Boulton and Watt, and believed English intelligence was embodied in such people and their environment. He particularly admired the systematic and practical nature of their applied reason. William Strutt, a cotton factory owner in Derby, who was a leading member of the radical local Philosophical Society that had Erasmus Darwin as its president, attempted to articulate this intelligence. He claimed, 'inventing is only looking at all sides of a thing and putting it in different points of view and by long habit and a great store of ideas this becomes almost mechanical.' Dupin sought to capture this analytical industrial mind from observations made on his promiscuous visits to leading English sites of industry and business.[10]

To visit English factories was as popular a task for a philosopher as going to an important geological spot, an exotic distant country, pointing a telescope at the moon, or examining wood lice under a microscope. In July 1809 England's leading astronomer, William Herschel, accompanied by his son John Herschel, arrived in the manufacturing city of Derby to view the local industry. Strutt proudly took them on a tour of his cotton factory, which the younger Herschel described in his diary as 'extremely beautiful, on account of the elegant machinery employed. The impulse is given by a small steam-engine, and thence communicated.' He then proceeded to give a detailed description of the machine. The following month the Herschels observed a vast cloth-manufacturing site, 'where we saw the whole process of making the cloth, from the wool to the last finish.' In July 1810, they visited the famous Boulton and Watt Soho Foundry in Birmingham, and were shown around by James Watt. John Herschel enthused that the foundry was 'the source and fountain of every improvement in machinery which has displayed the power and ingenuity of man.' Its engine house, he claimed, 'is one of the most magnificent sights I ever remember to have seen.' Again, Herschel proceeded to give a very detailed description of the machinery and layout.[11]

After completing their extensive tour Watt invited the Herschel's back to his home for dinner. In between mouthfuls of roast beef and Brussels sprouts the young Herschel sat mesmerized by the elderly Watt's memory: 'A memory stored with every part of elegant, useful, and in many cases profound science.' His mind was so well organized that it could handle efficiently any issue or object it confronted. Indeed, Herschel believed Watt's mind was in a state of permanent, productive, intellectual fertility: 'an invention ready in conceiving the most complicated plans of an activity, prompt in their execution, these are even separately very rare, but united they form a prodigy.' Here was the machinery of reason that Dupin so admired and sought to describe. Herschel similarly saw, in his factory visits, not just the ideal arrangement for material production, but also the blueprint of the human mind's process of production. Like a factory, the mind had to be correctly organized to be efficient at intellectual production. Through a combination of well-arranged memory and mental analysis, the mind too was more efficient at processing information and intellectual production. For Herschel, Watt's mind was organized exactly like the environment of Soho – to view it was to see a great mind. He concluded, 'very few are the individuals who have been as so vast utility to society in general and to the nation in particular as Mr Watt.'[12]

As a student at St John's College Cambridge, John Herschel had become a close friend of Charles Babbage, who was also deeply fascinated by machines and systems of manufacture. Indeed, he went on to spend a great deal of time analysing processes of production that culminated in the publication of his celebrated *Economy of Machinery and Manufactures* in 1832. As is equally well known Babbage became committed to industrializing human intelligence through his work on a calculating machine. This quest began with Herschel at Cambridge, where they set out to strip the brain naked and describe the operations of its correct process of reasoning. They both evangelically believed that the powerful tool of algebraic analysis could describe the structure of this logic.[13] Babbage and Herschel, following a particular version of the Scottish conjectural histories, believed that an industrial society was the ultimate stage of civilization. Consequently, as the apex of social formation, the intelligence that underpinned it was the logic that led to genuine knowledge.[14]

To Herschel, therefore, the factory visit represented a pilgrimage into man's ingenuity and a celebration of his power to create. Like many, Babbage's friend, the celebrated Whig political economist Nassau Senior, also enjoyed an educational day out at the factory. In 1825 he viewed Marsland's Stockport factory and was so impressed by what he saw that he concluded: 'if the power of directing inanimate substances, at the same time to exert the most tremendous energy, and to perform the most delicate operations, be the test, that dominion and power are nowhere so strikingly shown as in a large cotton manufactory.' The mechanics lecturer and factory propagandist, Andrew Ure, revelled in man's ability to organize inert matter into an intelligent system as manifested in the structure of a factory: 'it is there that the elemental powers have been made to animate millions of complex organs, infusing into forms of wood, iron, and brass an intelligent agency,' and he held up Thomas Robinson's Power Loom factory at Stockport as a good example.[15]

Like the French engineer, Pierre Lesage, Dupin was particularly impressed with Portsmouth dockyard and, in particular, with the blockmaking machinery. The wood blockmaking complex was established in 1802 and consisted of a number of carefully arranged steam-powered machines designed to manufacture wooden blocks used in the construction of ships. The architect of the system was Samuel Bentham and the machines used were designed and built by Marc Isambard Brunel and a young machine maker, Henry Maudslay. The hordes of visitors to Portsmouth dockyard stood aghast at Bentham's division of dockyard labour and application of machinery. From the start he had deliberately disregarded the 'artificial, but common classification of works according to trades or handicrafts', because 'it stood particularly in the way when the object was the contrivance of a

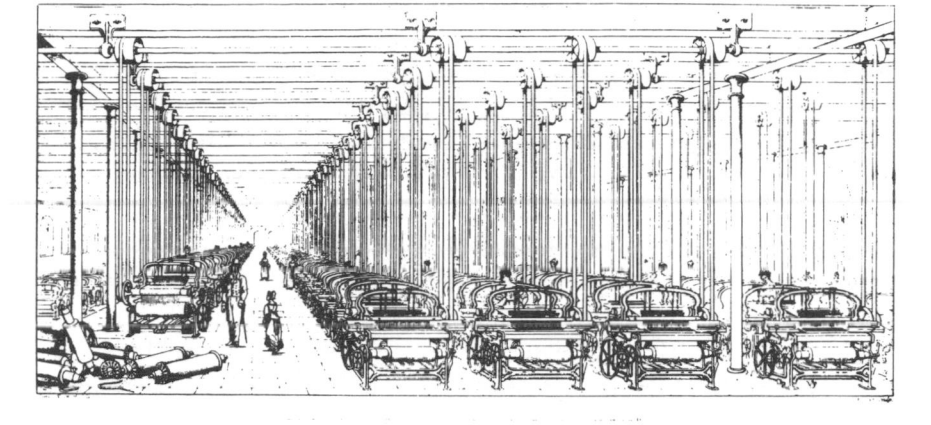

Figure 3.1 Thomas Robinson's Power Loom Factory near Stockport, as illustrated in A. Ure, *The Philosophy of Manufactures* (London, 1835).

good system of machinery.' He began by redefining the various operations required for the labour process, and when these had been classed, he started work on the contrivance of machines by which they might be performed – without the need for skill in the workmen. By this means the traditional 'mysteries' of the labour process were objectified and made visible within a new spatial organization, and wherever possible built into machines like those comprising the wood block-making system. The assemblage consisted of specialized and co-ordinated machines arranged in a carefully ordered arrangement that manufactured some 130,000 blocks per year – aided by ten unskilled men as opposed to the former 110 skilled workers. This saved the Admiralty £17,000 per year with an initial investment of £54,000.[16]

Make no mistake, Bentham had deliberately encouraged a high profile for the blockmaking system by ensuring that the final machines were visually impressive, and making sure that they were all publicly visible. In this way, insisting on making the system public helped legitimate it. Bentham made virtue and enlightenment mean visibility that was in stark contrast to the secretive and decaying world of the *ancien regime* both in politics (Old Corruption) and in work:

> I had considered it highly conducive to the hastening of the introduction of a general system of machinery, that public opinion should be obtained in its favour, and that this was likely to be more surely effected by a display of well arranged machines, for the accomplishing of one particular object, I determined, as the machines which it might be expedient to employ exclusively for blockmaking, admitted of a pleasing arrangement in point of appearance as well as use.

The importance of public display was similarly used by his brother Jeremy in his planned prison Panopticon, and applied by other contemporary industrialists. At a general level the public display of machines would help allay fears that the increase of power would degenerate into tyranny, while simultaneously giving the reasoning that underpinned its epistemological status. It was merely applying on earth what was apparent in the heavens. However, for certain guardians of the traditional social order, the public display of such industrially driven technological power was, as Stewart has shown, a potential political threat.[17]

The tension generated by the machine as a symbol of social improvement or of despotism had reared its head several times in the eighteenth century. For example, early in the second half of the eighteenth century there had been two labour disputes involving coal heavers and sawyers in London both over the introduction of new machines, riots against Hargreaves' first jenny in 1767 and 1769, Arkwright's 'patent machines' and larger jennies in 1779, and machine breaking at Portsmouth during Bentham's reforms in the late 1790s. Indeed, many of the defining themes had already been established in the west England woollen industry since 1776 and in Yorkshire from the early 1790s. Despite such signals and prophetic samples of things to come, numerous others remained undisturbed and continued to press forward with the argument that the machine was a symbol of progress that would cleanse the system of manufacture (as well as the mind and polity), improve the efficiency of production and lead to greater economic growth. The Luddite actions of 1811–13 certainly focussed attention more acutely on this matter but, as Marx later reflected, it took time for the Luddite movement and its sympathizers to realize that the target of their anger was not the machine, but, rather, 'The form of society which utilizes those instruments.' This meant recognizing the integral relationship between capitalist objectives, its most stark physical representation (such as steam-powered machines), notion of knowledge, and the subsequent shape of society.[18]

Economy of Mind, Body and Machine

As we have seen, a visit to a manufacturing site in England had become a necessary and fundamental part of a philosopher's education. These weird, awesome spectacles of human ingenuity were the symbols of English wealth, power, and intelligence. By 1835, the engineer James Martineau could tell the Liverpool Mechanics Institute that machinery was 'rapidly supplanting human labour and rendering mere muscular force . . . worthless . . . That natural machine, the human body, is depreciated in the market. But if the *body* have lost its value, the *mind* must get into business without delay.'[19] According to Martineau's dramatic and exaggerated comments the body's external functions had become deflated through mechanization. Therefore the most valuable human organ was now the mind. However, even this human tool was being challenged by mechanization.

Perhaps the clearest and most visible impact of the machine was in the very arena of industrializing the operations of intelligence. Here the machinery of reason probably appeared in its clearest manifestation. Debates over the replication of human intelligence have less to do with what it is to be human and far more to do with making it fit the criteria of a prevalent culture – be it religious, or, in this case, the machine. Thus attempts at inscribing the workings of human intelligence into a machine were (and are) ultimately about making humans appear to think like machines too and then claiming it as 'natural'.

Inspired by the work of the French mathematician, Gaspard de Prony, Charles Babbage attempted to build the mental division of labour, which the Frenchman had applied to the calculation of tables, into a machine. He wrote: 'The proceeding of M. Prony, in this celebrated system of calculation, much resembles that of a skilful person about to construct a cotton or silk mill, or any similar establishment.' Prony (like an Arkwright, Watt, Strutt or Bentham) was the logic behind the system describing the process of production (in this case numbers) – he planned it. Following the hierarchy of a factory, the next section after the designers were those equipped to operate, understand and maintain the machinery – the engineers. Finally there came a class of unskilled workers organized to perform their assigned task in the manufacturing process – the operatives. Again the factory was equated with the ideal organization of the mind. Babbage wrote in 1832:

> the arrangements which ought to regulate the interior economy of a manufactory, are founded on principles of deeper root than may have been supposed, and are capable of being usefully employed in preparing the road to some of the sublimest investigations of the human mind.

For Babbage and others, to view the application of mechanical reason was also to see the reason of the mind. For others, most notably Babbage's contemporary, Marx, it was to see the shape of capital:

> What is lost by the specialised workers is concentrated in the capital which confronts them . . . This process of separation . . . is completed in large-scale industry, which makes science a potentiality for production which is distinct from labour and presses it into the service of capital.[20]

When it came to getting the most productive work out of the human body (and mind), Babbage emerged from a long tradition. The dominant form of power during the eighteenth and well into the nineteenth century was muscle power, and discussions concerning machines were invariably linked with debates over human-powered work. Men of science and industry conducted experiments to compare the work rate of water wheels, wind sails, steam engines, animals and human labour. As Alan Morton has argued: 'Their conclusions, and opinions, about the relationship between the powers of men and machines, and the differing merits of various types of machines, provided important new knowledge about machines.' Morton has also shown the implicit relation, in certain places, between the emergence of wage levels and attempts to measure work during the eighteenth century.[21]

The eighteenth century is littered with experiments concerning the work rate of humans and horses. The aim of these studies was to measure the maximum exertion per day one could expect from a horse or man. As early as 1699, a paper appeared in the first volume of the *Memoirs of the French Academy* by Philippe de La Hire, in which La Hire deduced geometrically that the horizontal pushing power of a man was twenty-seven pounds. He then derived from this that a horse pulled horizontally as much as did seven men. In the same volume Guillaume Amontons presented a study of a glass polisher, whose polishing action moved the 'pad back and forth a foot and a half in a one-second cycle for ten hours a day.' He concluded from this that a man's force was twenty-five pounds, while his ratio with a horse was six rather than La Hire's seven to one. Interestingly, a figure of 5.87, the hundredth of a unit reflecting an increased emphasis on precision, was given by Abraham Rees's popular *Cyclopaedia* in 1818. Interpretations of human work power often drew heavily upon racial stereotypes. For example, the naturalized English Newtonian experimental philosopher, John Desaguliers, proudly claimed that five Englishmen were the equivalent to one horse, while in France and Holland it was seven to one. In 1744 he showed how a man could raise 140 pounds up a height of twenty-one feet twice a minute. To achieve this, Desaguliers recommended a 'Tavern-Drawer', running up a certain number of stairs and returning on a descending platform. The aim in the long run was to define a measurement for human work to enable labour to be calculated, regulated and controlled.[22]

Such practical studies were being emphasized elsewhere. While Dupin was busy admiring English manufactures and applied reason, English engineers and men of science drew upon his studies. Indeed, an immediate resource for Babbage was Dupin's published lectures that first appeared in France in 1826, and probably contained the most detailed overview of studies on human labour then available. He presented an array of information collected from different countries concerning the performance of animals and humans, coupled with an analysis of fatigue and the most efficient economic return on employment. Dupin claimed that as

> industry progresses more machines are used and more intelligent workmen are needed and thus we must pay attention not only to develop proper movements of workers' bodies but also improve their sense and intelligence. This will become increasingly necessary as industry advances at a more and more rapid pace.[23]

The reorganization and development of machinery required a contiguous rearrangement of human skills, intelligence and thus an agenda of appropriate education. The workers had to be made as much as the machines.

Babbage later applied his studies of human labour to the science of shovelling in his *Exposition of 1851*. He set out to demonstrate that the most productive use of the spade could be established through observation and calculation. It was not simply a product of brute strength, activity or skill. The labourer, he claimed, should first 'ascertain that a *given* weight of earth raised at each shovelful, together with a certain number of shovelfuls per hour, would be more advantageous for his strength than any other such combination.' It was via calculation and experiment involving the shape of the shovel, the repetitions, the height of the shovel lifted above the wheelbarrow, and 'if the barrow had upright sides, it would require more exertion to turn out its load than if its sides were much inclined.' Babbage advised that for a labourer to get the best out of his or her prescribed task, the person should ideally first become acquainted with their tools and particular tasks from child-hood.[24]

One of Babbage's most important resources was the French savant and one time industrial spy, Charles Augustin Coulomb. Coulomb reduced the question 'to a search for a way to combine the different degrees of force, of speed, and of time, so that a man, with equal fatigue may furnish the greatest quantity of action.' This would enable one to find, he claimed, the quantity that expressed the maximum of action relative to the level of fatigue. Drawing upon results provided by his colleague, Jean Charles de Borda, Coulomb tried to calculate a 'fair day's work' based on a soldier climbing to the peak of Tenerife (a height of 2,923 metres), the time taken to ascend (7.75 hours), and an average body weight (70 kilograms). He calculated his result by multiplying the height of the mountain by the average body weight to give a figure of 204,610 kilogram-meters. As Eugene Ferguson has shown, calculations for a 'fair days work' based on such an approach were wildly different. Take, for example, Desagulier's result of 416,500 kilogram-meters in comparison to the figure derived by the Scottish natural philosopher John Robison of 553,000 kilogram-meters. For Coulomb the next stage was finding the maximum load a person could carry at any given time to gain the optimum result per day.[25]

The kind of experiments detailed above saw the human body as a machine; they were designed to measure the maximum work that could be squeezed out of the body at the most sustainable rate. To ensure that the desired work rate was achieved required a more stringently policed and accountable labour process. It was in conjunction with this, as we shall see in the final two sections, that a more rigid form of accounting was devised. It was not surprising that the body or mind could eventually be represented as taking on the values and characteristics of a machine.

As well as impregnating the workplace, the machinery of reason was also success-fully informing the state's views towards social punishment.

'Mere Automata': Treading the Mill of Discipline

The 'system of the Treadmill,' declared Sir John Cox Hippisley, a Bencher of the Inner Temple, 'is altogether a system of UNMITIGATED TERROR, and *is meant to be so*; a system that looks no further than to an actual and present infliction upon the body.' For Hippisley such a contraption subjected the human body and mind to unnatural movements, compelled by 'the tortuous altitude and uneasy motion manifestly displayed in mounting the endless will of this mighty cylinder.' Not only did this lead to physical injuries but also a 'castigation that may sink deep into the mental as well as the bodily feelings of the culprit, and haunt his memory long after his release.' The eminent physician, John Mason Good, agreed completely and similarly claimed that the treadmill subverted 'the order of nature'. Such a machine, he concluded, may well be appropriate for 'turn-spit dogs and squirrels, which use their forefeet as well as their hind; but it is most preposterous for *man-kind*, to say nothing of the moral effects of degrading them into mere *automata*.' Their views, however, were not in the majority.[26]

The factory was frequently compared to a prison. However, in the case of the latter control and subordination of the body could, at least for a time, be experi-mented upon with much greater freedom. Treadmills, or as they were also known by contemporaries, 'discipline mills', are a good example of where the human body, machines, knowledge and morality met in the early nineteenth century. They also capture the mechanical voice of calculation prescribing the motion of labour and machines as one. Peter Barlow, Professor at the Woolwich Royal Military Academy, expressed this when he lauded over the virtues of the treadmill as a tool for 'the correction and improvement of the morals of the idle, vicious, and dis-orderly part of the community'. He further rejoiced, 'few who have had a full trial of this labour are willing to expose themselves to it a second time'.[27]

The political philosopher, Jeremy Bentham, had long advocated a form of the prison treadmill to power the planned introduction of his brother's machines into his proposed Panopticon prison. The idea had been to install large walking wheels, kept in perpetual motion through shift work by 1,000 convicts, generating enough energy to power his brother's machines. As Samuel Bentham enthusiastically wrote: 'The labour not only of the awkward and unpractical but of the blind and the lame may be called in and a value given to it little if at all short of that which the most skilful and experienced artist bears at present.' In the event the Bentham brothers' prison was never built, at least not one overseen and designed exactly to their specifications, but the early nineteenth century witnessed a flood of treadmills into British prisons.[28]

The English engineer William Cubitt is usually accredited with the invention of the discipline mill while he was chief engineer at Ransomes, a Quaker ironworks in Ipswich. His plan was to make prisoners industrious and useful by putting their labour to grinding corn. He declared in 1820: 'The operations of the convicts would be precisely the same as those which are now effected by the ordinary powers of wind, steam, or horses, and they would have no more concern with the object of the machinery, or manufacture than any of the above named agents.' A few years earlier he had patented a self-regulating wind sail.[29]

The magistrate at Ipswich had sought a mechanism for hard labour, and Cubitt's machine seemed to provide an ideal solution. He applied his mechanical reasoning to develop a system in which the power flowing from the prisoner could be controlled and regulated by the prison authorities. Another version of the treadmill was devised by John Millington, Professor of Mechanics at the Royal Institution in London, for use in the Bedfordshire House of Correction. In 1822 the smug journalist and clergyman, Sydney Smith, criticized the Preston prison regime for its far too useful application of prison labour and enthused about the virtues of the tedium imposed by a treadmill mentality. He particularly admired the fact that the prisoner could feel absolutely no satisfaction or stimulation in his or her work. 'We would banish all the looms of Preston gaols, and substitute nothing but the tread-wheel, or the capstan, or some species of labour where the prisoner could not see the result of his toil,   where it was monotonous, irksome, and dull as possible.' This view received the backing of numerous figures in social authority, perhaps none more so than Robert Peel.[30]

Cubitt's first treadmill was installed at the Suffolk County gaol in Bury St Edmunds at a cost of £6,913 3s. 6d. This, like the Portsmouth blockmaking machinery, was deliberately designed to be a popular tourist attraction. Indeed it inspired poems and a stage production entitled 'The Tread Mill, or Tom and Jerry at Brixton'. The device consisted of two wheels some twenty feet in length and five feet in height, with each wheel having twenty-four stepping boards. It employed twenty-eight prisoners who climbed forty-eight to fifty steps per minute for ten hours in the summer and eight hours in the winter. The power was sold at sixpence per bushel of corn to the local miller who used the power to move his millstones. In 1821 a massive ten-wheel Cubitt treadmill was built at the new Brixton House of Correction in South London. It worked one hundred and twenty-six prisoners and was used to power a gristmill, water pump, and speed-regulating fan. The treadmill proved extremely popular. David Shayt has noted that 'within 2 years, according to government surveys, 37 jails in England, Wales, and Scotland were using over 1,400 inmates on 134 treadmills. By 1842, treadmills were employed in 109 of 200 jails and houses of correction.'[31]

Each treadmill regime was classified as the equivalent of climbing a well-known mountain. For example, at York it was 'equal to walking up Mount Ararat

(6,000 feet) every day', while at Stafford it was a massive 16,630 feet assent – over half the height of Mount Everest. The local authorities kept careful statistics of the treadwheels, which provided extensive information on human work of a nature far more accurate than earlier studies. Details were recorded of the number of steps taken per minute, the number of hours that the convicts turned the wheel, the height of the steps, the number of revolutions turned in a day, and certain other data. This information was annually published in the *Yearly Digest of Gaol Returns* and presented in clear statistical tables. From this knowledge new techniques were designed in order to effect the operations of the treadmill. For example, breaks, windsails and bellows were devised to control the revolutions of the wheel, slide rules were adopted to calculate the work-rate and clock bells were installed to ring at the end of a treading stint.[32]

A typical discipline mill was W. M. Hase's well-known 'patent improved tread mill' of 1824, which was presented specifically for the 'employment of prisons'. The pump engine adjoining the tread wheels was put in motion by human force. Hase enthused over the potential of his machine:

> The power produced by this machine is exactly in proportion to the number of men employed. And the beauty of the machine was that whether the manufacturer – often beyond the prisons walls – required it or not, was not a particular problem since as soon as the Cock of the Pressure Engine is stopped, the Centrifugal Balls open another cock at the Prison Pump Engine; and continue to regulate the water into the same cistern or well from whence it was taken, and produce a continued round of hard Labour for any number of Prisoners; just the same as if the Engine at the Manufactory was at work. By this means labour to any extent can be obtained for any number of Prisoners, as the Pump Engine can be regulated so as to produce labour for 1 or 2, and from that to 100, 150 or even 200 Prisoners.[33]

Hase's description also included an extensive outline of Robert Bate's 'gyro-meter or calculator' – a device designed to record the work done on the treadmill. Bate was an instrument maker to the Board of Excise, who had made a fortune supplying the Excise Department with official hydrometers used to gauge spirits. The gyrometer was 'very closely shut from the prisoner, and at any time when the superintendent asks to examine the labour done by the prisoner, he will unlock the circular door.' Thus the inspector would always know what work had or was being done. Bate's gyrometer provided a means of giving greater accuracy to calculation, and supplying a means for visiting magistrates to check the general level of labour performed over a particular period of time. A similar device, invented around the same time, was introduced into textile factories to ascertain the vigilance of the patrolling watchman and was known as a 'tell-tale'. By hitching an unseen clock to a mechanism placed at a certain part of the watchman's round, the owner could monitor his regularity. At a particular spot along his walk he would have to pull a string attached to the mechanism that would record the regularity of his movements.[34]

The precise measurement of prison labour enabled the miller to adjust the work rate (subject to human resources), while Bate's gyrometer meant that the prison governor could both measure and monitor the work rate to ensure prisoners were not over or under performing. The Society for the Importance of Prison Discipline (SIPD) reported in 1824:

> In following up the calculations on the measurement of tread wheel labour by a few examples, it was conceived that as the several details vary one with another in regular proportion, they might be very conveniently laid down upon a scale in a logarithmic series.

Bate's gyrometer allowed the management of the treadmill to 'be conducted upon one regular system throughout the kingdom'.[35]

The reading from the gyrometer, coupled with known variables such as the proportion of working and resting men, the total time of labour expended per day, and the height of the steps, enabled everything to be controlled and measured. In short, the machine introduced a method for determining the velocity of the treadwheel. The two hands of the gyrometer were set together at the first point of the scale, and on completing the treadmill labour the observer noted the point or division last passed over by the small hand. This would indicate how many thousands and hundreds of revolutions had taken place, while the long hand pointed to the number of single revolutions. Not only could the machine be used to control and measure labour: it provided an unseen eye to constantly monitor and record the work rate of the prisoners. Hase concluded: 'the management of the Tread-mill . . . may, by the aid of the Sliding Scale [a slide rule used to calculate the result of all the specified variables], be conducted upon a very uniform system of operation.' Further, the device could compensate for the varying hours desig-nated for labour in English prisons; while the 'quantity of actual labour to the individual prisoner may, by the use of the scale, be rendered very nearly uniform at every prison where the Tread-mill is in operation – an object of much importance to the prison discipline of the country.' This required a set of boundaries to be drawn regarding the amount of labour that could be safely and efficiently squeezed out. The SIPD recommended, 'the best practical limit may with safety be fixed at 12,000 feet; and the lowest, for men, might be placed at 10,000 feet per day'.[36]

Architects of Production

Elsewhere, most notably at the vanguard of English industry, changes in the organization of labour had brought with it an urgent need to make the human body accountable in a way not so dissimilar to the prison treadmill. The maturing of the labour theory of value was accompanied by a more sophisticated technique of policing and accounting for labour. The shape of the ideal architecture of production was a theorized construct of the machinery of reason. As Marx tried to describe it: 'A spider conducts operations which resemble those of the weaver, and a bee would put many a human architect to shame by the construction of its honeycomb cells'. However, the underlying process was very different, 'what distinguishes the worst architect from the best of bees is that the architect builds the cell in his mind before he constructs it in wax . . . Man not only effects a change of form in the materials of nature; he also realises his own purpose in those materials.' In other words the environment came to embody the dominant form of objectives as shaped by the imperatives of its form of social reason. In this sense the machine was a product of a social ideology that found mechanization ideal to its needs.[37]

At the forefront of the new view towards labour gaining in strength and popularity in the late eighteenth- and early nineteenth-centuries were the architects of production. Designing the most efficient way to perform a certain activity, the ability to extract the optimum work and make sure that work was done, were increasingly seen to be possible only if part of a system visible to a technology of accounting. Babbage certainly emphasized the need for industrialists to keep accurate cost and time data on all manufacturing processes in his *Economy of Machinery and Manufactures*, and advised a number of quality policing procedures. 'That the master manufacturer by dividing the work to be executed into different processes, each requiring different degrees of skill or of force, can purchase exactly that precise quantity of both which is necessary for each process.' This axiom subsequently became known as the 'Babbage principle'. Central to this aim were standardized data on the history of work operations. Leading figures of industry and science during this period came increasingly to rely on accumulated records, calculation, and analysis as an important prerequisite to stable decision making.[38]

The impact of machines and the increasing sophistication of methods devised to measure labour, penetrated the production methods of a number of important industrialists including Wedgwood, Darwin, Boulton, Watt, the two sons of the latter partnership, the Strutts, John Marshall, Samuel Oldknow, and later James Nasmyth. They employed many of the same techniques of management and production that we saw Samuel Bentham also deploy at Portsmouth dockyard in the late 1790s and early 1810s. Efficient material and intellectual production in any practice was not to be gained through a change of people but, as Samuel Bentham emphasized, on a change of system based on the machinery of reason. Organizational change both informed a developing form of accountancy and was advised by the desire for an effective system of accounting.[39]

Neil McKendrick's study of Josiah Wedgwood and cost management provides a useful early example. Wedgwood set out to find, as he wrote in August 1772, the 'proper data, and methods of calculating the expense of manufacturing, Sale, loss etc. to be laid upon each article of our manufacture . . . it will be of the greatest use to us to establish some such scale as I have now been attempting to examine all our new articles by, that we may not fix the prices so high as to prevent sale, nor so low as to leave no profit upon them.' Wedgwood accounted for depreciation (wear and tear), administrative costs, the expense of sale, and the interest on capital in trade in his breakdown of production costs. He claimed his analysis showed that expenses such as modelling and moulds

> move like clockwork, & are much the same whether the quantity of goods be large or small, you will see the vast consequence in most manufactures of *making the greatest quantity possible in a given time* . . . Modelling & Moulds, and the expense of Scale wd not be much Increas'd if we cd sell double the quantity at our Rooms in Town, which lowering some of the prices may enable us to do.

To improve the economy, profit and control of the labour process, Wedgwood attempted to systematically observe all the production operations. Like a machine all the component parts should be – if not visible – ideally open to observation and measurement at some level.[40]

Once Wedgwood established the cost of a new technique he was in the position to make necessary changes if the circumstances arose. For example, through a reduction in wages per piece or, in times of depression, a reduction in the actual price of the product. This could be assisted by a shift in the quality of labour – for instance apprentices cost a third less than adult workers did, while women and children cost even less. He used these detailed calculations in fixing the piece rates for his workers. The cotton manufacturer, Samuel Oldknow, also kept detailed records of his employees including the work they were doing and the time it took them. This provided him with a detailed record over time displaying the work-level of any particular person at work on a particular frame. 'At a glance,' writes Robert B. Williams, 'Oldknow was made aware of the production of each machine and each machine attendant.'[41]

Decision making and planning via bookkeeping was now no longer simply a process of value exchange, but a detailed record of the movement in which the various forms of property passed. A record traced the history of the raw material from the storeroom to the shop, and the materials it united with along its path. In addition, records were kept of the labour and functional services, followed by the subsequent transfer of the newly priced units of product into stock to await value exchange. The precise observations of these operations were then, in turn, applied to future decision making. As an early historian of accounting wrote, the basic need for accounting 'is management's continuing need, in order to make next decisions, to be able to review accumulated results of its prior decision-actions.' The Wedgwood enamel works at Greek Street were designed so that a conveyor belt moved through the works threading them together. Wedgwood arranged his men on the same basis, 'the same hands cannot make *fine, & coarse – expensive & cheap* articles so as to turn to any good account to the Master.' Men had to be trained to fit the system or, as he famously remarked, to 'make such *machines* of the *Men* as cannot err.' The activities of Wedgwood, Samuel Bentham, and as we shall see the sons of Matthew Boulton and James Watt, demonstrate the emergence of cost management (calculating the cost make-up of respective products) as an evolving decision-making technology, which in turn, respecified the environment it sought to account for. The nemesis of this emerging form of accountancy was the stubbornly ingrained opaque nature of customary work practices.[42]

At the new Boulton and Watt Soho Foundry the standards of engineering were applied to both machine and as far as possible to the human body. The production process was logically designed to link up in a systematic cycle devised to avoid spatial inefficiency, and consisting of as many standardized component parts as possible. In principle, being self-sufficient and having central and co-ordinated control over the manufacturing process gave greater control over the speed and quality of the product and the workmen. Most subcontraction was ended and labour processes were, whenever possible, regularized. All the machines were accompanied with statements of their present speeds and the proposed new speeds calculated to serve as standards. The machines and workmen were then placed in their specific shops, strategically located in the production flow, and assigned their particular operations. A paper, dated 1801, entitled, 'Arrangement of Workmen and Distribution of Work at Soho Foundry', gives a list of the fixed and measurable standard jobs applicable to each worker. For example, 'to each fitter or group of fitters only one article or group of similar articles was assigned.' The calculations applied to measure the action of the men were based on observations of a good worker paid by the piece.[43]

Human and machine performance was observed and measured over a number of tasks between 1800 and 1802 when the Soho manufactory was being expanded. The aim was to produce standards 'to evaluate the weight of castings produced per man per month,' and thus to 'establish time-based piece rates in procedures such as turning and boring, and to rate tenders submitted by inside contractors in the manufactory.' Watt Jr. later enthused that since the foundry had been 'put upon Piecework, has been doing at the rate of 314 ^{Tons} 14 ^{cwt} per Qr which is about $^1/_2$ more than it did in the three preceding Quarters, which average 194 Tons.'[44]

Of course Watt senior had already applied this form of analysis in his work on perfecting his steam engine. Watt had managed to devise a measure for his steam engines via their diameter and stroke. Using an instrument that he had designed, called a 'counter', he could record the seesawing motion of the main beam. For his rotative engines he took the figure of 33,000 ft lb as his standard for one horse power, and during the 1790s devised with George Lee another device termed the 'indicator'. This was used to measure the highest and lowest cylinder pressures to estimate how much power would be needed to move particular machines such as a group of spinning jennies. John Southern, the manager of Boulton and Watt's engine concerns at Soho, then adapted the system in 1796 to record an engine's pressure on paper, by replacing the indicator's pointer with a pencil which, in turn, could trace a line on a piece of paper showing the pace of the piston. In this way a picture was formed plotting the pressure against the displacement of the piston. Once the appropriate scale was agreed upon the average pressure could be found by observing the mean distance between the base and top lines of the figure. Watt and Lee enthusiastically took up Southern's innovation and soon found they could use the indicator diagram to give a direct measure of an engine's power subject to certain requirements. Through this instrument a means was eventually established that could solve the problem of matching an appropriate steam engine to the machines it was supposed to drive.[45]

Similarly, what is clear in the design of the Soho system is the use Boulton Jr. and Watt Jr. made of prior records to inform their estimates of how much work was needed from their workers to perform a task, and where the prospective parts of the new production process should ideally be. It was the use of these records that informed the production layout and time-sequence and, as such, it was analytically preplanned. It was first planned in the head before being applied. A list of all the shops was drawn up with each part specifying exactly the machinery and its designated use, as well as the required operations and speed of the machine. Accompanying this organizational change was also the methods of wage payment. As a result of the introduction of a greater use of machinery, it became much easier to measure and standardize the time taken for the various operations inscribed in the system of production. This was crucial in fixing piece-rate levels and was carried out, as Eric Roll points out, in addition to 'a greater specialization of labour and a breaking up of the different classes of workmen into many groups of varying degrees of skill'.[46]

The standardized system of payment at the Soho foundry was based on an analysis of detailed job records and subsequent calculations taken from them. The cost of fitting each sized engine was then reduced to a permanent standard. New statistical books were started, enabling greater accuracy in drawing up estimates for future contracts, and ascertaining the profit realized in each completed contract. These books covered, for example, the cost of materials, the direct labour cost, and indirect costs such as fuel and lighting. The spatial and temporal organization of production now operated to the pattern and method desired for accounting. It therefore supplied what all industrialists desired, namely, a degree of foresight, through its ability to cost for future changes. The time sheets kept at the different shops, in principle, allowed the managers of Soho to adjust the system of production flow rate, as well as the computation of new wage rates.[47]

Conclusion: The Sinews of Machine Philosophy

This chapter has been concerned with a mode of reasoning developed in studies of machines and human power – in particular, its application at certain sites of manufacture, its role in forging a particular notion of intelligence, and its impact upon social punishment during the early nineteenth century. Implicit within this thinking was a corresponding view of the economy of man and machine. To ensure that a desired and planned work rate was achieved required a more stringently policed and accountable labour process. This is not to say all such changes worked – far from it – but as I have sought to show, it was more than just rhetoric. Indeed, as we have seen, such an approach undoubtedly penetrated certain places at the vanguard of English industry, and should not be dismissed just because it was not as dominant, successful, or economically productive as once thought.[48] Moreover, the entrance of a machine philosophy clearly entered other areas, and, crucially, was absorbed into the public consciousness.

Within this context certain historians have persuasively shown, in different ways, how the machine also became embedded in the making of political economy, political reform, and a guiding metaphor of aspects of government socio-economic policy. In addition, it became a key component of contemporary Christian evangelical thought, a blueprint for the workings of the human mind, and no doubt much more. The machine penetrated far deeper than merely everyday working practices, and intensified its representation simultaneously as a symbol of progress and a model of God's legislation, while appearing as a threat to livelihoods and a sign of moral decay. For many political radicals, conservative thinkers, and factory workers the mechanical heart that lay at the core of Enlightenment libertarianism had degenerated into an enslaving project.[49]

Notes

1. A. Randall, *Before the Luddites: Custom, Community and Machinery in the English Woollen Industry, 1776*–1809 (Cambridge: Cambridge University Press, 1991); L. Stewart, 'A Meaning for Machines: Modernity, Utility, and the

Eighteenth-Century British Public', *The Journal of Modern History*, 1998, 70: 259–94; M. Berg, *The Machinery Question and the Making of Political Economy 1815–1848* (Cambridge: Cambridge University Press, 1980). For a general survey of the reception of machines during this period see M. Berg, 'Workers and Machinery in Eighteenth-Century England', J. Rule (ed.), *British Trade Unionism 1750–1850: The Formative Years* (London: Longman, 1988), pp. 52–73, J. Rule, *The Age of Manufactures, 1700–1820: Industry, Innovation and Work in Britain*, 2nd edition (London: Faber and Faber, 1994), pp. 180–2.

2. J.G.A. Pocock, *Politics, Language and Time: Essays in Political Thought and History* (Chicago: University of Chicago Press, 1989), chapter three; J. G. A. Pocock, *The Machiavellian Moment: Florentine Political Thought and the Atlantic Republican Tradition* (Princeton: Princeton University Press, 1975), pp. 498–502; J. G. A. Pocock, *Virtue, Commerce, and History: Essays on Political Thought and History, Chiefly in the Eighteenth Century* (Cambridge: Cambridge University Press, 1985), chapter six; Berg, *The Machinery Question*, pp. 136–44; A.W. Coats, 'Changing Attitudes to Labour in the Mid-Eighteenth Century', *Economic History Review*, 1958, 2nd ser., 11: 35–51.

3. L. Stewart, *The Rise of Public Science: Rhetoric, Technology, and Natural Philosophy in Newtonian Britain, 1660–1750* (Cambridge: Cambridge University Press, 1992), part 3. But for a greater emphasis on the history of intellectual developments as the driving force see M. C. Jacob, *Scientific Culture and the Making of the Industrial West* (Oxford: Oxford University Press, 1997).

4. Stewart, *The Rise of Public Science*, and 'A Meaning for Machines', p. 262 and p. 292. For machines, economic growth and the repeal of the old legislation see A. Randall, 'New Languages or Old? Labour, Capital and Discourse in the Industrial Revolution', *Social History*, 1990, 15: 195–216, on p. 212 and p. 215, and *Before the Luddites*, p. 223 and pp. 256–7. For political economy and the machine see Berg, *The Machinery Question*.

5. C. Behagg, 'Secrecy, Ritual and Folk Violence: The Opacity of the Workplace in the First Half of the Nineteenth Century', R. D. Storch (ed.), *Popular Culture and Custom in Nineteenth-Century England*, (London: Croom Helm, 1982), pp. 154–79, on p. 174, and *Politics and Production in the Early Nineteenth Century* (London: Routledge, 1990), pp. 104–57; J. Rule, 'The Property of Skill in the Period of Manufacture', P. Joyce (ed.), *The Historical Meanings of Work* (Cambridge: Cambridge University Press, 1987), pp. 99–118, on p. 113; K. Marx, *Capital: A Critique of Political Economy*, vol. 1 (Harmondsworth: Penguin, 1990), p. 481.

6. Randall, *Before the Luddites*, pp. 2–3, pp. 7–8, pp. 26–7 and p. 44. For the regional aspect to the reception of the machine see also Berg, 'Workers and Machinery', p. 54 and p. 58, and *Age of Manufactures*, pp. 180–2.

7. Randall, *Before the Luddites*, pp. 47–8.

8. A. Randall, 'The Philosophy of Luddism: the Case of the West of England Woollen Workers, ca. 1790–1809', *Technology and Culture*, 1986, 27: 1–17, on p. 10, and 'New Languages or Old?' p. 201 and p. 206; Berg, *The Machinery Question*; A. Charlesworth, 'From the Moral Economy of Devon to the Political Economy of Manchester, 1790–1812', *Social History*, 1993, 18: 205–17. For Owen see G. Claeys, *Machinery, Money and the Millennium: From Moral Economy to Socialism, 1815–60* (Oxford: Oxford University Press, 1987), pp. 53–4 and p. 59.

9. J. R. Harris, *Industrial Espionage and Technological Transfer: Britain and France in the Eighteenth Century* (Aldershot: Ashgate Press, 1998); J. R. Harris, 'Movements of Technology Between Britain and Europe in the Eighteenth Century', D. J. Jeremy (ed.), *International Technology Transfer: Europe, Japan and the USA, 1700–1914* (Aldershot: Elgar Press, 1991), pp. 9–30; M. Bradley, 'Engineers as Military Spies? French Engineers come to Britain, 1780–1790', *Annals of Science*, 1992, 49: 137–62, on pp. 139–41; J. Horn and M. C. Jacob, 'Jean-Antoine Chaptal and the Cultural Roots of French Industrialization', *Technology and Culture*, 1998, 39: 671–698.

10. C. Dupin, *Two Excursions to the Ports of England, Scotland, and Ireland, in 1816, 1817, and 1818; with a description of the Breakwater at Plymouth, and of the Caledonian Canal* (London, 1819), p. 44. William Strutt is quoted in W. H. G. Armytage, *A Social History of Engineering* (London: Faber and Faber, 1976), p. 103.

11. John Herschel, 'Travel Diary, 1809–1810', 10 July, 22 August, 1809, and 17 July 1810, Herschel Papers, Harry Ransom Center, The University of Texas. Some examples of popular books describing factories are C. Babbage, *On the Economy and Manufactures* (London, 1832); A. Ure, *The Philosophy of Manufactures* (London, 1835); P. Barlow, *A Treatise on the Manufactures and Machinery of Great Britain* (London, 1836); G. Dodd, *Days at the Factories and the Manufactory Industry of Great Britain Described* (London, 1843); William Cooke Taylor, *Factories and the Factory System* (London, 1844).

12. Herschel, 'Travel Diary', 17 July, 1810. For Herschel and the industrialization of the human mind see W. J. Ashworth, 'Memory, Efficiency and Symbolic Analysis: Charles Babbage, John Herschel, and the Industrial Mind', *Isis*, 1996, 87: 629–53.

13. Ashworth, 'Memory, Efficiency, and Symbolic Analysis'. For a convincing analysis of Babbage's notion of factory defined intelligence and its relationship to the development of his calculating engine see S. Schaffer, 'Babbage's Intelligence: Calculating Engines and the Factory System', *Critical Inquiry*, 1994, 21: 203–27.

14. J. Herschel and C. Babbage, *Memoirs of the Analytical Society* (Cambridge, 1813), p. xxi; J. Herschel, 'Mathematics', *Edinburgh Encyclopaedia*, 1830,

reprinted in S. S. Schweber (ed.), *Aspects of the Life and Thought of John Herschel* (New York: Arno, 1981), pp. 434–59, on p. 437. See also Ashworth, 'Memory, Efficiency, and Symbolic Analysis', pp. 639–41.

15. N. W. Senior, *An Outline of the Science of Political Economy* (London, 1836), p. 70 and quoted in Berg, *The Machinery Question*, p. 130; Ure, *Philosophy of Manufactures*, pp. 2; 9–11; 32.

16. M. Bradley and F. Perrin, 'Charles Dupin's Study Visits to the British Isles, 1816–1824', *Technology and Culture*, 1991, 32: 47–68, on p. 52 and p. 63; C. Cooper, 'The Portsmouth System of Manufacture', *Technology and Culture*, 1984, 25: 182–225, pp. 192–206; N. Cossons, *The BP Book of Industrial Archaeology* (Newton Abbot: David & Charles, 1975), p. 186; W. J. Ashworth, '"System of terror": Samuel Bentham, Accountability and Dockyard Reform during the Napoleonic Wars', *Social History*, 1998, 1: 63–79; M. S. Bentham, *The Life of Brigadier-General Sir Samuel Bentham* (London, 1862), p. 98.

17. Stewart, 'A Meaning for Machines', pp. 284–8; Ashworth, '"System of Terror"', pp. 71–2; Cooper, 'The Portsmouth System', pp. 192–3 and pp. 213–14; S. Bentham, *Services Rendered in the Civil Department of the Navy in Investigating and Bringing to Official Notice Abuses and Imperfections; and in Effecting Improvement in Relation to the System of Management* (London, 1813), p. 164.

18. Berg, *The Machinery Question*, p. 2; Berg, 'Workers and Machinery', p. 62, and *The Age of Manufactures*, p. 192; Stewart, 'A Meaning for Machines', p. 289; Marx, *Capital*, vol. 1, pp. 554–5. For eighteenth-century disputes concerning machines and human labour see Randall, 'New Languages or Old', pp. 202–3; A. Q. Morton, 'Concepts of Power: Natural Philosophy and the Uses of Machines in Mid-Eighteenth-Century London', *British Journal for the History of Science*, 1995, 28: 63–78, pp. 75–7; Ashworth, '"System of terror"', p. 70. For a compelling analysis of the impact of capitalism in shaping the environment see D. Harvey, *The Urban Experience* (Oxford: Oxford University Press, 1989) and *The Condition of Postmodernity: An Enquiry into the Origins of Cultural Change* (Oxford: Oxford University Press, 1989).

19. Quoted in Berg, *The Machinery Question*, p. 158.

20. Babbage, *The Economy of Machinery and Manufactures*, pp. 195–6 and p. 191; P. Barlow, *The Encyclopaedia of Arts, Manufactures, and Machinery* (London, 1851), pp. 44–5; Marx, *Capital*, vol. 1, p. 482; Berg, *The Machinery Question*, pp. 183–90; D. MacKenzie, 'Marx and the Machine', *History of Technology*, 1984, 25: 473–502, p. 485. Marx, of course, did not explicitly look at the impact of the division of labour on knowledge production.

21. Morton, 'Concepts of Power', on p. 66 and pp. 73–7.

22. E. S. Ferguson, 'The Measurement of the "Man-Day"', *Scientific American*, October 1971, pp. 96–103, on pp. 96–9; Morton, 'Concepts of Power', p. 72; Stewart, 'A Meaning for Machines', p. 27.
23. Dupin is quoted in J. Hardie Hoagland, *Charles Babbage – His Life and Works in the Historical Evolution of Management Concepts*, unpublished PhD dissertation, Ohio University, 1954, p. 297; I. Grattan-Guinness, 'Work for the Workers: Advances in Engineering Mechnaics and Instruction in France, 1800–1830', *Annals of Science*, 1984, 41: 1–34, on p. 27. For the importation of French physics and the concept of work and its measurement see M. N. Wise with C. Smith, 'Work and Waste: Political Economy and Natural Philosophy in Nineteenth Century Britain', *History of Science*, 1989, 27: 263–301; 391–449; 1990, 28: 221–61. Another close resource for Babbage was the lecturer at Woolwich dockyard and later fellow founding member of the Astronomical Society of London (1819–), Olinthus Gregory, whose published work included discussions of an array of German, French and British studies of animal and human work rates and associated techniques. See his *A Treatise of Mechanics, Theoretical, Practical, and Descriptive*, three vols (London, 1806), vol. 2, pp. 64–77; O. Gregory, *Mathematics for Practical Men: Being a Common-Place Book of Principles, Theorems, Rules and Tables, in Various Departments of Pure and Mixed Mathematics, with their Most Useful Applications; Especially to the Pursuits of Surveyors, Architects, Mechanics, and Civil Engineers* (London, 1825), especially pp. 64–77.
24. C. Babbage, *The Exposition of 1851, or, Views of the Industry, the Science, and the Government, of England* (London, 1851), pp. 1–5.
25. Coulomb quoted in Hoagland, *Charles Babbage – His Life and Works*, pp. 274–5. See also Gregory, *Mathematics for Practical Men*, pp. 377–8; C. Stewart Gillmor, *Coulomb and the Evolution of Physics and Engineering in Eighteenth Century France* (Princeton: Princeton University Press, 1971), p. 78; Ferguson, 'The Measurement of the "Man-Day"', pp. 99–100. For Coulomb's attempt to spy on Boulton and Watt's Albion's Mills, see Harris, *Industrial Espionage*, pp. 316–17 and pp. 494–5.
26. J. C. Hippisley, *Prison Labour: Correspondence and Communications Addressed to HM's Principal Secretary of State for the Home Department, Concerning the Introduction of Tread-Mills into Prisons* (London, 1823), p. 17, p. 62 and p. 106.
27. Barlow, *The Encyclopaedia of Arts*, p. 122.
28. U. Henriques, 'The Rise and Decline of the Separate System of Prison Discipline', *Past and Present*, 1972, 54: 61–93, on p. 66; Samuel Bentham is quoted in J. E. Semple, *Jeremy Bentham's Panopticon Prison*, unpublished PhD, London School of Economics and Political Science, 1990, p. 175. For Samuel's extraordinary career see I. R. Christie, *The Benthams in Russia, 1780–1791* (Oxford: Oxford University Press, 1993).

29. J. Bentham, *Panopticon; or, The Inspection House: Containing the Idea of a New Principle of Construction Applicable to any sort of Establishment . . . in a Series of Letters Written in the Year 1787, from Crecheff in White Russia, to a Friend in England* (London, 1791), p. 2; Society for the Improvement of Prison Discipline Society for the Improvement of Prison Discipline, 'Description of a Corn and Flour Mill, also a Pump Mill Adapted for the Employment of Prisoners' in *Rules Proposed for the Government of Gaols, Houses of Correction, and Penitentiaries* (London, 1820), p. 59. Both Bentham and Cubitt are quoted in D. Shayt, 'Stairway to Redemption: America's Encounter with the British Tread Mill', *Technology and Culture*, 1989, 30: 908–38, p. 911. See also P. Priestley, *Victorian Prison Lives: English Prison Biography 1830–1914* (London: Methuen, 1985), p. 125. Cubitt went on to oversee the construction of Crystal Palace in 1851.

30. M. Ignatieff, *A Just Measure of Pain: The Penitentiary in the Industrial Revolution 1750–1850* (Harmondsworth: Penguin, 1978), p. 177; M. E. DeLacy, 'Grinding Men Good? Lancashire's Prisons at Mid-Century', Victor Bailey (ed.), *Policing and Punishment in Nineteenth Century Britain* (London: Croom Helm, 1981), pp. 182–216, on p. 201; V.A.C. Gatrell, *The Hanging Tree: Execution and the English People 1770–1868* (Oxford: Oxford University Press, 1996), p. 577.

31. R. Byrne, *Prisons and Punishments of London* (London: Grafton, 1992), p. 137; Shayt, 'Stairway to Redemption', p. 917. A detailed description of prison treadmills is given in Barlow, *The Encyclopaedia of Arts*, pp. 122–6.

32. Priestley, *Victorian Prison Lives*, p. 127; Shayt, 'Stairway to Redemption', pp. 919–21.

33. W. M. Hase, *Description of the Patent Improved Tread Mill, for the Employment of Prisoners. Also of the Patent Portable Crank Machine, for Producing Labour of any Degree of Severity, In Solitary Confinement, For One, Two, or any Number of Prisoners: To Which is added, The Description of the Gyrometer or Calculator, By R.B. Bate*, (Norwich, 1824), p. 7.

34. *Ibid.*, pp. 10–11; R.D. Connor, *The Weights and Measures of England* (London: HMSO, 1987), pp. 257–99; A. McConnell, *R.B. Bate of the Poultry 1782–1847: The Life and Times of a Scientific Instrument Maker* (London: Scientific Instrument Makers Society, 1993), pp. 19–23. At the same time Bate was devising and marketing the gyrometer he was also advising the government on the construction of the 'new Imperial standard of weights and measure' introduced in an Act of 1824.

35. Society for the Improvement of Prison Discipline, 'Description of a Corn and Flour Mill', p. 165.

36. Hase, *Description of the Patent Improved Tread Mill*, p. 13 and pp. 23–4; Society for the Improvement of Prison Discipline, 'Description of a Corn and Flour Mill', p. 165.

37. Marx, *Capital*, vol. 1, p. 284, quoted in Mackenzie, 'Marx and the Machine', p. 477.
38. Babbage, *Economy of Machinery and Manufactures*, pp. 115–17 and pp. 175–285; Berg, *The Machinery Question*, p. 184; Coats, 'Changing Attitudes to Labour', pp. 47–8; MacKenzie, 'Marx and the Machine', pp. 484–5. For cost accounting in the industrial revolution see R. Fleischman and T. Tyson, 'Cost Accounting During the Industrial Revolution: the Present State of Historical Knowledge', *Economic History Review*, 1993, 46: 503–17; R. K. Fleischman and L. D.Parker, *What is Past is Prologue: Cost Accounting in the British Industrial Revolution, 1760–1850* (New York: Garland, 1997).
39. Ashworth, '"System of Terror"', p. 68. For the importance of the social in informing the technical practice of accounting and its role in turn in changing what it purports to describe, see A. G. Hopwood, 'The Archaeology of Accounting Systems', *Accounting, Organisations and Society*, 1987, 12: 207–34.
40. Wedgwood to T. Bentley, 23 August 1772, quoted in N. McKendrick, 'Josiah Wedgwood and Cost Accounting in the Industrial Revolution', *Journal of Economic History*, 1973, 45–67, on p. 49 and p. 55.
41. *Ibid.*, p. 57 and p. 58; R. B. Williams, *Accounting for Steam and Cotton: Two Eighteenth Century Case Studies* (New York: Garland Press, 1997), pp. 112–13 and p. 121.
42. A.C. Littleton, *Accounting Evolution to 1900* (New York: Institute Publishing Co., 1966) first published 1933, p. i; Behagg, 'Secrecy, Ritual and Folk Violence', p. 174, and *Politics and Production in the Early Nineteenth Century*, pp. 104–57; Rule, 'The Property of Skill in the Period of Manufacture', p. 113; E. Roll, *An Early Experiment in Industrial Organisation: Being a History of the Firm of Boulton and Watt, 1775–1805* (London: Frank Cass, 1968) first published 1930, p. 156; S. Pollard, *The Genesis of Modern Management: A Study of the Industrial Revolution in Great Britain* (Cambridge: Cambridge University Press, 1965), pp. 78–9.
43. J. Tann (ed.), *The Selected Papers of Boulton and Watt*, vol. 1 (London: Diploma, 1981), pp. 9–10; Fleischman and Parker, *What is Past is Prologue*, p. 198; Babbage, *Economy of Machinery and Manufactures*, p. 172; Berg, *The Machinery Question*, p. 191; Schofield, *The Lunar Society of Birmingham*, p. 429. Between 1830 and 1832 Watt Jr. corresponded with Babbage about his work and research on machines and manufactures.
44. Fleishman and Parker, *What is Past is Prologue,* p. 201; Williams, *Accounting for Steam and Cotton*, pp. 196–204.
45. R. L. Hills, *Power From Steam: A History of the Stationary Steam Engine* (Cambridge: Cambridge University Press, 1993), pp. 88–94.
46. Roll, *An Early Experiment in Industrial Organisation*, pp. 175-94; Fleischman and Parker, *What is Past is Prologue*, p. 34.

47. Roll, *An Early Experiment in Industrial Organisation*, pp. 244–9; Williams, *Accounting for Steam and Cotton*, pp. 220–1; Pollard, *The Genesis of Modern Management*, pp. 216–19; McNeil, *Under the Banner of Science*, p. 14; Berg, *The Machinery Question*, pp. 190–1; Fleishman and Parker, *What is Past is Prologue*, pp. 201–4.

48. For the limited and regional spread of machines see R. Samuel, 'Workshop of the World: Steam Power and Hand Technology in mid-Victorian Britain', *History Workshop*, 1977, 3: 6–72; Berg, *The Age of Manufactures*; C. Sabel and J. Zeitlin, 'Historical Alternatives to Mass-production: Politics, Markets and Technology in Nineteenth-Century Industrialisation', *Past and Present*, 1985, 108; M. J. Daunton, *Progress and Poverty: An Economic and Social History of Britain 1700–1850* (Oxford: Oxford University Press, 1995), Chapter five.

49. Berg, *The Machinery Question*; B. Hilton, *The Age of Atonement. The Influence of Evangelicalism on Social and Economic Thought 1785–1865* (Oxford: Oxford University Press, 1987); Randall, *Before the Luddites*; Wise with Smith, 'Work and Waste'; Stewart, 'A Meaning for Machines'; Schaffer, 'Babbage's Intelligence'; Ashworth, 'Memory, Efficiency and Symbolic Analysis'; Marx, *Capital*, vol. 1, p. 283.

−4−

The Governor and the Telegraph: Mental Management in British Natural Philosophy[1]

Elizabeth Green Musselman

Historians of Britain during the period 1750–1870 have found, unsurprisingly, that a considerable amount of the work done in physical science and technology at that time was directed at improving industrial mechanization and efficiency. So many of the leading lights in British physics and engineering at this stage − Michael Faraday, Charles Babbage, William Thomson, James Clerk Maxwell − devoted themselves to questions that had clear utility in the world of machines. It is tempting to exaggerate how exclusively mechanistic industrial-era physical and even biological science was. For decades, historians mistakenly sketched the Romantic, vitalist, or spiritualist as the exceptional spoilsport for mechanized, industry-minded science. The nineteenth century in British science wrongly came to seem like one unbroken exercise in increasing productivity, predictability, objectivity, determinism, and precision. Even now that many science studies scholars recognize that these values crystallized out of social constructions, we still tend to believe that such values mattered more to the sciences by the end of the nineteenth century than they did at the beginning.[2]

As true as much of this is,[3] I will argue in this chapter that we have missed − or at least have not paid enough attention to − an important part of the story. In this period, natural philosophers[4] keenly recognized that no matter how deep their desires for efficiency and objectivity ran, their ability to achieve those desires remained elusive. Not only that, but it seemed entirely possible, given humans' limited capacities, that such goals might stay elusive permanently. To truly understand the mentality and practice of British natural philosophy, I think it is crucial to recognize that its most cherished ideals were frequently understood as just that − ideals that remained unattainable for the near and perhaps even the distant future.

To substantiate this thesis, I will focus here on a problem that was particularly salient for industrial-era natural philosophers, namely the problem of how to improve the efficiency of bodily and mechanical labour (seen by most as two sides of the same coin). Most British natural philosophers in the early industrial period knew that, in practice, unsupervised mechanisms could not produce the best results. In a perfect world, a perfect machine might yield perfect outcomes. But, as we know from the history of industrial technology and thermodynamics, natural philosophers were learning to stop pining for that perfect world.[5] In reality, mechanisms needed managers: machines and workers needed supervisors; the *laissez-faire* market needed the occasional protectionist intervention; the natural world needed God; the body needed the mind.

In this chapter, I argue that the realistic management of mechanical imperfection in bodies and machines constituted as much (if not more) of the work of British natural philosophy from about 1780–1860 as did the idealistic pursuit of the perfectly oiled system. I will show how a pragmatism about the limits of machines reflected equivalent pragmatisms about the limits of the human body and of scientific epistemology. I will also make the case that natural philosophers thought of a particular part of the human body, the nervous system, as functionally similar to scientific and other forms of social organization.[6] By extension, the preventatives and palliatives that kept the nervous system in order could do the same for the sciences and the rest of society. When working properly, the nervous system literally embodied good scientific method. Simple sensations entered the body at its extremes; those sensations became gradually refined into facts, generalizations, and laws as information travelled through the nerves, into the brain, and finally entered the mind. The mind in turn directed the body, using the nervous system as its conduit. Ideally speaking, that division of labour was supposed to obtain on a macroscopic scale as well. For example, uneducated fact collectors were like the nerve endings that passed along unfiltered information to the more mentally sophisticated philosophers at the metropolitan centres, who in turn meted out orders for further research.[7] In the physiological and philosophical works of elite natural philosophers, both nervous physiology and scientific and other social organizations involved hierarchical systems of management.

I will use two episodes from the late eighteenth and early nineteenth centuries to make these points. In the first case, I show that just as steam-boiler explosions and other mechanical inefficiencies pointed to the need for governors and supervisors, natural philosophers also thought of their bodies as sensitive mechanisms that required the mind's regulation. In the second episode, we find that attempts to construct more efficient optical and electric telegraphic systems built on the knowledge that in a purely physiological sense, human perception was far from perfect. The minimally trained operators who formed the first line of communication along telegraphic routes required careful supervision, just as the nervous system's sensory errors required supervision by the diligent mind. In short, it behoved personal, scientific, and economic health to confront bodies and machines as imperfect objects. On their own, both kinds of mechanism failed to achieve perfect efficiency, and both required keen management. Perhaps they always would. What mattered for the moment was the effective management of disorder, rather than its ultimate elimination.

Mental Governors and the Management of Energy

An ideal Enlightenment system ran perfectly without interference – thus Laplace's lack of need for God as a 'hypothesis'.[8] Most mainstream to liberal British natural philosophers until about 1830 believed that nature and human economy existed in a kind of balance. Each system had a fixed centre; any disturbances to the system would naturally be righted, thus ensuring a 'timeless state of natural order'. Some philosophers placed more value in the system that constantly remained in balance, and others argued that oscillations (like earthquakes in geology or waves in dynamics) were an uneradicable element of an ordered system – and perfectly contained within a timeless order so long as the system, on average, continued to oscillate around an unchanging centre. The nineteenth century spawned a number of doubts that a perfectly balanced, unchanging system could ever exist. Natural philosophers turned their attentions from the achievement of perfect, frictionless, waste-free labour to the maximization of efficiency.[9] Just as studies of work showed that mechanisms required governance in order to produce maximum efficiency, physio-psychological researchers believed that the bodily mechanism required a governing mind.

The steam engine proved an especially useful tool for expressing the importance of management in the physical and medical sciences.[10] Even before the appearance of thermodynamics, we find frequent comparisons of the body to the engine, and more generally to a mechanical process that, like the factory, required careful management to achieve optimum efficiency. For instance, consider Sara Coleridge's musing that 'life is the steam of the corporeal engine; the soul is the engineer who makes use of the steam-quickened engine'.[11] Andrew Ure took this concept even further when he wrote that manufactures have

> three organic systems: the mechanical, the moral, and the commercial, which may not unaptly be compared to the muscular, the nervous, and the sanguiferous systems of an animal. They have also three interests to subserve, that of the operative, the master, and the state, and must seek their perfection in the due development and administration of each. The mechanical being should always be subordinated to the moral constitution, and both should co-operate to the commercial efficiency. Three distinct powers concur to their vitality, – labour, science, capital; the first destined to move, the second to direct, and the third to sustain. When the whole are in harmony, they form a body qualified to discharge its manifold functions by an intrinsic self-governing agency, like those of organic life.[12]

One point of this complex passage is to establish science and its practitioners as the nerve centre of the industrial nation's body. In the labour hierarchy Ure outlined, workers acted as automatons who performed the mechanical, muscular tasks the economy required. Scientific managers organized and directed labour so that as much as possible became available for the state's commercial enterprise. Without the efficient co-operation of each element, this manufacturing 'organism' died.[13]

A key component of any good organic or political system was thus management or discipline – without which bodies and engines left themselves vulnerable to collapse. In fact, much of the work that led to the new science of thermodynamics was directed at avoiding abrupt changes in velocity in machines.[14] After the appearance of Richard Trevithick's high-pressure steam engine, a number of sensational steam boiler explosions dramatically highlighted the importance of vigilance. Even when an engine's safety valve was left open, great quantities of steam could form so rapidly around the boiler that the boiler could not contain the pressure. The public complained that boilers had been pushed beyond their capacities and that they were monitored by untrained lackeys.[15]

Machinists developed a number of devices to overcome this problem. For instance, the steam-engine governor kept a machine running at a uniform rate, thereby simultaneously maximizing efficiency and safety. The governor consisted of two heavy balls attached to a spindle, whose rate of rotation depended on that of the fly wheel. If the fly wheel slowed, the balls moved together, thus opening the throttle valve and admitting more steam, speeding up the fly wheel again. An 1860s advertisement promised 'no more explosions', thanks to a governor that 'seems endowed with intelligence'.[16]

In the previous century, Soho manufactory founder Matthew Boulton had invented the mercurial siphon gauge, a meter that displayed the level of vacuum in the condenser. Without this 'outward and visible sign', he said, 'it is impossible to judge of ye inward & spiritual grace'. Boulton particularly enjoyed monitoring the grace of his machine by watching the mercury bob up and down in the gauge.[17] Supervising the health of a machine was a necessary, even an enjoyable, aspect of industrial management. Even with 'intelligent' governors in place, engines still required the supervision of a non-mechanical human.

Looking to discussions of human physiology, we find an equal conviction that the body required non-mechanical regulation for the sake of its health. While materialists had an important presence in British physiology, for most of the nineteenth century mainstream physiologists disdained both those who studied the body as though there were no mind, and spiritualists who committed the opposite error.[18]

With mainstream physiology and natural philosophy[19] committed to the governing power of the mind over the body, a key problem became how to use that configuration to maximize human, and especially scientific, work. To achieve extended 'intellectual operations' with minimum fatigue, William Carpenter recommended combining methodical training for the mind with the maintenance of bodily health.[20] With his concept of correlation of forces, William Robert Grove sought to identify 'scientific with social and economic progress' and to link 'this progress to the idea of the machine as an instrument of social discipline and control'. In his scheme, the experimental philosopher became like the factory manager.[21] Even the materialist Thomas Henry Huxley could not resist the powerful image of the body-engine guided by a regulatory intelligence. Defining the liberally educated man for a popular audience, he said such a man would have been

> so trained in youth that his body is the ready servant of his will, and does with ease and pleasure all the work that, as a mechanism, it is capable of; whose intellect is a clear, cold, logic engine with all its parts of equal strength, and in smooth working order; ready, like a steam engine, to be turned to any kind of work, and spin the gossamers as well as forge the anchors of the mind; whose mind is stored with a knowledge of the great and fundamental truths of Nature and the laws of her operations.[22]

The natural philosopher, whose mind was stored especially full with 'the fundamental truths of Nature and the laws of her operations', had to take special care not to run his or her own engine to the point of exhaustion. Intellectuals had long been thought prone to melancholy. Moderate exercise for the pure sake of exertion became increasingly popular during the nineteenth century as a means for lifting melancholic spirits.[23]

As a form of physical and mental exercise, scientific work could be beneficial to body and mind, but could also lead to exhaustion or injury if not indulged cautiously. In his *Economy of Machinery and Manufactures*, Babbage had emphasized the importance of 'uniformity and steadiness' for keeping a complex machine running smoothly. Just after discussing governors he noted that the fatigue brought on human muscles by work 'does not altogether depend on the actual force employed in each effort, but partly on the frequency with which it is exerted'.[24] Similarly, he wrote after his own run for a north London MP post that the House of Lords 'is to the political what the fly-wheel is to the mechanical engine. It ought to represent the average but not the extreme opinions of the people'.[25] Like the governor on a steam engine Babbage admired so much, the philosopher's and the parliamentarian's attention served the dual function of deeply understanding function and controlling abnormality.

When we look carefully at the lives of other British natural philosophers, we find widespread awareness of the connections between mental governance of the body and managerial governance of machines in the industrial system. In virtually every British natural philosopher's life, one can find instances of strain and anxiety, corrected (or not) by diligent attention to regulation. Early in his career, James Watt complained of a 'disease' in the 'boilers' of the 'engine which drives the works' of his body. His continued poor health led him to redirect his energies to invention.[26] Often natural philosophers' complaints emerged from the very strains of doing science. For example, the overwhelming spectacle of the early meetings of the British Association for the Advancement of Science taxed a few participants into a stupor: assistant secretary John Phillips had a nervous break-down after the 1837 Liverpool meeting. He found solace and renewed health in boating and climbing. The Bristol meeting of the same association seems to have been the proximate cause for chemist William Henry's suicide.[27] In the early 1840s, Michael Faraday also buckled under a rigorous workload. He had been maintaining a full schedule of public lecturing and private experiments, and some work with volatilized metals early in 1839 left him with severe eye inflammation. He told John Herschel that under those conditions he was 'obliged to use these organs very cautiously & for but short periods'. He found relief from the 'mental strain' at the theatre, on the beach in Brighton, and in Switzerland. Reflecting on Faraday's life several decades later, John Tyndall admired the great chemist's ultimate ability to regulate his energies:

> This, at one period or another of their lives, seems to be the fate of most great invest-igators. They do not know the limits of their constitutional strength until they have transgressed them. It is, perhaps, right that they should transgress them, in order to ascertain where they lie. Faraday, however, though he went far towards it, did not push his transgression beyond his power of restitution.[28]

In 1851, John Couch Adams worried about his mentor, Cambridge Observatory director James Challis, who had retreated to the country while 'getting over the effects of overwork'.[29] Astronomy popularizer Agnes Mary Clerke also pushed herself to the verge of exhaustion. She complained that the pool of astronomical facts grew larger each year, 'and the strain of keeping them under mental command becomes heavier'. The work she had written just prior to making this remark, *Problems in Astrophysics*, had so exhausted her that she could only labour at it for half-hours at a time.[30] In writing his mammoth *Principles of Psychology*, Herbert Spencer similarly buckled under the weight of his evidence. His 'nervous system finally gave way', and he could not work for a year and a half.[31] In 1861, William Thomson bemoaned his fractured thigh, which prevented him from attending the first meeting of the British Association's Committee on Electrical Standards, whose actions proved so important to the future of the telegraphy industry. Though the fall did not injure what he called his 'vis viva', the 'constant uniformity of my position prevents me from getting any refreshment and makes anything like head work to be avoided'.[32]

In fact, by the end of the century, Francis Galton deemed energy the 'most important quality to favour' in eugenic schemes, and found scientists extraordin-arily endowed with it. His own breakdown at Cambridge had made this conclusion quite personal. Galton interpreted his frightening experience through the by-then familiar model of body-as-engine/mind-as-governor:

I suffered from intermittent pulse and a variety of brain symptoms of an alarming kind. A mill seemed to be working inside my head; I could not banish obsessing ideas; at times I could hardly read a book, and found it painful even to look at a printed page . . . I had been much too zealous, had worked too irregularly and in too many directions, and had done myself serious harm. It was as though I had tried to make a steam-engine perform more work than it was constructed for, by tampering with its safety valve and thereby straining its mechanism. Happily, the human body may sometimes repair itself, which the steam-engine cannot.[33]

Galton's active mind gave him the capacity to manage his body by occasionally releasing the pressure. Touring, walks, mountaineering, and visits to spas relieved him. In fact, he became so convinced of his mind's directive power, that at one point he nearly asphyxiated himself. In an experimental attempt to 'subjugate the body by the spirit, and . . . determined that my will should replace automatism', Galton made his breathing dependent on his will, and had some difficulty rendering it automatic again.[34]

Let us consider one final example, this time an extended one, of a British natural philosopher relying on the powers of mental management. By the time John Herschel began experiencing strange visions in the 1840s, his astronomically accomplished aunt Caroline had already cautioned him 'not to overwork yourself like your dear Father [equally renowned astronomer William Herschel] did'. Soon after that, David Brewster had recommended 'the medicine that has saved me, – a calm life in summer and a devotion of yourself to rural efforts, or any other engrossing pursuits [that] will keep off the mind from the poison of its own abstractions'.[35]

It would seem at first that Herschel failed to heed this advice. In his popular writing, bodily needs frequently took a back seat to the mental appreciation of nature and its divinely designed intricacies. This meant not a denial of the body per se so much as its subservience to the reason and will. He deemed this approach important enough to make it the leading idea of his most famous and most popular work, *A Preliminary Discourse on the Study of Natural Philosophy*. Human dominance of the natural system seemed surprising, he wrote, when one considered only the physical frailty of the human constitution. But it was the exercise of reason, not brute strength, that allowed our dominion. A choice few had reaped from the faculty of reason even greater fruits than the satisfaction of bodily appetites:

> every one who passes his life in tolerable ease and comfort, or rather whose whole time is not anxiously consumed in providing the absolute necessaries of existence, is conscious of wants and cravings in which the senses have no part . . . [and] he will readily admit them to hold a much higher rank, and to deserve much more attention, than the former class.

These feelings held a higher rank because they led one to contemplate the perfection of God's creation.[36] This did not mean these faculties entirely transcended bodily cravings. Herschel thought of the mind's power of generalization as 'a ravenous and hungry mood grasping[,] swallowing[,] digesting and assimilating all that comes near and condensing and pocketing all that is over and above (like Sancho Panca at the wedding feast) for future use'.[37] The proper method for understanding God's creation was not to deny the body as an ascetic would, but to discipline it utterly as an industrial manager would.[38]

Though Joseph Agassi rightly called Herschel's philosophy in the *Preliminary Discourse* a 'philosophy of success', we should not conclude that he ignored the importance of failure.[39] In a work meant for a popular audience, Herschel understandably presented the natural philosopher in full vigour and perfect freedom from prejudice. In his more specialized and private writing, however, an important part of scientific method was knowing the self, warts and all. He argued in his 1841 review of William Whewell's *History of the Inductive Sciences* that disease provided unique opportunities for scientific study; by causing deviations from the bodily norm, it allowed scientists to obtain a clearer understanding of normal processes.[40] Study of one's occasionally abnormal body was one of the preconditions for the attainment of success.

As they did for his contemporaries, Herschel's musings packed a personal punch. At least as early as 1843, he began periodically to see floating, colourful disks of light which he at first called 'ocular spectra' or 'fortification patterns' (because of their fort-like shape). He later learned that several other prominent natural philosophers, like William Hyde Wollaston, David Brewster, and George Airy, had experienced these visual phenomena, akin to the visions we now associate with migraines. The condition came to be called *hemiopsy*.[41] In the meantime, Herschel furtively recorded these visions in his diary. His attacks began in the outside corner of his left eye as a 'singular shadowy appearance', which gradually moved to the centre of his field of vision. As it came into focus, the shadow took on sharper, zigzagged shapes, and frequently colour as well.[42]

Over time, fatigue – encouraged by the heavy doses of laudanum he took – became the clearest culprit behind Herschel's hemiopsy.[43] The weariness came largely from several horrible years that he spent as Master of the Mint. The Mint position and chronic bronchitis contributed to his nervous and physical collapse in the mid-1850s, after which the hemionopic visions increased in frequency. He spent much of his remaining fifteen years in bed or in a wheelchair enduring repeated bouts of bronchitis, rheumatism, and gout. He found himself in a 'state of languor & depression both of bodily & mental activity – which deprives me almost of the power of doing anything calling for consecutive thought or giving *anything* its due attention be it ever so pressing'.[44]

Herschel struck many as a sickly fellow. During an 1843 visit to the Herschel home at Collingwood, novelist Maria Edgeworth worried about her friend's wellbeing:

> He shewed us a Daguerreotype of the stand of the great instrument [William Herschel's 40-foot telescope] before it was taken down. He told us that the impression of that frame as it stood was so strong on his eyes that when it was gone he some time afterwards saw it in its place so plainly before him that he thought he could have touched it. There

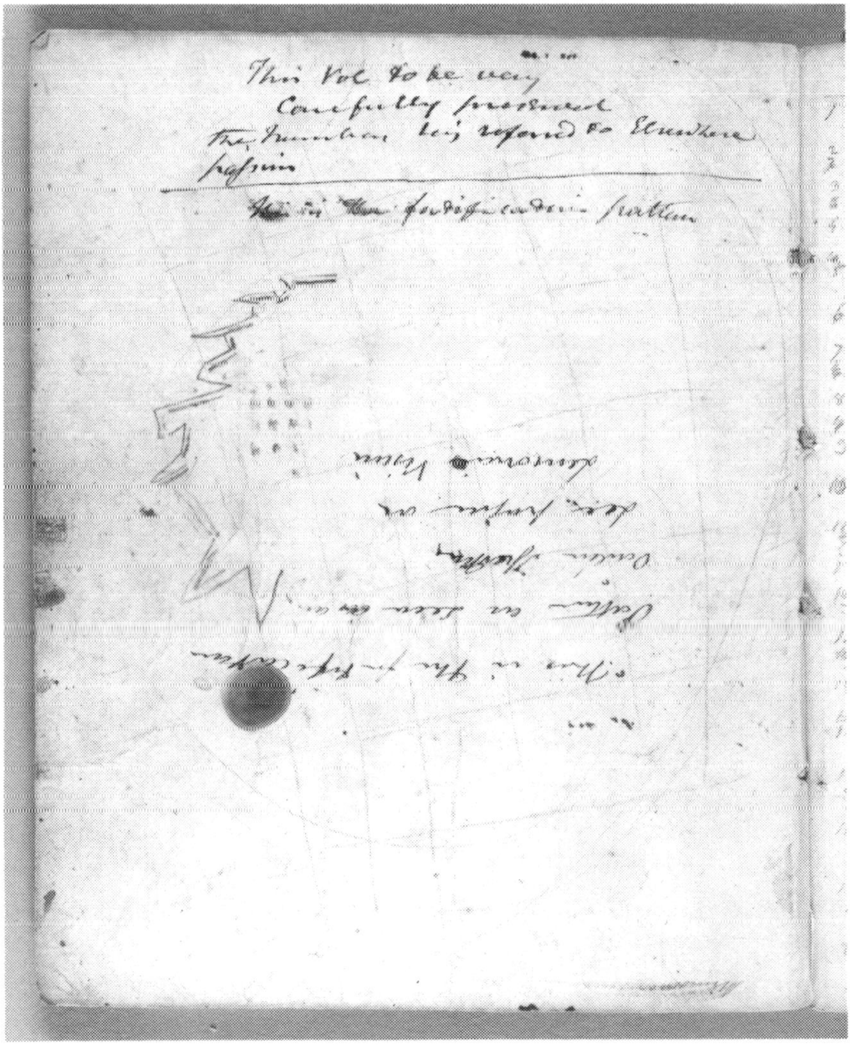

Figure 4.1 John Herschel hurriedly sketched this image of an 'ocular spectrum' experience in one of the notebooks he used to record his experiments with photographic developers. Harry Ransom Humanities Research Center, the University of Texas at Austin

it is still! I never saw so sensitive a person – almost too much for his health. He complains – no he never complains, but he told us of a strange delusion or disease of his sight which comes on at night sometimes when he is sitting up reading. The farthest part of the room vanishes and by degrees the circuit of sight diminishes so that he can at last see only the table before him and just the space occupied by the candles. This should warn him not to overwork and it does warn Lady [Margaret] Herschel to take all means to prevent his overstraining his great faculties.[45]

If perception were like photography – a science in which Herschel showed a keen interest – there was at least the hope of an explanation and the ability to control the situation. Indeed, Herschel spoke of his own visions as the result of a 'photographic process'.

In a more public effort to explain his visions, Herschel spoke in 1858 to the Leeds Literary and Philosophical Society on 'Sensorial Vision'. To this audience, he argued that his visions were the physical manifestation of an especially active mind.[46] Implied in his talk was the notion that anyone might suffer a nervous illness but the philosopher had the resources of reason and experience at his disposal, tools that could diagnose and even cure. For example, he argued that the subject of ocular spectra was

far from being exhausted, and it is to the habit of attention to such sensorial impressions, fostered by frequently watching the development of these spectra *under a variety of circumstances* in my own case, that I attribute my having been led to notice that other class of phænomena of which I shall presently speak, and which from their inconspic-uousness, I suppose, *escape the notice of most people.*[47]

In this statement, Herschel both validated his own authority on the subject of vision, and encouraged those with similar skills to inquire further. Privately, he wondered if his visions might indicate 'an intelligence working within us which is not our own'.[48]

For Herschel and many of his contemporaries, the analogies of the steam engine and factory management helped natural philosophers define how the mind interacted with the body. They found that such systems required diligent manage-ment. If they could not achieve perfect efficiency through autonomous mechanism, they could at least allow managers to guide these mechanisms toward maximum work. In the next section, we will see natural philosophers applying this directive power to long-distance communication.

Telegraphy and the Management of Communication

Modern peoples by printing, gunpowder, the compass and the language of telegraph signs, have made vanish the greatest obstacles which have opposed the civilization of men, and made possible their union in great republics. It is thus that the arts and sciences serve liberty.[49]

We might expect that the above accolade came from an English pundit, marvelling at Cooke and Wheatstone's 1837 invention of the electric telegraph. In fact, however, the speaker was Bertrand Barère de Vieuzac, a delegate to the National Convention in France, more than 40 years earlier. Speaking in 1794, the delegate had just witnessed the first official message passed along an *optical telegraph* line between Lille (on the border with the Austrian Netherlands) and Paris. That message reported the happy news that France was recapturing cities from the Austrians and Prussians. In 1801, Napoleon commissioned one of these optical telegraphs to facilitate an invasion of England, but later cancelled the attack.[50]

Figure 4.2 A German diagram of a Chappe optical telegraph and its alphabet of signals

The new technology already had found its way across the English Channel via a French prisoner of war.[51] In September 1794 the editors of the *Gentlemen's Magazine* shared a dispatch with its readers: the French inventor Claude Chappe had devised the means to 'transmit thoughts, in a peculiar language, from one distance to another, by means of machines, which are placed at different distances of between four and five leagues from one another, so that the expression reaches a very distant place in the space of a few minutes'.[52] The article set off a host of English inventors seeking to copy or approximate this device for 'communicating intelligence'. Using a budget of £3,000 and the design of John Gamble, chaplain to the Duke of York, the Admiralty established a line of 'telegraph hills' from London to Deal by January 1796. The Admiralty continued to operate and expand the lines throughout the Napoleonic Wars,[53] using them to transmit rapidly such news as the Spithead Mutiny from ship to headquarters and back again.[54]

Designs varied between the various optical telegraphs that developed, but generally they involved a system of several movable shutters or paddles (semaphores) attached to a base. The telegraph was darkly painted and placed on a tower, church, hill, or other high location so that its signals would contrast with the sky. Using a carefully guarded code book, a telegraph operator manoeuvred the shutters or semaphores to symbolize various letters, words, or phrases. Operators would read and relay these messages along a line of stations, which typically ran between a contested borderland and a major city. The stations sat in enough proximity to each other that their operators could easily read the signals from neighbouring stations using a simple telescope.[55]

Some immediately saw in the optical telegraph the potential for the Enlightenment dream of a universal language.[56] Abraham Edelcrantz, a Swedish nobleman second only to Chappe in the development of the optical telegraph, hoped that his code book might eventually serve as a universal dictionary, 'whereby people of all nations could communicate without knowing each other's language'.[57] Semaphoric code would thus join other languages that the natural sciences had developed to handle problems of idiosyncratic knowledge. These languages included technical vocabularies, rationalized nomenclatures, mathematics, training, and machines. For example, we can understand Babbage's difference engine as a hardware language for expressing his conception of universal mental operations.[58] We might also view the efforts of Cambridge's Analytical Society as an attempt to replace the uncommunicative features of Newton's fluxional calculus.[59]

As in the governor case, however, such ideals hardly represented the realities of mechanical operation. The difficulties of working with the optical telegraph again mirrored the difficulties of working with the nervous system. Natural philosophers soon saw that in both systems, communication errors frequently happened en route from source to destination. Apart from errors caused by unavoidable external conditions, most mistakes arose from the poorly managed 'automatons' who conveyed the messages. Stations thus required not only an observer (usually a lieutenant) to read incoming signals and a 'handyman' to reproduce those signals for the next station – but stations also had to keep a log of their communications so that they could be checked for errors by supervisors.[60] Telegraphy directors admonished their workers to correct for sensory inaccuracy by using the same mental powers of attention that were advised by the mental and moral philosophers of the period,[61] but ultimately errors were seen as unavoidable. Ignace Chappe, brother to the inventor, proclaimed it a sheer impossibility to have error-free transmissions down the telegraph system's long chain of stations.[62] Much of the work done to refine the optical telegraph's design during the Napoleonic Wars was directed at making the apparatus and coded language simple enough that a minimum of errors occurred, while keeping it complex enough that enemy spies could not decode the messages.[63] Because this research involved determining the minimum signalling legible with the least error over some distance, it prefigured later work on just noticeable differences and later connections between the nervous system and the telegraph.[64]

By the time electric telegraphs attracted significant attention in the 1840s–50s, the ground had been laid for thinking about the analogous difficulties of nervous and telegraphic communication. Since the nervous system was typically imagined as (at least like) an electrical system,[65] the analogy became especially apt with the arrival of the electric telegraph. William Fothergill Cooke, one of the electric telegraph's inventors and originally an anatomical wax modeller, even referred to breaks in his wires as 'injuries'.[66] In a particularly striking example of this analogy, an early American historian of the telegraph, George Prescott, wrote that the telegraph

> in its most common form, communicating intelligence between distant places, performs the function of the sensitive nerves of the human body. In the fire telegraph it is made to act for the first time in its motor function, or to produce effects of power at a distance; and this is also connected with the sensitive function, through a brain or central station, which is the reservoir of electric or nervous power for the whole system. We have thus an excito-motory system, in which the intelligence and volition of the operator at the central station come in to connect sensitive and motor functions, as they would in the case of the individual. The conditions of the municipal organization absolutely compelled the relation of circuits which has been described.[67]

Prescott's vivid juxtaposition suggests a number of reasons why the analogy made sense to telegraph engineers and physiologists alike. Not only did both the telegraph and the nervous system convey intelligence and sensitivity almost instantaneously, but they both also contained a central station that directed, connected and interpreted the proceedings. This supervisory organ still proved necessary, for although the electrical telegraphic system was certainly speedier than the optical version, it still relied on mechanical and human performance, neither of which achieved perfection. Telegraphers still had to translate code into legible messages, and at an even more basic level, a messenger boy had to run that legible message to the recipient. Only the non-mechanical attribute known as skill – skill in both designing and working the apparatus – improved the system's efficiency.[68]

To comprehend the depth of the nervous system-telegraph analogy, we need to examine its roots in several commitments that British natural philosophers tended to share in the early industrial period. For one thing, the problem of communication stood at the heart of concerns about provincialism and science. Linguistic differences mitigated against the formation of scientific laws from disparately communicated facts. Language, in all its complexity and diversity, upset what might have been a clear relationship between the provincial and the general, for if, on the one hand, language made public knowledge possible, it also might jam an interpretive wedge between nature and the mind, and between knowers.

Self-consciousness prevented that wedge from splitting scientific certainty asunder. If one knew one's own interpretative quirks, one could presumably eliminate them from the final public account.[69] Language – particularly the coded languages of telegraphy – foregrounded their own artificiality. The supervisor, the elite natural philosopher, and the factory manager then provided the nearly ineffable interpretive skills required to reach that final stage of good (if not perfect) knowledge. In fact, that management might even require national control: Parliament's 1868 decision to nationalize the various private telegraph systems reflected a long-standing concern that telegraphic messages were too important and profitable to be left to private enterprise.[70]

In short, natural philosophers learned through study of the nervous system and optical telegraphy that communication required supervised negotiation.[71] If signs had more than one meaning, if more than one description or perception could relate an experience, then arriving at the truth required managers to decide what would stand as an authoritative description of a phenomenon. Along with the new Biblical critics, scientists and physicians configured language and even sensations as signs. Proper interpretation was no longer inherent to the signs themselves, but rather came with experience and training.[72]

Beyond their concerns about the communication between province and metropole, natural philosophers in the eighteenth and nineteenth centuries cultivated a more general interest in epistemological problems having to do with mind, body, and the nervous connections between them. In particular, scientific epistemology and method frequently looked to nervous physiology to learn what was possible for human investigators.[73] In the period under discussion, anatomists, physiologists, and philosophers devoted substantial attention to understanding the nervous system and how it might structure understanding and communication.

The ideas of the philosophers and physicians of the Enlightenment-era Scottish Common Sense school set the agenda for much subsequent British mental-moral philosophy. The Common Sense philosophers, for instance, made what was considered an important distinction between sensation and perception. Sensation was the virtually unmediated mapping of the outside world onto the retina, whereas perception was the mind's active judgement of what the sensation was and what it meant.[74] This analytical distinction helped differentiate the totally physical and passive aspects of nervous physiology from the immaterial and dynamic nature of mental activity. A healthful life and science therefore required not only a well-kept body, but also the cultivation of mental and moral faculties such as reason, judgement, heightened attention, sympathy and sensibility.

In his 1749 *Observations on Man*, English physician David Hartley had made the explicit, associationist connections between nervous physiology and the mental-moral philosophy that would so dominate British thought. He argued that ideas arose and became connected through vibrations in the nerves and brain.[75] Following on Hartley's example, two of the most important early figures in the Scottish Enlightenment, William Cullen and Robert Whytt, had given their colleague's mental philosophy a more empirical basis in nervous physiology. Their approach emphasized the active nature of the mind – and therefore, the active nature of perception and other mental processes. Furthermore, they elevated the nervous system to the place of chief importance in physiology. Cullen informed his students at the University of Edinburgh that the nervous system, 'as the organ of sense and motion, is connected with so many functions of the animal œconomy, that the study of it must be of the utmost importance, and a fundamental part of the study of the whole œconomy'. He even made the muscles a subsidiary of the nervous system.[76] Popular texts through the first half of the nineteenth century reinforced the idea that the nerves acted not only as a route for sensations from the outside world, but also as the conduit for the mind's direction of the body. The popular and scientific literature on the nervous system considered its directive capacity to be of primary importance. For physician John Elliot, for example, the human body was

> a machine composed of bones and muscles, with their proper appendages, for the purpose of motion at the instance of its intelligent principle; from this principle nerves, or instruments of sensation, are likewise detached to the various parts of the body, for such information as may be necessary for determining it to those motions of the body which may be most conducive to the happiness of the former, and preservation of both.[77]

Members of a later generation like Charles Bell continued to challenge the passive model of the nerves maintained by Albrecht von Haller and other materialists. Bell insisted that the mind was not merely acted upon, but active during sensation and other nervous activities.[78] Historian Christopher Lawrence has made clear that the hierarchical organization imputed to the mind and nervous system 'served to sanction the introduction of new economic and associated cultural forms by identifying the landed minority as the custodians of civilization, and therefore the natural governors, in a backward society'.[79] Such ideas were easily adaptable to an industrial setting and its own conception of governors.

Such ideas about the hierarchical ordering of the body and society also made sense in light of the connections formed in the early nineteenth century between nervous impulses and other imponderable forces. If nervous impulses acted like electricity, for example, it stood to reason that the nerves existed in a continually active state. Luigi Galvani's connection between electrical and nervous impulse and Johannes Müller's law of specific energies both emphasized the extent to which the body could be understood via analogy with machines powered by imponderable forces. Just as varying stimuli (such as electricity, mechanical pressure) could garner the same response when applied to a nerve, so also machine technology was demonstrating the correlation of different kinds of forces.[80] By mid-century, London physician Henry Holland considered it a commonplace to liken nervous power to light, electricity, magnetism, heat, and chemical attraction. Important implications of this analogy for Holland were the continuity of material and mental phenomena, and the possibility that the rational will might still control the 'more automatic machinery which surrounds it'.[81] By the time Holland was flourishing, this image of the body as a machine governed by a mind had become quite popular. Not only epistemological idealists like William Whewell, but also many of his empiricist critics argued that the mind actively shaped knowledge of the world.[82]

Interest in the connections between mental philosophy and nervous physiology was widespread within the natural philosophical and medical communities.[83] A quick skim of any scientific periodical from this period demonstrates a keen fascination with bodily abnormalities and their mental effects and management. Goethe's *Zur Farbenlehre* (1810) and Brewster's *Letters on Natural Magic* (1832), are only the two best-known treatments of these phenomena.[84] Speculations and experiments on all manner of illusions and aches, phantasmagoria and pangs, appeared in the specialized and popular scientific literature. The *Philosophical Magazine* published an especially large number of notices about various nervous effects – understandably, given that that prolific student of optics David Brewster edited the journal from 1832 to 1868.[85] But more formal society transactions also appeased their readers' interest in experiences of nervous malfunction.[86] In their correspondence and private notes as well, natural philosophers noted their experiences with nervous disorder.[87]

In the last quarter of the nineteenth century, Hubert Airy (son of the Greenwich Observatory director George Airy) looked back over this vast literature, and proclaimed that natural philosophers were particularly qualified for the study of nervous disorder. Because of their particular education and experience, he argued, natural philosophers had *unique* claims to authority on the subject that surpassed even the claims of physicians.

> [T]he votaries of Natural Philosophy are especially qualified by their habits of accurate observation to contemplate attentively any strange apparition, without or within, and, I had almost said, are especially exposed to the risk of impairment (temporary or permanent) of the eyesight, by the severity of the eye-work and brain-work they undergo, and therefore possess especial advantages for the study of visual derangements; whereas the physician, unless personally subject to the malady, must depend, for his acquaintance with its phenomena, on the imperfect or exaggerated accounts of patients untrained to observe closely or record faithfully.[88]

According to Airy's logic, anyone who presumed that the physiology of the nervous system was the exclusive territory of physicians, thought wrong. Nervous physiology played too important a part in the methodology of natural philosophy. The natural philosopher not only valued the nervous system as a tool; he or she also often worked it to the point of impairment. Finally, he or she brought the necessary training to investigate accurately any physiological problems he or she might personally have. One's familiarity with epistemology, the science of imponderable forces, precision instrumentation, and optics made one a unique authority on nervous issues.

In sum, by the mid-nineteenth century, it had become clear that telegraphs and nervous systems faced the same managerial problems. The intelligence the two systems communicated was so vital that a supervisor or mind had to watch over and direct the accident-prone mechanical elements

Conclusion

Lorraine Daston and Ted Porter, among others, have demonstrated the widespread desire among nineteenth-century scientists to 'de-skill' their work, in order to guarantee the objectivity of the knowledge they produced. Indeed, devices as diverse as the photographic camera, the method of least squares, and the Royal Greenwich Observatory's standard forms were designed to reduce the extent to which idiosyncratic perceptions or theoretical prejudice entered scientific observation.[89] We should recognize, though, that claims to totally mechanical objectivity were *rhetorical strategies* or *goals*. In reality, the very same natural philosophers who argued against a scientific aristocracy and for the democratization of skill, in a pinch reserved for themselves a privileged status in the scientific community. As Richard Yeo phrased this idea, 'There was . . . a danger that this emphasis on the accessibility of inductive method could be construed to imply that scientific method was simply a matter of common sense.'[90] Likewise, a special place remained for society's other managers: God, the factory supervisor, the mind.

The quiet reassertion of what we might call an inductive hierarchy often seemed like the only way out of epistemological jams. The foot soldiers of inductivism – bodies, machines – did not always behave as they should. They sometimes provided inaccurate pictures of nature. Furthermore, the automatic controls designed to eradicate such errors rarely worked perfectly. When new technologies like the electric telegraph eventually eliminated these errors, new problems took their place. So, though ideally managers would not be necessary, real science required them. Fact gatherers and machines needed supervisors. Analogously, the body needed the mind.

Notes

1. The author thanks Iwan Rhys Morus for his helpful editorial comments and particularly his careful attention to bibliographical references.
2. The classic expression of this last perspective can be found in L. Daston, 'Objectivity and the Escape from Perspective', *Social Studies of Science,* 1992, 22: 597–618.
3. In the last decade, historians have rectified much of the neglect and abuse of Romantic and vitalistic science. See, for example, the classic in this field: A. Cunningham and N. Jardine (eds), *Romanticism and the Sciences* (Cambridge: Cambridge University Press, 1990).
4. In today's terms, natural philosophers would be those men and women who studied the sciences of matter and motion. Natural philosophy thus includes what we would now call the physical sciences, but also considered problems in what we now think of as physiology, psychology, and chemistry.
5. For example, see C. Smith, *The Science of Energy: A Cultural History of Energy Physics in Victorian Britain* (London: Athlone Press, 1998), pp. 77–99.
6. For a related argument, see A. Winter, *Mesmerized: Powers of Mind in Victorian Britain* (Chicago: University of Chicago Press, 1998).
7. That this vision itself rarely reflected reality is a point well made in A. Secord, 'Artisan naturalists: science as popular culture in nineteenth-century England', PhD thesis, University of London, forthcoming. Also see her 'Artisan Botany', N. Jardine, J. A. Secord and E.C. Spary (eds), *Cultures of Natural History* (Cambridge: Cambridge University Press, 1996); 'Science in the Pub: Artisan Botanists in early 19th-century Lancashire', *History of Science*, 1994, 32: 269–315.

8. R. Hahn, 'Laplace and the Vanishing Role of God in the Physical Universe', H. Woolf (ed.), *Analytic Spirit: Essays in the History of Science in Honor of Henry Guerlac* (Ithaca NY: Cornell University Press, 1981), pp. 85–95.

9. N. Wise with C. Smith, 'Work and Waste: Political Economy and Natural Philosophy in Nineteenth Century Britain', *History of Science*, 1989, 27: 263–301; 391–449; 1990, 28: 221–61.

10. Wise with Smith, 'Work and Waste', 221 61; N. Wise, 'Mediating Machines', *Science in Context*, 1988, 2: 79–92; R. L. Kremer, *The Thermodynamics of Life and Experimental Physiology, 1770–1880* (New York: Garland Press, 1990); C. E. Russett, *Sexual Science: The Victorian Construction of Womanhood* (Cambridge MA: Harvard University Press, 1989), pp. 104–29.

11. R. Porter and D. Porter, *In Sickness and in Health: The British Experience 1650–1850* (London: Fourth Estate, 1988), p. 51.

12. A. Ure, *The Philosophy of Manufactures; or, an Exposition of the Scientific, Moral, and Commercial Economy of the Factory System of Great Britain*, 3rd edn, (London, 1861), p. 55.

13. Ure, *Ibid.*, pp. 7–8; 20–3; 214–15; 311.

14. For example, see L. Carnot, *Essai sur les machines en general*, 2nd edn, (Dijon, 1786).

15. J. G. Burke, 'Bursting Boilers and the Federal Power', M. Kranzberg and W. H. Davenport (eds), *Technology and Culture: An Anthology* (New York: New American Library, 1972), pp. 98–9; L. C. Hunter, *A History of Industrial Power in the United States 1780–1930*, three vols, (Charlottesville, VA: University Press of Virginia 1985), vol. 2, pp. 353–92. Both sections describe incidents in Britain.

16. C. Wheatstone papers, Box 6, King's College London (KCL). Also see the second and third chapters particularly of C. Babbage, *On the Economy of Machinery and Manufactures*, 4th edn, (London, 1835).

17. H. W. Dickinson, *Matthew Boulton* (Cambridge: Cambridge University Press, 1936), pp. 116–17.

18. L. J. Daston, 'British Responses to Psycho-physiology, 1860–1900', *Isis*, 1978, 69: 192–208, on p. 206. For examples of such 'mainstream physiology', see H. Holland, *Chapters on Mental Physiology* (London, 1852), pp. 65–8; W. B. Carpenter, *Principles of Mental Physiology; with their Applications to the Training and Discipline of the Mind, and the Study of its Morbid Conditions*, 4th edn (New York, 1877), pp. 1–28; P. G. Tait, *Lectures on Some Recent Advances in Physical Science; with a Special Lecture on Force*, 2nd edn (London, 1876), pp. 24–6.

19. See the next section for a discussion of natural philosophers' commitment to the mind as governor.

20. Carpenter, *Principles of Mental Physiology*, p. 389.

21. I. R. Morus, 'Correlation and Control: William Robert Grove and the Construction of a New Philosophy of Scientific Reform', *Studies in History and Philosophy of Science*, 1991, 22: 589–621, on pp. 597; 610.

22. T. H. Huxley, 'A Liberal Education, and Where to Find It', *Science and Education* (New York, 1896), p. 86. Huxley delivered this lecture in 1868.

23. B. Haley, *The Healthy Body and Victorian Culture* (Cambridge MA: Harvard University Press, 1978); C. H. Flynn, 'Running Out of Matter: the Body Exercised in Eighteenth-century Fiction', G. S. Rousseau and R. Porter (eds), *The Languages of Psyche: Mind and Body in Enlightenment Thought* (Berkeley and Los Angeles: University of California Press, 1987), pp. 147–85; A. Warwick, 'Exercising the Student Body: Mathematics and Athleticism in Victorian Cambridge', C. Lawrence and S. Shapin (eds), *Science Incarnate: Historical Embodiments of Natural Knowledge* (Chicago: University of Chicago Press, 1998), pp. 288–326.

24. Babbage, *Economy of Machinery and Manufactures*, pp. 27; 30.

25. C. Babbage, *A Word to the Wise* (London, 1833), quoted in A. Hyman, *Charles Babbage: Pioneer of the Computer* (Princeton: Princeton University Press, 1983), pp. 86–7.

26. Smith, *Science of Energy*, p. 43.

27. J. Phillips to W. W. Currie, 7 November 1837, Fitzwilliam Museum, Perceval bequest, J.123; W. V. Farrar, K. Farrar and E. L. Scott, 'The Henrys of Manchester, part 2; Thomas Henry's Sons: Thomas, Peter, and William', *Ambix*, 1974, 21: 179–207; both quoted in J. Morrell and A. Thackray, *Gentlemen of Science: Early Years of the British Association for the Advancement of Science* (Oxford: Oxford University Press, 1981), pp. 128–36; 402.

28. J. Tyndall, *Faraday as a Discoverer* (New York, 1880), pp. 75–8; M. Faraday to J. Herschel, 14 February 1839, L. P. Williams (ed.), *The Selected Correspondence of Michael Faraday,* two vols (Cambridge: Cambridge University Press, 1971), vol. 1, p. 335. Dalton feared that Faraday might have had lead poisoning, as he thought he had himself four decades earlier. See J. Dalton to M. Faraday, 3 September 1840, Royal Institution, reprinted in A. Thackray, *John Dalton: Critical Assessments of His Life and Science* (Cambridge MA: Harvard University Press, 1972), pp. 171–2.

29. J. C. Adams to G. Airy, 8 May 1851, RGO 6/373.180, Cambridge University Library (CUL).

30. A. M. Clerke, *Modern Cosmogonies* (London, 1905), p. 160; M. L. M. Huggins, *Agnes Mary Clerke and Ellen Mary Clerke: An Appreciation* (private publication, 1907), pp. 18–20.

31. H. Spencer, *An Autobiography*, vol. 20–1 of *The Works of Herbert Spencer* (Osnabruck, 1966), vol. 20, p. 543, first published 1904.

32. W. Thomson to G. G. Stokes, 16 January and 14 February 1861, K122 and K124, CUL. On the standards committee, see B. J. Hunt, 'The Ohm is Where the Art is: British Telegraph Engineers and the Development of Electrical Standards', *Osiris*, 1994, 9: 48–63.

33. F. Galton, *Inquiries into Human Faculty and Its Development*, 2nd edn (London, 1892), pp. 17–19; F. Galton, *Memories of My Life* (London, 1909), pp. 78–9. Also see K. Pearson, *The Life, Letters and Labours of Francis Galton*, 3 vols (Cambridge: Cambridge University Press, 1914), vol. 1, 166–73.

34. Galton, *Memories*, pp. 154–9; 191–2; 276–7; 290. Galton's case is also discussed in Warwick, 'Exercising the Student Body', pp. 296–8.

35. C. Herschel to J. Herschel, 14 July 1823, Egerton ms. 3761, British Library (BL); D. Brewster to J. Herschel, 2 December 1825, J. Herschel correspondence, Royal Society of London (JHC–RSL) 4.259.

36. J. Herschel, *A Preliminary Discourse on the Study of Natural Philosophy*, ed. J. Secord (Chicago: University of Chicago Press, 1987), p. 3, first printed 1830.

37. J. Herschel to C. Babbage, 19 March 1820, JHC–RSL 2.130.

38. See William Ashworth's chapter in this volume, and his 'Memory, Efficiency, and Symbolic Analysis: Charles Babbage, John Herschel, and the Industrial Mind', *Isis*, 1996, 87: 629–53.

39. J. Agassi, 'Sir John Herschel's Philosophy of Success', *Historical Studies in the Physical Sciences*, 1969, 1: 1–36.

40. [J. Herschel], 'Whewell on the Inductive Sciences', *Quarterly Review,* 1841, 68: 182.

41. E. Green Musselman, 'Persistence of Sight: Problems of Idiosyncratic Vision and Knowledge in British Natural Philosophy, 1780–1860', PhD dissertation, Indiana University, 1999, pp. 78–155; H. Airy, 'On a Distinct Form of Transient Hemiopsia', *Philosophical Transactions of the Royal Society of London,* 1870, 160: 247–64.

42. J. Herschel diary, 11 June 1846, MS.584, RSL. Also see entries for 11 May 1853, 20 February 1854, 18 August 1855, 7 February 1858, 12 February 1865, 29 July 1866, 24 February and 5 May 1868; 22 June, 7 August, and 11 October 1869; 16 April, 17 July, and 5 September 1870; 'Optical MSS. – Unidentified Material', 4 January 1852, W0354, Harry Ransom Humanities Research Center (HRC); J. Herschel, 'On Sensorial Vision', in *Familiar Lectures on Scientific Subjects* (London, 1867), pp. 406–7.

43. J. Herschel, 'Miscellanea', 12 May 1820, M-W0070, HRC; J. Herschel and J. South, 'Observations of the Apparent Distances and Positions of 380 Double and Triple Stars', *Philosophical Transactions of the Royal Society of London*, 1824, 114: 15; G. Buttmann, *The Shadow of the Telescope: A Biography of John Herschel*, trans. B. E. J. Pagel (New York: Charles Scribner's Sons,

1970), pp. 181–2; J. Herschel, 'Optical MSS.'. Laudanum was the tincture of opium and used widely without regulation until 1868. Herschel acknowledged that the drug might have exacerbated his visions, but remained convinced that the true cause lay elsewhere.

44. J. Herschel to M. Somerville?, n.d., L0760, HRC. On Herschel's ill health, also see G. Airy to J. Herschel, 3 February 1839, JHC–RSL 1.76; J. Herschel to G. Airy, 16 April 1856(?), JHC–RSL 1.331; F. Baily to J. Herschel, 9 January 1841, JHC–RSL 3.197; J. Herschel to F. Baily, 1 March 1837 and 26 January and 11 October 1841, JHC–RSL 3.138, 198, 218; I. Herschel to E. Sabine, 6 April 1855, MS.258.639, RSL; M. Herschel to J. W. Lubbock, 20 October 1855/6(?), H.364, RSL; J. Herschel diary, MS.584-6, RSL; Buttmann, *Shadow of the Telescope*, pp. 154–5.

45. M. Edgeworth to M. P. Edgeworth, 26 November 1843, in C. Colvin (ed.), *Maria Edgeworth: Letters from England 1813–1844* (Oxford: Oxford University Press, 1971), pp. 594–5. Also see a reporter's description of Herschel's gaunt appearance in 1838 in 'Sir John Frederick William Herschel', *Daily News* (13 May 1871), pp. 5–6.

46. Herschel, 'Sensorial', pp. 407; 411–12.

47. Herschel, 'Sensorial', p. 402; emphasis mine.

48. J. Herschel to W. B. Carpenter, 23 November 1858, JHC–RSL 5.195.

49. See G. J. Holzmann and B. Pehrson, *The Early History of Data Networks*, 1994, URL: http://www.it.kth.se/docs/early_net/toc.html, accessed 20–21 May 1999.

50. Holzmann and Pehrson, *Data Networks*, Chapter 2.

51. Actually, investigations into optical telegraphy had a history dating to at least the seventeenth century – among others, Robert Hooke had invented a kind of semaphore device – but Chappe was the first to develop a system for extensive use. See Holzmann and Pehrson, *Data Networks*, Chapter 1; J. Gamble, *An Essay on the Different Modes of Communication with Signals; containing an History of the Progressive Improvements in this Art, from the First Account of Beacons to the Most Approved Methods of Telegraphic Correspondence* (London, 1797), pp. 16–56.

52. [Editorial Response], *Gentlemen's Magazine*, 1794, 64: 815.

53. In fact, the Admiralty closed these lines only after the advantages of the electric telegraph became clear in 1847. See T. W. Holmes, *The Semaphore: The Story of the Admiralty-to-Portsmouth Shutter Telegraph and Semaphore Lines 1796 to 1847* (Ilfracombe: Stockwell, 1983) pp. 103–4.

54. Holmes, *Semaphore*, pp. 32–41; Holzmann and Pehrson, *Data Networks*, Chapter 5; Gamble, *Communication with Signals*.

55. Holmes, *Semaphore*.

56. For example, see J. Locke, *An Essay concerning Human Understanding*, ed. Peter H. Nidditch, (Oxford: Oxford University Press, 1975), pp. 397–401, first published 1689; H. Aarsleff, *The Study of Language in England, 1780–1860* (Princeton, NJ: Princeton University Press, 1967); U. Eco, *The Search for the Perfect Language* (Oxford: Blackwell, 1995).

57. A. N. Edelcrantz, *A Treatise on Telegraphs: and Experiments with a New Construction Thereof*, trans. G. J. Holzmann and B. Pehrson, URL: http://www.it.kth.se/docs/early_net/ch-1-4.html, accessed 20–21 May 1999, first published 1796; R. E. Rider, 'Measure of Ideas, Rule of Language: Mathematics and Language in the Eighteenth century', T. Frängsmyr, J. L. Heilbron, and R. E. Rider, *The Quantifying Spirit in the Eighteenth Century* (Berkeley and Los Angeles: University of California Press, 1990), pp. 125–32.

    Interestingly enough, Edelcrantz was an avid, but ultimately unsuccessful suitor to Maria Edgeworth, whose father, Richard Lovell Edgeworth, had been working on his own 'tellograph'. Edelcrantz also won high acclaim in Britain for his invention of a safety valve for steam engines. See Holzmann and Pehrson, *Data Networks*, Chapter 3.

58. Ashworth, 'Memory'; S. Schaffer, 'Babbage's Intelligence: Calculating Engines and the Factory System', *Critical Inquiry*, 1994, 21: 203–27, C. Babbage, 'Notes on Mechanical Drawing and Lettering', Add. ms. 37204.1–61, BL.

59. K. C. Knox, 'Dephlogisticating the Bible: Natural Philosophy and Religious Controversy in Late Georgian Cambridge', *History of Science*, 1996, 34: 167–200.

60. Holmes, *Semaphore*, pp. 52–3; 139–40; 155; Holzmann and Pehrson, *Data Analysis*, Chapter 2, Appendices B, C.

61. For example, see D. Stewart, *Elements of the Philosophy of the Human Mind*, vol. 2, W. Hamilton (ed.), *Collected Works of Dugald Stewart* (Edinburgh, 1877); T. Brown, *Lectures on the Philosophy of the Human Mind* (Hallowell, 1850); Holland, *Mental Physiology*; Carpenter, *Principles of Mental Physiology*.

62. Holzmann and Pehrson, *Data Networks*, Chapter 2.

63. For example, see Edelcrantz, *Treatise on Telegraphs*.

64. Gamble, *Communication with Signals*, pp. 78–91; 96–7; T. Lenoir, 'Helmholtz and the Materialities of Communication', *Osiris*, 1994, 9: 185–207; I. R. Morus, 'The Electric Ariel: Telegraphy and Commercial Culture in Victorian England', *Victorian Studies*,1996, 39: 339–78, on p. 375.

65. E. Clarke and L. S. Jacyna, *Nineteenth-Century Origins of Neuroscientific Concepts* (Berkeley and Los Angeles: University of California Press, 1987), pp. 157–211.

66. W. F. Cooke, *Extracts from the Private Letters of the Late Sir William Fothergill Cooke, 1836–39, relating to the Invention and Development of the Electric Telegraph* (London, 1895), p. 9.

67. G. B. Prescott, *History, Theory, and Practice of the Electric Telegraph* (Boston, 1860), p. 242; quoted in I. R. Morus, '"The Nervous System of Britain": Space, Time, and the Electric Telegraph in the Victorian Age', *British Journal for the History of Science*, 2000, 33: 471. For many other examples of the analogy, see the remainder of Morus's article; J. J. Fahie, *A History of Electric Telegraphy, to the Year 1837* (London, 1884), pp. 239; 303–4; T. Standage, *The Victorian Internet* (London: Wiedenfeld and Nicolson, 1998), pp. 87; 98; 151–2; 160.

68. Standage, *Victorian Internet*, pp. 62–4; 93–5; 122–5.

69. S. Schaffer, 'Astronomers Mark Time Discipline: and the Personal Equation', *Science in Context*, 1988, 2: 115–45; R. Benschop and D. Draaisma, 'In Pursuit of Precision: the Calibration of Minds and Machines in Late Nineteenth-century Psychology', *Annals of Science*, 2000, 57: 1–25; L. Daston, 'Knowledge of the Invisible, the Ineffable, and the Intuitive', unpublished paper, History of Science Society conference, Atlanta, October 1994; E. Carbutt, 'An Essay on the Signs of Ideas; or, the Means of Conveying to Others a Knowledge of our Ideas', *Memoirs and Proceedings of the Manchester Literary and Philosophical Society*, 1819, 3: 241–70.

70. J. Kieve, *The Electric Telegraph: A Social and Cultural History* (Plymouth: David and Charles, 1973), pp. 36; 119–54.

71. For a modern philosopher's explanation of how scientific communication necessarily entails negotiation, see D. Gooding, 'How do Scientists Reach Agreement about Novel Observations?' *Studies in History and Philosophy of Science*, 1986, 17: 205–30.

72. Aarsleff, *Study of Language*.

73. Roger Smith first made these connections in his excellent paper, 'The Background of Physiological Psychology in Natural Philosophy', *History of Science*, 1973, 11: 75–123.

74. Stewart, *Elements of the Philosophy of the Human Mind*; Brown, *Lectures on the Philosophy of the Human Mind*; R. Olson, *Scottish Philosophy and British Physics, 1750–1880: A Study in the Foundations of the Victorian Scientific Style* (Princeton: Princeton University Press, 1975).

75. D. Hartley, *Observations on Man, His Frame, His Duty, and His Expectations* (London, 1749).

76. W. Cullen, *Institutions of Medicine; Part 1, Physiology; for the Use of the Students in the University of Edinburgh*, 3rd edn (Edinburgh, 1785), pp. 23; 61–77; 101–2; R. Whytt, *Observations on the Nature, Causes and Cure of Those Diseases Which Are Commonly Called Nervous, Hyperchondriac or Hysteric; to Which Are Prefixed Some Remarks on the Sympathy of Nerves* (Edinburgh, 1764); R. K. French, *Robert Whytt, the Soul, and Medicine* (London: Wellcome Institute, 1969).

77. J. Elliot, *Elements of the Branches of Natural Philosophy Connected with Medicine* (London, 1782).

78. C. Bell, *Idea of a New Anatomy of the Brain* (London, 1811); Whytt, *Observations*; K. M. Figlio, 'Theories of Perception and the Physiology of Mind in the Late Eighteenth Century', *History of Science*, 1975, 13: 178.

79. C. Lawrence, 'The Nervous System and Society in the Scottish Enlightenment', B. Barnes and S. Shapin (eds), *Natural Order: Historical Studies of Scientific Culture* (London and Beverly Hills: Sage, 1979), pp. 20.

80. J. Muller, *Handbuch der Physiologie des Menschen fur Vorlesungen*, two vols (Koblenz, 1837–40).

81. Holland, *Mental Physiology*, pp. viii; 65–6; 239–301, especially p. 272.

82. W. Whewell, *The Philosophy of the Inductive Sciences; Founded upon their History*, 2nd edn, two vols, (London, 1847), vol. 1, pp. 26–7; 33–7.

83. Also see Iwan Rhys Morus's chapter in this volume.

84. J. W. von Goethe, *Theory of Colours*, trans. Charles Eastlake, (Cambridge: MIT Press, 1970), first published 1840; D. Brewster, *Letters on Natural Magic, Addressed to Sir Walter Scott, Bart.* (London, 1832).

85. For example, see R. Addams, 'An Account of a Peculiar Optical Phenomenon', *Philosophical Magazine*, 1834, 5. 373–4, D. Griffin, 'On an Unusual Affection of the Eye, in which Three Images were Produced', *Philosophical Magazine*, 1835, 6: 281–4; R. T. Cranmore, 'On Some Phænomena of Defective Vision', *Philosophical Magazine*, 1850, 36: 485–6; and many others.

86. For example, see D. Stewart, 'Some Account of a Boy Born Blind and Deaf, Collected from Authentic Sources of Information; with a Few Remarks and Comments', *Transactions of the Royal Society of Edinburgh*, 1814, 7: 1–78; P. M. Roget, 'Explanation of an Optical Deception in the Appearance of the Spokes of a Wheel Seen through Vertical Apertures', *Philosophical Transactions of the Royal Society of London*, 1825, 115: 131–40; W. Scoresby, 'An Inquiry into some of the Circumstances and Principles which Regulate the Production of Pictures on the Retina of the Human Eye', *Proceedings of the Royal Society of London* (22 December 1853), 380–3, (15 June 1854), 117–22; and many others.

87. For example, see J. Herschel to J. D. Forbes, n.d. April 1842, JHC–RSL 22.115; A. de Morgan to G. B. Airy, 2 September 1844, RGO 6/368.263, CUL; W. Whewell to G. B. Airy, 11 August 1850, RGO 6/372.439–40, CUL; C. Wheatstone, 'Binocular Vision' and 'Colour', Box 3, File 17–18, Wheatstone papers, KCL.

88. Airy, 'Transient Hemiopsia', 247.

89. T. M. Porter, *The Rise of Statistical Thinking 1820–1900* (Princeton NJ: Princeton University Press, 1986); Z. G. Swijtink, 'The Objectification of

Observation: Measurement and Statistical Methods in the Nineteenth Century',
L. Krüger (ed.), *The Probabilistic Revolution*, two vols (Cambridge MA: MIT
Press, 1987), vol. 1, pp. 261–85; Schaffer, 'Astronomers Mark Time'; Daston,
'Objectivity'; L. Daston and P. Galison, 'The Image of Objectivity', *Representations*, 1992, 40: 81–128; H. Rothermel, 'Images of the Sun: Warren De
la Rue, George Biddell Airy and Celestial Photography', *British Journal for
the History of Science*, 1993, 26: 137–69; M. N. Wise (ed.), *The Values of
Precision* (Princeton NJ: Princeton University Press, 1995).
90. R. R. Yeo, 'Scientific Method and the Rhetoric of Science in Britain, 1830–
1917', J. A. Schuster and R. R. Yeo (eds), *The Politics and Rhetoric of
Scientific Method: Historical Studies* (Dordrecht: Reidel, 1986), p. 267.

A Grand and Universal Panacea: Death, Resurrection and the Electric Chair

Iwan Rhys Morus

From very early in its history, natural philosophers recognized a particularly intimate link between electricity and the body. Electrical experimenters routinely incorporated their own and others' bodies in their spectacular demonstrations of electricity's powers.[1] Electricity rapidly became a way of performing with and on the human body, of making it do strange things or, even more subversively, getting it do quite normal things like moving a limb or blinking an eye. Performances like this were subversive, this chapter suggests, because they brought about new kinds of understandings of the human body's place in culture and decisively shifted the boundary between bodies and machines. There was nothing new of course about regarding the body as a kind of machine, as previous chapters have demonstrated, but electrical performances made the machinelike body particularly vivid.[2] Using electricity, natural philosophers could make human bodies act like machines as well as make machines act like human bodies. Paradoxically, electrical performances could simultaneously situate the body within culture whilst removing it from culture at the same time. Electrical experimentation provided a means of disciplining and managing the body, making sense of it by taking it out of nature and putting it into culture. Electrical performances provided a new set of tools for making the individual body universal – for making 'the body' as a trans-historical, acultural object for inquiry.

Electricity could be used to provide a stark illustration of Cartesian dualism. By graphically demonstrating how mind could be divorced from body, electricity provided a key element in inaugurating a sharp disjunction during the eighteenth century in the ways in which people thought of their bodies and themselves. The Abbé Nollet's famous (or infamous) experimental demonstration of electrical conduction by shocking a line of Carthusian monks into leaping into the air simultaneously might have been designed with the French Royal Court's amusement and edification in mind, but it was also a telling example of Cartesianism in action.[3] Using electricity Nollet could wrest control over their own bodies away from his experimental subjects' minds and direct them for himself instead. Experiments like these made the mind's separation from the body brutally apparent. Nollet was placing himself in the position of a puppet master, or of Jacques de Vaucanson with respect to his automata (or maybe even the position an absolutist French monarch might like to be in with regard to his subjects) – able to control others' bodies at will.[4] Electricity was crucial in introducing new ways of not only understanding mind-body dualism, but of making it real. As such it was to become an increasingly powerful instrument for bodily management and control for the rest of the eighteenth and throughout the nineteenth century.

Electricity also played an important role in redefining a number of seemingly well-established and inviolable bodily boundaries. Natural philosophers could use electricity to chip away at previously clearly defined categories. Whilst the gap between mind and body was widened and solidified, the distinction between bodies and machines became significantly more porous. Machines that could simulate animal or human activity were an Enlightenment obsession.[5] The French engineer and instrument maker Vaucanson was feted for his mechanical duck that could allegedly quack, eat and even shit like the genuine article. It provided grist for the mill of radical materialists like Julien Offrey de la Mettrie who wanted to take Descartes to his logical conclusion and deny the existence of the immaterial soul.[6] Electricity seemed to challenge the boundary between life and death as well. If electricians like Alessandro Volta or Henry Cavendish could make an artificial electric fish, then that challenged the distinction between the alive and the dead, as well as the boundary between body and machine.[7] By the beginning of the nineteenth century it looked to many as if electricity offered a means of restoring life to the dead, if not even creating artificial life from inanimate matter.[8]

This chapter takes up electricity at the beginning of the nineteenth century and follows it through to the century's close. It starts by looking at the performative constructions of the electrical body at the beginning of the century. When Luigi Galvani's nephew, Giovanni Aldini, embarked on his Grand Tour of Europe in the early 1800s he was not only acting to defend his eminent uncle's philosophical reputation; he was constructing the electrical body as he went along, experimenting on animal and human corpses in Paris and London. It was through a series of local performances such as these and others in Europe and America that the electrical body became an universal object of philosophical enquiry and literary speculation. The chapter follows the cultures of galvanism through the mid-century, looking at electricity's role in radical politics, hospital and fringe medicine and the ways in which electricity contributed to making the human body a focus for the increasingly metrological scientific culture of the second half of the century. It shows how electricity remained at the centre of efforts to rearticulate the relationship between animate bodies and inanimate machines and argues that electrical experiments and performances provided crucial resources for the construction of new boundaries between animate and inanimate objects.

The chapter closes with an overview of debates surrounding the introduction of electrocution as a new and scientific means of execution at the end of the nineteenth century. Electrocution was both celebrated as the ultimate expression of scientific civilization, providing as it did a truly scientific way of death, and condemned for putting science at the service of barbarity. The section focuses on the ways in which the successful practice of electrocution required the complete integration of the body into electrical machine culture. Just like any other electrical experiment, electrocution depended on standardization.[9] To work, the electric chair needed its own physics. The period around the first electrocution in 1890 saw an upsurge of interest in the physics of electrical life and death. The mechanics of death by electricity became an object of careful scrutiny as experimenters worked to find out just what kind of item of electrical apparatus the human body was. This chapter suggests however that electrocution also provided a tangible demonstration of the limits of the electrical body. In the end, all the careful preparations and efforts to predict and control the behaviour of the body in the electric chair ended in failure. The electrical body did not turn out to be as amenable to managerial discipline as its promoters hoped.

Performing the Body Electric

When the Italian professor Luigi Galvani announced his discovery of animal electricity in 1791 he triggered a wave of renewed interest in the relationship between electricity and the body across Europe. Galvani, a medical practitioner and Professor of Practical Anatomy and of Obstetrics at the University of Bologna, had found that frogs' legs twitched in the presence of electrical discharges. He interpreted his findings as evidence of a distinct kind of electricity in animal tissue. The ensuing dispute with his fellow-Italian Alessandro Volta over the origins of this electricity focussed experimenters' attention on re-examining the relationship between electricity and the processes of life.[10] Electrical experiments like those of Galvani and his supporters and protagonists aimed to find evidence for the existence or otherwise of a particularly close relationship between electricity and life. They were efforts to make dead flesh act as if it were still living. Experimenters laboured to coax spontaneous movement from bits of dissected animal flesh as proof of the existence of an innate animal electricity. Experimental performances like this in different locations across Europe – and often in public – played a key role in establishing the body as a subject of inquiry. The electrical body was made sense of and articulated through such local experimental performances.

Galvani's Italian supporters, particularly his nephew Giovanni Aldini as well as others such as Andrea Vassali-Eandi soon focussed their attention on experiments on human bodies in their efforts to establish the relationship between electricity and life.[11] Experimenting on the corpses of recently executed criminals Vassali-Eandi and his co-experimenters tried to find ways of conclusively demonstrating the continuing sensitivity of human flesh to electrical stimulation and that it was a source of electricity. They described how, by 'arming the spinal marrow by means of a cylinder of lead introduced into the canal of the cervical vertebrae, and then conveying one extremity of a silver arc over the surface of the heart, and the other to the arming of the spinal marrow', they could exhibit 'very visible, and very strong contractions' of the corpse's heart. Crucially, the 'experiments, as seen, were made without any intervention of the pile, and without any armature applied to the heart.'[12] By producing contractions without using an external source of electricity they could argue that the body itself was the source of power. Aldini tried to convince the First Class of the National Institute of France in Paris with similar experiments carried out on decapitated oxen as he toured Europe in his campaign to defend his uncle's reputation.[13]

Aldini concluded his European Grand Tour with experimental performances in London and Oxford. He performed experiments 'in the presence of his excellency the ambassador of France, general Andreossi, lord Pelham, lord Roxburgh, lord

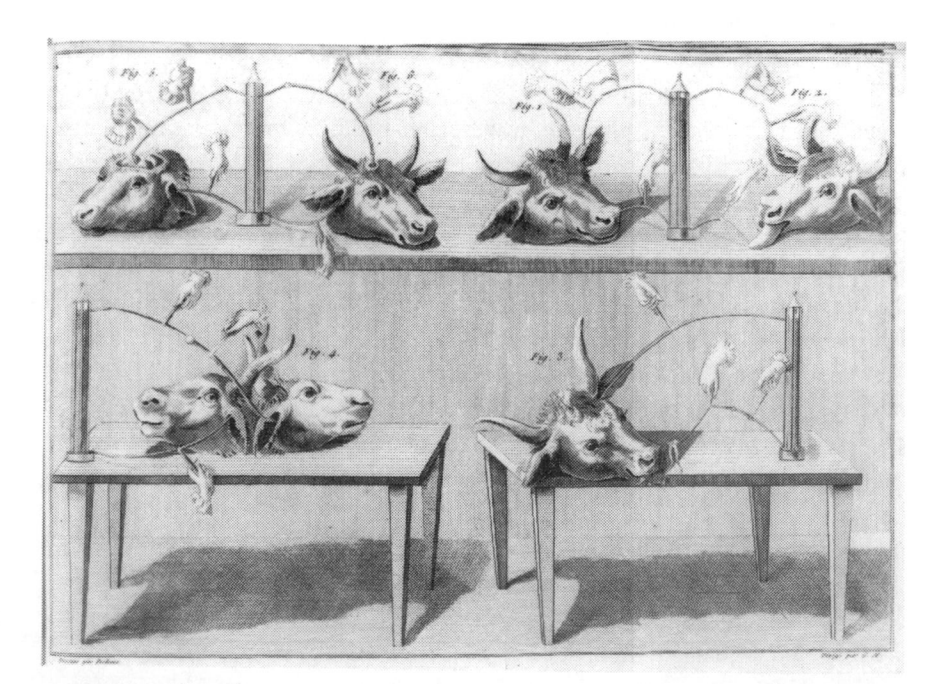

Figure 5.1 Giovanni Aldini's experiments on the electrical properties of animal bodies. Note the use of frog's legs to indicate the presence of electricity. G. Aldini, *Essai Theorique et Expérimental sur le Galvanisme* (Paris, 1804)

Castlereagh, lord Hervey, the honourable Mr. Upton, Mr. Cholmondely, Mr. Anchora, Mr. Elliot, and several other gentlemen of rank.'[14] On another occasion the experiments were performed for the edification of the Prince of Wales. The highlight of Aldini's English visit was his electrical dissection of an executed murderer on the 17 January 1803, in the presence of the President of the Royal College of Surgeons. Using a large galvanic battery, Aldini produced a spectacular exhibition of grimaces and convulsions: 'On the first application of the process to the face, the jaw of the deceased criminal began to quiver, the adjoining muscles were horribly contorted, and one eye was actually opened. In the subsequent part of the process, the right hand was raised and clenched, and the legs and thighs were set in motion.'[15] Aldini might later deplore the use of electricity 'to convulse the remains of human bodies, as a mechanic deceives the common people by moving an automaton by the aid of springs and other contrivances' as a 'prostitution of galvanism' but it was clearly the feature of his experimental performances that his fashionable audiences found most intriguing and shocking.[16] His London perform-ances fitted well into a local English culture of public experimentation as a source of entertainment and edification. Performed as they were under the aegis of the Royal College of Surgeons they also meshed well with the punitive medico-juridical role of Regency surgery.[17]

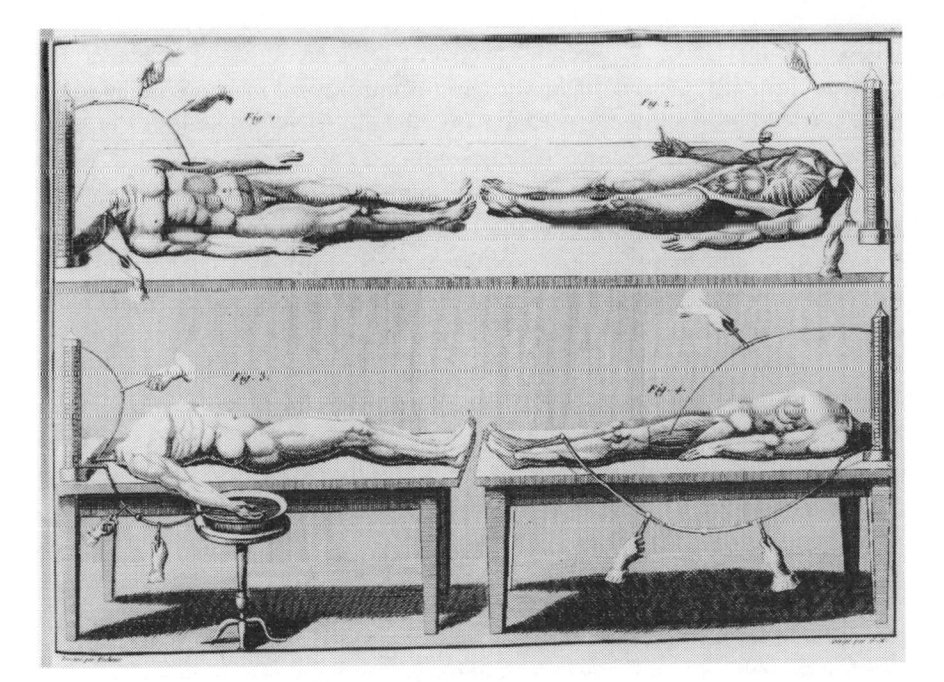

Figure 5.2 Aldini carrying out electrical experiments on the corpses of decapitated criminals. G. Aldini, *Essai Theorique et Expérimental sur le Galvanisme* (Paris, 1804)

Similar experiments to those of Aldini were repeated fifteen years later in Glasgow by the Scottish chemist and enthusiast for the factory system, Andrew Ure. On 4 November 1818 Ure carried out a series of electrical experiments on the body of Clydesdale, executed for murder earlier that day. By applying electricity to the body Ure, like Aldini, could produce a whole range of convulsions: 'Every muscle of the body was immediately agitated with convulsive movements, resembling a violent shuddering from cold.' When electricity was applied to the face

> every muscle in his countenance was simultaneously thrown into fearful action; rage, horror, despair, anguish, and ghastly smiles, united their hideous expression in the murderer's face, surpassing by far the wildest representations of a Fuseli or a Kean. At this period several of the spectators were forced to leave the apartment from terror or sickness, and one gentleman fainted.[18]

The descriptions, like the performances themselves were clearly aimed at shocking the audience. By placing the electrified corpse's gesticulations in the context of the stylized gesturings of Regency stage and art, Ure was also reminding his audience, as had Aldini with his experiments, that electricity seemed to hold out the very real possibility of restoring the dead to life.

Romantic natural philosophers in the German lands were also intrigued by the possibilities that Galvani's experiments opened up for investigating the borderland between electricity, life and death. Alexander Humboldt and Johann Wilhelm Ritter both carried out extensive experiments on the electrical properties of organic tissue. Humboldt made electrical batteries from piles of 'animal substances'. Ritter at the Romantic citadel of Jena placed the study of electricity at the centre of his experimental investigations of the life force. He even experimented on himself, showing how electricity applied to different parts of his body could be used to augment or diminish the senses.[19] Like Aldini and Ure he was convinced that electricity could be a means of restoring life to the dead. The American electrician Joseph Henry also carried out experiments on the corpse of a recently executed criminal in New Jersey in 1827.[20] Another American experiment was reported a little over a decade later when 'Coleman, a mulatto, who murdered his wife' was executed in New York in 1839. The description of the experiments bear a striking resemblance to those by Ure more than twenty years previously:

> Every muscle in the grim murderer's countenance was thrown into the most horrible contortions: rage, horror, anguish, and despair, the most rapid smiles, the most hideous expressions of contempt and hatred, by turns were depicted on his countenance, and gave a fearful wildness to his face, which far surpassed even the most vivid imagination from Fuseli's brain, or Kean's scenic display that we ever witnessed.[21]

The similarities with Ure's description are far too close to be coincidental. This kind of language was coming to be the standard lexicon of the electrical body.

Mary Shelley's novel *Frankenstein*, published as it was in 1818, appeared at a time when raising the dead by means of electricity seemed a very real possibility. Shelley's text was ambivalent on the precise method whereby Victor Frankenstein produced his monster and made only passing reference to electricity. There can be little question however that both she and her husband were aware of ongoing experiments on electricity and life. Percy Bysshe Shelley's doctor, William Lawrence, was involved in a vicious debate with John Abernethy on the physical origins of life. Percy Shelley was himself an enthusiast for galvanic experimentation and galvanism was certainly one of the topics discussed during the late-night conversations with Byron and Dr Polidori that inspired Mary to write her Gothic horror.[22] *Frankenstein* underlined both the potential horrors and the fascination of early nineteenth-century audiences for the possibility of creating artificial life. The Monster's rampages provided a graphic warning that galvanic experimentation might have consequences beyond the experimenter's capacity to control. The novel's play with the boundaries between living and non-living matter, between bodies and machines, was made plausible and relevant by its readers' knowledge of the already established possibilities of the electrical body.[23]

Those possibilities were revisited two decades later by a short story in the scurrilously Tory *Fraser's Magazine*. The anonymous author took his readers on a knowing tour of Europe's galvanic hotspots with his tale of a German student's efforts to revive Frankenstein's Monster.[24] The student studied at Leipzig and Paris, where he was persuaded that 'all our sentiments are nothing more than a subtle kind of mind, and that mind itself is only a modification of matter.' He repeated Andrew Crosse's notorious experiments producing insect life from electrified volcanic debris.[25] He recalled 'the effect produced at Guy's Hospital on the medical students, when the corpse of a criminal, under the effect of a powerful galvanic battery, opened its eyes, made one step from the table against which he was placed, erect, and stiff, and fell among them.' Finding that the Monster 'had only a talismanic existence – was a mere automaton – a machine – a plant without the faculty of motion,' our hero set out to provide it with a mind, which he did by literally ransacking the brains of a rogue's gallery of European intellectuals from Goethe and Schelling to Coleridge, using a pair of electrodes.[26] The tale ended as the student and the Monster were dragged down to Hell for his blasphemy and the narrator awoke to find that it was all, disappointingly, a dream.

Edgar Allan Poe had similar fun with the possibilities of galvanic animation or reanimation with 'Some Words with a Mummy', in 1845. An Egyptian mummy was brought back to life for the amusement of a late-night dinner party with the aid of a judicious dose of the galvanic fluid. The party made an incision over the outside of the exterior *os sesamoideum pollicis pedis*, and thus got at the root of the *abductor* muscle. Re-adjusting the battery, we now applied the fluid to the bisected nerves – when, with a movement of exceeding life-likeness, the Mummy first drew up its right knee so as to bring it nearly in contact with the abdomen, and then, straightening the limb with inconceivable force, bestowed a kick upon Doctor Ponnonner, which had the effect of discharging that gentleman, like an arrow from a catapult, through a window into the street below.[27]

Poe was both lampooning and drawing upon his readers' knowledge (or half-knowledge) that there was good reason for supposing such events to be within the realms of possibility. As he did in others of his 'science fiction' writings, like his famous 'Balloon-hoax', he was careful to draw on contemporary understandings and contexts in constructing his fictions. Like his contemporary, P. T. Barnum, he challenged audiences to re-examine their perceptions of what might or might not be plausible.[28] Electrical bodies could be used to fool Poe's audience precisely because they were reckoned to be within the boundaries of the plausible.

Poe's or Shelley's fictions worked because the electrical body had a secure foundation as a plausible and universal object of experimental investigation. That it was so was the outcome of the multiplicity of local performances like those of Aldini, or Ritter or Ure. It was just through these kinds of experiments that the early Victorian sense of the body as a machine was put together. The electrical body as an element in an electrical universe was constructed out of such perform-ances and their contexts too. In this sense the electrical body was part of the contemporary technology of display – a part of the repertoire on which natural philosophers, electricians and others could draw to articulate and display the powers of nature. It was part of the routine at London shows of practical science at the Adelaide Gallery or Royal Polytechnic Institute where visitors were promised 'artful snares laid for giving galvanic shocks to the unwary' or where even as eminent a visitor as the Duke of Wellington could fall into a galvanic trap.[29] As well as building on these performative contexts, fictions like Shelley's or Poe's added to them too, proliferating the contexts where the electrical body appeared.

The Royal Polytechnic Institute, one of London's premier sites of scientific edification and amusement, provided the forum for Benjamin Ward Richardson's rearticulation of the electrical body in the early 1860s. Richardson wanted to turn the electrical body on its head. Where Aldini and Ure had argued that electricity was a stimulant, capable of restoring life to dead bodies, Richardson argued that it was a soporific. Far from revitalizing the inanimate body, Richardson aimed to show that what electricity did, after the initial excitement was over, was cause it to sink even further into torpor. 'If we wish to create a semblance of life without a reality', he argued we may use galvanism. If the body is yet warm, we may, for a few minutes, excite any amount of muscular contraction. We may excite on the dead face a sardonic smile, or make the index finger point to any quarter of the compass. We may exhort a deep gasp or startling sigh; but we are doing nothing, or if we are doing anything, it is an act which is unpardonable in its horror; we are restoring a momentary intelligence which we cannot sustain, and we are enabling the prostrate body to look into life only to sink again into cold oblivion.[30]

Richardson aimed to demonstrate that in the long term, far from being a revivifying agent, electricity was destructive to the human mechanism. It might briefly restore a spark of life but its continued application would destroy the body's delicate balances. Muscles would cease to contract and nerves would stop conducting. Electricity was an anaesthetic not an animator. He conducted meticulous researches on anaesthetized animals to demonstrate that repeated application of electricity to the body produced paralysis and death not resuscitation.

Richardson, a London doctor and enthusiastic natural philosophical operator, underlined his findings with a series of spectacular presentations at the Royal Polytechnic.[31] He made use of the Polytechnic's massive induction coil, weighing 15 cwt with a primary wire of 3,770 yards and a secondary wire 150 miles in length.[32] The product of these dramatic demonstrations was a meticulous examination of electricity's effect on animal bodies and tissues whilst it simultaneously sought to reproduce lightning inside the Polytechnic's lecture theatre. Richardson looked at and demonstrated the effects of different kinds of electrical discharges from different sources on organic tissue. Tracing the electric current's path through the different organs and tissues of the body he used the latest in the electricians' technology of display to demonstrate the animal body's variable resistance to his audience. Using 'Gassiott's [sic] electric fountains or cascades' he could show his Polytechnic audience

how beautiful is the light as it streams over the glass within the globe . . . now, the light is decreased, and the current from the coil, instead of making its way silently, flies across from a point to a point; we have interposed our tube containing fat, and the current resisted by that, flies across. See, again, the fountain is nearly as beautiful as at first; we have removed our tube holding fat, and interposed blood . . . Lastly we see a difference between blood and spinal cord.[33]

All the experimenters discussed here were in a certain sense performing the electrical body into being even as they took opposing views as to how that body was organized and on how electricity impacted on the human frame. They displayed their mastery over criminal corpses, rabbits, frogs or bits of disembodied tissue by making them parts of assemblages of electrical apparatus that they could reliably control. Control over one's apparatus, the tools of the electrical showman's trade, was the mark of a successful public experimenter. Electricians could demonstrate their mastery of the electrical universe by showing their audiences how they could reliably manipulate their experimental apparatus. By making the electrical body part of their experimental repertoire they were demonstrating their authority over it as well. Aldini and Ure could reanimate the dead by means of electricity, Richardson could rob the living of their senses in the same way. Their audiences – as well as those of Shelley, Poe, or the anonymous author of the 'New Frankenstein' – were being invited to understand what was performed in front of them in terms of a homology between the dead and the undead, the natural and the artificial, the mechanical and the organic. Each could be made to model the other. This was a common tactic amongst Regency and Victorian experimenters – making a model of something was a way of mastering it.[34] The key to understanding the electrical body was to make it and its components interchangeable with other items of the electricians' technology of display as parts of the same networks of scientific production and consumption.

Cultures of Galvanism

Electricity was a malleable cultural resource. Early nineteenth-century practical electricians like William Sturgeon or Henry Noad argued that electricity was the key to understanding and mastering the universe. The cosmos was a vast electrical machine that could be understood and manipulated in much the same way as they understood and manipulated the electrical machines and artefacts with which they plied their trade. That understanding encompassed the organic as much as the inorganic. Human bodies were part of the electrical universe too.[35] The electrical universe and the electrical body that went with it could be potent political tools in early nineteenth-century English culture. Radical materialists quickly picked up on its potentialities. Later in the century as the new-fangled electric telegraph proliferated, it seemed a promising way of making sense of the electrical body as well. That homology, too, had important political and cultural ramifications.[36] Towards the end of the century, the electrical body was increasingly integrated into the metrological culture of Victorian physics. The key to understanding – and disciplining – the body in this respect was standardization. Just as other items of electrical apparatus and equipment needed to be standardized to operate effectively within the new networks of power, so did the electrical body.[37]

For the English electrician and popular lecturer William Sturgeon, electricity was the central power that governed the universe. The cosmos was constituted of just the same kind of apparatus as made up his stock in trade. 'Nature's laboratory is well stored with apparatus of this kind, aptly fitted for incessant action', he maintained, 'and the insignificance of our puny contrivances to mimic nature's operations, must be amply apparent when compared with the magnificent apparatus of the earth.'[38] Electrical enthusiasts like the flamboyant Colonel Francis Maceroni, former aide-de-camp to Murat, inventor of a patented steam coach and physical force radical, made good use of such analogies, likening the earth to a complex battery and comparing both to the physical structures of organized beings.[39] During the 1830s the Owenite lecturer Thomas Simmons Mackintosh toured Mechanic's Institutes and Halls of Science with his 'Electrical Theory of the Universe', arguing that 'the animal system is a bundle of circles, each connected with the others, like the wheels of a watch, or like the different parts of a steam engine . . . and that the nervous circle is actuated by electricity.' According to Mackintosh, the 'roots of moral action' lay in the nature of man as 'an organized machine'.[40]

The political agitator Richard Carlile was an enthusiast for electricity.[41] Whilst he was incarcerated for his political activities during the 1830s, his mistress Eliza Sharples deployed the language of the electrical body to bolster the anti-clerical message of her Isis lectures at the London Rotunda. Arguing on the basis that the human body was a 'self-acting electrical machine, sustained by currents of atmospheric air and liquids' she mounted an all-out assault on Anglican dogma. 'The conceit that spirit can retain an identity without the aid of the body, is that of superstition and madness', she declaimed, because 'All electricity depends upon certain arrangements of materials, without which it cannot exist; so that the imagination of life without body, is like the creation of all things out of nothing.'[42] Carlile's friend, the radical Welsh doctor Thomas Williams, who carried out the public dissection of his body following his death in 1843, shared his enthusiasm for electricity.[43] He published in the *Lancet* his electrical experiments in support of Marshall Hall's highly controversial theories of reflex action, showing how much nervous activity took place automatically, without the intervention of conscious will.[44]

Political radicals were not the only ones to latch on to the possibilities of the electrical body. One of the most far-reaching and comprehensive mid-nineteenth-century English articulations of the electrical nature of life was the work of Alfred Smee, Tory and firmly orthodox Anglican. His *Elements of Electro-Biology* laid out a comprehensive framework for the electrical understanding of the body.[45] He argued that animal and human bodies should be recognized as complex networks of electrical batteries and other electrical apparatus. He carried out extensive experiments showing how different kinds of electrical instruments could be used to mimic the actions of the senses, detecting light, smell, sound and so on. Far from seeing the electrical body as the tool of political radicals, Smee argued that it was a bulwark of orthodoxy. He could show how the idea of God (of the orthodox Anglican variety) arose naturally from the complex electrical organization of the human brain. He could show how disorders in that same complex electrical structure led to mental derangements ranging from Catholicism to Chartism. Critics mocked his pretensions, accusing him of electrical charlatanery and challenging him to produce a real 'living, moving, feeling, thinking, moral, and religious man, by a combination of voltaic circuits.'[46]

The accusation of charlatanery must have been a sore point. Promises of electrical miracle cures proliferated during the second quarter of the century. Another of Richard Carlile's friends, the mesmerist William Hooper Halse, combined medical galvanism with his mesmeric performances.[47] Halse's pamphlets offered cures for 'all kinds of nervous disorders, asthma, rheumatism, sciatica, tic douloureux, paralysis, spinal complaints, long-standing headaches, deficiency of nervous energy, deafness, dulness of sight, liver complaints, general debility, indigestion, stiff joints, epilepsy, and recent cases of consumption.'[48] Dawson Bellhouse made similarly ambitious claims for his electrical regimen, exhorting his clients that 'there is no remedy more powerful, and beneficial in its effects, than Medical Galvanism, when properly administered.'[49] A W. Hardy from Harrogate sang the praises of his 'infused sulphur water and electro-chemical baths.'[50] Galvanic rings were very much in vogue during the second half of the 1840s and, by the 1850s, galvanic belts were increasingly the fashion. William Piggot touted his belts as 'a beautiful instance of Art aiding Science to produce the highest beneficial result', comparing their action on the 'marvellous machinery of man himself' to the effect of a compensation balance on a chronometer.[51] Hard-pressed medical practitioners complained themselves blue in the face at this proliferation of arrant quackery.[52]

Medical galvanists in the second half of the century offered their services in discreetly curing the deleterious results of youthful indiscretions. According to James Beresford Ryley, electricity could restore the flagging tissues: 'By the one quality it removes the products of inflammation . . . and by the other it operates on those genetic forces the suspension or diminution of which constitute complete or relative impotency.'[53] Such a course of treatment could revolutionize the patient's entire self-image. Describing the response of one patient to electric treatment, Ryley related how

> He had such pride in his physical development while under treatment, that for some time after he invariably invited his friends to feel his chest and biceps muscles, and to that end, struck an attitude, à la Sandow, and at the same time doubled up his arm in the usually approved manner for that purpose.[54]

By the end of the century, electrical medicine was big business, with companies like the Pall Mall Electric Association or C. B. Harness's Medical Battery Company raking in a fortune with their electric belts and corsets.[55] Such devices could give wonderful support and vitality to the internal organs of the body, improve the figure, prevent chills, impart new life and vigour to the debilitated constitution, stimulate the organic action, promote circulation, assist digestion, and promptly renew the vital energy the loss of which is the first symptom of decay.

Advertisements promised that electric belts could 'stimulate the functions of various organs, increase their secretions, give tone to muscle and nerves, relax morbid contractions, improve nutrition, and Renew Exhausted Nerve Force.'[56]

Despite medical electricity's cultural connections with materialism and political radicalism and its reputation as the province of quacks and charlatans, a hard core of doctors worked to make electrotherapy part of orthodox hospital practice. They argued that under proper medical direction electricity could prove to be a vital tool in regulating unruly bodies. At Guy's Hospital in London from 1836, Golding Bird oversaw the electrical treatment of patients for diseases like paralysis and chorea, especially 'those occurring in young women, in whom the disease assumes somewhat of a hysterical character, and those protracted cases in boys in whom other remedies have been tried ineffectually.'[57] Thomas Laycock concurred that electricity could prove to be the therapy of choice in treating hysterical women. Electrotherapy could return to normality the bodies of those whom hysteria had transformed from the 'gentle, truthful, and self-denying woman', into victims of 'insane cunning, destructiveness, infanticidal impulses, morbid appetites, &c.'[58] By the 1880s more metropolitan hospitals were opening electrical departments. The Cambridge-trained William Edward Steavenson was placed in charge of the new electrical department at St Bartholomew's Hospital in 1882, William Henry Stone administered electricity at St Thomas's Hospital and Armand de Watteville ran the electrical department at St Mary's Hospital. These were men who worked to make the medical application of electricity part of the world of electrical engineering as much as it was part of hospital medicine.[59]

Outside the large and prestigious metropolitan general hospitals electricity had its place in the new breed of specialist hospitals as well. Harry Lobb had opened a short-lived Galvanic Hospital in 1861, castigated by the *Lancet* as being as useful as 'an Hospital for Treatment . . . by the Excrement of Boa-Constrictors.'[60] The German emigré Julius Althaus made electricity an important part of the therapeutic regime at the Hospital for Diseases of the Nervous System that opened in Marylebone in 1866. He emphasized the importance of professional oversight, stressing against the hordes of irregular practitioners that electricity was 'not one of those remedies which, if they do no good, can do no harm; but on the contrary, it may, in the hands of an inexperienced operator, do a great deal of mischief.'[61] The anti-quack message was echoed by Herbert Tibbits, founder of the West-end Hospital for Diseases of the Nervous System, Paralysis and Epilepsy who insisted that 'the medical practitioner who prescribes electricity should, as a general rule, and with

Figure 5.3 A doctor demonstrating medical electricity on a young woman to an audience of colleagues. Print of engraving after Daniel Urrabieta Ortiz y Vierge. Wellcome Library, London

few exceptions, either administer it himself or cause it to be administered by a skilled operator.'[62] The Institute of Medical Electricity, established as a joint-stock company in 1888 by a consortium including several eminent members of the Institute of Electrical Engineers was, as much as anything else, an effort to impose some of the disciplines of their own profession on the treatment of the electrical body.[63]

One reason why electrical engineers saw electrotherapeutics as an area where their own expertise was relevant was because they recognized the electrical body as being made up of the same kind of components, organized into the same kind of system as that on which they plied their trade. Analogies between the human nervous system and the Victorian telegraph network were ubiquitous and stretched back to the telegraph's origins in the 1840s. Smee in his *Elements of Electro-Biology* had described nerves as 'bio-telegraphs'. Andrew Wynter, explaining the telegraph's operations to the *Quarterly Review*'s readership, described the Electric Telegraph Company's Lothbury headquarters as 'the great brain – if we may so term it – of the nervous system of Britain.'[64] Another writer looked forward to the day when the telegraph would 'like the great nerves of the human body, unite in living sympathy all the far-scattered children of man.'[65] The physicist George Gabriel Stokes averred that 'Nowadays the whole earth resembles, in measure, one of our own bodies. The electric wires represent the nerves, and messages are conveyed from the most remote regions to the central place of government, just as in our bodies, where sensations are conveyed to the sensorium.'[66] It was an important feature of the analogy that it worked both ways. The nervous system could be used to cast light on the mysteries of the telegraph just as much as the telegraph explained the operations of the nerves.[67]

Measurement, according to late nineteenth-century physicists and electrical engineers, was the key to understanding and controlling the telegraph system. It was no surprise therefore that many of them argued that measurement was the key to understanding and controlling the electrical body too. By making the electrical body subject to metrological discipline – by making it part of the mensurational culture of late nineteenth-century physics – it could be made manageable. The German Wilhelm Erb insisted that 'the human body is nothing more than a large conducting mass of definite resistance; and the laws controlling the distribution of electricity in large conducting masses therefore apply to it without any limitation.'[68] Armand de Watteville concurred, describing the body as 'a vessel bound with poorly conducting material (the skin) unequally packed with non-conducting solid particles, the interstices being filled up with a saline fluid of fair conductive power.'[69] The key to understanding the action of electricity on the body was therefore Ohm's law of the distribution of electrical resistance. At just the same time in the late 1880s when physicists and electrical engineers were preoccupied with the problem of standardizing the ohm – of defining a standard and exchangeable unit of electrical resistance – medical electricians like William Henry Stone and electrical engineers like Henry Newman Lawrence at the Institute of Medical Electricity were setting out to provide accurate measurements of the electrical resistance of the human body as well.[70]

Accurate measurement was an important consideration for practical therapy according to these men. Julius Althaus argued that 'Doses of electricity require to be exactly measured to suit the different constitution, age and sex of the patient.'[71] William Henry Stone appealed to the Institution of Electrical Engineering for their help in making medical electricity a mensurational science. 'You can be of very great service to us physicians and physiologists by giving us suggestions, especially in the department with which you are most conversant (more conversant than we are), viz., the department of measurement,' he argued.[72] The issue was one of skill, or more precisely of what kind of skill should be regarded as being relevant to the care of the electrical body. Inextricably tied to the issue of skill was the question of ownership. If electrical engineers were to legitimately portray themselves as authorities on the care of the electrical body then they had to make sure that body belonged to them, that it could be made subject to the same disciplinary regimes that pertained to any other part of their practice. In other words they needed to be able to show that dealing with the electrical body was just the same as dealing with a piece of telegraph cable.

The electrical body was a contested site throughout the nineteenth century. It could be a powerful argument for revolutionizing society or just as powerful a statement in favour of maintaining the moral and political order. Irregular practitioners, doctors and electrical engineers argued over the kinds of skills and expertise that might be deemed sufficient to lay claim to expertise over the electrical operations of the body. Running through many of these debates was the perennial Victorian concern with bodily management and discipline. Electricity promised to be a tool that could be used to make the body docile. This was one of the reasons why the telegraphic metaphor was so potent. It linked questions of bodily management with issues of social control. It was also a tool that linked the cultures of metrology and consumerism. Both aimed at producing a standardized, homogenous electrical body. Just as Harness's electrical belts promised the consumer a body just like anybody else's, electrotechnology offered a body that could be fully integrated into the electrical universe, standardized like any other item of electricians' apparatus.

A Scientific Way of Death

Metrologically minded medical electricians worked hard to try and bring the human body within the purview of electrical engineering. New electrical industries were taking off in a big way during the final quarter of the nineteenth century. As they did so – and as more people came into frequent contact with the new networks of electrical power – electrical fatalities proliferated as well. Death brought a new urgency to discussions of the body's electrical mechanism. Electricity's death-dealing capacities offered other possibilities as well. Penal reformers as well as electrical enthusiasts were keen to promote electricity as a new and scientific means of execution. Managing electrocution – a new word coined in the 1890s – meant finding new ways of managing the electrical body as well. Before, during and after the first electrocutions in 1890, debates raged over the ethics of electrical killing, its practicalities and its mechanism. Enthusiasts hailed electricity as a civilized and sanitized means of killing fit for a scientific century. Opponents damned electrocution as a misuse of science's powers. Proponents and opponents alike worked at constructing a physics of electrocution. To make their case either for or against, they needed to find out the mechanism of electrical death. To make electrocution manageable – or to demonstrate its ultimate intractability – the workings of the electrical body had to be laid bare.

Accidental death from contact with electrical currents was becoming increasingly common during the 1880s as systems of electrical power transmission developed and became pervasive features of American and European urban geographies.[73] Popular and professional electrical magazines carried frequent accounts of electrical workers – and customers – coming into fatal contact with the electric current. The publicity surrounding such cases highlighted the potential culpability of electrical companies as well as the need to understand the mechanism of death. A London Coroner's Court jury in 1896 noted that

> we think the City of London Electric Light Company have not taken proper precautions to prevent their employés [sic] meeting with accidents of this character; we also wish to express our opinion that the men are not properly paid; and also that notices as to the dangerous nature of the work should be posted at every station.[74]

Sentiments like these only underlined the social as well as the physical dangers of out-of-control electricity. Finding ways of understanding the electrical body was increasingly becoming an electrical engineering imperative if electrical companies were to be able to protect their shareholders profits as well as the lives of their workers. The 'physiology of death by electric shock' was soon a common topic of heated debate in electrical engineering circles.

The 'physiology of death by electric shock' had another potential application as well, however. From the late 1880s the possibility of introducing electricity as a means of capital punishment was increasingly being canvassed. In 1889 the New York Medico-Legal Society hailed the prospect that electrical executions would do away with 'the ghastly struggles of the condemned, with the executioner, and the revolting scene of men strangled by bungling in adjusting the rope.'[75] A law making electricity a legitimate means of execution for capital crimes had already passed through the New York State Legislature in the previous year. All that remained was the development of a practical technology of electrical death. The matter was soon embroiled in the notorious 'battle of the systems' between advocates of alternating and continuous current systems of electrical power. Proponents of continuous current systems, notably Edison and his companies, agitated in favour of employing alternating currents as the vehicle for execution, arguing that experimental evidence demonstrated that the human body was more susceptible to death from alternating that it was from continuous currents.[76] Edison's protégé Harold P. Brown conducted highly publicized demonstrations in which cattle, dogs and even horses were killed by electricity to demonstrate the efficiency of alternating currents in the matter.[77]

The first electrical execution took place in Auburn Prison, New York on the 6 August 1890, using a system devised by the medical electrician and specialist on nervous diseases Alphonso David Rockwell.[78] The victim was William Kemmler, convicted of murdering his fiancée, Tillie Ziegler. The event took place in a carefully controlled setting before witnesses. As the *New York Times* reported the previous day, the 'death machinery has been adjusted. Those in charge of it declare that it is in perfect working order, and all the preparations that are deemed necessary for the successful killing of the criminal have been completed.'[79] The result was a graphic example of the recalcitrance of the electrical body. Despite the operators' best efforts, it took two shocks before the doctors present felt safe in pronouncing Kemmler dead. On the second application

> the witnesses were so horrified by the ghastly sight they could not take their eyes off it . . . Blood began to appear on the face of the wretch in the chair. It stood on his face like sweat . . . An awful odor [sic] began to permeate the death chamber, and then, as though to cap the climax of this fearful sight, it was seen that the hair under and around the electrode at the base of the spine was singeing. The stench was unbearable.[80]

The public response to Kemmler's execution and the others that followed was mixed. The *New York Times* lambasted the state legislature and called for an end to electrocution. In Britain, the *Lancet* condemned the decision to continue the 'experiment' as repugnant: 'Could anything more uncertain or unsatisfactory be conceived, anything more painful be recorded on the face of the history of modern medicine? The best minds will stand astounded that any medical man or men could be found ready to dip their hands into any part of such fearful work.'[81] They maintained that the evidence of successive electrocutions was at least sufficient to raise doubt as to whether or not the procedure was always as painless as it was advertised. They argued in any case that painlessness was insufficient to mitigate the barbarity of the proceedings and the impropriety of applying science in such a fashion: 'The death in this case is reported to have been painless, and we have no doubt on that point. It was as painless as death from a blow with a club. But what a display of scientific refinement for such a deed!'[82] The electrical press was far less hostile, particularly the *Electrical Review* which increasingly expressed positive enthusiasm for electrocution. Their complaints were on the one hand directed at the failure of the 'electrocutionists' themselves to carry out the procedure with sufficient precision and on the other towards those such as the editors of the *Lancet*, who attacked the application of electricity to death as barbaric.[83]

The *Electrical Review* was vituperative in its condemnation of the *Lancet*, in particular, for its stance on electrocution. Their position was portrayed as anti-scientific, sentimental and broaching on the hysterical: 'It is an attitude quite inconsistent with that which becomes a great organ of medical and surgical science and such observations . . . resemble more the hysterical ravings of an anti-vivisectionist.'[84] The choice of insult was revealing. Opposition to electrocution was on the same level of obscurantist anti-scientism as the then flourishing anti-vivisection campaigns.[85] The *Review* made its point even more succinctly a few years later:

We are compelled to outrage the English language and to coin a new word to express the utterly hopeless condition of our contemporary, the *Lancet*. Over the subject of electrocution in the United States, it has sunk into the most maudlin state of old-womandom that it is conceivable for any leading organ to fall into.[86]

The *Review* had no qualms concerning the 'experimental' nature of electrocution. On the contrary, it would provide new evidence concerning the nature of the electrical body. Opposition was on a par with any other attempt to block the freedom of experiment. It was to be taken as a challenge to scientific progress.

Critics and proponents alike drew attention to the importance of detailed knowledge of the body's response to electricity as the basis for future proceedings. Even before the execution, the *Electrician* had opined that it was crucial to

Let humanitarians and members of the medical profession first study the human body as an electrical apparatus, and a very delicate one; let them follow the current in each of its numerous paths inside the body, and ascertain what its effect is on each organ, each membrane, each nerve, &c., and then, if they think well, let them arrange to execute by electricity.[87]

What was wanted was a thoroughgoing physics of electrocution that could show just what happened when electricity passed through the body. That was what proponents of electrical execution like Harold P. Brown and Edward Tatum amongst others were aiming at with their animal experiments in the late 1880s.[88] It was also the aim of Carlos MacDonald, head of New York's Lunacy Commission and one of Rockwell's collaborators in devising the state's electrocution apparatus, when he presented a report on electrocution to the New York Academy of Medicine in 1892. He argued that 'the fact that this method of executing criminals may now be said to have passed beyond the experimental stage, would seem to justify, if not indeed to demand, the presentation of an authentic summary of the practical results thus far obtained by some one whose data and conclusions would be derived from actual observation and experience in the application of the statute.'[89]

Throughout the 1890s investigators in America and Europe worked hard at the physics of electrocution. MacDonald had concluded that electrocution was 'the surest, quickest, most efficient, and least painful method of inflicting the death penalty that has yet been devised.'[90] In a series of letters to the *Lancet* in the mid-1890s, initiated by W. S. Hedley, a number of correspondents aired their views concerning the mechanics of death from electricity.[91] The correspondence shows clearly just how wide a range of opinions could be plausibly entertained concerning the 'physiology of death by electric shock' and the breadth of experimental evidence that could be marshalled to support various positions. At the end of the decade researchers were still struggling to determine just exactly what the

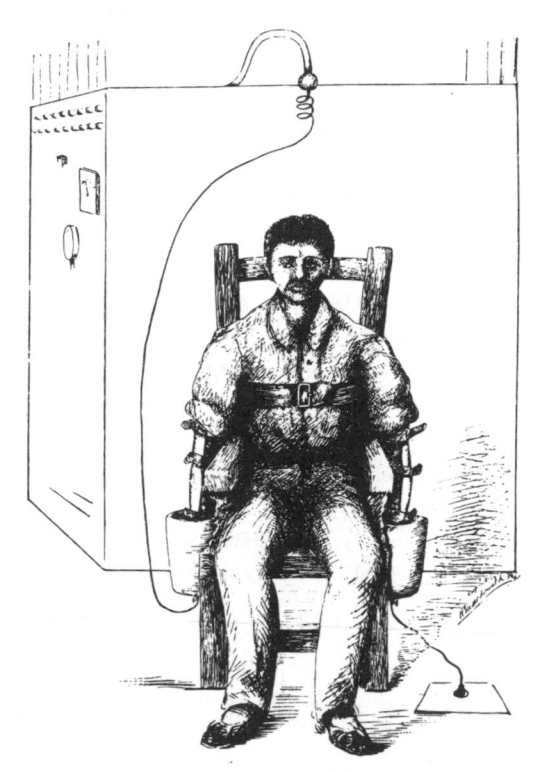

Figure 5.4 Charles McElvaine, prepared for electrocution at Sing Sing Prison on the 8th February 1892. C. F. MacDonald, *The Infliction of the Death Penalty by means of Electricity* (New York NY, 1892)

mechanism of death in electrocution was. The electrical body seemed to defy standardization. Just as experimenters during the 1880s had struggled to pin down the human body's resistance to electric current, their counterparts a decade later were still faced with a bewildering range of animal and human bodily responses to the passage of electricity. Much of the debate also took place within the context of an electrical engineering profession whose members routinely swapped anecdotes of their own individual prowess in taking and surviving massive doses of electrical current.

Increasingly, the question was not 'how does electricity kill?' but 'does electricity really kill at all?' The French medical physicist Arsenne d'Arsonval, known for his experiments with high-tension electricity on the body, suggested two mechanisms of electrical death: 'By producing mechanical lesions of the vessels and nervous system', or 'By inhibiting the great functions wholly or partially (stoppage of respiration, of the heart, of the exchanges between tissues and the blood &c.' In particular, he suggested that respiratory failure was the most common cause of death from electric shock. On this basis, d'Arsonval claimed electrocution to be a 'complicated, barbarous, and unreliable proceeding.'[92] Henry Lewis Jones, one of London's foremost practitioners of medical electricity, suggested that death from electricity occurred as a result of heart failure: 'it is certain that electrical discharges can kill a man as dead as a doornail.'[93] A few years later experiments by two physiologists at the University of Durham appeared to confirm Lewis Jones's claim. A series of experiments on dogs and rabbits using alternating currents seemed to suggest that death occurred by heart failure rather than asphyxiation. The doctors pointed as well to anecdotal evidence from workmen suggesting that those fatally injured working with electrical wires continued breathing for some time after being shocked.[94] The debate was still ongoing in 1899 when Prevost and Battelli summarized the state of play and their own findings in the *Journal de Physiologie et de Pathologie Générale.*[95]

The early and mid-1890s saw the emergence of the first protocols laying out the proper response to cases of electric shock. W. S. Hedley was a particular advocate of the use of artificial respiration in such cases, following on from d'Arsonval's suggestion that respiratory failure was the most common cause of death. In his view, 'in cases of accidental contact with electric-light wires the condition is generally one of suspended animation – of only apparent death – and that by the timely use of artificial respiration real and actual death can often be averted.'[96] He was keen to point out that the dangers of electricity should not be overestimated: 'It is not always so easy as might be supposed to kill an animal by electricity.'[97] As Hedley put it:

> the sequence of events may perhaps be imagined as follows:- Entering the skull, a current diffuses itself though the brain, sweeping away the faculties of sensation, intellect and will; concentrating itself, it makes for the foramen magnum, smiting in its path that vast collection of conducting fibres and nerve centres - the medulla oblongata. The delicate mechanism by which vital functions (respiratory, vaso motor, cardio-inhibitory &c.) are governed is thus destroyed, and it is on the balanced relationship of such functions that life depends.[98]

The *Electrical Review* and other professional journals mounted a campaign to persuade the Board of Trade to issue guidelines on the proper treatment of electric shock casualties. In the meantime, the *Electrical Review* issued its own recommendations and circulated them to every electrical power company in London. These 'simple directions for restoring animation' were couched in language that would be 'capable of being understood even by an ordinarily intelligent labourer.'[99]

Arthur Conan Doyle poked fun at the continuing uncertainties surrounding electrocution and electricity's relationship to life and death in a short story in 1894. In his scenario the citizens of Los Amigos decided to adopt electrocution as their favoured means of execution and, scornful of the puny doses of electricity adopted by effete Easterners in their efforts, determined that when an irreclaimable came their way he should be dealt handsomely by, and have the run of all the big dynamos. And what the result of that would be none could predict, save that it must be absolutely blasting and deadly . . . Some prophesied combustion, and some disintegration, and disappearance.[100]

The final result, predictably enough, was the opposite of the townfolks' intention. The victim's 'hair and beard had shredded off in an instant, and the room looked like a barber's shop in a Saturday night. There he sat, his eyes still shining, his skin radiant with the glow of perfect health, but with a scalp as bald as a Dutch cheese, and a chin without so much as a trace of down.' As the town critic pointed out to the disappointed onlookers, 'What you have done with your electricity is that you have increased this man's vitality until he can defy death for centuries . . . Electricity is life, and you have charged him with it to the utmost.'[101]

Afterthoughts

Doyle, clearly, was exploiting the ongoing uncertainty surrounding the relationship between electricity and the body. Electricity occupied an ambiguous place in the public imagination as both a life-giving and death-dealing technology.[102] A century that had commenced with speculation concerning electricity's power to overcome death had ended with the electric chair and the drawing up of guidelines to prevent death by electricity. The transformation serves as a striking illustration of the malleability of the electrical body. The ways in which the boundaries between the animate and the inanimate – the machine and the organic – could be put together and articulated were in a constant state of flux throughout the century. There was nothing self-evident about the ways in which connections between electricity and the body could be made. Such linkages were always up for grabs. Particular ways of articulating the relationship were a function of time and place as well. They were a product of specific cultural spaces. Sustaining any given account of the electrical body was a business that required work and effort. Forging the network of conceptual and material links that was needed to keep the electrical body stable required ongoing labour.

Making the electrical body a viable cultural construct was a matter of making it blend into its surroundings. The body gained its significance in the same way as any other technological artefacts that inhabited the same space. It mattered therefore for the sense of Aldini's or Ure's versions of the electrical body that they were articulated in a dissecting room. In just the same way it mattered that Richardson's performances took place at the Royal Polytechnic Institution or that electrocution took place using the latest paraphernalia of electrical engineering. These were the places and contexts within which the electrical body could be seen

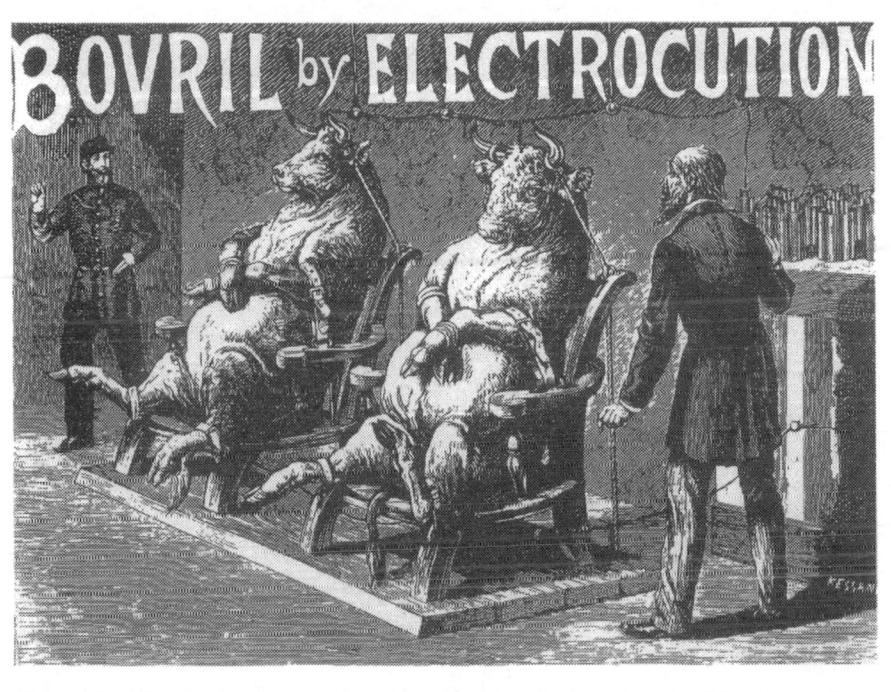

Figure 5.5 A Bovril advertisement draws attention to the latest technology. Like Arthur Conan Doyle's short story, "The Los Amigos Fiasco," the image plays on the late Victorian dual perception of electricity as both life-giving and death-dealing technology. *The Graphic*, 1891

to make sense. Outside such places the electrical body could only survive if the cultural regime governing activity inside could be extended to the outside world as well. This is what the *Electrical Review* was trying to do with its instructions to the 'ordinarily intelligent labourer' on how to revivify an electrocuted body. Making the human body fit for participation in new technological networks as they emerged during the last century meant making sure that the boundary between bodies and machines could be kept permeable enough for the disciplines that pertained to machines to apply to the body as well.

Doyle's satire also highlighted the problems of calibration and standardization that surrounded the electrical body's relationship to technology. Successfully integrating the body into new technological networks meant finding ways of making sure that the human body acted in reliable and predictable ways when it was placed within those networks. The electric chair was – in this respect at least – a good example of the electrical body's limitations. Despite their best efforts, its promoters could not get the chair to work. The body remained recalcitrant and relatively immune to their efforts at calibration.[103] Far from responding reliably, William Kemmler's body and those of his fellow victims, resisted standardization. They did not act as electrical engineers said they should. That was what happened in Doyle's short story as well. There were clearly limitations to what kinds of disciplines could be imposed on the body. In many ways however the electrical body's recalcitrance could itself be turned into a powerful argument in favour of electrical expertise.[104] It was in the end just because the body could not be trusted to behave reliably that electrical experts were needed. Electrical expertise was itself embodied after all in the bodies of its practitioners. It was precisely their hands-on knowledge of the electrical body that was needed to keep it docile.

Notes

1. S. Schaffer, 'Natural Philosophy and Public Spectacle in the Eighteenth Century', *History of Science*, 1983, 21: 1–43.
2. O. Mayr, *Authority, Liberty and Automatic Machinery in Early Modern Europe* (Baltimore MD: Johns Hopkins University Press, 1986).
3. For Nollet see J. Heilbron, *Electricity in the Seventeenth and Eighteenth Centuries: A Study of Early Modern Physics* (Berkeley and Los Angeles CA: University of California Press, 1979).
4. Electricity might be regarded as a means of producing what the sociologist Harry Collins calls 'behaviour-specific' or 'machine-like' action in its subjects. See H. Collins, *Artificial Experts: Social Knowledge and Intelligent Machines* (Cambridge MA: MIT Press, 1990), Chapter 3 in particular. For contemporary interest in producing these kinds of regimented actions see M. Foucault, *Discipline and Punish* (Harmondsworth: Penguin Books, 1977), pp. 135–41.
5. S. Schaffer, 'Enlightened Automata', W. Clark, J. Golinski and S. Schaffer (eds), *The Sciences in Enlightened Europe* (Chicago IL: University of Chicago Press, 1999), pp. 126–65; J.-C. Beaune, 'The Classical Age of Automata: An Impressionistic Survey from the Sixteenth to the Nineteenth Century', M. Feher, R. Naddaff and N. Tazi (eds), *Fragments for a History of the Human Body, Part One* (New York NY: Urzone Inc, 1989); A. Chapuis and E. Droz, *Automata: A Historical and Technological Study* (Neuchâtel: Éditions du Griffon, 1958).
6. L. Cohen Rosenfield, *From Beast-Machine to Man-Machine: Animal Soul in French Letters from Descartes to La Mettrie* (New York NY: Octagon Books, 1968).
7. Heilbron, *Electricity*. For Volta see M. Pera, *The Ambiguous Frog: The Galvani-Volta Controversy on Animal Electricity* (Princeton NJ: Princeton University Press, 1992).

8. J. A. Secord, 'Extraordinary Experiment: Electricity and the Creation of Life in Victorian England', D. Gooding, T. Pinch and S. Schaffer (eds), *The Uses of Experiment* (Cambridge: Cambridge University Press, 1989), pp. 337–83; I. R. Morus, *Frankenstein's Children: Electricity, Exhibition and Experiment in Early Nineteenth-century London* (Princeton NJ: Princeton University Press, 1998), Chapter 5.

9. For an overview of nineteenth-century approaches to exactitude and standardization see M. N. Wise (ed.), *The Values of Precision* (Princeton NJ: Princeton University Press, 1995).

10. Pera, *Ambiguous Frog*. For early discussions of electricity and life see H. E. Hoff, 'Galvani and the Pre-Galvanian Electrophysiologists', *Annals of Science*, 1936, 1: 157–72; W. C. Walker, 'Animal Electricity before Galvani', *Annals of Electricity*, 1937, 2: 84–113; R. Home, 'Electricity and the Nervous Fluid', *Journal of the History of Biology*, 1970, 3: 235–51. For Galvani's arguments and experiments see N. Kipnis, 'Galvani and the Debate on Animal Electricity', *Annals of Science*, 1987, 44: 107–42; M. Bresadola, 'Exploring Galvani's Room for Experiments', M. Bresadola and G. Pancaldi (eds), *Luigi Galvani International Workshop: Proceedings* (Bologna: Universita di Bologna, 1999), pp. 65–82. For some European responses see M. Trumpler, 'From Tabletops to Triangles: Increasing Abstraction in the Depiction of Experiments in Animal Electricity from Galvani to Ritter', Bresadola and Pancaldi (eds), *Galvani.*, pp. 115–45; C. Blondel, 'Animal Electricity in Paris: From Initial Support to its Discredit and Eventual Rehabilitation', Bresadola and Pancaldi (eds), *Galvani.*, pp. 187–209.

11. 'Report presented to the Class of the Exact Sciences of the Academy of Turin, 15th August 1802, in regard to the Galvanic Experiments made by C. Vassali-Eandi, Giulio, and Rossi, on the 10th and 14th of the same Month, on the Head and Trunk of three Men a short Time after their Decapitation', *Tilloch's Philosophical Magazine*, 1803, 15: 38–45.

12. 'Report', pp. 40–1.

13. Blondel, 'Animal Electricity in Paris'.

14. 'Animal Galvanism', *Tilloch's Philosophical Magazine*, 1803, 15: 93–4, on p. 93.

15. 'Galvanism', *Tilloch's Philosophical Magazine*, 1802, 14: 364–8, on p. 367.

16. J. Aldini, *General Views on the Application of Galvanism to Medical Purposes; principally in cases of Suspended Animation* (London, 1819), p. 26.

17. For more details of Aldini's London tour see Morus, *Frankenstein's Children*, pp. 127–8; C. Sleigh, 'Life, Death and Galvanism', *Studies in the History and Philosophy of the Biological and Biomedical Sciences*, 1998, 29: 219–48. R. Richardson, *Death, Dissection and the Destitute* (Harmondsworth: Penguin, 1988) discusses the punitive role of Regency surgeons and working-class fears of dissection.

18. A. Ure, 'An Account of some Experiments made on the Body of a Criminal immediately after Execution, with Physiological and Practical Observations', *Quarterly Journal of Science*, 1819, 6: 283–94, on p. 289; p. 290.
19. H. A. M. Snelders, 'Romanticism and Naturphilosophie and the Inorganic Natural Sciences 1797–1840: An Introductory Survey', *Studies in Romanticism*, 1970, 9: 193–215; W. Wetzels, 'Johann Wilhelm Ritter: Romantic Physics in Germany', A. Cunningham and N. Jardine (eds), *Romanticism and the Sciences* (Cambridge: Cambridge University Press, 1990), pp. 199–212; Trumpler, 'Tabletops to Triangles'.
20. N. Reingold (ed.), *The Papers of Joseph Henry* vol. 1 (Washington DC: Smithsonian Institution Press, 1972), Joseph Henry to John Torrey, 4 October, 1827, p. 199.
21. 'Galvanic Experiments on the Body of an Executed Murderer', *Annals of Electricity*, 1839–40, 4: 78–9, on p. 79, extracted from the *Jersey Times and Naval and Military Chronicle*.
22. M. Shelley, *Frankenstein, or, the Modern Prometheus*, with an introduction by M. Butler (London: Pickering and Chatto, 1993). For the Lawrence-Abernethy debate see also O. Temkin, 'Basic Science, Medicine and the Romantic Era', *The Double Face of Janus and other Essays in the History of Medicine* (Baltimore MD: Johns Hopkins University Press, 1977), pp. 345–72.
23. The literature on *Frankenstein* is vast. See C. Baldick, *In Frankenstein's Shadow: Myth, Monstrosity and Nineteenth-Century Writing* (Oxford: Oxford University Press, 1987); S. Bann (ed.), *Frankenstein, Creation and Monstrosity* (London: Reaktion Books, 1994).
24. Anon., 'The New Frankenstein', *Fraser's Magazine*, 1837, 17: 21–30.
25. 'New Frankenstein', p. 22. For Crosse see Secord, 'Extraordinary Experiment'; Morus, *Frankenstein's Children*, pp. 139–43.
26. 'New Frankenstein', p. 23.
27. E. Allan Poe, 'Some Words with a Mummy', Harold Beaver (ed.), *The Science Fiction of Edgar Allan Poe* (Penguin: Harmondsworth, 1976), pp. 154–70, on p. 158. First published in the *American Whig Review*, 1845.
28. For Barnum see N. Harris, *Humbug: The Art of P. T. Barnum* (Boston MA: Little and Brown, 1973), in particular his notion of Barnum's 'operational aesthetic'.
29. For the technology of display see I. R. Morus, 'Currents from the Underworld: Electricity and the Technology of Display in early Victorian England', *Isis*, 1993, 84: 50–69. For the technology of display and the constitution of the electrical universe see Morus, *Frankenstein*, pp. 125–52.
30. B. Ward Richardson, 'Researches on the Treatment of Suspended Animation', *British and Foreign Medico-Chirurgical Review*, 1863, 31: 478–505.

31. For the Polytechnic see R. Altick, *The Shows of London* (Cambridge MA: Harvard University Press, 1978); Morus, *Frankenstein*; I. R. Morus, 'Manufacturing Nature: Science, Technology and Victorian Consumer Culture', *British Journal of the History of Science*, 1996, 29: 403–34.

32. B. Ward Richardson, 'On Research with the Large Induction Coil of the Royal Polytechnic Institution, with Special Reference to the Cause and Phenomena of Death by Lightning', *Medical Times and Gazette*, 1869, 38: 511–14; 595–9; 39: 183–86; 373–6.

33. Richardson, 'Induction Coil', p. 598. Gassiot's 'electric fountains' were presumably a reference to the discharge-tube experiments recently conducted by John Peter Gassiot and William Robert Grove in England and Julius Plücker in Germany, in which the passage of electricity through attenuated gases in glass tubes caused the gases to glow.

34. Morus, *Frankenstein*, pp. 47–53; 130–9; I. R. Morus, 'Different Experimental Lives: Michael Faraday and William Sturgeon', *History of Science*, 1992, 30: 1–28; S. Schaffer, 'Fish and Ships', unpublished manuscript, 1999.

35. Morus, *Frankenstein*, Chapter 5.

36. I. R. Morus, '"The Nervous System of Britain": Space, Time and the Electric Telegraph in the Victorian Age', *British Journal for the History of Science*, 2000, 33: 455–75. Noakes's chapter in this collection also discusses the bodily ramifications of telegraphy in the context of the socially and politically fraught culture of spiritualism.

37. T. P. Hughes, *Networks of Power: Electrification in Western Society* (Baltimore MD: Johns Hopkins University Press, 1983); I. R. Morus, 'The Measure of Man: Technologizing the Victorian Body', *History of Science*, 1999, 37: 249–82.

38. W. Sturgeon, 'A General Outline of the Various Theories which have been Advanced for the Explanation of Terrestrial Magnetism', *Annals of Electricity*, 1836–37, 1: 117–23, on p. 123.

39. F. Maceroni, 'An Account of some Remarkable Electrical Phenomena seen in the Mediterranean, with some Physiological Deductions', *Mechanics' Magazine*, 1831, 15: 93–6; 98–100, on p. 94.

40. T. S. Mackintosh, *The Electrical Theory of the Universe* (Manchester, 1838), p. 371.

41. J. Wiener, *Radicalism and Freethought in Nineteenth-Century Britain: The Life of Richard Carlile* (Westport CT: Greenwood Press, 1983), pp. 250–2.

42. [E. Sharples], 'An Inquiry how far the Human Character is Formed by Education or External Circumstances', *The Isis* 1832, 1: 81–5, on p. 85; [E. Sharples], 'Fifth Discourse on the Bible', *The Isis*, 1932, 1: 241–7, on pp. 242, 244.

43. S. Wilks and G. T. Bettany, *A Biographical Dictionary of Guy's Hospital* (London, 1892), pp. 428–9.

44. T. Williams, 'On the Laws of the Nervous Force, and the Functions of the Roots of the Spinal Nerves', *Lancet*, 1847, ii: 516–17. For doctors and political radicalism in early nineteenth-century Britain see A. Desmond, *The Politics of Evolution* (Chicago IL: University of Chicago Press, 1989).
45. A. Smee, *Elements of Electro-Biology* (London, 1849).
46. Anon., 'Instinct and Reason', *British and Foreign Medico-Chirurgical Review*, 1850, 6: 522–4, on p. 522.
47. W. H. Halse, *On the Extraordinary Remedial Efficacy of Medical Galvanism, when Scientifically Administered* (London, n.d.). On Halse's connections with Carlile see Wiener, *Radicalism*. For Victorians' fascination with mesmerism see A. Winter, *Mesmerized: Powers of Mind in Victorian Britain* (Chicago IL: University of Chicago Press, 1998).
48. Halse, *Medical Galvanism*, p. 1.
49. Professor Bellhouse, *Medical Galvanism and its Properties as a Curative Agent for all Diseases of the Human Body* (Liverpool, n.d.), p. 1.
50. W. Hardy, *The Infused Sulphur Water and Electro-Chemical Baths* (Harrogate, n.d.).
51. W. P. Piggott, *Galvanic Belt and Galvanism* (London, n.d.).
52. J. C. Christophers, 'Anaesthesia Treated by Electro-magnetism', *Lancet* 1846, ii: 144–5. See Morus, *Frankenstein*, Chapter 8; I. R. Morus, 'Marketing the Machine: The Construction of Electrotherapeutics as Viable Medicine in early Victorian England', *Medical Electricity*, 1992, 36: 34–52.
53. J. B. Ryley, *Physical and Nervous Exhaustion in Man. Its Etiology and Treatment by 'Electro-Kinetics'* (London, 1892), p. 60.
54. Ryley, *Nervous Exhaustion*, p. 32.
55. L. Loeb, 'Consumerism and Commercial Electrotherapy: The Medical Battery Company in Nineteenth-Century London', *Journal of Victorian Culture*, 1999, 4: 252–75.
56. Advertisement for Harness's Electropathic Belts, pictured in L. de Vries, *Victorian Advertisements* (London: John Murray, 1968), p. 15. Originally from the *Illustrated London News* of 1890.
57. H. M. Hughes, 'Digest of One Hundred Cases of Chorea treated in the Hospital', *Guy's Hospital Reports*, 1846, 4: 360–94, on p. 388.
58. T. Laycock, 'On the Treatment of Cerebral Hysteria, and Moral Insanity in Women, by Electro-galvanism', *Medical Times*, 1850, 1: 57–8, on p. 58. For some of the literature on hysteria, electricity and women's bodies see Morus, *Frankenstein*, Chapter 8; J. Oppenheim, *Shattered Nerves: Doctors, Patients and Depression in Victorian England* (Oxford: Oxford University Press, 1991); C. E. Russett, *Sexual Science: The Victorian Construction of Womanhood* (Cambridge MA: Harvard University Press, 1989).
59. Morus, 'Measure of Man'.

60. 'The March of Specialism', *Lancet*, 1863, i: 183. For the complex cultural context of specialist hospitals see M. J. Peterson, *The Medical Profession in mid-Victorian England* (Berkeley and Los Angeles CA: University of California Press, 1978), pp. 244–82.

61. J. Althaus, *A Treatise on Medical Electricity, Theoretical and Practical* (London, 1859), p. 344.

62. H. Tibbits, *A Handbook of Medical and Surgical Electricity* (London, 1877), p. 247.

63. For the Institute of Medical Electricity see T. Uycama, 'Capital, Profession and Medical Technology: The Electro-therapeutic Institutes and the Royal College of Physicians, 1888–1922', *Medical History*, 1997, 41: 150–81.

64. [A. Wynter], 'The Electric Telegraph', *Quarterly Review*, 1854, 59: 118–64, on p. 132.

65. G. Wilson, *Electricity and the Electric Telegraph* (London, 1855), p. 77.

66. 'Dinner of the Institution of Electrical Engineers', *Electrician*, 1889, 24: 12–15, on p. 13.

67. Morus, 'Nervous System'.

68. W. Erb, *Handbook of Electro-therapeutics*, trans. L. Putzel (New York NY, 1883), p. 19.

69. A. de Watteville, *Practical Introduction to Medical Electricity* (London, 1884), p. 45.

70. S. Schaffer, 'Late Victorian Metrology and its Instrumentation: A Manufactory of Ohms', R. Bud and S. Cozzens (eds), *Invisible Connections: Instruments, Institutions and Science* (Bellingham: SPIE Press, 1992), pp. 23–56; S. Schaffer, 'Metrology, Metrication and Victorian Values', B. Lightman (ed.), *Victorian Science in Context* (Chicago IL: University of Chicago Press, 1997); Morus, 'Measure of Man'.

71. Althaus, *Medical Electricity*, pp. 347–8.

72. W. H. Stone and W. J. Kilner, 'On Measurement in the Medical Application of Electricity', *Journal of the Society of Telegraph Engineers and of Electricians*, 1882, 11: 107–28, on p. 109.

73. Hughes, *Networks of Power*; D. Nye, *Electrifying America: Social Meanings of a New Technology* (Cambridge MA: MIT Press, 1990).

74. 'The Recent Death from Electric Shock', *Electrical Review*, 1896, 39: 148.

75. 'Electricity vs. the Hangman', *Medico-Legal Journal*, 1889, 6: 106.

76. Hughes, *Networks of Power*, pp. 106–9.

77. See for example H. P. Brown, *The Comparative Danger to Life of Alternating and Continuous Electrical Currents* (New York NY, 1889).

78. A. D. Rockwell, *Rambling Recollections: An Autobiography* (New York NY: Paul B. Hooker, 1920), pp. 221–32; 'Dr. A. D. Rockwell Dies in 93rd Year', *New York Times*, 13 April 1932, p. 17.

79. 'Kemmler's Last Night', *New York Times*, 6 August 1890, p. 1.
80. 'Far Worse than Hanging', *New York Times*, 7 August 1890, p. 1.
81. 'Capital Punishment by Electricity', *Lancet*, 1891, ii: 943–4, on p. 943.
82. 'Another Electrocution', *Lancet*, 1891, ii: 1349.
83. 'The Current that Kills', *Electrical Review*, 1892, 30: 723–4; 759–60; 793–4; 1892, 31: 9.
84. 'Capital Punishment by Electricity', *Electrical Review*, 1891, 29: 495.
85. R. French, *Antivivisection and Medical Science in Victorian Society* (Princeton NJ: Princeton University Press, 1975); N. Rupke (ed.), *Vivisection in Historical Perspective* (London: Routledge, 1990).
86. 'The *Lancet* and Electrocution', *Electrical Review*, 1895, 36: 310.
87. S. F. Walker, 'Execution by Electricity', *Electrician*, 1889, 23: 288–9, on p. 289.
88. Brown, *Comparative Danger*; E. Tatum, 'Death from Electrical Currents', *New York Medical Journal*, 1890, 51: 207–9.
89. C. F. MacDonald, *The Infliction of the Death Penalty by Means of Electricity, Being a Report of Seven Cases* (New York NY, 1892), p. 1.
90. MacDonald, *Death Penalty*, p. 37.
91. For a detailed discussion see J. Senior, 'Rationalizing Electrotherapy in Neurology, 1860–1920', PhD thesis, Oxford University, 1994, pp. 95–101.
92. 'Deaths and Accidents Caused by High Tension Currents', *Electrical Review*, 1893, 32: 374.
93. H. L. Jones, 'The Lethal Effects of Electrical Currents', *British Medical Journal*, 1895, i: 468–70.
94. T. Oliver and R. Bolam, 'On the Cause of Death by Electric Shock', *British Medical Journal*, 1898, i: 132–5.
95. J.-L. Prevost and F. Battelli, 'La Mort par les Courants Électriques', *Journal de Physiologie et de Pathologie Générale*, 1899, 3: 399–442.
96. W. S. Hedley, 'The Pathology and Treatment of Electric Accidents', *Lancet*, 1894, ii: 437.
97. W. S. Hedley, 'Death by Electricity', *Electrical Review*, 1898, 42: 207–8, on p. 208.
98. W. S. Hedley, 'The Painlessness of Electric Death', *Electrical Review*, 1897, 41: 205–6, on p. 206.
99. 'Accidents from Shock, and their Treatment', *Electrical Review*, 1894, 35: 733–4, on p. 734.
100. A. Conan Doyle, 'The Los Amigos Fiasco', *Round the Red Lamp, being Facts and Fancies of Medical Life* (London, 1894), pp. 281–94, on p. 282.
101. Doyle, 'Los Amigos', pp. 289–90; p. 293.
102. C. Marvin, *When Old Technologies were New* (Oxford: Oxford University Press, 1988), pp. 109–51.

103. For the sociology of calibration see H. Collins, *Changing Order: Replication and Induction in Scientific Practice* (London: Sage Publications, 1985), pp. 100–6. For calibration and electrical bodies see Morus, 'Measure of Man'.
104. See Green Musselman's contribution to this collection for further discussion of the limits of Victorian views on the machinelike body.

−6−

'Instruments to Lay Hold of Spirits': Technologizing the Bodies of Victorian Spiritualism

Richard Noakes

Can machines establish the existence of disembodied spirits? Many Victorians thought so. In the second half of the nineteenth century, several leading British scientific practitioners, engineers, spiritualists, and journalists used simple mechanical contraptions, precision electrical apparatus, vacuum tubes, photographic plates, and self-recording instruments to try to establish whether the striking physical phenomena produced through spiritualist mediums derived from known or unknown causes. In the seventeenth and eighteenth centuries mechanical measures of immaterial entities and spirits had been criticized as self-contradictory, dangerous, and risible, but by the mid-nineteenth century, 'spirits' appeared to be manifesting themselves in such gross physical ways – from coded raps on tables to materialized figures – that they were seen as plausible subjects for close scrutiny with the material resources of laboratories.[1]

The complex relationship between nineteenth century cultures of spiritualism and machines has been the subject of many recent historical studies.[2] These emphasize experimental and symbolic connections between new technologies for receiving and transmitting signals from distant intelligences and the development of spiritualistic and psychic practices for exchanging messages with the souls of the dead and living. Precision electrical instruments and practical routines for measuring faults in telegraph cables were used to determine the authenticity of spirit manifestations. Just as the electric telegraph annihilated spatial and temporal gulfs between continents, so the 'celestial telegraph' was upheld as a bridge between this world and the next; and just as photographs, telephones, and phonographs embodied the voices of the distant living, so mediums were seen as instruments that embodied the appearances and utterances of the distant dead.

Spiritualism was thus no different from other Victorian cultures in which the human body was increasingly represented in terms of such burgeoning technological systems as the electric telegraph and electrical power transmission. Human bodies were not only more closely integrated with and disciplined by such systems but were increasingly represented by medical and scientific practitioners as machines whose performance could be measured by instruments.[3] For some historians, it was disenchantment with such materialistic conceptions of the human body and the effects of technological systems on society that prompted many Victorians to turn to spiritualism and psychical research for solutions to deep moral, intellectual, and religious anxieties.[4] This chapter shows, however, that this analysis underestimates the extent to which investigators and supporters of spiritualism embraced late nineteenth-century machine cultures. They saw technology as a symbol of social progress but also believed that diverse forms of technology – from simple mechanical contraptions to precision laboratory instruments – had a plausible and important role in the progress of spiritualistic 'science'.[5] The period in which spiritualistic investigators pushed hardest for instrumental measures of séance 'manifestations' – the 1860s–1870s – was not coincidentally that witnessing a dramatic rise in the status of precision measurement and mechanized observation in the sciences. The development of highly sensitive instruments and the establishment of teaching laboratories for inculcating expertise in precision measurement were integral parts of Victorian scientists' strategies to bolster trust in their claims and to furnish Britain with the scientific skills and resources that would reinforce its industrial and economic might.[6] Leading Victorian scientific investigators of spiritualism such as William Crookes and Cromwell Varley shared their scientific colleagues' faith in the long-term economic benefits of 'accurate investigation' and moreover, insisted that employing the same techniques in the séance would produce evidence of phenomena that would be of long-term intellectual and spiritual benefit to mankind.[7]

This chapter builds on much recent scholarship demonstrating the importance of the proper conduct of investigators' bodies in controversies over scientific knowledge.[8] Disputes about the constituents of natural knowledge were also fights over the bodily gestures and conventions considered appropriate to the making of such knowledge. This was especially true in Victorian spiritualism where disagreements between spiritualists and their critics over the reality of manifested spiritual bodies were also conflicts over what constituted proper scientific conduct of bodies in the séance. Spiritualists sought to defend the conventions of the spirit circle by appealing to analogies between séance bodies and scientific instruments although this did little to thwart spiritualism's fiercest opponents. Magicians and popular showmen sought to show that mediumistic performances could be replicated and debunked by stage machinery, optical illusions, and simple conjuring. Physiologists and medical men, on the other hand, developed sophisticated theories of mental mechanism that appeared to explain the sloppy procedures that underpinned physical scientists' evidence for spiritualistic manifestations. Facing such criticism, scientific investigators of the séance recognized that the authority of their claims had to shift from the troublesome bodies of the séance to instruments.

Several studies have illustrated the importance of self-recording instruments in the nineteenth century sciences.[9] Simon Schaffer has stressed how these technologies 'distract attention from the person of the experimenter' and promise to produce more robust evidence of the external world.[10] Similarly, Lorraine Daston and Peter Galison have argued that evidence produced in this way offered 'freedom from will – from the wilful interventions that had come to be seen as the most dangerous aspects of subjectivity'.[11] The quest for objective evidence of psychic and spiritualistic manifestations, devoid of 'interventions' from tricky mediums or deluded investigators, characterizes the troubled enterprises of William Crookes and William Henry Harrison. These practitioners used precision instruments and routines of physics laboratories to produce disembodied and therefore more trustworthy measures of spiritualistic powers. However, it was this shift from the individual to the instrument that many spiritualists found objectionable and I will be suggesting that this helps explain why laboratory technology fulfilled only a limited role in their sciences of the séance.

The Troubled Bodies of Spiritualism

Questions of bodies dominated 'modern spiritualism' which spread from America to Britain and the Continent in the early 1850s. By the 1870s millions of people worldwide believed that their experiences of spiritualism, from domestic séances to public lectures given by entranced mediums, had convinced them of the truth of spiritualism's controversial claims: that the spiritual body survived the death of the natural body which was itself a mere 'machine' of the spiritual body, that spirits progressed in the 'other world' at a rate commensurate with earthly sins, and that spirits of the dead could, under certain conditions, manifest themselves to the living.[12] Spiritualism's claims and practices threatened many religious, intellectual, and social positions: it abolished hell fire, it suggested that evidence for the spiritual body and the 'future life' could be gained through the natural as well as the supernatural faculties, and most significantly, by emphasizing 'personal experience' of spirit, it threatened the authority of the Christian establishment.[13]

Despite agreement between spiritualists on these claims, Victorian spiritualism was extremely heterogeneous. It appealed to men and women from all classes for diverse, and often contradictory, reasons: it furnished people of all classes with evidence of the survival of deceased relatives and of personal immortality; it provided Christians with welcome evidence of the plausibility of Biblical miracles; anti-Christian plebeian autodidacts used it to forge democratic and empirical routes to spiritual salvation independently of the national church; women mediums used their skills to gain power and independence within and without the stifling domestic sphere; enterprising conjurors and showmen exploited spiritualism as a lucrative topic for exposure and ridicule; and some bourgeois Victorian physiologists and physicists seized on séance occurrences as fertile territory for probing new forces and powers of the mind.[14]

The most spectacular and controversial aspect of spiritualism was undoubtedly the physical and mental phenomena associated with professed spirits of the dead and the spiritualist 'mediums'. These became more complex as the century progressed. In the 1850s, they included tables that turned, furniture that rapped, and objects and mediums that levitated under the apparent influence of spirits, and mediums who had clairvoyant visions and became channels for spirits that wrote, spoke and administered cures. By the 1870s, spiritualism boasted spirit photography, spirits who wrote and spoke directly without the need of mediums, and most spectacular of all, spirits that materialized in darkened wooden cabinets and emerged as fully formed human figures that walked, chatted, and interacted with séance participants. For many séance goers, trickery, hallucination, self-deception and a host of other mundane explanations offered by scientific, religious, and intellectual critics, were insufficient to account for all the 'facts' of the séance and supported the plausibility of the existence of disembodied spirits. Although spiritualists emphasized the long-term importance of the 'higher' mental phenomena of spiritualism, the grosser and thus more controversial physical phenomena still furnished the very 'evidence of the senses' with which spiritualists believed they could combat materialism and make the spiritual body amenable to physical measurement.[15]

The practices developed by spiritualists to convince their publics of the credibility of their claims were strongly dependent on bodies – both that of the séance-goer and the medium – whose peculiar constitution and 'sensitivity' were held to make them especially good 'instruments' for relaying intelligence and displaying physical effects.[16] The séance was undoubtedly the most revered institution in spiritualism and spiritualists worked hard to negotiate and enforce 'rules and conditions' of séances that would improve the chances of contacting, exhibiting, and investigating spirits who appeared to be as capricious and 'self-willed' as living humans or who might, as the medium Daniel Dunglas Home warned, 'choose not to manifest themselves'.[17] The basic thrust of many published séance rules is best summed up by the spiritualist Newton Crosland who pointed out in 1873 that 'behaviour and disposition' at the séance determined 'the character of the manifestations'.[18] The best sitters were polite, passive and friendly because their sympathetic mental and bodily states created the harmonious stream of imponderable 'elements' with which the spirits were believed to manifest themselves.[19] For this reason, genial conversation, singing in unison, and praying were encouraged as the most important first steps in achieving communion with capricious spirits. The worst sitters, according to the leading spiritualist publisher James Burns, were the 'dogmatic', the 'vicious and crude', or those whose 'temperaments' conflicted with those in the circle, and these were generally held to cause manifestations of a correspondingly unsatisfactory or low character.[20] For this reason, spiritualists resented scientific investigators of spiritualism more for their arrogant, prankish and generally 'unscientific' behaviour in the séance (notably towards mediums) than their verdicts on 'manifestations'.[21] Most mediums were women and individuals of delicate health, so spiritualists also berated séance goers who did not treat the focus of spiritualistic activity with the civility that women and the sick enjoyed outside the darkened room. Published rules and conditions also emphasized that some experimenting with the order of the 'spirit circle' and other arrangements might be required for the best results.

Spiritualists' claim that spirits used electrical and magnetic powers to manifest themselves influenced their choice of metaphors for managing bodies in the séance room. Thus, one leading spiritualist insisted that participants of opposite temperaments constituted the 'positive and negative elements' of a spiritualistic battery and suggested that a 'strongly positive temperament or disposition' should be excluded 'as any such magnetic spheres emanating from the circle will overpower that of the spirits'.[22] Similarly, spiritualists not only spoke in terms of the 'celestial telegraph' to the spirit world and used a 'telegraphic' alphabet of raps to communicate with spirits, but believed that reliable interactions between terrestrial and spiritual intelligences depended on a well-managed séance 'apparatus' as much as successful telegraphic communication required proper working instruments As one spiritualist saw it:

> If your apparatus for telegraphing is imperfect – if there is 'contact' or 'deflection of needles', how liable the receiver is to misunderstand the messages, although the sender may transmit it as correctly as he possibly can under the circumstances; but who would condemn the sender of the message because the apparatus was imperfect? And just so I apprehend the messages from the spirit-world are defective, or are often considered false, because the right conditions are not provided.[23]

Over twenty years later William Fletcher Barrett, the experimental physicist who helped launch the Society for Psychical Research (SPR) in 1882, used a similar instrumental analogy to defend the role of mediums. He insisted that

> Physical science affords abundant analogies of the necessity for a medium, or intermediary, between the unseen and the seen. The waves of the luminiferous ether require a material medium to absorb them before they can be perceived by our senses; the intermediary may be a photographic plate, the rods and cones of the retina, a blackened surface, or the so-called electromagnetic resonators, according to the respective length of those waves; but *some* medium, formed of ponderable matter, is absolutely necessary to render the chemical, luminous, thermal, or electrical effects of these waves perceptible to us.[24]

The power of sensitive photographic plates to mediate between the seen and the unseen was doubly useful in spiritualism. It not only made plausible the claim that photographic plates could reveal spiritual entities invisible to the naked eye but justified spiritualist notions of mediums as human analogues of those plates.[25]

Spiritualists worked hard to create the séance environment in which mediums could work best although critics held that these were the very conditions that were designed to prevent fair enquiry. An anonymous *Saturday Review* journalist spoke for many disenchanted Victorian spiritualistic investigators when, in 1871, he lamented the fact that séances were

> never performed in a straightforward open way, like any honest experiment. They are either done in the dark, or only before known believers and confederates, or within a specially prepared place; and even when they are done in the daylight, the operator is full of tricks to distract attention, and to produce mysterious bewilderment.[26]

Indeed it was because the success of séances appeared to be so contingent on the specific bodies and conditions that other critics could emphasize differences between séances and technology. Henry Dircks, a civil engineer, and as we will see in the following section, co-inventor of a famous phantasmagorical illusion, made this point succinctly in 1872 when he pointed out that nothing was performed in spiritualism

> without a *séance*, and an amazing amount of childish jugglery. If I promised to convulse a man's joints, I produce a small battery at any time and in any place, and the thing is done, even though every man should be a profound disbeliever and inveterate opponent. Besides, I never fail. Man, woman, or child, old or young, alike are all convulsed on their connecting the poles of the galvanic battery. Let spiritualists take this for their guidance, and if they then succeed they will never after have to complain of irritating and taunting discussions and correspondence.[27]

The very alacrity with which spiritualists promulgated the séance rules illustrates their ongoing struggles to manage this aspect of their culture and to convince sceptics that adherence to the rules would eventually give séances the reliability on which Dircks insisted. Reports of séances in Victorian spiritualist periodicals testify to the frequent occasions when order broke down in the darkened room. This was often caused by disagreements between séance goers over the balance between conditions needed for conducting satisfactory tests and those demanded by the medium for producing her phenomena. For some séance goers, the latter conditions were so contrived that they had to be broken in the interests of truth. In 1873, for example, the lawyer William Volckman attended a séance in Hackney given by the young medium Florence Cook, whose *pièce-de-resistance* was the production of a fully-formed materialized spirit, 'Katie King', from within a darkened cabinet adjoining the séance room.[28] At one point during the séance Volckman grew so suspicious of the physical similarity between Miss Cook and 'Katie King' that he seized the spirit form and declared it to be the medium masquerading as her ghost. For Volckman and his allies, this constituted a satisfactory exposure of a star medium, but Miss Cook's supporters, who had established confidence in her genuineness over a long series of séances, vigorously defended their medium and denounced Volckman. Miss Cook's supporters were as outraged by Volckman's behaviour as his sensational revelation about the medium. Since Volckman had broken his agreement to behave in a civil and polite fashion in the séance and decided to grab the female 'spirit form' he had disqualified himself as a credible investigator and undermined the reliability of his evidence. His actions were not only judged improper but dangerous: since spiritualists believed that the materialization process involved spirits borrowing energy and matter from the medium, intrusions (whether by people or rays of light) on the bodies of the spirit or medium were thought to seriously harm or even kill the medium. This hypothesis was frequently invoked by spiritualists to explain why the spirit manifestations looked suspiciously like their mediums and bore such gross and crude physical attributes as beating hearts, illiteracy, and onion-smelling breath. Few critics, however, were convinced by this argument and found it hard to reconcile these attributes with their notions of the refined 'spiritual' body.[29]

Despite their confidence in Miss Cook's credibility and Volckman's disingenuousness, Miss Cook's supporters were deeply wounded by the incident and needed to produce and promulgate more satisfactory evidence that the medium and her spirit form were bodily distinct. Their chief strategy was to appeal to the authority of William Crookes, the distinguished analytical chemist and scientific journalist who had by 1873 already established himself as one of the least hostile scientific investigators of spiritualism. Crookes developed a close friendship with Miss Cook, 'Katie', and her allies and convinced them that, unlike Volckman, his strategies for investigating the medium and spirit would respect the fact that both needed to be treated as 'ladies'. Indeed, he was so effective at convincing spiritualists of the honour of his intentions, that he was able to bend séance rules to meet his own notions of adequate testing: he gained Miss Cook and Katie's consent to enter the darkened cabinet where he claimed to see the spirit form standing next to the medium, he was allowed to clasp and kiss the spirit form and observe how its body differed from Miss Cook's, and he took a series of photographs of 'Katie' illuminated by powerful electric light.[30]

This achievement raised Crookes's status among Miss Cook's defenders and many other spiritualists, but it threatened it in other quarters. What provoked scorn was Crookes's dubious behaviour towards the medium. The friendship and intimacy with Miss Cook which Crookes believed was crucial for conducting important spiritualistic experiments caused numerous rumours to spread within and without spiritualist circles regarding the propriety of his actions. Many spiritualists believed he had, unlike most scientific men, treated mediums with the proper respect, but others feared this was at the cost of proper experimental practice. Charles Maurice Davies, the non-conformist clergyman and wry *Times* commentator on Victorian London's 'mystic' cultures, saw many Crookes-Cook séances and thought the 'effusive Professor' had developed an intimacy and dangerous 'prejudice' towards his experimental subject that was 'scarcely becoming a F.R.S'.[31] The Victorian conjuror John Nevil Maskelyne was more savage and thought Crookes's account of 'Katie's' physical beauty revealed that the scientist was 'too far gone for "investigation"'.[32] As in early Victorian cultures of mesmerism, the performance of investigators was at least as important in public judgements of spiritualism as the startling phenomena themselves.[33]

Despite their efforts to regulate the behaviour of séance-goers and to defend the genuineness and innocence of mediums, spiritualists faced mounting criticism that the bodies on which they depended could not be trusted. At no period was this more acute than in the 1860s and 1870s, which witnessed the development of the grossest materializations of the spirit body, a string of exposures of celebrity mediums, and the most savage attacks on the reliability of Crookes and other scientific investigators of the spirit world. As we shall see in the following section, the most potent attacks on spiritualism's bodies concerned their relationship with and similarity to machines.

Machines and Illusionists/Ghosts and Mediums

In 1858 an American Unitarian minister explained that his conviction in the genuineness of spiritualistic manifestations was partly based on the fact that despite searching for 'machinery, jugglery, or imposture' in the séance room where he witnessed the manifestations, he failed to 'find something mundane a sufficient cause for all these wonders'.[34] His reference to machinery undoubtedly alluded to the fact that since their first appearance in ante-bellum America, spiritualistic phenomena had not only been widely compared to the tricks of ancient and modern wizards, but had been explicitly imitated by illusionists and showmen using clever 'machinery'. Some of the greatest magicians and showmen of the nineteenth century – including P. T. Barnum, Robert Houdin, 'Professor' John Henry Pepper, 'Professor' John Henry Anderson, John Nevil Maskelyne and George Cooke – exploited Victorian audiences' taste for spectacle, mystery, and the supernatural and staged fake spiritualist phenomena that they believed were not only more thrilling than mediums' dark séances but more honest because, unlike mediums, they drew attention to the technology behind spirits.

The performances of the celebrated nineteenth-century Scottish conjuror, 'Professor' Anderson, the 'Wizard of the North', powerfully illustrate the uses to which Victorian showmen put machinery in their bid to destroy the livelihoods of mediums.[35] During an American tour in the late 1840s, Anderson vowed to 'discover the mechanism' of what he regarded as the spiritualistic 'imposture' and on returning to Britain, practised what he preached in numerous shows that purported to reveal the chicanery behind mesmerism, table turning and spirit rapping.[36] As suggested by the following account of a performance in London, Anderson believed that by replicating spiritualistic phenomena with visible machines, he could distinguish himself from 'conjurors in disguise' who concealed the machinery by which they produced 'spirit' manifestations for fee-paying customers.

> Suspending two glass bells from the ceiling, placing a table on a platform extended across the centre of the pit, and setting up an automaton figure on the stage, [Anderson] made each in turn answer every question that he put as to the number of letters composing a given word, or the number of pips on a card drawn from the pack. The bells answered by ringing, the table by raps, and the automaton by signs. The means by which the replies were obtained was not stated. Anderson merely informed the audience that they were purely mechanical, and not more so than those employed by the Spiritualists, whom he denounced as impostors.[37]

To protect their livelihoods, however, conjurors could not be completely open about their stage mechanisms and this encouraged speculation on the source of their astonishing skills. Although they claimed to show how spiritualism was done with simple prestidigitation and such resources as ropes, wires, false doors, mirrors, and phosphorescent powder, many spectators were still puzzled by the extraordinary performance. Indeed, many spectators found it difficult to distinguish between conjurors and mediums and some spiritualists even believed magicians were mediums in disguise.[38] Charles Maurice Davies summed up the these dilemmas when, after attending several séances and magic shows in the mid-1870s, he reflected that one conjuror's mechanical imitation of spiritualistic phenomena was 'quite as wonderful as anything I have ever witnessed at a séance', another was too 'lumbering' to count as a satisfactory 'reproduction', but that both the conjuror and the spiritualist 'claims to be Moses, and denounces the others as mere magicians'.[39]

Davies's remarks were part of a much broader commentary on the anti-spiritualist illusionists of Victorian London many of whom, like 'Professor' Pepper and Maskelyne and Cooke, made machines central to their acts. The immensely successful phantasmagorical apparatus that Pepper billed as 'Pepper's Ghost' was a joint invention with Henry Dircks whose primitive 'Dircksian Phantasmagoria'

Figure 6.1 'Pepper's Ghost' or the 'Dircksian Phantasmagoria' used to startling effect in a Victorian stage play. The invention required the construction of a hidden stage beneath the main stage. Light from an artificial lamp is directed on a spectrally-clad actor or actress who cannot be seen by spectators. The image of the actor is projected via a trap door onto a pane of glass held at a steep angle to the stage. Spectators see through the glass and gain the impression of a spectral figure behind the pane. *The World of Wonders: A Record of Things Wonderful in Nature, Science, and Art*, 2 vols. (London, 1895–97). Reproduced with permission of the British Library.

Pepper helped Dircks turn into a popular stage effect.[40] The invention involved shining a bright lamp onto an actor who played out his or her role in a compartment beneath the main stage. Light from the actor was projected onto a large pane of glass held at an angle to the front of a stage where, from the perspective of audience members, there appeared a spectral image that appeared to manifest itself out of nowhere. It was first demonstrated in 1862 at London's Royal Polytechnic Institution, a popular metropolitan hall of science where Pepper also enjoyed fame for spectacular displays of optical illusions, magic lanterns, chemical reactions, and electrical machines.[41] Despite their later fierce priority dispute, Pepper and Dircks agreed that 'The Ghost' served their mutual interests in promoting rational entertainment and to distinguish them from what Pepper called 'traders in spirits'. For Dircks, 'The Ghost' fitted squarely within the tradition of David Brewster's

Letters on Natural Magic (1833) and other eighteenth- and nineteenth-century works that reduced apparently supernatural phenomena and miraculous machines to discernible operations of light, sound and other natural forces.[42] Unlike ancient wizardry and modern spiritualism, the natural magic embodied in the 'Ghost' made

> no pretension to an occult science, but on the contrary tends to dissipate many vulgar errors, by disabusing the public mind, even on matters long considered supernatural. Concave mirrors, magic lanterns, phantasmagoria, and similar optical instruments, afford ample illustration of the happy tendency of modern investigation over the once degrading employment of superior knowledge only to impose on rather than enlighten the public.[43]

Like the conjurors with whom they competed for audiences, Dircks and Pepper mechanized and demystified phenomena that spiritualists claimed were genuinely novel.[44] However, it was audiences' understanding of the mechanism of the 'Ghost' that appears to have led, in the early 1870s, to its fall in popularity and eventual demise. However, this did not stop Dircks from continuing his war against spiritualism and other 'Chimerical Pursuits,' or Pepper from his alternative theatrical strategies of upstaging spiritualism with bogus 'manifestations'.[45]

Pepper's principal venue for performances of 'fake séances' was the Egyptian Hall, Piccadilly, 'England's Home of Mystery' whose tradition of mechanizing spirits would be continued by late-Victorian Britain's most celebrated illusionist double-act, Maskelyne and Cooke. The 'Royal Illusionists and Anti-Spiritualists', Maskelyne and Cooke, established their reputation for unmasking mediums in the mid-1860s when they used clever conjuring to replicate the public performances of the Davenport brothers, two American mediums who caused a sensation in mid-Victorian society with their apparent ability to levitate objects outside a darkened cabinet in which the performers were tied to chairs. A watchmaker by training, Maskelyne spent much of his career 'constructing apparatus for scientific, optical, and mechanical illusion' and with the help of Cooke, an ex-cabinet maker, used similar apparatus to replicate levitations, disembodied hands, materialized figures and a host of other séance phenomena.[46] Maskelyne and Cooke prided themselves on the fact that, unlike mediums, many of their 'séances' occurred under bright illumination and that they allowed audience members to inspect whether there were any tricks or non-mechanical agencies involved in the production of the astonishing effects. Although Maskelyne and Cooke were ridiculed by spiritualists for producing poor imitations of spiritualistic manifestations, the immense and sustained popularity of their performances raised the reputation of conjurors among Victorian intellectual and scientific circles as important experts to consult on the performances of mediums. By collapsing the distinction between spirit 'manifestations' and machine-generated spectacles, they shifted attention from

Figure 6.2 An 1873 advertisement for performances of Maskelyne and Cooke at the Egyptian Hall, Piccadilly. This represents the 'light' séances in which they claimed they could replicate some of the standard phenomena of dark spiritualistic séances – floating mediums, levitating tables, disembodied hands – with simple machinery, optical illusions, and conjuring. Despite such claims, Maskelyne and Cooke's advertisements usually failed to depict such backstage processes. This strategy was undoubtedly informed by their need to maintain a degree of mystery about their performances which not only attracted theatre-goers but collapsed the distinction between conjurors and mediums. Guildhall Library, London, GR.2.57, page 75/342. Reproduced with permission of the Guildhall Library, Corporation of London

what mediums appeared to do using allegedly supernatural means to what conjurors could accomplish with deft bodily skills and the technological resources of a magician's cabinet. This cultural shift is powerfully illustrated by the activities of the intellectuals and scientists who ran the early SPR. In their investigations into the 'physical' phenomena of spiritualism, they appealed to the authority of Maskelyne and other conjurors whose analyses of mediums' performances were valued as much as the 'accurate' investigations of the physical scientists in the Society.

Spirits of Mental Machinery

The similarity between mediums and conjurors was given considerable intellectual respectability by leading Anglo-American physiologists, psychologists, and medical practitioners who, throughout the mid- to late-Victorian period, developed the most potent scientific arguments against the credibility of the evidence for spiritualism. Developing early nineteenth-century medical and philosophical works that reduced apparitions and other 'supernatural' occurrences to hallucinations, nervous disorders and other mundane causes, they developed sophisticated psycho-physiological theories that stressed the ways in which the involuntary actions of the mind and body made spiritualistic witnesses unable to distinguish fact from fancy and which were exploited by wily mediums in their allegedly supernatural feats of mind and body.

One of the most outspoken and eloquent defenders of this position, and the savant whose psycho-physiological researches formed the core of the Anglo-American medical and scientific bulwark against late-Victorian spiritualism was the physiologist and physician William Benjamin Carpenter.[47] As Alison Winter has shown, from the late 1840s Carpenter plied his physiological expertise in phenomena of altered mental states.[48] Building on Marshall Hall's claim that many bodily actions responded involuntarily to sensory stimulation via a separate 'excito-motory' nervous system centred on the spinal column, Carpenter, Thomas Laycock and other early Victorian physiologists, developed analogous accounts of mental reflexes. Carpenter argued that many mental responses to ideas or intellectual stimuli took place without the guidance of will and led to involuntary 'ideo-motor' actions centred on the cerebrum. As Carpenter put it in 1852, an individual subjected to such involuntary actions had become a 'mere *thinking automaton*, the whole course of whose ideas is determinable by suggestions operating from without'.[49] Carpenter believed his theory satisfactorily accounted for a range of abnormal mental phenomena including hysteria, somnambulism, 'trance' behaviour, mesmerism, electrobiology, and table turning. These were not the result of some external agency such as the mesmeric fluid, electricity, or spirits, but involuntary mental activity caused by concentrating on an idea or external suggestion provided by a mesmerist, electrobiologist, or medium. Carpenter fought harder to vanquish what he believed was the public's delusion about table turning and at the height of its popularity in 1853, he sought to demonstrate, with the help of a simple mechanical apparatus designed by Michael Faraday, that the force of table turning derived not from disembodied spirits but from the table turners themselves who involuntarily pushed the table in response to the strong expectation or wish that the table would move. Not everybody judged Faraday's demonstration and Carpenter's theories to be a decisive explanation of spiritualism.[50] Indeed, much to Carpenter's disgust, table-turning was just a prelude to the 'epidemic delusion' of spiritualism.[51] From this period until the early 1880s, in reviews in periodicals, public lectures, his best-selling textbook *Principles of Mental Physiology* (1874) and other forums, Carpenter used his theories of mental mechanism to indict the credibility of spiritualism's witnesses. One of the key problems was that evidence of spiritualistic manifestations derived from individuals who erroneously regarded their bodies as unproblematic instruments for gauging the external world. As he argued in 1875:

> Nothing is more common at the present time, than for the advocates of Spiritualism to appeal to 'the evidence of their own senses' as conclusive in regard to anything done by 'the spirits'; and to claim that their testimony and that of other witnesses to what Common Sense rejects as altogether preposterous and incredible: such persons being altogether ignorant of the fact well known to the Physiologist and Psychologist, that, when the Mind has been previously possessed by a 'dominant idea', *nothing is more fallacious* than the 'evidence of the senses'.[52]

For Carpenter, most spiritualistic witnesses entered séances already possessed by the expectation that spirits would appear. It was this mental fixation that weakened the regulating power of the will over the senses and left séance goers unable to make informed judgements of what they experienced. In this condition, séance goers were more likely to deceive themselves, hallucinate, suffer from crucial lapses in concentration, and fall prey to mediumistic legerdemain. Given that spiritualism contradicted such well-established or 'common sense' notions as the laws of gravity and that the necessarily overwhelming evidence in its favour was decidedly wanting, it was more likely that the senses of spiritualists than the sense of their scientific critics was at fault, and that 'so-called spiritual communications come from *within*, not from *without*, the individuals who suppose themselves to be the recipients of them' and 'that they belong to the class termed 'subjective' by physiologists and psychologists'.[53]

Carpenter's theories allowed him to protect the honour of spiritualistic witnesses, many of whom were esteemed scientific colleagues such as Crookes, the telegraphic engineer Cromwell Varley, and the naturalist Alfred Russel Wallace. These savants had not wilfully deceived their audiences but had fallen victim to unconscious mental processes that, to one degree or another, were present in everybody. The difference between good and bad scientific investigators of spiritualism was a difference of mental discipline. Carpenter insisted that physiologists and medical practitioners were 'fully qualified for the task by habits of philosophical discrimination, by entire freedom from prejudice, and by a *full acquaintance with the numerous and varies sources of fallacy which attend this particular department of inquiry*'.[54] Crookes and many other scientists, on the other hand, only had a narrow technical education which may have served them well in their own scientific fields, but signally failed to prepare them for the study of mediumistic and self-deception. Their limited mental training explained why they had accepted the 'spiritual' theory of manifestations on shaky evidence and had woefully misplaced notions of the relationship between experimenter and subject in the séance. As Carpenter warned in 1876, the trouble with most physical investigators of spiritualism was their 'ignorance of the nature *of their instruments of research*; putting as much faith in tricky girls or women, as they do in their thermometers or electroscopes'.[55] The most significant instrument of research for Carpenter and many other medical men, however, was the physical scientist himself whose failure to conduct himself in a manner appropriate to the scientific study of tricky mediums spectacularly demonstrated the effects of wrongly regulated mental machinery.

Carpenter's long campaign against spiritualism drew frequent and violent responses from spiritualists and non-spiritualists. In their opinion, there were plenty of manifestations that could not be attributed to the bodily and mental actions of witnesses or to mediumistic deception. Indeed the launch and steadily rising membership of the SPR suggests that not all British scientists and intellectuals were satisfied that Carpenter's was the last word on spiritualism. In their quest to give intellectual respectability to the investigation of psychic, spiritualistic and other abnormal psychological phenomena, the SPR leaders forged a midway position between Carpenter and spiritualism that appropriated physiologists' and psychologists' language of mental machinery and left a place for spiritual agencies. Like Carpenter, they held that mediums or what they strategically called 'automatists' did experience motor and mental actions that were beyond their conscious will, but believed psychical research revealed how a 'subliminal' or subconscious part of the medium's self as well as discarnate spiritual agencies could take temporary control over the medium's sensory and motor functions.[56] The SPR's collapse of so much 'spiritual' phenomena into mental mechanisms exasperated most spiritualists. But as we shall see in the next section, they were also sceptical of attempts to collapse 'spiritual' truths into real machines.

Spiritualism without Mediums: William Crookes's Instruments of Psychic Force

We have seen that bodies and machines posed thorny problems for Victorian investigators of spiritualism. Investigators had to regulate their bodies in conformity with séance conventions that were designed to produce reliable evidence of new powers associated with the body of the medium. However, this kind of self-control was also criticized for threatening the bodily performances necessary for making séance investigations objective and scientific. More damaging, the performances of the human and spiritual bodies of the séance were replicated, explained, and ridiculed by the real and metaphorical machinery of conjurors, physiologists, and medical men. By the 1870s, however, there were many scientific practitioners who attacked conjurors and physiologists because their explanations of spiritualism were not based on scrupulous investigation or a comprehensive knowledge of all the 'facts' of the séance. Few articulated such arguments more vociferously than William Crookes and William Henry Harrison, two experimental scientists whose forays into the séance are among the most significant nineteenth-century examples of technology being used to resolve the troubles of spiritualism's bodies. Their researches spectacularly showed how laboratory instruments could be pitted against the machines of the stage and mind in the cause of demonstrating spiritualistic facts.

Crookes's notorious investigations into spiritualism have attracted much attention from scientists, spiritualists, psychical researchers and historians since their inception in the late 1860s.[57] By this time, Crookes was widely recognized as an analytical chemist of considerable skill and a leading science journalist. Trained at the Royal College of Chemistry in his native London, Crookes built his scientific reputation by plying chemical expertise in the rapidly growing fields of photography, spectroscopy, science journalism, and industrial chemistry. In the 1860s his enterprises had secured him a Royal Society Fellowship for the spectroscopic discovery of the chemical element thallium, and power and income as editor of the widely circulated *Chemical News*. The thallium researches informed his strong conviction that scientific discovery, especially of new elements and forces, was a promising if risky way of raising his standing in Victorian science. There was more than just a purely intellectual or altruistic reason for Crookes insisting, in 1871, that 'New forces must be found, or mankind must remain sadly ignorant of the mysteries of the universe'.[58]

Crookes's decision to investigate spiritualism may have been prompted by the tragic death of a younger brother although it owed a great deal to the testimony and example set by such respected chemist colleagues as Robert Angus Smith and Walter Weldon. As he explained to John Tyndall in late 1869, one such colleague had 'witnessed phenomena alleged to be spiritual, which he was unable to explain by any known physical force, and advised me to take the first opportunity of witnessing such things for myself and forming my own judgement upon them'.[59] By this time Crookes was in fact already attending séances in London and returning with a similar verdict but unlike his chemist colleagues, he was convinced the phenomena were too important to be left to private scientific discussion.

Crookes was in a powerful position to make spiritualism a topic for public scientific debate. As editor of the best-selling *Quarterly Journal of Science* (*QJS*), he was used to publicizing the exciting new frontiers of scientific research and the importance of scientific expertise in solving host of pressing social problems, and in July 1870 he outlined a similar solution to the burgeoning problem of spiritualism. Crookes urged that it was the 'duty of scientific men who have learnt exact modes of working, to examine phenomena which attract the attention of the public, in order to confirm their genuineness, or to explain if possible the delusions of the honest and to expose the tricks of deceivers.' What qualified the 'scientific man' above the 'pseudo-scientific spiritualist' and anybody else was his insistence on 'precautions and tests' in matters 'marvellous and unexpected,' and the 'delicacy of the instrumental aids' which far surpassed the 'natural senses' in providing 'experimental proof' of spiritualist phenomena.[60]

By this time Crookes had already secured the help of one of the few mediums whom he judged trustworthy enough to conduct 'careful scientific testing experiments'.[61] The medium was Daniel Dunglas Home who, despite being the subject of fierce criticism and ridicule in Victorian periodicals, enjoyed patronage and testimonials from several British and European savants including the astronomer Lord Lindsay and Crookes's colleague, the chemist Alexander Boutlerow. From April 1870 Home gave a long series of séances in the dining room of Crookes's London residence and performed many of his usual feats including self-levitation and the handling of hot-coals. By holding his séances in the light of gas lamps and allowing male investigators to conduct thorough searches of his body, Home gradually convinced Crookes that the kinetic and gravity-defying phenomena were linked with a strange wavering force associated with his body. What particularly impressed Crookes was that despite accepting Home's invitation to be searched as if he were a conjuror, the medium did not appear to employ 'simple instrumental aids' and displayed phenomena that would 'baffle the skill' of such conjurors as Houdin and Anderson 'backed with all the resources of elaborate machinery and the practice of years'.[62] In late May 1871 Crookes began a series of test séances in which he sought to produce evidence fit for presentation to scientific audiences. His most dramatic step was transforming the topology of the séance. From the small physical laboratory next to his dining room, he brought several simple machines and instruments for making crude measurements of the wavering force, notably a self-registering spring-balance that produced an automatic record of the greatest measured weight while enabling the experimenters to scrutinize other parts of the apparatus. He invited his friend, William Huggins, the eminent astronomer and Royal Society Vice-President, to share the tasks of closely observing and recording what happened. Crookes's main goal was to examine Home's apparent skills in exerting a force at a distance without any mechanical aid. Having verified and further investigated Home's ability to levitate and play an accordion without touching the instrument, the experimenters proceeded to the principal part of the test. This involved observing the mechanical effect of Home's force on a thin wooden board, one end of which rested on a piece of wood on a table edge while the other was suspended from a self-registering spring-balance. After inviting Home to place his fingers lightly on the table end of the board, Crookes and Huggins watched the medium carefully and observed that the automatic register initially oscillated slowly and then registered a maximum downward weight of 6½ pounds. To bolster his conviction that Home could not have done this by simple lever action, Crookes calibrated his machine against his own body: he 'stepped upon the table and stood on one foot at the end of the board' and even when he 'jerked up and down' on it, he saw that he could only cause the spring balance to display one third of the maximum force that Home had exerted. This bolstered Crookes's conviction that he had 'conclusively' established 'the existence of a new force, in some unknown manner connected with the human organisation, which for convenience may be called the Psychic Force.'[63]

Crookes eagerly sent detailed reports of his experiment to the Royal Society and prepared a version for the July 1871 *QJS* that, according to one commentator, 'set all London on fire, and the Spiritualists rabid with excitement'.[64] Crookes's researches certainly divided circles of spiritualists and non-spiritualists. Many scientists, spiritualists and medical practitioners were impressed by his courage and evidence, although many spiritualists insisted that he had only demonstrated what they already knew from domestic séances. James Burns, the editor of the leading spiritualist weekly, *Medium and Daybreak*, was much more sceptical. He agreed that Crookes's investigations would raise the profile of spiritualism among non-spiritualists but denied that they were of the 'slightest assistance to Spiritualists', or that they were 'scientific' because they more resembled normal séance procedures than laboratory practices. Burns's position reflected what he perceived to be sharp differences between what he held to be proper spiritualist science and that practised by the likes of Crookes. In 1870 he argued that since the principal goal of spiritualistic science was elucidating the 'psychological' cause of manifestations, then laboratory apparatus were of limited use in this 'science'. 'Could all the paraphernalia of Mr. Crookes's workshop reveal to him the presence of a spirit?' Burns asked rhetorically, and insisted that 'The chemist and electrician may be of great service in investigating the nature of the means used and the material phenomena developed,' but the 'cause of the Spiritual phenomena' required 'mind-power and mind-appliances in the form of those highly developed organisms wherein spiritual consciousness and psychological function bring the sentient being into relation with the natural facts far above the apprehension of the senses.'[65] Burns was not alone in upholding the medium as the only instrument with the requisite psychological sensitivity to ascend to the 'natural' facts of spiritualism. In 1869 the eminent American spiritualist Epes Sargent doubted whether 'scientific men' were 'best qualified' because they

> have no instruments to lay hold of spirits, no chemical tests by which to detect their presence. Retorts and galvanic batteries are here of no avail. A simple woman, like Joan of Arc or the Seeress of Prevorst, may be the true expert here.[66]

From the perspective of spiritualists *and* such redoubtable spiritualistic assailants as Carpenter, physical scientists lacked the proper mental appliances for discerning the truth of spiritualism.

Burns and his supporters made the body of the medium the most important instrument of the scientific séance, but other critics of Crookes's researches believed it was one of the biggest liabilities. Most telling were the views of George Gabriel Stokes, the physicist and powerful Royal Society Secretary to whom Crookes had sent his psychic force researches, and whose support was crucial in the chemist's ongoing struggles to build his reputation.[67] Stokes warned Crookes that his apparatus did not preclude the possibility of Home using lever action to achieve the 'psychic' effects and only agreed to inspect the apparatus in the medium's absence. Stokes, however, does not appear to have kept his promise and this owed much to the fact that he, like many Victorian scientists, had 'heard too much of the tricks of Spiritualists' to consider mediums a legitimate instrument of scientific research.[68] Others were more concerned with the body of the experimenter himself. The physicist Balfour Stewart told *Nature* that it was likely that Home had exerted an 'electro-biological' influence over Crookes who had subsequently mistaken a subjective for an objective impression of psychic force.[69] In the most damning of all responses, William Benjamin Carpenter agreed with many critics that Crookes's choice of apparatus and protocol were totally inadequate for evading Home's trickery, and denied that 'psychic force' was a reality and threatened existing medical and scientific knowledge of bodily powers. As we have seen, however, Carpenter went further than anybody else in linking Crookes's failure as a competent séance scientist to wrongly disciplined judgement, an attack that prompted Crookes's fiercest defences of the importance of his physical expertise in the séance.[70]

Judging by his subsequent *QJS* publications on spiritualism, it was the criticisms from fellow scientists that Crookes took most seriously. They put his experimenter's body on trial as much as Home's mediumistic one, and forced Crookes to develop several strategies for shifting the evidential context of psychic force away from these troublesome bodies.[71] Responding to Stokes's worry that

Home could have secretly used lever action, he told the physicist that he was 'fitting up an apparatus in which contact is made through water only, in such a way that transmission of mechanical movement to the board is impossible; and I am also arranging an experiment in which Mr. Home will not touch the apparatus at all.'[72] This first change in apparatus probably owed a great deal the early nineteenth American chemist and spiritualist Robert Hare who had built an apparatus in 1858 to counter Michael Faraday and William Benjamin Carpenter's argument that the mechanical forces exerted by 'spirits' derived from unconscious muscular action of séance participants.[73] Crookes was satisfied that any muscular power exerted by Home on the board could be eliminated by placing a copper vessel filled with water between Home's hands and the board, and with this arrangement again observed the end of the board oscillating slowly under the influence of a strange force. In a second, and more dramatic change in strategy, Crookes constructed an instrument in which Home held his hand well above a lever whose responses to the fluctuating psychic force were inscribed on a smoked-glass plate that was moved horizontally by a clockwork mechanism. With this instrument,

FIG. 10. (Section.)

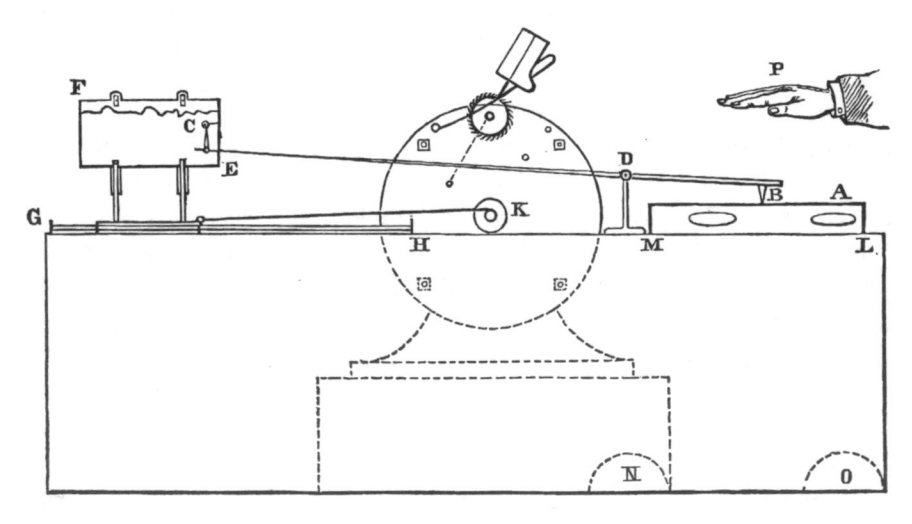

Figure 6.3 Crookes's apparatus for registering 'psychic' force without contact between medium and machine. Lever CB is arranged to respond to a force presumed to emanate from the medium's hand P and which impact upon a piece of thin parchment stretched across a circular hoop of wood, ALM. Pointer C is attached to a light lever pivoted at D and counterbalanced by a weighted vertical needle B which touches the parchment. Vertical oscillations of the parchment are transmitted from B to C which touches EF, a smoked glass plate pulled in the direction HG by a clockwork mechanism K. W. Crookes, 'Some Further Experiments on Psychic Force', *Quarterly Journal of Science*, 1871. Reproduced with permission of Leeds University Library Special Collections

Crookes believed he had answered Stokes's, Stewart's and Carpenter's grave doubts, because it ensured no contact between medium and machine and produced physical records of the fluctuating 'psychic force' that could not be called subjective impressions due to Home's 'influence' or weak judgement.

Crookes's third strategy was arguably the most significant. Sensitive to Stokes's aversion to mediums, he explained in late June 1871 that he proposed 'to make a delicate apparatus, with a mirror and reflected ray of light, to show fractions of grains. Then I hope to find this [psychic] force is not confined to a few, but is, like the magnetic state, universal.'[74] In other words, this instrument would allow Crookes to demonstrate psychic force in everybody and remove the need for the mediums who were greatly endowed with the force. Crookes appears to have made rapid progress on this front because by November he entered an *Echo* controversy about his psychic force experiments with the news that:

> Some recent experiments in my laboratory lead me to believe that I have compassed an instrument as purely physical as a thermometer or electroscope, which will enable me to detect the presence of some hitherto unknown form of force or emanation from the fingers of everyone with whom I have tried it.[75]

The 'recent experiments' to which Crookes referred were his intense investigations of an apparently new force associated with radiation that appeared to alter the weight of or repel bodies, investigations that were themselves prompted by his acclaimed attempt to produce an accurate measurement of the atomic weight of thallium in a vacuum.[76] At this stage, Crookes was convinced that *both* spiritualistic and radiation researches would fulfil his quest for a new force that modified gravity and that would further his scientific reputation. In January 1872, having recently suffered the humiliation of having his psychic force papers rejected by the Royal Society, it was even more important that Crookes embody the capricious force in a non-mediumistic instrument. Accordingly, Crookes used the skills and material resources that had had proved so successful with the atomic weight researches – notably glass blowing techniques and powerful Sprengel vacuum pumps – to construct highly evacuated glass vessels in which he suspended delicate pith indicators. Satisfied that there was insufficient gas inside the vessels to produce the convection currents by which bodily radiation normally transmitted force to the indicator, Crookes still observed that the indicators were deflected when approached by the body. By March, Crookes was eagerly inviting fellow scientists to demonstrations of the new instrument. One spectator was the biometrician Francis Galton who in late March told his cousin Charles Darwin that

> What will interest you very much, is that Crookes has needles (of some material not yet divulged) which he hangs *in vacuo* in little bulbs of glass. When the finger is *approached* the needle moves, sometimes [?] by attraction, sometimes by repulsion. It is not affected

REPULSION RESULTING FROM RADIATION. 5ɔ9

to exhaust temporarily, heating the straw by passing a spirit-flame along the tube, so as to drive off moisture. If, as is almost certain to be the case, one end becomes heavier

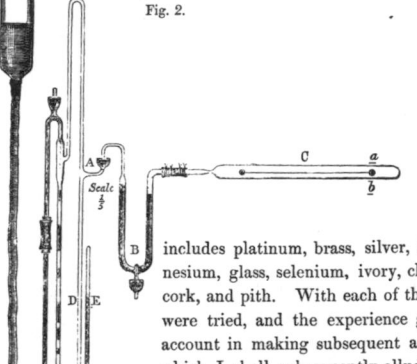

Fig. 2.

than the other, equilibrium can be restored, without much difficulty, by holding the spirit-flame for a few seconds under the heavier end, so as to slightly char the straw or other material. When in good adjustment and sufficiently sensitive the balance is ready for experiment.

25. The material with which I formed the masses at the ends includes platinum, brass, silver, lead, bismuth, aluminium, magnesium, glass, selenium, ivory, charcoal of different kinds, straw, cork, and pith. With each of these a large series of experiments were tried, and the experience gained with each was turned to account in making subsequent apparatus*. Certain differences, which I shall subsequently allude to, were noticed according to the material forming the gravitating mass; but as soon as I succeeded in obtaining the requisite degree of delicacy, the chief results were as decided as they were unexpected.

26. The most delicate apparatus for general experiment is made with a straw beam having pith masses at the end. The general apparatus is shown in the annexed figure (fig. 2):—

A is the tube belonging to the Sprengel pump †. B is the desiccator, full of glass beads moistened with sulphuric acid. C is the tube containing the straw balance with pith ends. It is drawn out to a contracted neck at the end connected with the pump, so as to readily admit of being sealed off if desired at any stage of the exhaustion. D is the pump-gauge, and E is the barometer.

27. The whole being fitted up as here shown, and the apparatus being full of air to begin with, I passed a spirit-flame across the lower part of the tube at *b*, observing the movement by a low-power micrometer; the pith ball (*a b*) descended slightly, and then immediately rose to considerably above its original position. It seemed as if the

* It is only fair to acknowledge here the assistance which I have received during the progress of these experiments from my young friend and pupil, Mr. CHARLES H. GIMINGHAM. Without his skill with the blow-pipe and delicacy of manipulation with complicated apparatus, it would have been difficult for me to have carried out this investigation during the limited time I am able to devote to original research.

† For a full description of this pump, with diagrams, see Phil. Trans. 1873, vol. clxiii. p. 295.

MDCCCLXXIV. 3 Y

Figure 6.4 Apparatus built by Crookes and his laboratory assistant for investigating an apparent new force associated with the body. C is one of the many 'delicate' instruments for exploring this force: this one is a glass vessel containing a horizontally pivoted straw balance with pith-ball ends. The other parts of the diagram show some of the instruments used to evacuate the vessel, notably a Sprengel pump (three leftmost tubes) and a chemical dessicator B. Removing gases and vapours from the vessel was crucial because this reduced the possibility of confusing 'psychic' force with the effects of convection currents. When the pressure in the vessel was judged to be at its lowest point (measured by the height of the mercury in the barometer E) the vessel was sealed off from the rest of the apparatus. When placed near the human body and sources of radiation the pith balls were strongly repelled, even though it was assumed that convection currents in the vessel were not present in sufficient quantity to cause such motion. W. Crookes, 'On Attraction and Repulsion Accompanying Radiation', *Philosophical Transactions of the Royal Society of London*, 1874. Reproduced with permission of Leeds University Library.

at all when the operator is jaded but moves most rapidly when he is bright and warm and comfortable after dinner. Now different people have different power over the needle and Miss F[ox] has extraordinary power. I moved it myself and saw Crookes move it, but I did not see Miss F[ox] (*even* the warmth of the hand cannot radiate through glass). Crookes believes he has hold of quite a grand discovery and told me and showed me what I have described quite confidentially, but I asked him if I might say something about it to you and he gave permission.[77]

Although there was still a medium present during this trial (Kate Fox), what undoubtedly impressed Galton, Darwin and many others was the possibility of a machine for displaying a force without mediums and dark séances and which would remove spiritualism from a world of quacks and impostors. 'If Mr. Crooks [sic] succeeds in making his apparatus', Darwin replied to Galton in April 1872

& can get some instrument-maker to sell it, then everyone could buy one & try for himself. This would settle the question at once, whether any power does come out of the human body of certain or many individuals. It w^d undoubtedly be a very grand discovery.[78]

With this instrument, Crookes could have sanitized and commodified a spiritualistic truth. However, still smarting from the Royal Society's rejection of his work, he sought harder evidence that the bodily force moving the 'delicate needles' was completely novel. By mid-1873, Crookes had used a wide range of inorganic sources – thermal, electrical, and magnetic – to see if he could imitate the effect of the body on his instruments. As he explained in 1875, these procedures ultimately convinced him that there was not the 'slightest action exerted by my own or any other person's hand which I could not entirely explain by an action of heat'.[79] While upholding his evidence for psychic force, he now believed his delicate instruments were registering something more mundane and not necessarily associated with the body. The 'grand discovery,' Crookes concluded, was an anomalous action of radiation, and it was his attempt to explore and display this action that led to his construction of his famous radiometer. As Darwin shrewdly anticipated, Crookes sold copies of his radiometer to the public through instrument makers and thereby sparked another scientific debate about strange forces. Although some spiritualists were keen to emphasize the 'psychic' ancestry of this radiation instrument, Crookes shrewdly emphasized distinctions between his physical and psychical enterprises and enjoyed the fact that the Royal Society, once so sceptical of psychic force, awarded him accolades and funds for pursuing what he regarded as an equally mysterious radiation force.[80]

As I have shown elsewhere, this was not Crookes's only attempt to make workshop 'paraphernalia' the means of generating reliable evidence of spiritualistic phenomena.[81] In 1874 he borrowed an electrical apparatus that Cromwell Varley had built for testing the mediumship of Florence Cook and in early 1875 adapted it for assessing Annie Eva Fay, an American medium notorious for her ability to levitate musical instruments and other objects outside a darkened cabinet.[82] In Varley's test, the medium was placed in an electrical circuit comprising many of the resources of new physics laboratories and electrical engineering workshops – a mirror-galvanometer, a battery, and resistance coils calibrated in British Association units. Her bodily movements – notably, whether she broke the circuit and faked spirit manifestations – could thus be monitored on the galvanometer by observers placed well outside the darkened cabinet where the medium sat.[83] Before the test séances, Varley and Crookes took the crucial step of calibrating the apparatus against the body: they invited mediums and scientific colleagues to attempt to escape from the circuit and concluded that this was impossible without causing violent motions of the galvanometer. What impressed Crookes about the test was not simply that Florence Cook and Annie Fay performed their feats without causing suspicious galvanometrical readings, but that not even two Fellows of the Royal Society, with their greater knowledge of precision instruments, could evade the test.[84] His results, which appeared in several spiritualist periodicals, impressed few scientific practitioners but many spiritualists, who believed he had provided an 'experimental demonstration' of the spiritual provenance of Mrs Fay's powers.[85]

Crookes's association with Miss Fay, however, was deeply troublesome. Like Florence Cook, she was one of the 'tricky girls' that Carpenter and several leading conjurors publicly claimed had evaded Crookes and his apparatus with clever legerdemain. Although Crookes stood by the results of this and earlier experimental séances, these attacks compounded his growing disillusionment with 'fruitless' spiritualistic controversy whose effects on his scientific reputation were proving dangerous.[86] After mid-1875 Crookes significantly toned down his private spiritualistic investigations and avoided too many references to such work in public. Although he later participated in the activities of the SPR, his campaigns to elucidate strange forces now focussed on such delicate instruments as the radiometer rather than mediums' bodies.

William Harrison and the Natural Laws of Mediumship

The considerable impact of Crookes's spiritualistic investigations on late Victorian public debate owed at least as much to Crookes's association with widely circulated periodicals as the controversial content of his work. Crookes not only adapted experimental reports for his *QJS* but enjoyed the fact that his researches were regularly championed by William Henry Harrison of the *Spiritualist*. Historians have recognized Harrison's prominent role in the organization of late-Victorian spiritualism – notably his famous newspaper and his part in the launch and running of Britain's first national spiritualist society, the British National Association of Spiritualists – but they have overlooked the ways in which his notorious organizing zeal extended to creating a scientific spiritualism that drew heavily on the routines and resources of late-Victorian spaces for the sciences.[87]

Born in London in 1841, Harrison initially worked as a clerk and manager for a telegraph station at Haverfordwest where he began his life-long career in journalism. Harrison quickly established himself as a major photographic expert and combined his talents to become a prominent contributor to the *British Journal of Photography* and other scientific periodicals. His telegraphic work brought him in contact with Cromwell Varley who, in 1868, gave him opportunities of witnessing the spiritualistic phenomena produced through the mediumship of Varley's wife.[88] These experiences convinced him of the reality and spiritual provenance of the phenomena, and further experience of the cultures of spiritualism prompted him to launch, in November 1869, the monthly (later weekly) *Spiritualist: A Record of the Progress of the Science and Ethics of Spiritualism*. One of the most successful spiritualist newspapers of the 1870s, the *Spiritualist*, as its subtitle suggests, boasted vastly more scientific content than its rivals, notably articles by scientific practitioners on spiritualism, reports of scientific meetings, extracts of and correspondence on scientific researches that seemed to give credence to the possibility of unknown forces and powers. In 1871, for example, it featured Varley's description of experiments (using the sensitive galvanometer he had used in his telegraphic work) designed to refute the common spiritualist claim that the human body could produce electricity and that this was one of the forces involved in spiritual manifestations.[89] Varley's report was soon criticized in the *Spiritualist* by Henry Collen, who insisted that Varley's experiments were inconclusive. But like many spiritualists seeking scientific authority for their claims regarding the possibilities of bodily forces, Collen appealed to the warning made by the eminent German physiologist Emil Du Bois Reymond in an 1866 Royal Institution lecture that it would be 'rash' to dismiss the notion of 'electricity being concerned, and even playing a prominent part in the internal mechanism of the nerves'. For Collen this illustrated the dangers of drawing firm conclusions about 'recondite phenomena' of the human body because the body was 'so complex in its construction, the actions going on it so infinitely delicate' and because 'we are so totally unconscious of many of them'.[90]

With a strong background in science journalism, Harrison worked harder than most Victorian spiritualists to encourage this kind of scientific debate and to promulgate scientific approaches to spiritualism. Harrison set the scientific agenda in his very first editorial where he boasted that 'Systematic scientific research' would establish the 'physical and mental laws' governing manifestations and he envisioned an 'Institution of Scientific Spiritualists' that would 'collect a large mass of authenticated facts' about spiritualism including the type and causes of manifestations.[91] Although he eagerly publicized the steps that Crookes and other scientific practitioners appeared to be making in this direction, Harrison's plans were underpinned by deep dissatisfaction with the attitude of the 'scientific world' towards spiritualism. Like most spiritualists, he regularly scorned scientists for their poor conduct in the séance and for taking the unscientific step of denouncing spiritualism without having first-hand experience of it. Other opponents of spiritualism were equally unscientific and disingenuous in his view. In 1873, for example, he described his visit to a fake séance staged by Maskelyne and Cooke at the Crystal Palace. Turning the tables on the conjurors, he presented mechanical and optical explanations of how he believed their 'clumsy' imitations were produced, and waspishly noted that the bogus scientific information presented during the performance was 'as reliable and scientific, as Dr. Carpenter's explanation of spiritual phenomena'.[92]

Throughout the 1870s Harrison elaborated on how 'Systematic scientific research' could 'push on Spiritualism as a science'.[93] His 1872 suggestions for work to be conducted by a 'psychological society' in séances for producing disembodies voices demonstrates the prominence of instruments in his campaign.

> At voice circles considerable changes in the temperature of the hands and feet of the sitters often take place, and more especially is this the case with the medium. The amount and order of these changes require observing and registering, and as some of the most remarkable of the physical manifestations take place in the dark, the changes of temperature from minute to minute could perhaps be registered by means of thermopiles let into the woodwork of the table under the hands of the sitters, with conducting wires communicating with reflecting galvanometers and self-recording photographic cylinders fixed in another room.[94]

These suggestions do not appear to have been adopted by spiritualism, although Harrison's uses of his photographic apparatus and expertise were more substantial. In 1872 he caused a sensation in spiritualist circles by exposing the fraudulence of the spirit photographer William Hudson, but this reflected Harrison's interest in protecting the credibility of photography in spiritualism rather than his desire to denigrate spirit photography *per se*.[95] Indeed, in 1875 he collaborated with Varley on an (unsuccessful) experiment to photograph the luminous 'odic' flames that the early nineteenth century German chemist Karl von Reichenbach claimed that 'sensitive' people could see around magnets. What was so appealing about this was that, like Crookes's 'delicate apparatus,' this promised to produce objective records of spiritualism independently of darkened séances, sensitives and mediums. 'If such action could be proved', Harrison insisted,

> we Spiritualists would then be able to go the scientific world and say, 'You have hitherto denied the reality of the emanation from magnets revealed by Baron Reichenbach's

sensitives half a generation ago, but these flames can now be photographed at any time by the process which is laid before you'.[96]

Measuring mediums was nevertheless an important part of Harrison's project. Harrison shared the common spiritualist assumption that mediums could be regarded as instruments for transmitting manifestations but believed this analogy had to be pushed further. He was acutely aware of the suspicions aroused by the corporeality of 'spirit forms' and their bodily similarity to their mediums, and recognized that the contributions of the medium and spirit to manifestations had to be distinguished. Harrison's proposed solution drew implicitly upon the example of the 'personal equation' in astronomical observation, a measure of the error introduced into an observer's judgement of transit times caused by his personality.[97] The only way of determining the 'message of the communicating spirit in its original purity' was to establish 'the amount of error introduced by the transmitting instrument'.[98] Harrison's analysis appears to have informed a more elaborate argument of the American spiritualist William Gunning. In 1871 Gunning argued that 'To give these revelations from the unseen world any scientific value, we must, as in the revelations from material worlds through the astronomer, get the personal equation of the medium, and correct the manifestation by it.' Just as Hermann von Helmholtz and F. C. Donders could produce accurate determinations of the personal equation of an astronomer so, Gunning insisted, similar practitioners could weigh, measure, and time a medium and clearly distinguish between the forces and manifestations deriving from within and those 'assimilated in Nature from without'.[99]

Victorian spiritualism may not have got its Helmholtz or Donders but between 1878–9 Harrison and his colleagues at the Scientific Research Committee of the British National Association of Spiritualists (BNAS) did take up Gunning's challenge to weigh mediums using the kind of self-recording instruments promoted by Helmholtz in physiological research.[100] Harrison had played prominent roles in the foundation of the BNAS (founded 1873) and its research committee (founded 1876). The latter was established to fulfil the Association's aim to provide spiritualists with the 'positive results' of 'systematic investigation into the facts and phenomena called Spiritual [and] Psychic' and was run by Cromwell Varley, Desmond Fitzgerald and other scientific practitioners with spiritualistic interests.[101] Thanks to donations from such wealthy BNAS members as Charles Blackburn, the Committee paid several well-known instrument makers – notably, James Prescott Joule's assistant, John Benjamin Dancer, and Varley's brother, Frederick – to build self-recording instruments or 'machinery' that would register the weight changes of medium when he was materializing a spirit.

Similar to the Varley and Crookes electrical tests, Committee members believed their weight test would provide an indirect way of establishing the bodily

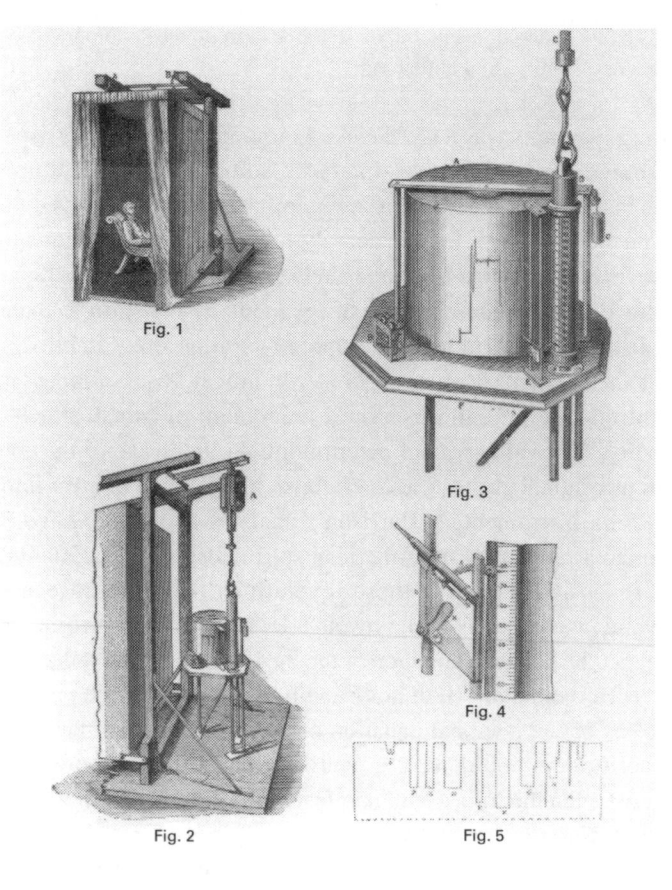

Figure 6.5 Frederick Henry Varley's 'self-recording machinery for registering changes in the weight of the bodies of mediums during the production of spiritual manifestations'. 'Fig. 1' shows a wooden cabinet suspended from a 'two-armed iron scale beam' with iron rods A and B. 'Fig. 2' shows how motions of the suspended cabinet are transmitted to the self-recording apparatus. A is an iron weight which counterbalances the empty cabinet, and below it is a screw and hook gear connecting the lever arm to a spring balance. 'Fig. 3' is a close-up of the self-recording apparatus. A is the recording drum to which is clipped a 4 foot length of white paper. DE is the spring balance, B is the clockwork mechanism which, with the counterweight C, turns the drum through a complete revolution in 2 hours. 'Fig. 4' shows an arm of the spring balance A connected to a brass plate EHD which transmits the vertical motions of the balance. The pencil is affixed to the to the top of the plate which can move vertically between two brass slide rods (F and F). 'Fig 5' shows Harrison's rough sketch of the inscription made by the instrument during a test séance with the medium Mr. Haxby. The irregular drops in the curve show the sustained falls in weight of the cabinet which Harrison and his colleagues correlated with the appearance of a materialized spirit form outside the cabinet. Crucially, the dips in the curve never reached the dotted line suggesting that there was always some weight of the medium left in the cabinet, the rest of it being used to constitute the body of the materialized spirit. W. H. Harrison, 'New Discoveries in Spiritualism', *Spiritualist*, 1879. Reproduced with permission of the British Library

relationship of medium and spirit, without breaking such séance conditions as entering the darkened cabinet. The weight test involved suspending a darkened cabinet from a two-armed scale beam to one end of which was attached a spring balance. The self-recording apparatus rested on a stand behind the cabinet and its pencil was connected to the indicator of the spring balance. Changes in weight of the cabinet were thus transmitted to a pencil, which traced a curve on paper calibrated in minutes and pounds. During the test séances, the medium sat on a chair in his darkened cabinet, committee members vocalized their observations from chairs near the cabinet, and a 'recorder' sat in another sealed cabinet in the room where, by the light of a lamp, he noted the content and time of such observations. Shortly after the medium entered the cabinet, the lights were extinguished in the room, the clock mechanism of the self-recording instrument started, and committee members began to describe a range of physical phenomena including the occasional appearance of fully formed materialized spirits that moved some distance in front of the medium's cabinet.[102]

The most important part of the investigation was the interpretation of the fluctuating graph of weight change and its correlation with the recorded observations. Committee members emphasized that the appearance of the spirit correlated with periods when the weight of the medium was lowest. Moreover, they emphasized that the residual weight never reached zero (as it might have done had the medium left the cabinet to masquerade as his spirit form) but was at least a substantial fraction of the medium's original weight. These trials raised the confidence of Harrison and his colleagues in the interpretations that they had reached using less sophisticated versions of the apparatus on other mediums. As Harrison informed a BNAS audience, they established that the materialized spirit was not bodily identical to its medium but temporarily borrowed 'more or less of the healthy living organism' of the medium so that it could manifest itself 'on the plane of matter'. Harrison was as keen to confirm spiritualists' faith in materialization mediums as to counter potent scientific arguments against materialization *per se*. Noting how physicists had objected to the fact that spiritualistic phenomena appeared to breach energy conservation laws, he insisted that the weight trials had shown that 'when phenomena are presented at one part of the séance-room, weight and energy are correspondingly abstracted from the medium', and this pushed a spiritualistic 'fact . . . from the region of miracle into the domain of law'.[103]

Given that Harrison only seems to have presented these researches to spiritualist audiences, it is unsurprising that they had little impact among physicists, let alone other scientific practitioners but the weighing instruments were not much more successful among spiritualists. Far from providing 'a superior method of testing genuine phenomena' they appear to have fallen into disuse by early 1881.[104] I suggest that there were at least three reasons for this. First, some spiritualists suggested ways in which the test could have been evaded by a wily medium – the latter possibility becoming more plausible when one of the tested mediums (Charles Williams) was exposed as a fraudster shortly after the BNAS trials.[105] Second, Harrison's principal means of propagating his science of spiritualism were wrecked during the period 1879–81: his fierce disagreements with and eventual expulsion from the BNAS lost him wealthy and powerful allies and, owing to fierce competition from the spiritualist weekly *Light*, the *Spiritualist* finally collapsed in 1881. A third and arguably most telling reason for the failure of Harrison's programme is that much as spiritualists valued scientific investigators' evidence for the physical phenomena of spiritualism, they still harboured grave reservations about the place of such investigators' machines and instruments in the séance. In 1874, for example, the editor of the *Spiritual Magazine* warned that, however satisfactory Varley's electrical tests had been, they

> can only be employed by men of science, with scientific appliances; and it would be still more satisfactory if simpler and equally effective tests could be devised which could be more generally applied; and for the majority of investigators no tests are so satisfactory as the ordinary ones of sight and touch.[106]

Even if spiritualists could have had greater access to such devices as Crookes's 'delicate apparatus', they would have raised the strong objection, voiced most eloquently by Burns and Sargent, that it was the humble medium, not the precision laboratory instrument, that was ultimately the best appliance for elucidating the psychological cause of manifestations. In many ways, spiritualists' scepticism of machines and instruments reflects what Logie Barrow and Perry Williams regard as a deep conflict between spiritualists' 'democratic' epistemology and the elitist 'liberal' epistemology promulgated by scientific and academic investigators of spiritualism, many of whom founded and dominated the SPR.[107] With its emphasis on the personal and intuitive, the 'democratic' epistemology was at odds with the 'liberal' epistemology, which upheld impersonal, bureaucratic, and machine-mediated systems of producing evidence of strange mental and bodily powers. Like the scientific experts at the SPR with whom spiritualists increasingly came into conflict, machines and instruments subverted the authority of the individuals to make judgements about their personal experiences of spirit.

Conclusion

This chapter has demonstrated the important extent to which the heterogeneous world of Victorian spiritualism overlapped with the contemporary cultures of machines and instruments developed in the new spaces for scientific research and teaching. My focus on bodies and machines is also an attempt to develop a more satisfactory framework for understanding the fate of 'spiritualism and science' in the nineteenth century. The ultimate exclusion of spiritualism from cultures of scientific practice and learning has usually been attributed to the inherently 'pseudo-scientific' nature of spiritualistic enquiry.[108] There is now a growing literature demonstrating the implausibility of such stories about spiritualism and a range of other 'fringe' sciences.[109] This chapter shows that conflicts between spiritualism's supporters, investigators and adversaries were disputes over competing notions of scientific practice and authority in the séance as much as the existence of disembodied spirits. Questions of practice and authority were in turn questions of how bodies should perform in the séance, what constituted the proper mental discipline for an investigator, and whether laboratory apparatus were better at mediating the spirit world than mediums.

Crookes and Harrison were unable to produce solutions to these questions that would satisfy notions of proper séance science promoted by spiritualists and their adversaries. As we have seen, this reflected the increasing epistemological differences between spiritualists, who privileged the personal experience of mediumistic instruments, and 'orthodox' scientists, who privileged the testimony laboratory apparatus and scientifically trained experts. This difference was present in the radically opposed notions of experimental subject promulgated in spiritualism and in the different experimental psychologies being developed in late nineteenth-century America and Europe.[110] Despite their differences, experimental psychologists held that reliable psychological evidence derived from experimental subjects whose responses were standardized by careful training or who were completely subordinate to the experimenter. It was just this mechanization and subordination of the body of the psychological subject that spiritualists found so abhorrent. For them, the bodies of spiritualism could only be technologized so far – they could be represented but not replaced by technology.

In many ways, the limited scientific appeal of the enterprises of Crookes, Harrison and other séance scientists owed much to their failure to control their uncertain and 'tricky' experimental subjects to the extent demanded by psychologists and practitioners of other scientific disciplines. Nonetheless their enterprises may have informed the technological strategies by which early twentieth century practitioners sought to make psychical research more appealing to a scientific audience. In 1920, for example, the enterprising American inventor, Thomas Alva Edison, planned to furnish psychic investigators with an apparatus worked on the electric valve principle that was 'so delicate' that it could be 'operated on by personalities which have passed on to another existence'.[111] In the same year, the German engineer and psychical researcher Fritz Grünewald designed a precision automatic electric balance to produce better measures of an entranced medium's weight changes. And in 1923, Harry Price, founder-manager of Britain's National Laboratory for Psychical Research (a rival to the SPR), built an 'electrical chair' in which he controlled and measured mediums throughout séances.[112] Although these strategies did not produce the decisive results sought by scientific audiences, they illustrate how, in a period when most psychical researchers favoured psychological tests of abnormal mental powers over investigations of physical 'manifestations', others, like Crookes, Harrison and other Victorian predecessors, believed that laboratory instruments had become so precise that they could produce unrivalled measures of the spirit body or replace mediums altogether.[113]

Notes

1. For seventeenth and eighteenth century controversies over mechanical measures of spirit see S. Shapin and S. Schaffer, *Leviathan and the Air Pump: Hobbes, Boyle, and the Experimental Life* (Princeton: Princeton University Press, 1985), pp. 207–24; S. Schaffer, 'Priestley and the Politics of Spirit', R. G. W. Anderson and C. Lawrence (eds), *Science, Medicine, and Dissent: Joseph Priestley (1733–1804)* (London: Wellcome Trust/Science Museum, 1987), pp. 39–53; J. R. R. Christie, 'Laputa Revisited', J. R. R. Christie and S. Shuttleworth (eds), *Nature Transfigured: Science and Literature, 1700–1900* (Manchester: Manchester University Press, 1989), pp. 45–60. I would like to thank Iwan Morus, Graeme Gooday, Kevin Knox and John Christie for their generous help in preparation of this paper. Permission to quote from and reproduce unpublished material has been granted by the British Library, Leeds University Library Special Collections, the Guildhall Library, Corporation of London, the College of Psychic Studies, and Dittrick Medical History Centre, Case Western Reserve University.

2. R. J. Noakes, 'Telegraphy is an Occult Art: Cromwell Fleetwood Varley and the Diffusion of Electricity to the Other World', *British Journal for the History of Science*, 1999, 32: 421–59; K. Staubermann, 'Tying the Knot: Skill, Judgement, and Authority in the 1870s Leipzig Spiritistic Experiments', *British Journal for the History of Science*, 2001, 34: 67–80; A. Hessenbruch, 'Science as Public Sphere: X-Rays Between Spiritualism and Physics', C. Goschler (ed.), *Wissenschaft und Öffentlichkeit in Berlin, 1870–1930* (Stuttgart: Franz Steiner, 2001), pp. 89–126; B. E. Carroll, *Spiritualism in Antebellum America* (Bloomington: Indiana University Press, 1997), pp. 65–71; S. Connor, *Dumbstruck: A Cultural History of Ventriloquism* (Oxford: Oxford University Press, 2000), pp. 362–93; P. Thurschwell, *Literature, Technology and Magical Thinking, 1880–1920* (Cambridge: Cambridge University Press, 2001).

3. I. R. Morus, 'The Measure of Man: Technologizing the Victorian Body', *History of Science*, 1999, 37: 249–82; C. Marvin, *When Old Technologies Were*

New: Thinking About Electrical Communication in the Late Nineteenth Century (Oxford: Oxford University Press, 1988), pp. 109–51.

4. For spiritualism as an anti-industrial movement see B. Wynne, 'Physics and Psychics: Science, Symbolic Action and Social Control in Late-Victorian England', B. Barnes and S. Shapin (eds), *Natural Order: Historical Studies of Scientific Culture* (Bath: Sage, 1979), pp. 167–86

5. For a typical example of a spiritualist appreciation of technological progress see Anon., 'Review of Recent Progress', H. Tuttle and J. M. Peebles, *The Year-Book of Spiritualism for 1871* (Boston: William White and Co., 1871), pp. 60–1.

6. S. Schaffer, 'Late Victorian Metrology and its Instrumentation: a Manufactory of Ohms', R. Bud and S. Cozzens (eds), *Invisible Connections: Instruments, Institutions and Science* (Bellingham, 1992), pp. 23–56; G. Gooday, 'Precision Measurement and the Genesis of Physics Teaching Laboratories in Victorian Britain', *British Journal for the History of Science*, 1990, 23: 23–51.

7. C. Varley, 'Evidence of Mr. Varley', *Report on Spiritualism of the Committee of the London Dialectical Society* (London: J. Burns, 1873), pp. 157–72 on p. 164.

8. S. Schaffer, 'Self-Evidence', *Critical Inquiry*, 1992, 18: 327–62; S. Schaffer, 'Experimenters' Techniques, Dyer's Hands and the Electric Planetarium', *Isis*, 1997, 88: 456–83; A. Winter, *Mesmerized: Powers of Mind in Victorian Britain* (Chicago: Chicago University Press, 1999), esp. pp. 60–108, Morus, 'Measure of Man.'

9. Schaffer, 'Self-Evidence'; L. Daston and P. Galison, 'The Image of Objectivity', *Representations*, 1992, 90: 81–128; T. L. Hankins and R. J. Silverman, *Instruments and the Imagination* (Princeton: Princeton University Press, 1995), pp. 113–14; S. de Chadarevian, 'Graphical Method and Discipline: Self-Recording Instruments in Nineteenth-Century Physiology', *Studies in History and Philosophy of Science*, 1993, 24: 267–91.

10. Schaffer, 'Self-Evidence', p. 62.

11. Daston and Galison, 'Image', p. 83.

12. For bodies as spirit 'machines' see, for example, Anon., 'The Spirit and the Body', *Spiritualist*, 1872, 2: 65–7, on p. 65.

13. [J. Burns], Editorial Note, *Medium and Daybreak*, 1873, 3: 39.

14. J. Oppenheim, *The Other World: Spiritualism and Psychical Research in Britain, 1850–1914* (Cambridge: Cambridge University Press, 1985); L. Barrow, *Independent Spirits: Spiritualism and the English Plebeians, 1850–1910* (London: Routledge and Kegan Paul, 1986); A. Owen, *The Darkened Room: Women, Power, and Spiritualism in Victorian England* (London: Virago, 1989).

15. N. Crosland, *Apparitions: An Essay, Explanatory of Old Facts and a New Theory to which is Added Sketches and Adventures* (London, 1873), pp. 9–10.

16. For mediums as instruments see [W. H. Harrison], 'Spirit Forms', *Spiritualist*, 1873, 3: 451–4, on p. 451.

17. C. F. Varley, 'Mr. C. F. Varley and the "Times" Discussion', *Spiritualist*, 1873, 3: 75–6, on p. 75; D. D. Home, 'Spiritualism and Science', *The Times*, 31 December 1872, p. 10.

18. Crosland, *Apparitions,* p. 14.

19. [J. Burns], 'The Philosophy of the Spirit-Circle', *Medium and Daybreak*, 1870, 1: 308.

20. J. Burns, 'How to Investigate Spiritual Phenomena', *Report on Spiritualism of the Committee of the London Dialectical Society* (London: J. Burns, 1873), pp. 399–403, on p. 401.

21. See, for example, William Henry Harrison's attack on John Tyndall's séance antics: [W. H. Harrison], 'Professor Tyndall at a Spirit Circle', *Spiritualist*, 1871, 1: 156–7.

22. E. Hardinge [Britten], 'Rules to be Observed for the Spirit Circle', *Human Nature*, 1868, 2: 49–52.

23. 'H. S.', 'Magneto-Electricity and the Spirit-Circle', *Medium and Daybreak*, 1872, 2: 303.

24. W. F. Barrett, 'Science and Spiritualism', *Light*, 1894, 13: 583–5, on p. 585.

25. For mediums as photographic plates see, for example, N. B. Wolfe, *Startling Facts in Modern Spiritualism*, 2nd edn (Chicago, 1875), p. 461. For spirit photography see J. Tucker, 'Photography as Witness, Detective, and Impostor', Bernard Lightman (ed.), *Victorian Science in Context* (Chicago: Chicago University Press, 1997), pp. 378–408.

26. Anon., 'Spiritualism', *Saturday Review*, 21 October 1871, 518–19, on p. 519.

27. H. Dircks, 'Spiritualism and Science', *The Times*, 2 January 1873, p. 12.

28. For this episode and extensive discussion of the fraught relationship between Victorian spiritualistic investigators and women mediums see Owen, *Darkened Room*, esp. pp. 41–74.

29. For cynical treatments of the physicality and crudities of spirit manifestations see J. N. Maskelyne, *Modern Spiritualism: A Short Account of its Rise and Progress, with Exposures of So-Called Media* (London, 1876), pp. 70–9; C. M. Davies, *Mystic London; Or, Phases of Occult Life in the Metropolis* (London, 1875), p. 319.

30. W. Crookes, 'Spirit-Forms', *Spiritualist*, 1874, 4: 157–8; W. Crookes, 'The Last of Katie King: The Photographing of Katie King by the Aid of the Electric Light', *Spiritualist*, 1874, 4: 270–1.

31. Davies, *Mystic London*, p. 319.

32. Maskelyne, *Modern Spiritualism*, p. 145. For Crookes and Florence Cook see T. H. Hall, *The Spiritualists: The Story of Florence Cook and William Crookes* (London: Gerald Duckworth & Co., 1962); R. G. Medhurst and K. M.

Goldney, 'William Crookes and the Physical Phenomena of Mediumship', *Proceedings of the Society for Psychical Research*, 1964, 54: 25–156, on pp. 48–74.

33. Winter, *Mesmerized*, pp. 64–6.

34. Allen Putnam cited in R. Hare, *Experimental Investigation of the Spirit Manifestations, Demonstrating the Existence of Spirits and their Communion with Mortals* (New York, 1855), p. 59.

35. Cited in Dawes, *Great Illusionists*, p. 112.

36. T. Frost, *The Lives of the Conjurors* (London, 1876), pp. 249–50.

37. For Anderson see Dawes, *Great Illusionists*, pp. 108–17. Frost, *Conjurors*, p 252.

38. See, for example, the views of the spiritualist Benjamin Coleman cited in Maskelyne, *Modern Spiritualism*, p. 67.

39. Davies, *Mystic London*, pp. 355–6; 359.

40. Dawes, *Great Illusionists*, pp. 83–90.

41. J. H. Pepper, *The True History of the Ghost; and all About Metempsychosis* (London, 1890); Dawes, *Great Illusionists*, pp. 83–90. For the Royal Polytechnic Institution see R. D. Altick, *The Shows of London* (Cambridge MA: Harvard University Press, 1979), pp. 375–89; I. R. Morus, *Frankenstein's Children: Electricity, Exhibition, and Experiments in Early-Nineteenth Century London* (Princeton: Princeton University Press, 1998), pp. 75–83.

42. Pepper, *True History*, p. 28. For this tradition see Altick, *Shows*, pp. 211–20; T. Castle, 'Phantasmagoria: Spectral Technology and the Metaphorics of Modern Reverie', *Critical Inquiry*, 1988, 15: 26–61; Hankins and Silverman, *Instruments*, pp. 37–71; S. Schaffer, 'Deus et Machina: Human Nature and Eighteenth Century Automata', *La Lettre de la Maison Française*, 1997, 9: 30–58.

43. H. Dircks, *The Ghost! As Produced in the Spectre Drama, Popularly Illustrating the Marvellous Optical Illusions Obtained by the Apparatus Called the Dircksian Phantasmagoria: Being a Full Account of its History, Construction, and Various Adaptations* (London, 1863), p. 41.

44. For discussion of a comparable situation in 1890s Berlin see Hessenbruch, 'Science as Public Sphere'.

45. H. Dircks, *Scientific Studies: Or Practical in Contrast with Chimerical Pursuits; Exemplified in Two Popular Lectures* (London, 1869). For Pepper's mock séances see [Harrison], 'Professor Pepper'.

46. G. A. Jenness, *Maskelyne and Cooke, Egyptian Hall, London, 1873–1904* (Enfield: G. A. Jenness, 1967), p. 31.

47. For this reaction see S. E. D. Shortt, 'Physicians and Psychics: The Anglo-American Medical Response to Spiritualism, 1870–1890', *Journal of the History of Medicine*, 1984, 39: 339–55; Oppenheim, *Other World*, pp. 236–49.

48. Winter, *Mesmerized*, pp. 276–305.
49. W. B. Carpenter, 'On the Influence of Suggestion in Modifying and Directing Muscular Movement, Independently of Volition [1852]', *Proceedings of the Royal Institution of Great Britain*, 1851–54, 1: 147–53, on p. 147.
50. Winter, *Mesmerized*, pp. 290–4.
51. W. B. Carpenter, *Principles of Mental Physiology, with Their Applications to the Training of the Mind, and the Study of its Morbid Conditions* (London, 1875), pp. 312–15.
52. Carpenter, *Principles*, p. 628. Carpenter's emphasis.
53. [W. B. Carpenter], 'Spiritualism and its Latest Converts', *Quarterly Review*, 1871, 131: 301–53, on p. 308. Carpenter's emphasis.
54. Carpenter, *Principles*, p. 626. Carpenter's emphasis
55. W. B. Carpenter, 'Spiritualism', *Spectator*, 14 October 1876, pp. 1281–2, on p. 1282. Carpenter's emphasis.
56. F. W. H. Myers, *Human Personality and its Survival of Bodily Death*, two vols, (London, 1903), vol. 1, pp. 220–97, vol. 2, pp. 139–188. For discussion see A. Gauld, *The Founders of Psychical Research* (New York: Schocken Books, 1968), pp. 288–93.
57. Compare F. Podmore, *Modern Spiritualism: A History and Criticism*, 2 vols, (London, 1902), vol. 2, pp. 140–60; Hall, *Spiritualists*; Oppenheim, *Other World*, pp. 338–54; R. J. Noakes, '"Cranks and Visionaries": Science, Spiritualism, and Transgression in Victorian Britain', unpublished PhD dissertation, University of Cambridge, 1998, Chapter 4.
58. W. Crookes, *Psychic Force and Modern Spiritualism: A Reply to the 'Quarterly Review' and Other Critics* (London, 1871), p. 5.
59. Crookes to Tyndall, 22 December 1869, cited in M. R. Barrington (ed.), *Crookes and the Spirit World* (London: Souvenir Press, 1972), pp. 232–34, on p. 232.
60. W. Crookes, 'Spiritualism Viewed by the Light of Modern Science', *Quarterly Journal of Science*, 1870, 7: 316–21, on pp. 317–19.
61. W. Crookes, 'Experimental Investigation of a New Force', *Quarterly Journal of Science*, 1871, 1: 339–49, on p. 339.
62. W. Crookes, 'Notes of an Enquiry in to the Phenomena Called Spiritual, During the Years 1870–73', *Quarterly Journal of Science*, 1874, 3: 77–97, on pp. 80–1.
63. Crookes, 'Experimental Investigation', p. 339.
64. The editor of the *Birmingham Morning News* reported in Anon., 'Spiritualism and the Newspapers', *Spiritualist*, 1871, 1: 189.
65. [J. Burns], 'About Scientific Spiritualism', *Medium and Daybreak*, 1870, 1: 201–2, on p. 201.
66. E. Sargent, *Planchette; Or, the Despair of Science* (Boston, 1869), p. 26.

67. On the Crookes-Stokes relationship see D. B. Wilson, *Kelvin and Stokes: A Comparative Study in Victorian Physics* (Bristol: Adam Hilger, 1987), pp. 191–209.

68. Stokes, 'Report on Mr. Crookes's Paper', published in Crookes, 'Some Further Experiments on Psychic Force', *Quarterly Journal of Science*, 1871, 1: 471–93, on pp. 481–2.

69. B. Stewart, 'Mr. Crookes on the "Psychic Force"', *Nature, 1871, 4: 237.

70. [Carpenter], 'Spiritualism'; Crookes, *Psychic Force*.

71. Cf. Schaffer, 'Self-Evidence'. For 'evidential context' see T. J. Pinch, 'Towards an Analysis of Scientific Observation: The Externality and Evidential Significance of Observational Reports in Physics', *Social Studies of Science*, 1985, 15: 3–36.

72. Crookes to Stokes, 20 June 1871, cited in Crookes, 'Some Further Experiments', p. 478.

73. Hare, *Experimental Investigation*, especially plates I–IV.

74. Crookes to Stokes, 20 June 1871, cited in Crookes, 'Some Further Experiments', p. 478.

75. W. Crookes, 'Mr. Crookes's "Psychic Force"', *Echo*, 10 November 1871, p. 2.

76. R. K. Dekosky, 'William Crookes and the Quest for Absolute Vacuum in the 1870s', *Annals of Science*, 1983, 40: 1–18; Noakes, 'Cranks and Visionaries', Chapter 4.

77. Galton to Darwin, 28 March 1872, cited in K. Pearson (ed.), *The Life, Letters and Labours of Francis Galton*, three vols (Cambridge: Cambridge University Press, 1914–30), vol. 2, pp. 63–4; 63.

78. Darwin to Galton, 21 April [1872], Robert M. Stecher Collection, Dittrick Medical History Centre, Case Western Reserve University.

79. W. Crookes, 'On Repulsion Resulting from Radiation – Part II', *Philosophical Transactions of the Royal Society of London*, 1875, 165: 519–47, on p. 526.

80. Anon., 'A New Discovery by Mr. Crookes', *Medium and Daybreak*, 1875, 6: 298.

81. Noakes, 'Telegraphy', pp. 450–8.

82. [J. Burns], 'A Scientific Séance – The Electrical Test for Mediumship', *Medium and Daybreak,* 1875, 6: 161–3, on p. 161.

83. Cf. Gooday's chapter in this volume, which discusses the bodily techniques used by nineteenth-century physicists and engineers to 'read' galvanometers.

84. W. Crookes, 'A Scientific Examination of Mrs. Fay's Mediumship', *Spiritualist*, 1875, 6: 126–8.

85. [Burns], 'A Scientific Séance'; [W. H. Harrison], 'Electrical Tests Popularly Explained', *Spiritualist*, 1875, 6: 135–6.

86. Medhurst and Goldney, 'William Crookes', p. 115.

87. Harrison is discussed in Podmore, *Modern Spiritualism*, vol. 2, pp. 168–9; Oppenheim, *Other World*, pp. 45–6.

88. Anon., 'The Presentation of the Harrison Testimonial', *Spiritualist*, 1876, 8: 53–7.

89. C. F. Varley, 'Electricity, Magnetism and the Human Body', *Spiritualist*, 1871, 1: 137.

90. H. Collen, 'Electricity, Magnetism, and the Human Body', *Spiritualist*, 1871, 1: 159. For further discussion of an earlier manifestation of this debate see Winter, *Mesmerized*, pp. 293–4.

91. [W. H. Harrison], 'Opening Address', *Spiritualist*, 1869, 1: 5.

92. [W. H. Harrison], 'Stage Imitations of Spiritual Phenomena', *Spiritualist*, 1873, 3: 136–9, on p. 138.

93. W. H. Harrison, 'The Scientific Research Committee of the National Association of Spiritualists', *Spiritualist*, 1876, 9: 193–4, on p. 193.

94. W. H. Harrison, 'The Work of a Psychological Society', *Spiritualist*, 1871, 1: 206–7, on p. 206.

95. [W. H. Harrison], 'Real and Sham Spirit Photographs', *Spiritualist*, 1872, 1: 75–6.

96. W. H. Harrison, 'New Experiments on Odic Flames from Magnets', *Spiritualist*, 1875, 7: 97–8, on p. 97.

97. Schaffer, 'Astronomers Mark Time'.

98. [W. H. Harrison], 'Seeing Mediumship', *Spiritualist*, 1870, 1: 69.

99. W. D. Gunning, 'The New Sciences – Their Bearing on Spiritualism', Peebles and Tuttle, *Year-Book*, pp. 32–47, on pp. 42; 45. Gunning's emphasis.

100. My account is based on Harrison's *Spiritualist* reports of the experiments: 'Weighing a Medium During the Production of Spiritual Manifestations', *Spiritualist*, 1878, 11: 210–16; 'Variations in the Weight of a Medium During Manifestations', *Spiritualist*, 1878, 11: 235; W. H. Harrison, 'Weighing Mediums During Séances', *Spiritualist*, 1878, 11: 268–70; 'Self-Registering Apparatus for Weighing Mediums During Manifestations', *Spiritualist*, 1878, 12: 115; W. H. Harrison, 'New Discoveries in Spiritualism', *Spiritualist*, 1879, 13: 186–91. For Helmholtz and self-recording instruments see Chadarevian, 'Graphical Method'.

101. Minute Books of the British National Association of Spiritualists, College of Psychic Studies, Book 1, 17 August 1874.

102. Harrison, 'New Discoveries'.

103. Harrison, 'Weighing Mediums', p. 269.

104. Harrison, 'Weighing Mediums', p. 270. Minute Books of the British National Association of Spiritualists, College of Psychic Studies, Book 2, 8 March 1881.

105. Podmore, *Modern Spiritualism*, vol. 2, pp. 110–11.

106. Anon., 'Electrical Tests with Miss Cook when Entranced', *Spiritual Magazine*, 1874, 9 (New Series): 161–8, on p. 167.

107. Barrow, *Independent Spirits*; J. P. Williams, 'The Making of Victorian Psychical Research: An Intellectual Élite's Approach to the Spirit World', unpublished PhD dissertation, University of Cambridge, 1984.

108. Oppenheim, *Other World*; R. Brandon, *The Spiritualists: The Passion for the Occult in the Nineteenth and Twentieth Centuries* (London: Weidenfeld and Nicolson, 1983).

109. Winter, *Mesmerized*; Noakes, 'Cranks and Visionaries'.

110. K. Danziger, *Constructing the Subject: Historical Origins of Psychological Research* (Cambridge: Cambridge University Press, 1990); D. J. Coon, 'Standardising the Subject: Experimental Psychologists, Introspection, and the Quest for a Technoscientific Ideal', *Technology and Culture*, 1993: 34: 753–83. For a penetrating discussion of the complex relationship between late-nineteenth century German experimental psychology and scientific investigations of spiritualism see Staubermann, 'Tying the Knot'.

111. Edison cited in A. C. Lescaraboura, 'Edison's Views on Life and Death: An Interview with the Famous Inventor Regarding His Attempt to Communicate with the Next World', *Scientific American*, 1920, 123: 446, 458–60, on p. 446. See also M. Josephson, *Edison* (London: Eyre and Spottiswoode, 1961), pp. 439–40.

112. H. Price, *Fifty Years of Psychical Research* (Longmans, Green, & Co., 1939), pp. 234–40.

113. For the investigative priorities of nineteenth- and twentieth-century psychical researchers see Gauld, *Founders*; B. Inglis, *Science and Parascience: A History of the Paranormal, 1914–39* (London: Hodder & Stoughton, 1984).

Spot-watching, Bodily Postures and the 'Practised Eye': the Material Practice of Instrument Reading in Late Victorian Electrical Life

Graeme Gooday

The lamp-light falls on blackened walls,
And streams through narrow perforations;
The long beam trails o'er pasteboard scales,
With slow decaying oscillations.
Flow, current! flow! set the quick light spot flying
Flow, current! answer, light spot! flashing, quivering, dying.

O look! how queer! how thin and clear,
And thinner, clearer, sharper growing.
This gliding fire, with central wire
The fine degrees distinctly showing.
Swing, magnet, swing! advancing and receding;
Swing, magnet, answer, dearest, what's your final reading?

O love! You fail to read the scale
Correct to tenths of a division;
To mirror heaven those eyes were given,
And not for methods of precision.
Break, contact! break! Set the free light-spot flying!
Break, contact! Rest thee, magnet! Swinging, creeping, dying.

James Clerk Maxwell, 'A Lecture on Thomson's Galvanometer.'[1]

When nineteenth-century experimentalists spoke of 'reading' an instrument, this was shorthand for the older usage of (taking a) 'reading off' a number from the instrument's scale.[2] This paper looks at the 'reading' of electrical instruments, especially the mirror-galvanometer, as a hitherto neglected instance of the body-technology nexus. Previous studies of the quantitative 'reading' of instruments have addressed the topic in terms of the abstract social politics of replication or of error analysis.[3] With the single important exception of Otto Sibum's study of thermometry, such studies have been dominated by the concerns of political or epistemological *theory*, drawing either on Pierre Duhem's account of the theory-ladenness of experiment or Gaston Bachelard's analysis of instruments as 'embodied theory'.[4] Historians of the material culture of qualitative electrical 'display' technologies have, however, cogently challenged this obsession with the abstract. And I extend their arguments to show that reading late Victorian quantitative instruments was also a *bodily* rather than merely cerebral encounter.[5] This encounter, I contend, concerned more than just the physiological apparatus of vision: the 'reading' technology (such as scales and dials) of such devices embodied assumptions about a user's bodily posture, proximity and observational skill.[6]

In what sense, then, could there have been a *bodily* issue for a Victorian experimenter reading a number off the distant scale of a Thomson mirror galvan-ometer?[7] We can get a valuable clue by looking at James Clerk Maxwell's satiric verse of a lecture on how to read this volatile instrument. More than just illustrating his literary prowess in skilful borrowing from Tennyson's famous poem 'The Splendour Falls . . .,'[8] Maxwell alludes in a subtly gendered fashion to the way that the precision methods of reading depended on the (intrinsic) qualities of the observer's eyes. After cashing out Maxwell's claims on the role of the eye in use of the mirror galvanometer, I show below how Maxwell and his contemporaries actually treated the bodily nature of instrument reading as encompassing more than just the visual. Posture and the attentive gaze were as crucial in configuring the user-galvanometer nexus. But whereas Maxwell's figurative galvanometer readers are indifferent to the passage of time, I show also that the rather more urgent industrial prerogatives of Victorian lighting engineers led them to develop alternative reading practices. These were premissed on a rather different spatio-temporal understanding of the body-instrument relationship. Moreover I suggest that the distinctive nature of such bodily reading practices made them an import-antly constitutive feature of the *self-identity* of the electrical engineer.

In addressing this topic of 'reading' I shall resist the reductionist temptation to treat instruments simply as 'texts' ripe for literary deconstruction.[9] Rather, by drawing on the work of Roger Chartier and Robert Darnton, we can see very useful analogies between the *activities* of reading instruments and of reading texts.[10] First, the history of reading practices go well beyond histories of production; for example, the refined instrument reading technique discussed by James Clerk Maxwell in his 1873 *Treatise on Electricity and Magnetism* was not trivially entailed by the intentions of the designers or makers of instruments that he used. Second, the competent reading of an instrument involves the conventionalized application of interpretative resources to decode the symbolic meaning of the conjunction of scale against moving needle or light spot. For example, users of mirror galvanometers could be trained to read the moving light spot either as a pulsed telegraphic message and or as representing the magnitude of a transient current. Third, such conventionalized reading was not merely a matter of mental training, but a bodily act conditioned by the spatio-temporal and economic constraints of everyday life. Important challenges to conventions thus arose when instruments were redeployed in technological contexts operating with unprecedented forms of spatio-temporal regime. Finally, the conventions of reading instruments or texts can be specific to distinct reading communities. I will show below how practitioners with backgrounds in telegraphy and mechanical engineering could hold rather different expectations about proper reading practices, especially on the appropriateness of evenly spaced instrument scales and on mirror-based reading techniques.

Maxwell, Duhem and the 'Practised Eye' in Reading the Mirror Galvanometer

[Experiment] consists in the first place in the observation of certain phenomena. To make this observation, it is enough to be attentive and to have sufficiently quick senses. It is not necessary to understand physics. In addition, the experiment consists in the *interpretation* of the observed facts. To be able to make this interpretation, it is not sufficient to be alert and to have a practised eye. You must know the accepted theories. You must understand how to apply them. You must be a physicist. Anyone who sees clearly can follow the movements of a spot of light on a transparent scale, and see if it moves to the right or to the left, or if it comes to rest at such and such a point. There is no need to be very learned to be able to do that. But if you are ignorant of electrodynamics, you will not be able to complete the experiment. You will not be able to measure the resistance of the coil.

Pierre Duhem, 'Some Reflections on the Subject of Experimental Physics', 1894.[11]

In his 1894 essay for *Revues des Questions Scientifiques* Pierre Duhem played down the significance of the embodied observer in instrument reading. He argued that the result of a physics experiment should be regarded primarily as an 'abstract and symbolic judgement' rather than the application of dextrous manual technique to contigently assembled apparatus. In his idealist schema, a tangent galvanometer was not so much an assembly of threaded copper, silk-covered wires and suspended needle but the circumference of a circle carrying a current with a magnet at the centre. Similarly the battery was not essentially a vessel containing certain solids immersed in certain liquids, but more importantly a conceptual entity (*être de raison*).[12] Given the ubiquity of theory in all experimental matters, Duhem contrasted the overriding necessity for experimentalists to be theoretically well versed with the insufficiency of alertness and the 'practised eye' (*l'oeil exercé*) to get any more than observations. To illustrate his point he cited an experiment that involved several coils in an electrical circuit plus a mirror arrangement for taking readings from a moving iron piece. The iron piece oscillated in and out of one of the coils, and a mirror on its back registered this movement by reflecting a moving light spot onto a transparent celluloid scale – a technique borrowed directly from the mirror galvanometer. Duhem surmised that an untutored visitor to the laboratory would misconstrue this as an experiment on the oscillations of the iron. Only an expert suitably qualified in *theory* would recognize this experiment for what it really was, namely, a determination of the electrical resistance of a test coil.

In espousing the sovereignty of theory, Duhem maximized the rhetorical force of this claim by wasting no time in explaining *how* the flickerings of the light spot over the scale could be recorded and then interpreted theoretically so as to yield a value for the unknown resistance. He rather left his audience with the impression that this task was so simple and easy that any of them could do it. In quoting this example from Duhem's work, N. R. Hanson and others have recapitulated this message concerning the theory-ladenness of experiment as if this were the only important feature of making a measurement.[13] Importantly, though, Duhem's theory-centred rhetoric glossed over two interrelated implications in the passage above about the relative importance of theoretical and practical skill. Theoretical knowledge was *necessary* to know how to set up such a complex experiment and then how to interpret the readings of light-post movement, but it was also *insufficient*.

Within the terms of Duhem's own account, in order to have any empirical data to interpret at all it was also *necessary* (but equally insufficient) to have bodily alertness and a practised eye. Duhem's equivocation over the omnipotence of theory was resolved in the version of this measurement experiment using mirror methods that later appeared in *La Théorie physique, son sujet at sa structure*. In this account Duhem repeated this example, adding the telling concessionary clause that 'the director of the laboratory may be less skillful in this matter of observation than the assistant' (*peut être moins habile que le garçon*).[14] What could have been the auxiliary skill involved here? Why did Duhem now consider it worth mentioning at all? We have to consult contemporary textbooks by Maxwell and Kohlrausch to find that the experiment cited by Duhem employed the method of 'logarithmic decrement' – a time consuming procedure that required considerable optical proficiency. The difficulty in this resistance damping experiment concerned the tracking of the light spot swinging rapidly through ever diminishing arcs. The laboratory technician had to use the 'practised' eye to identify the succession of positions at either end of on the scale at which the lightspot reached its turning point, recording these all the while without losing track of the spot's motion. The sustained fidelity of the observational 'eye' was crucial here since the subsequent process of logarithmic calculation was made using data on the precise *difference* between successive extremum deflection values rather than on the absolute value of such deflections.

Clearly, then, the refined bodily skill of the technician was needed to supplement the powers of the professorial mind and, moreover, such a technician would also need some distinct training and practice in the subtleties of this reading technique in order to do better what the laboratory director could not.[15] Evidently for Duhem, the provincial professor of physics and political-religious conservative, this division of labour was awkward to represent in depictions of laboratory life. Yet Duhem's unease in this matter was certainly not shared by all other late nineteenth-century physicists, especially not those in the Scottish tradition of natural philosophy. For the genteel James Clerk Maxwell, the skilled bodily labour of reading instruments was an integral part of the electromagnetic endeavour. His rarely discussed writings on measurement instruments in his *Treatise on Electricity and Magnetism* first published in 1873 show how an expert electrical theorist was by no means compelled to adopt Duhem's idealist reductionism about experimental practice. Any reader of Maxwell's *Treatise* would quickly find that quite a number of chapters are devoted to experimental matters, among which there are several lengthy accounts of the challenges of using and reading measuring instruments, especially in the use of mirror methods and galvanometers.

Before the *Treatise* was published Maxwell had in fact at least a decade's experience in the theory and bodily practice of dealing with the Thomson mirror galvanometer. He had used it in September 1864 to test his contention that the ratio of electrostatic and electromagnetic units was intimately related to the velocity of light, and to calculate the results he developed a sophisticated algebraic analysis of the period and mean value of the light beam's oscillations.[16] In preparing material for the *Treatise* in 1869 he undertook a specialist study of galvanometry,[17] and by July 1871 he was advising John Strutt, the prospective Lord Rayleigh, on how a carpenter should install a mirror galvanometer in his domestic laboratory at Terling. Maxwell's letter to Strutt reveals how far matters of material and bodily configuration were of great importance to users of the mirror galvanometer:

> If you have more than one window and all in one wall, the space between two windows is probably the best to erect a reflecting galvanometer à la Thomson. About 7½ feet (according to your height) from the ground fasten a frame of wood the length of the flat part of the wall and say two feet broad to hang things from . . . In front of the wooden frame hang a curtain rod and have 2 dark or black curtains which may be drawn to meet. They need not hang down more than 3 or 4 feet. Thus you may have a darkish but easily accessible tent. You hang the lamp a little above your head[;] fix the bracket at a height so that you can see it well and your scale at the proper place, which will be a good height to read when standing in the tent . . . It is difficult to imagine exactly your condition. I have put down what happened to be in my head.[18]

Here Maxwell explicitly links the optimum arrangement for reading the galvanometer to a very specific user posture and environment. A carefully curtained cubicle is required to ensure that the user can see the reflected light beam falling clearly on the galvanometer scale. Moreover the physical height of the instrument user is an important factor in determining the location of the associated fittings so that the scale could be seen 'well' and thus easily 'read' by the user standing in the tent. Such specifications were not matters of luxurious self-indulgence for a wealthy experimenter. If an observer was placed to get the best view of the scale, readings from it could be recorded with greatest accuracy, especially important for long periods of observation in which the risk of fatigue induced error could be significant.

Maxwell's interest in the bodily implications of reading instruments was not merely ergonomic in character. During the period 1871–2 he was also studying the relationship between colour vision and the physiology of the retina.[19] This research of the physical optics of the human eye evidently impinged on his *Treatise* analysis of the central role of the 'eye' in taking in the invaluable mirror method. Although Maxwell locates his account of the 'theory of the mirror method' of instrument reading in his chapter on magnetic measurements (*Treatise*, Chapter VII, Book 2), he contends that the observational techniques involved are of 'great importance in many physical researches'. In an account written for a mathematically literate audience Maxwell gave a detailed treatment of both static and moving magnet-based mirror devices.[20] There he wrote explicitly on the optimum optical and bodily arrangements for an observer to 'see' the motions of a mirror-galvanometer, drawing on his earlier writings on the optimum optical arrangements for instruments.[21]

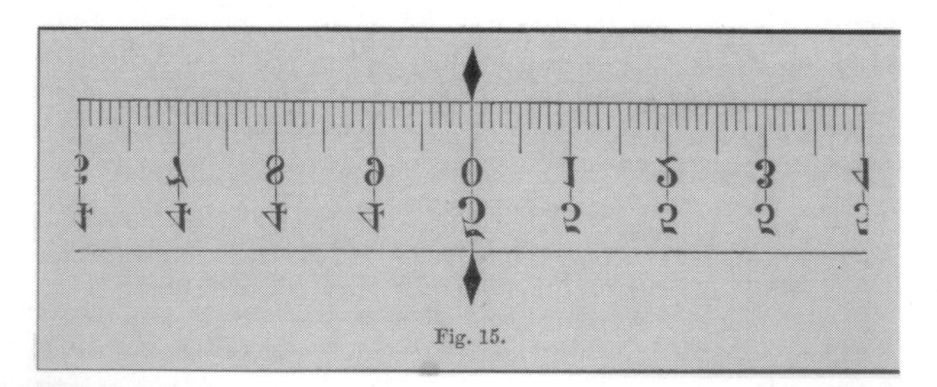

Fig. 15.

Figure 7.1 Scale for mirror galvanometer calibrated in centimetres and subdivided into 'tenths of a division'. Note that the scale is both inverted and reversed to facilitate viewing via a mirror and telescope combination. J. C. Maxwell, *Treatise on Electricity and Magnetism*, vol.2, 3rd edition (Oxford, 1891)

In the *Treatise*, Maxwell imputes the central agency of taking accurate readings to the action of the observer's 'eye' – suitably aided, as needed, by auxiliary technologies. Noticeably for Maxwell the action of the eye is often represented not in terms of binocular vision but in singular terms as 'an eye' or 'the eye'. Partly this is because some of the instruments he discusses, such as the telescope, presuppose monocular vision. However, it is also clear that the precise geometry of an instrumental set-up required the specification of the position of one eye alone. For example, to gauge the positions of the ends of a rotating magnetic needle Maxwell specifies these could be 'read off' a divided circle 'by an eye placed in a plane through the suspension thread and the point of the needle'. His requirement for optical resolution was that a scale calibrated in millimetres should be 'seen distinctly by reflexion' at a distance of several metres from the mirror, and he gave detailed instructions on how to achieve this goal. See the inverted mirror-image scale marked in centimetre divisions with millimetre subdivisions for use with an inverting telescope (Figure 7.1).[22] Circumstantially these would appear to represent the 'tenths of a division' that are beyond the resolving power of the hapless student in Maxwell's 'Lecture on a Thomson Galvanometer'.

For most cases, and especially for slow movements of the magnet apparatus, he recommended that observations should be made on a rotating scale with an inverting telescope in a fixed position. The observer seated in fixed orientation at the telescope 'sees the image of the scale' moving to right or to left past the vertical wire of the telescope, and uses a clock to record both when that wire coincided with a given scale point and the extremities of motion. For faster motions, however, Maxwell noted that it 'becomes impossible to read the divisions of the scale' except at the extremities; thus he recommended a designated spot be marked on the scale to facilitate accurate observation of the transit. Thirdly he dealt with the important case envisioned in the arrangements he recommended for Strutt's laboratory, and to which Maxwell made allusion in his Tennysonian parody of 1872. If the magnet's motion were both swift and variable, attempts to observe it through a telescope would be 'useless'. The observer should instead use the mirror device in a darkened room and look at the scale directly to observe the reflected motions of the image of a vertical wire thrown on the scale by a nearby lamp:

> A bright patch of light crossed by the shadow of the wire is seen on the scale. Its motions can be followed by the eye, and the division of the scale at which it comes to rest can be fixed on by the eye and read off at leisure. If it be desired to note that instant of the passage of the bright spot past a given point on the scale, a pin or a bright metal wire may be placed there so as to flash out at the time of passage.[23]

In contrast to the later writings of Duhem, Maxwell had taken great trouble to analyse the practical problems of reading instruments, and offered his audience of the *Treatise* some specialized techniques he had developed to deal with particularly challenging cases of 'reading' moving mirror/magnet combinations. It is clear, moreover, from the above passage the extent to which Maxwell construed reading galvanometer deflections as a bodily matter. For him it was the observer's *eye* that was necessarily engaged both to track its motions and then fix on its final position, and manual intervention was recommended to augment the instrument to enhance the eye's facility for capturing the precise timing of a particular magnitude of scale deflection. This latter advice was crucial because, in contrast to taking the comparatively straightforward 'final' reading of a static galvanometer, the reading of a moving light spot was the part of galvanometric practice that was the most difficult and potentially error prone. In a later section of the *Treatise* on 'electromagnetic measurement', Maxwell deals significantly with the particularly problematic case of measuring transient currents that are produced by an 'operator' attempting to measure their magnitude. Notwithstanding the way in which the operator would have 'his eye on the motion of the magnet', Maxwell gives his readers an equation to gauge the operator's likely *underestimate* of the correct current from the observer's inevitable 'failure' to act immediately at the 'proper instant'.[24]

It is important to emphasize that the facility of the 'eye' for accurate reading was not a trivial point of mere marginal interest to Maxwell. His 'Lecture on Thomson's Galvanometer' published under his characteristic cypher dp/dt in *Nature* for May 1872, elaborates on the case of a notional student – the 'Single Pupil in an Alcove with Drawn Curtains' – who falls short of the bodily competences of galvanometer reading outlined in the *Treatise*. This jocular verse was written for *Nature* readers presumed, I suggest, to be familiar with Tennyson's poetry, the challenges of using a mirror galvanometer and contemporary concerns about women's education. Throughout Maxwell adheres to the moral, metrical form and typography of the poet laureate's original. Maxwell's first two stanzas dextrously transmute Tennyson's sunbeamed splendour into the searching lamplight of the galvanometer, and the decaying yet sharpening bugle echoes become the ever clearer but relentlessly oscillating cross-wire shadow. In the third stanza Maxwell's narrator-lecturer finds that the student's observation of the galvanometer – just like Tennyson's bucolic interrogator of the bugle – yields only undulations that fade evasively into heavenly eternity.

In this last stanza, however, we also find, I suggest, an oblique gendered comment on the contemporary emergence of the (Cambridge) female undergraduate.[25] In significant contrast to Tennyson's bucolic reverie, Maxwell locates the private lecture in a quasi-romantic setting of an alcove behind drawn curtains (cf. Strutt letter above), introduces a pupil to whom Maxwell's lecturer exclaims 'O love!' just in Tennyson's original). And this student is made responsible for the absence of a final galvanometer reading: through deficiency of bodily competence, she is unable to read the galvanometer scale 'correct to tenths of a division' – to the nearest millimetre division. It is alleged that his student's eyes were not 'given' for the methods of precision documented in Maxwell's soon to be published *Treatise*: these eyes were apparently destined rather for the passive 'feminine' role of aesthetically mirroring heaven. This last stanza, can be linked to other features of Maxwell's contemporary career as a university lecturer. However flippant its tone, it is hard to avoid the impression that this poem was Maxwell's sceptical comment on the potential physiological (in)capacity of female students to learn to read such a crucial instrument as the Thomson mirror galvanometer. Indeed, while Maxwell was director of the Cavendish laboratory (1874–9), no female students were ever allowed to study there.[26]

Having shown the ubiquity of bodily issues in Maxwell's account of reading the mirror galvanometer, I turn in the next section to look beyond Maxwell's work at the more general problems encountered in later nineteenth-century efforts to harness bodies and technologies to the task of 'reading' electrical performance.

Solving the Body-instrument Problem: Discipline, Automation and 'Care'

> We use instruments as an extension of our hands and they may serve also as an extension of our senses. We assimilate them to our body by pouring ourselves into them. And we must realize then also that our own body has a special place in the universe: we never attend to our body as an object in itself. Our body is always in use as the basic instrument of our intellectual and practical control over our surroundings.
>
> Michael Polanyi, *The Study of Man*.[27]

How might we generalize beyond the Maxwell case discussed above? Shapin and Lawrence have shown the fertile consequences of following Polanyi in considering the bodies of experimenters to be 'instruments' just as much as their auxiliary hardware.[28] Yet we need not uncritically accept all of Polanyi's claims on this matter. I would argue that we should not accept the suggestion that an 'external' instrument is *necessarily* linked to the experimenter's body by simple 'extension' or 'assimilation'. In examining the instrument-body nexus Don Ihde argues that it helps to distinguish between two distinctive forms of instrument-body relations: 'embodiment' and 'hermeneutic'. When instruments perform as an unproblematic augmentation of the user's capacities the instrument indeed becomes effectively assimilated: in its 'embodied' role it performs its assigned task transparently without drawing the user's attention to its 'otherness'. But this 'normal' scenario assumed in Polanyi's account is not the only one to be considered. Instruments can at other times behave in unexpected or pathological ways, producing recalcitrantly autonomous performances that themselves become the subject of investigation. Ihde argues that the discordance in the body-tool relationship for such cases is resolved 'hermeneutically' by iterative refinements to arrive at a new understanding and more stable management of the contingencies of the body-instrument nexus.[29] In this regard the work of Schaffer and Dörries shows how the historian can learn much about how instrumental-technique is diachronically refined from episodes epitomizing this 'hermeneutic' mode.[30]

For a dedicated explorer of instrumental technique like Maxwell, this 'hermeneutic' mode might in fact not have been any less typical than the 'embodiment' mode. After all, the *Treatise* account of how to use a mirror-based technology followed nearly a decade of trial and error in attempts to find the optimum means of conjoining eye and galvanometer to produce satisfactory readings. Importantly the non-contiguous nature of the eye-galvanometer ensemble makes it difficult to characterize *any* practice of galvanometer 'reading' in Polanyi-Ihde terms as a simple instance of 'embodiment'. Maxwell's *Treatise* neither presents the mirror galvanometer as extending any bodily capacity to gauge electrical currents, nor does he characterize the galvanometer as being assimilated into the bodily relations of the observer. Indeed, in contrast to Polanyi we might interpret 'reading' as the co-ordination of two *separate* and *spatially separated* instruments – bodily and artefactual – that are not necessarily ever completely merged in a unitary ensemble. This is especially pertinent since during the period covered by this chapter, physiologists, physicists and electricians were starting to interpret the action of the human body in electro-mechanical terms. Maxwell was not alone in representing the human eye as a distinct instrument in its own right.[31]

In the absence of controlled embodiment relations, how did instrument users cope with the spatio-temporal degrees of freedom between the two instruments of eye and external device? We can see that procedural *conventions* were adopted to establish a configuration of body-instrument ensemble trusted to produce 'readings' free of significant error. Schaffer, for example, has shown how nineteenth-century astronomers borrowed two conventionalizing techniques from contemporary industry to manage the potentially disruptive contingencies of the body-telescope nexus. Airy introduced the personal equation to compensate for the individual physiological idiosyncrasy of Greenwich observers, and automation to replace the fallible fatigue-prone observer by self-registering apparatus that transformed instrumental readings into 'objective' textual inscriptions. Maxwell indeed enthused in his *Treatise* about how the mirror galvanometer had been adapted at Kew Observatory to maintain a continuous photographic record of perpetual changes in terrestrial magnetism.[32] Yet neither this nor the personal equation was applicable to the sort of one-off reading of a galvanometer or ammeter most commonly conducted by the telegraph or electrical engineer. Nor were such practitioners concerned with the large-scale universalizing epistemology of Airy et al., but rather with knowledge of the particular performance of a particular technology in particular circumstances. Such technological experts did not look to the factory discipline of the overseer or machine to guarantee or validate their readings but rather to the conventions of *self-discipline*.

At the time Maxwell wrote his *Treatise* there were two very different sets of conventions for self-discipline in reporting instrument readings. Widespread among Germanic practitioners was the post-experimental statistical reporting of 'probable' error of observations. Experimenters in Britain tended, by contrast, to emphasize the amount of laborious manual 'care' that was enacted before and during the measurement to pre-empt all possible sources of error in observational arrangements – especially misalignments and parallax effects. Such misleading results could be prevented by time-consuming precautions taken both in setting up measurement apparatus and then in managing procedures during measurement. For example, Maxwell enjoins *Treatise* readers seeking to determine the axes of a magnet and of terrestrial magnetism to adjust 'carefully' the stirrup holding the suspended magnet to ensure its motion conformed to a particularly useful analytic formula. The epistemological significance of this 'care' was evident in Maxwell's comments on the arrangements for measuring magnetic force: complicating higher orders of a particular analytical expression could be neglected if the measurements were 'carefully made', thus creating a less error-prone relation between the scale reading and the quantity being measured.[33]

Maxwell's self-disciplined practice of experimental care drew not just on access to ideal resources set up in the optimum manner – something that Maxwell could afford as a wealthy laird with a well-equipped private laboratory (ditto Strutt). It also presupposed an indefinite amount of time was available to prepare and implement precautionary means, undertake a range of elaborate auxiliary checks and to undertake detailed mathematical reduction of the results. Thus it was that Maxwell could both exhort his *Treatise* audience to 'read off at leisure' the final position of a galvanometer light spot – and leave his fictional lecturer student lingering indefinitely over the galvanometer in the curtained alcove. We can see the extraordinary level of refinement he attained in a later section of the second *Treatise* volume devoted to electromagnetic measurements that stipulated that *final* scale-reading was far from sufficient for proper galvanometric measurements. Maxwell additionally expected measurers to take readings at 'definite divisions of the scale', at particular phases of vibration, the logarithmic decrement of the vibrations and the overall time of vibration too. Only by painstakingly taking all these distinct kinds of readings could a truly reliable result be calculated.[34]

Maxwell himself could expend the time necessary for such a fastidious regime of care whilst writing this part of the *Treatise* because he was a private individual without academic duties to press upon his time. However, the time-consuming fastidiousness of Maxwell's instrumental reading methods exasperated those who worked in the field of power and light engineering that emerged around the time of Maxwell's death in 1879 – especially his techniques for measuring electro-magnetic self-induction. A 'pleasant way of spending an afternoon' was how William Ayrton and John Perry in 1887 described Maxwell's 1865 method, which required two readings of a galvanometer's maximum deflection. The double adjustment bridge methods documented in the *Treatise* were so time consuming and awkward as to be deemed 'nearly hopeless' for the busy engineer.[35] We shall see in the next section how the technologies of telegraphy and especially electrical lighting brought an urgency to the reading of electrical instruments that inspired new practices and technologies for reading currents and voltages.

The Spatio-temporality of Witnessing: Reading Instruments in Technological Settings

For my own part, I made my way, in accordance with an invitation from Willoughby Smith, to the electrician's [Test] room . . . they have not been averse to a few visitors. Mr Gooch is looking on; Professor Thomson be sure is there, a worthy 'Wizard of the North'; Cyrus Field could no more be absent than the cable itself . . . [All] have in their several ways a great interest in every movement of Willoughby Smith and his brother (and able assistant) Oliver; and, when the core of the cable is stripped and the heart itself – the conducting wire – is fixed on the instrument . . . these two electricians bend over the galvanometer in patient watching.

Robert Dudley, 'Testing the recovered Atlantic Cable', *Illustrated LSondon News*, 13 October 1866.

The industrialization of instrument reading followed the pattern of the factory-based industrialization of manual labour a century earlier in reducing the degrees of freedom within which body-instrument relations could be configured. The new disciplining agency of temporal constraints on instrument reading derived from what was *at stake* in the act of reading an instrument, notably the economizing of effort, risk and resources. The stakes were also financial for managers, customers and shareholders, and the reading of instruments and responses to those readings had to be undertaken within a time-scale commensurate with those interests. Given the collective nature of such financial interests the need for reading technologies to allow multiple witnessing became more important. The pressing nature of industrial timekeeping and scrutiny in galvanometer reading is manifest in a famous moment of Atlantic telegraphy on board the *Great Eastern* on 1 September 1866.[36] In journalist Robert Dudley's narrative for the *Illustrated London News*, and in the accompanying illustration (Figure 7.2), the ship's electricians stand over the galvanometer in the electrician's test room, accompanied by a dozen eminent shipboard witnesses. All anxiously await confirmation that the 1865 cable recently retrieved from the ocean bed had been reconnected in readiness for full commercial operation.

Unlike Maxwell's leisurely disinterest in galvanometer reading, every person in the electrician's room had some financial and or professional stake in the outcome of this reading – especially in the wake of the disastrously costly failures both of the previous year and in 1857. Importantly, though, the sensitive reading marine galvanometer allowed only a few individuals directly to witness the spot flickering that indicated a tiny signal current. Accordingly, the 'wizardly' brothers Willoughby and Oliver Smith were depicted bending over the galvanometer patiently awaiting movement from the lightspot, Willoughby as the senior of the two overseeing the operation. Witnesses stand away from the instrument so that their collective presence and movement do not disturb the lightspot: unable to get a direct view of the light spot, they take great interest in 'every movement' of the electricians' bodies instead. At the juncture captured by Dudley and the ILN portraitist, the parties present had already been waiting patiently and still for three hours. The intensity of the drama increased after the time at which an agreed signal would be sent from the end of the cable. The test room's 'accustomed stillness' documented by Kempe then deepened, and the ticking of the chronometer became

Figure 7.2 Willoughby and Oliver Smith testing the recovered Atlantic Cable with mirror galvanometer in the electrician's room on the Great Eastern on 1st September 1866. *Illustrated London News*, 1866

'monotonous': nearly a quarter of an hour had passed and no signal came. Suddenly, though, Willoughby Smith threw off his hat and the 'British hurrah' burst forth 'from his lips'. The entire room then broke out in cheers and soon the ship's crew was firing celebratory guns and rockets to let the consort ships know that the instrument had signalled the cable's restoration and reconnection.

Although hardly representing the typical everyday case, this episode illustrates that posture, secularity and multiple witnessing were important issues for the self-disciplined telegraphic user of the mirror galvanometer. The nature of the self-discipline required was somewhat dependent on which of the many kinds of mirror galvanometer was being used. The 'ironclad' marine galvanometer employed onboard the *Great Eastern* was shielded and desensitized to ensure that the heaving and bustle of the shipboard environment did not introduce stray vibrations to the signals encoded in the lightspot's movement. For precise electrical testing, the original and more sensitive mirror galvanometer was employed. As the post office electrician Harry Kempe explained in a series of articles in the *Telegraphic Journal* in 1874–5, it fell to the user to exclude disturbances that might affect the instrument's readings.[37] To get any useful results the instrument should be set up on a 'very firm' table in a stable basement room away from any moving iron. It would be almost 'almost useless' in an upper room as the ubiquitous vibrations would send the spot of light 'dancing and vibrating to and fro' making it impossible to take a final reading.[38] The self-disciplined user would also carry no iron keys or knives in any pockets since if 'he moves about much' these would 'very much affect' the performance of the galvanometer.[39] Kempe did, however, allow the galvanometer user some scope for latitude. The telegraphic practitioner stood over the table on which the instrument body was placed – in contrast to the seated posture implied in Maxwell's account – and Kempe allowed that the height of the table could depend 'a good deal on the fancy of the experimenter'. But in his contention that a 'good average height' of such a table was between three and a half to four feet, it is fairly clear that the experimenter was meant to be able to view the spot of light moving over the scale not far below eye level. As we shall see shortly however, such a regimented posture for telegraphic 'spot-watching' was not easily assimilated within the much busier world of power engineering.

The temporal basis of reading practice contrasts radically between telegraphic and power engineering. While the Smith brothers could wait for hours just to see a single galvanometer flicker signalled from a remote station, electrical lighting engineers in the 1880s had no such leisure. They dealt with systems that required a much more 'pan-optical' scrutiny of many different instruments to ensure that domestic consumers could enjoy continuing stable electrical supply without the interruptions or surges that were commercially catastrophic.[40] In such contexts the quavering mirror galvanometer proved unusable as whirling dynamos flung it into perpetual vibration.

Accordingly some engineers sought a speedy response by using evaluative skills embodied in hand, eye and ear. When James Swinburne first installed a lighting system in Antwerp for the Swan company in December 1881, he assessed the voltage load on a dynamo by using the manual 'touch' of a filament lamp that became hotter as the voltage increased. One of Maxwell's former students at the Cavendish, J. E. H. Gordon, advised readers of his *Practical Treatise on Electrical Lighting* in 1883 that they should trust their visual judgement of brightness to gauge the potential drop across a lamp, keeping a lamp in a separate circuit as a standard against which other lamps could be compared. By contrast, there was no comparatively safe or convenient bodily means of gauging the huge currents used in lighting engineering. Before excess current could be heard from straining machinery or seen in red hot wiring, it was usually too late to avert disaster. Mrs J.E.H. Gordon reported of her husband's alternator trials for the Telegraph Construction and Maintenance Company in early 1883 that by the time an overloaded current generator could be heard to 'scream,' the omens were ill. By the following day, the remaining fragments of the exploded machine could be picked up with a shovel.[41]

As I have explained elsewhere, electrical engineers in the 1880s dealt with such problems by developing new reading technologies that could instantaneously register changes in currents or voltages. Their aim was that a single glance of the eye could attain an instant 'direct' reading of voltage or current from more than one instrument.[42] This clearly involved a radical break with the reading technology and bodily decorum of the mirror galvanometer. Power station engineers could not, like Maxwell or the Smith brothers, devote their gaze exclusively to a single instrument, especially not one that required a constrained posture, or commit themselves to close proximity in a specially darkened environment and set aside time to wait for light spots to settle. The new direct reading instruments enabled an engineer or power-station operative needing to register a sudden change in consumer demand or machine performance that required compensating intervention in machinery settings.

By the time that Swinburne lectured the Institution of Civil Engineers on 'Electrical Measuring Instruments' in April 1892 the new reading technology was well established. He contended that all devices in electrical engineering should be direct-reading: 'the index should point to the pressure or current'. There should be no 'turning of buttons on the tops' – as in the case of the 'null-reading' Siemens electrodynamometer (see next section) – nor 'reference to tables' as used in that instrument or other older devices for which no attempts at permanent calibration could be trusted. Although dynamometers were invaluable for high accuracy testing and calibration, he declared that they 'should be avoided in central-station work.' Swinburne's point was that central generating stations operated under especially strenuous conditions because the attendants and superintendents had to monitor many different instruments simultaneously – quite unlike the electrician at the telegraph station. Thus he pronounced that all instruments should have 'bold and visible scales', with vertically mounted dials, so that it was unnecessary to go up 'close' to the switchboard to take a reading.[43]

To see the extent to which Swinburne's wisdom represented common practice in the electrical industry much can be learned from a representation published in the *Engineer* for 1893 of the engine house at a London a.c. generating station (Figure 7.3). At the centre we see a superintendent responsible for ensuring that sufficient steam engine-alternator units (connected by belts) were switched on or off to meet the changing consumer demand registered on the switchboard. The hierarchy of responsibility is clear: attendants manage the engines and alternators in response to instructions from the superintendent, who also advises the switchboard attendant when, for example, to switch new alternators in or out. His task is to make swift interventions to ensure that individual alternators do not become overloaded, thus while being very close to the instruments on the switchboard, the latter is not able to read all the instruments simultaneously – only the instrument for the particular circuit he is attending. The superintendent by contrast has a (partial) pan-optical

Figure 7.3 The Engine House at the Amberley Road Electric Lighting Station, West London, showing layout of generating machinery, meters on the switchboard, and operative staff all superintended by station foreman. *The Engineer,*1893

perspective of all two dozen the circuit instruments and can, by appropriate changes of posture, read all their dials from some distance away in the centre of the room whilst monitoring staff and generating machinery. Thus the instrument dials are large and direct reading, evidently designed to be read quickly by viewers either nearby or some distance away who might also be concerned with other concurrent tasks.[44]

We can see that assumptions about the instrument user, the appropriate mode of reading and the user environment are thus evidently built into the reading technology of these specialized switchboard instruments (albeit with a trade off for the mirror galvanometer's sensitivity). The technological and temporal constraints – the fewer degrees of freedom   for instrument reading in the power station are manifested in a more regimented reading technology for such instruments rather than in narrowly configuring the bodily action of the observer as did the (ideal) operation of the mirror galvanometer. Moreover switchboard instruments were designed, unlike mirror galvanometers, to be robust enough to perform in a stable fashion with humans walking near them and tons of whirling metal nearby. Nevertheless, the power generating station was an extreme case of technological-managerial constraint on the reading of electrical instruments. We shall see in the next section that ordinary diagnostic instruments for electrical engineering were not quite so heavily constrained in their reading technologies. Yet several issues remained open for debate in the design of reading technologies: the appropriateness of even-spacing of scales on direct-reading instruments and of using mirror reading techniques in the practice of 'heavy' electrical engineering.

Contested Reading Practices 1: the Spacing of Scale Markings

> For years designers have been devoting unlimited ingenuity to making instruments with equally-divided scales. An equally-divided scale is of no value, and, to secure approximately proportional readings, other important considerations in the design may have to be sacrificed.
>
> James Swinburne, *Lecture to the Institution of Civil Engineers* (London, 1892).[45]

One important question in developing new kinds of engineering instruments in the 1880s concerned the appropriate complementarity between the complexity of the reading technology and the user's (presumed) levels of embodied skill. As with all techniques in instrument design and instrument reading there was a trade off between these two considerations. Earlier instruments were relatively simple in construction but produced relatively complex 'signals' so that users had to apply sophisticated visual discernment and adopt a particular scrutinizing posture (as well as theoretical *nous*) in order to 'read' the motion of the light spot. The mirror galvanometer had the simplest – and lightest – possible design but presupposed a user with a high degree of visual adeptness as well as composure to track its long-persisting oscillations. By contrast the daily routines and responsibilities of lighting engineers did not allow for such spatio-temporal liberty, and designers sought to compensate for this in the more complex design of direct-reading ammeters and voltmeters. They were fitted with technical contrivances that quickly stabilized the position of an indicating needle against a particular point of the instrument scale so that reading could be swiftly made by an observer without coming especially close or adopting a special posture. Yet as indicated in the quote from James Swinburne above, there was lingering disagreement about the best *form* of scale against which the user should gauge the indicator position in taking such an 'immediate' reading. This reflected divergent convictions about the proper location of trust in instrument design. Was it more prudent to trust the visual abilities of a skilled observer in reading scales of any complex form, or to trust an indicating mechanism to produce deflections that could be easily read but whose greater complexity rendered it more fallible?[46]

For some, especially for those with untrained eyes, the easiest scale to 'read' was one engraved with *evenly* spaced markings. This format was normal in telegraphic instruments that generally had scale divisions marked either in angular degrees (for example, for the tangent galvanometer), or in millimetres like the mirror galvanometer . Electricians had to calculate the final 'reading' of such devices from an algebraic formula or (daily revised) calibration chart, but were evidently accustomed to such elaborate procedures in indirect reading. They would nevertheless have expected an evenly spaced scale so that when the needle or light spot fell between markings, they could use simple linear interpolation to arrive quickly at a 'raw' reading. A senior post office telegraph engineer, Harry Kempe, certainly assumed this capacity in his discussion of degree-calibrated galvanometers in his canonical *Handbook of Electrical Testing* of 1876 (many editions). The assumption is apparent in his argument that electricians should be able to read these devices to within $\frac{1}{4}°$. Practitioners (should) have the visual capacity to judge not only when a needle was exactly midway between two scale markings ($\frac{1}{2}°$), but then also infer 'without difficulty' (by eye alone) whether the needle was nearer to the degree scale marking or the midway half-degree point.[47] Electricians who adopted such assumptions about normal reading practices using evenly spaced scales might thus be described as belonging to the 'telegraphy paradigm'. It was those who sought to extend this paradigm to direct-reading instruments developed for electric lighting in the 1880s that were the target of Swinburne's jibes.

The two professors Swinburne accused of devoting 'unlimited ingenuity' to developing direct-reading instruments with even-spaced scales were William Ayrton and John Perry. Both were self-styled acolytes of Sir William Thomson, and Ayrton in particular had gained experience in the use of mirror galvanometer under him at Glasgow University in the late 1860s, and was thereafter engaged in telegraphic work in Britain, India and Japan.[48] It was as professors at Finsbury Technology College in 1881 that Ayrton and Perry first developed direct-reading and 'proportional' instruments for current and voltage measurements in electrical lighting work. In so doing they sought to extend the telegraphy paradigm of evenly spaced scales, and from 1884 these read directly in amperes or volts – allegedly no calculation or reference to calibration charts was needed. Yet this user-friendly technology proved very difficult to accomplish in a reliable fashion. Not only did the hitherto mental calculation operation have to be embedded in the instrument's deflection mechanism, but this mechanism had to be sophisticated enough to operate reliably so that any change in voltage or current could produce an exactly proportionate needle movement all along its scale. As I have explained elsewhere, various different models of the Ayrton and Perry instrument were popular among some early electrical engineers but regarded as notoriously unreliable among others.[49]

Swinburne's position, by contrast, was that reading scales should be made to fit the instrument and not vice versa. To use instruments with a contrived mechanism for proportional deflections just to be able to equip them with an evenly spaced scale was a pointless sacrifice of trustworthiness for the sake of convenience. In his *Practical Electrical Measurement,* of 1888, Swinburne noted, for an example, that an Ayrton and Perry spring ammeter he had tested was 'right' at two points at either end of its scale but read as much as 8 per cent too high in the middle of its range. For him it was *always* preferable to have instruments with a trustworthy calibration however awkward it was to acquire the visual acuity to read results from a non-linear scale. In this paradigm of instrument reading the visual skill of the user was assumed to be sufficient to make a non-linear interpolation when the needle fell between two scale divisions. Importantly this approach did not stem simply from criticisms of Ayrton and Perry instruments. Swinburne's disposition stemmed, as did that of Ayrton from a training in the reading techniques distinctive of a specialized area of engineering – only it was not the same area as Ayrton's training. Like many others who entered electrical engineering in the 1880s Swinburne, was a trained mechanical engineer, and had served his apprenticeship in Manchester locomotive shops and Tyneside shipyards. And like all mechanical engineers he was accustomed to reading steam pressure gauges, such as the Bourdon gauge, which were by no means necessarily proportional in operation.[50]

By daily practice in reading such gauges, Swinburne and his 'mechanical' ilk would have become well versed in what I call the 'steam technology' paradigm of instrument reading: the ability to reading at a glance the deflection of an indicator needle against an unevenly spaced scale. Swinburne and other erstwhile 'mechanicals' carried this embodied visual skill in non-linear interpolation into the new world of electrical engineering and expected their instruments to match. For example, at the very opening of his 1892 ICE lecture Swinburne noted with approval that electrical engineers' methods of measurement were becoming ever more like those of the mechanical engineer – diverging from the 'practice of the experimental physicist'. Thus while Swinburne later praised the Ayrton and Perry spring ammeter as being 'remarkable', he was critical of the 'unlimited ingenuity' they had extended to developing the equally divided scale. When Ayrton complained of being 'derided' in the discussion that followed this lecture Swinburne retorted that the instrument should not be 'tampered' with to make it fit the scale, but the scale engraved to 'suit the instrument'. An instrument maker, Sydney Evershed, agreed that for the last five to six years major manufacturers had done just that. This has been the standard practice among engineering instrument makers ever since.[51]

That being said, while the 'telegraphy paradigm' of reading evenly spaced scales was thus widely rejected by the majority electrical engineers who had been apprenticed into the embodied visual skills of mechanical engineers, there was greater disagreement about the appropriateness of importing 'spot-watching' techniques from mirror galvanometry.

Contested Reading Practices 2: Posturing and Spot-watching

We do not think that engineers who have once worked with a good d'Arsonval galvanometer will ever part with it in favour of instruments with pointers. Readings can, of course, be taken to greater accuracy with the spot than a pointer. The sensitiveness of the reflecting galvanometer is absolute . . . [and it] is easily made to cover the whole of the requirements of a [work]shop by means of a single instrument.

Captain H. R. Sankey and R.V. Andersen, discussion at IEE, November, 1891.[52]

In the late 1880s the international community of electrical engineers paid much attention to a remarkable new industrial form of mirror-based ammeter and voltmeter developed by French *electriciens* Jacques Arsène D'Arsonval and Marcel Deprez. This device registered currents using the same reading technology as a Thomson reflecting instrument, albeit equipped with a direct-reading scale and housed in a vertical iron tube to shield it from external magnetic disturbances. Notwithstanding the enormous range of currents that could reliably be gauged by this device, James Swinburne was unimpressed by the first version of the Deprez-d'Arsonval instrument that he encountered. He reported in his 1888 book *Practical Electrical Measurement* that such reflecting devices were, like the Thomson mirror galvanometer, fit only for the laboratory and were 'not suitable' for work in power engineering. Thus he could not recommend to his readers the policy adopted by his recent employer R. E. B. Crompton, the eminent Chelmsford dynamo manufacturer, for using this galvanometer to test the performance of the company's incandescent lamps. Notably, however, Swinburne was more sympathetic to the newly manufactured direct-reading 'industrial' form with a mechanism damped to become 'perfectly deadbeat' – not wavering endlessly like the Thomson device discussed by Maxwell. Unsurprisingly, though, Swinburne advised prospective users to calibrate the device for themselves rather than trust the fallible scale supplied by the manufacturer.[53]

Just as Swinburne published his advice in 1888, Crompton introduced the d'Arsonval instruments to the Willans and Robinson company. This was Britain's pre-eminent supplier of high-speed steam engines to Cromptons and rival fellow dynamo manufacturers, and indeed their engines powered the electric lighting at Buckingham Palace from 1884. Willans and Robinson soon – and somewhat controversially – made them their standard testroom instruments. This was a major decision to make because the company already had a high reputation for efficient machines and reliable testing methods. In 1887 Willans had commissioned his electrical staff, Captain Sankey and F. V. Andersen to extend such tests to determine the efficiency with which his company's engines converted steam power into electrical power when driving his customer's dynamos – data his clients were evidently keen to have. To match existing company standards they sought instruments that could be read reliably to within $1/5$ per cent, and that *all* dynamo manufacturers could trust to produce such readings. Moreover, they should do so instantaneously in a way that enabled customers to stand next to company staff in the test room to corroborate the results of the efficiency tests as they proceeded.

It was this issue of *witnessing* instrument reading that posed greatest difficulties for the Willans and Robinson staff, for each company that sent its dynamos to the Thames Ditton test room wanted the readings to be taken with that particular company's own favoured instruments. Yet to maintain parity of results between companies, Willans and Robinson had to adopt a single set of instruments for all tests. Initially his staff adopted the compromise of using the Siemens electro-dynamometer since most agreed that its absolute calibration hardly ever drifted. This dynamometer operated as a 'zeroing' balance instrument: to determine a current or voltage registered by the instrument, the user manually twisted a torsion-head to whatever angular position would restore the deflection to zero. Then by consulting an accompanying calibration sheet this position could be converted into a 'reading' of current or voltage. Yet the very 'null' technology that guaranteed the reliability of its readings also made it ineffective for the real-time multiply witnessed readings sought by clients of Willans and Robinson. According to Sankey and Andersen this device was 'troublesome' because its time-consuming operation was discontinuous and required intermittent bodily intervention: neither they nor their customers could monitor and thence average out the current fluctuations that mattered greatly in high-accuracy dynamo tests. According to Willans, trying to use such a dynamometer to measure an ever-changing current was like trying to weigh a horse and cart while they were riding over the balance.[54]

Given the publicity accorded to the unprecedented accuracy, sensitivity, range and robustness of the industrial D'Arsonval reflecting instruments in 1888–9, and its recommendation by Crompton, it is not surprising that Willans's staff adopted this instrument to meet company standards of robustness and accuracy. Moreover the use of a large calibrated proportional scale place five feet from the mirror instrument enabled visitors to witness continuously and simultaneously the moving spot image projected by the D'Arsonval instrument to an extent hardly possible with either a dynamometer or a standard dial ammeter/voltmeter. In a paper that they presented at the IEE in November 1891 Sankey and Andersen explained how they used these instruments in their dynamo-electrical tests with adjustments for different sizes of current achieved by varying the circuit resistance. At its most sensitive setting, the galvanometer's illuminated spot would register a change as small as one ten-millionth of an ampere. Having taken 'great care' in setting up this arrangement, Sankey and Andersen claimed to be able to read currents for ordinary work to within 0.3 per cent of error. Such was the force of the results that Willans even reduced by 1 per cent his claims for the maximum efficiencies that could be achieved by coupling dynamos to his company's engines.[55]

Ironically, in the discussion that followed this paper at the IEE, few challenged the accuracy of these claims, but there was warm debate on the appropriateness of extending mirror-based reading methods to the everyday work of electrical engineers. Both Crompton and William Ayrton entirely sympathized with the use of d'Arsonval instruments, although the latter criticized details of Sankey and Andersen's procedures. Typically in disagreement with Ayrton, James Swinburne congratulated Sankey and Andersen for results of great value but disagreed with their choice of instrumental technique. To the extent that Swinburne was occasionally involved in delicate telegraph work he appreciated the large range and 'fair accuracy' that could be accomplished with this instrument. He did not, however, regard a reflecting galvanometer as a *bona fide* engineering instrument. As an engineer he objected to the practice of 'spot-watching'. The editor of the *Electrician* and Cambridge natural sciences graduate Alexander Trotter generally agreed. Trotter emphasized that Willans's staff had accomplished only laboratory-style measurements and had not shown their IEE audience how their methods could be 'converted' into proper electrical engineering measurements. The rationale for such a conversion, according to Trotter, was that 'spot watching' was a practice that the engineer would only adopt with 'considerable dislike'. Indeed he contended that the d'Arsonval galvanometer was not an instrument that had 'come to stay for engineering purposes'. Much more fitting for engineering work he contended was a 'needle-reading' commercial instrument that could be read to one part in a thousand.[56]

Peter Willans then stepped forward to defend his employees' choice of reading technologies. He contended that averaging out a fluctuating spot reading by Sankey's method was better than either accurate but relatively uninformative 'null' methods or Ayrton's more instantaneous but naive method of placing 'trust' in each successive scale deflection meaning 'always the same thing'. A further advantage of the spot-watching approach was that it enabled their customers to witness and corroborate the results in ways hard to achieve by any other method. A spot of light was at least something that 'two people can see' and they could make independent records of the results at the same time, prior to the final averaging of half an hour of results. Thus the Willans team was frankly 'surprised' that Swinburne, Trotter and others did not accept this instrument for engineering work. To counter this they offered aesthetic and quantitative arguments in its favour. Andersen considered that the spot method of reading was 'simply charming', and now that oil lamps had been replaced by electric lights in the reflecting arrangement, this method was 'far superior' to the 'reading of currents with pointers'. Once engineers had worked with a good D'Arsonval galvanometer, they would not part with it in favour of instruments with pointers because readings could be taken to 'greater accuracy' with the spot than a pointer.[57]

Swinburne was however, unmoved by their suggestion that engineers who had worked with a 'good' d'Arsonval galvanometer would never part with it 'in favour of instruments with pointers'. Five months later in his lecture on electrical measuring instruments at the Institution of Civil Engineers, he reiterated his conviction (shared by Trotter) that engineering instruments ought to have 'clear' index pointers. He made no mention of reflecting instruments at all, and indeed the only D'Arsonval instrument to which he gave explicit approval for engineering work was a conventional dial-reading device made by Weston. Tellingly, though, Swinburne was most concerned to criticize the misleading use of evenly spaced scale markings and did not even try to dissuade engineers from using mirror-based devices. Although he himself disliked the postural implications of 'spot watching' and, like Trotter, envisaged that other 'engineers' would not take them up, there was evidently a persistent pluralism in the choice of reading technologies. As Swinburne admitted, so long as D'Arsonval instruments had been calibrated and used with all due care, they raised no particular problems of inter-practitioner trust. The question was more about whether *as engineers* they could tolerate technologies that challenged their pre-existing bodily expectations of how to take readings, or whether like Sankey and Andersen they could learn to derive the same sort of aesthetic *satisfaction* from spot watching that Maxwell had derived twenty years earlier. For at least a vocal minority including Swinburne and Trotter, the answer was a clear 'no'.

Conclusion

Looking at the material and spatio-temporal features of work with electrical instrument shows that the late Victorians did not regard the reading of such instruments as merely an abstract encounter between intellect and (reified theory). James Clerk Maxwell was a major theoretical expert committed to exploring and articulating the role of the body – especially the eye – in taking readings by the 'mirror method'. His writings on the use of this technique reveal both overt prescriptions and tacit assumptions about the active visual capacities, bodily dis/position and leisured contemplation of the instrument user in relation to this 'reading technology'. Those working in industrial telegraphy and especially (later) power engineering departed from his account of the protracted nature of instrument reading. Indeed the disparity of views on instrument reading as a kind of body-technology encounter emerge in discussions of the appropriateness of particular kinds of body posture, of linear versus non-linear scale calibrations, of light-spot vis-à-vis needle reading methods, and the best means of simultaneous witness 'reading'. This disparity can be understood by reference to the different spatio-temporal constraints on reading practices in telegraphy and power generation, and the various traditions within the latter industry of what constituted appropriate bodily labour.

We can thus return to the Bachelardian notion of instrument as embodied theory, and argue that the design of electrical instruments embodies not only analytical theories of electromagnetism, but some (tacit) expectations about how the embodied user ought to engage with the 'reading technology' of that instrument. But we should also look beyond instrument design to an independent consideration of instrument use – and non-use. From the objection of some engineers to 'spot watching' we can surmise that a practitioner's decision about whether to adopt a new kind of instrument was not determined (solely) by the trustworthiness of the theories embedded in its design. The reading practices associated with a particular instrument *configured* the embodied user in particular ways, so the question became whether such a configuring could readily be accommodated within the other pre-existing embodied practices of the prospective user's daily work. Given Swinburne's objections to the ways in which the d'Arsonval reflecting galvanometer threatened to turn the engineer into a 'spot watcher', the issue of readiness here was perhaps primarily a question of the user's *identity*. Would the posture required in using such an instrument be *particularly* inconvenient or demeaning for the bodily constituted self? In the above account I have shown this no trivial issue, but a major theme in the self-fashioning of the electrical engineer as a specialist distinct from the physicist or telegraphic electrician.

Returning to the case of the unfortunate pupil in Maxwell's 1872 lecture, whether a galvanometer user was 'given' to a using a *particular* method of precision reading was clearly not a matter of physiological pre-destination nor just a matter of optical expertise. To recover more generally how instruments were used in the past, we need instead to understand how technical training, work cultures and technological environments moulded bodily expectations and dispositions about how instruments ought to be read.

Notes

1. 'dp/dt', [J. C. Maxwell], 'A lecture on Thomson's Galvanometer: Delivered to a Single Pupil in an Alcove with Drawn Curtains', *Nature*, 1872, 6: 46. This was entitled 'Lectures to Women on Physical Science: I' in L. Campbell and W. Garnett, *Life of James Clerk Maxwell* (London, 1882), p. 631. It is reproduced with the former title in S. P. Thompson, *Life of Lord Kelvin* (London, 1910), two vols, vol. 1, p. 349. For the coded (thermodynamic) explanation of the signature dp/dt, see Campbell and Garnett, *Life of Maxwell*, pp. ix–x.
2. See etymological discussion of 'reading' in relation to instruments (especially astronomical variety) in *Oxford English Dictionary*, 2nd edition, (Oxford: Oxford University Press, 1989).
3. S. Schaffer and S. Shapin, *Leviathan and the Air-pump: Hobbes, Boyle and the Experimental Life* (Princeton: Princeton University Press, 1985); H. Collins, *Changing Order: Replication and Induction in Scientific Practice* (London: Sage, 1985); K. Olesko, *Physics as a Calling: Discipline and Practice in the Königsberg Seminar for Physics* (Ithaca NY: Cornell University Press, 1991); S. Schaffer, 'Late Victorian Metrology and its Instrumentation: a Manufactory of Ohms', R. Bud and S. Cozzens (eds), *Invisible Connections: Instruments, Institutions and Science* (Bellingham: SPIE Optical Engineering Press, 1992), pp. 24–55. O. Sibum 'Reworking the Mechanical Value of Heat: Instruments of Precision and Gestures of Accuracy in early Victorian England', *Studies in History and Philosophy of Science*, 1995, 26: 73–106.
4. G. Gooday, 'Instrument as Embodied Theory', A. Hessenbruch (ed.) *Reader's Guide to the History of Science* (London: Fitzroy Dearborn, 2000), pp. 376–8. Sibum, 'Mechanical Value of Heat'.

5. C. Marvin, *When Old Technologies Were New: Thinking about Commun-ications in the Late Nineteenth Century* (Oxford: Oxford University Press, 1988) and I. R. Morus, *Frankenstein's Children: Electricity, Exhibition and Experiment in Early-Nineteenth Century London* (Princeton NJ: Princeton University Press, 1998).

6. In this approach I draw support from historians of physiology who have shown how late Victorians represented visual 'attention' as bodily matter, and even accounted for bodily action using metaphors drawn directly from electrical technology. T. Lenoir, 'Models and Instruments in the Develop-ment of Electrophysiology, 1845–1912', *Historical Studies in the Physical Sciences*, 1986, 17: 1–54; J. Crary, *Suspensions of Perception: Attention, Spectacle and Modern Culture* (Cambridge MA: MIT Press, 1999), especially pp. 153–5, 176–7. Also important is A. Briggs's treatment of 'The Philosophy of the Eye' in his *Victorian Things* (Harmondsworth: Penguin, 1990), pp. 103–41.

7. In this regard Sibum has shown that the problem of bodily proximity in Joule's reading of delicate thermometers required very self-disciplined practice to prevent readings being compromised by the proximity of his or other's bodies. Sibum, 'Mechanical Value of Heat'. For related study of the Victorian microscope as a visual treatment for which disciplined bodily training was required see G. Gooday, '"Nature" in the Laboratory: Domestication and Discipline with the Microscope in Victorian Life Science', *British Journal for the History of Science*, 1991, 24: 307–41.

8. Tennyson's 'The Splendour Falls . . . ' was composed in 1848 and published in the second edition of *The Princess* in 1850. Maxwell's poetic corpus is republished in Campbell and Garnett, *Life of Maxwell*, pp. 577–651. For general discussion, including Maxwell's further borrowing from *The Princess* in his 1878 Rede lecture on the telephone, see G. Beer, *Open Fields: Science in Cultural Encounter* (Oxford: Clarendon Press, 1996), pp. 213–5.

9. For analysis of thermometer readings as a form of 'text' see P. Heelan, *Space-perception and the Philosophy of Science* (Berkeley and Los Angeles: University of California Press, 1983), p. 193. For a more sceptical analysis see D. Ihde, 'This is not a "Text", or , do we "Read" Images', *Expanding Hermeneutics: Visualism in Science* (Evanston IL: Northwestern University Press, 1998), pp. 88–97.

10. R. Chartier, The Order of Books, 'Communities of Readers' in (1992/4); R. Darnton, 'First Steps to a History of Reading', *The Kiss of Lamourette: Reflections on Cultural History* (New York: Norton, 1990), pp. 154–87; 171–3; 187. My thanks to Jon Topham for directing me to these sources.

11. P. Duhem, 'Some Reflections on the Subject of Experimental Physics', Roger Ariew and Peter Barker (trans. and ed.) *Pierre Duhem: Essays in the History*

and Philosophy of Science (Indianapolis: Hackett, 1996), pp. 75–111; quotation on p. 76. The original was published in 'Quelque réflexions au sujet de la physique expérimentale', *Revues des Questions Scientifiques*, 1894, 36: 179–229.

12. Duhem 'Some Reflections' pp. 88–90. Compare with the slightly revised version in *The Aim and Structure of Physical Theory*, 2nd ed. 1914 (trans. Philip Wiener, 1954), p. 145.

13. This passage was directly cited in N. R. Hanson's classic study of the theory-laden nature of observation *Patterns of Discovery: an Inquiry into the Conceptual Foundations of Science* (Cambridge: Cambridge University Press, 1961), pp. 17 18.

14. P. Duhem, *La Théorie Physique, son objet – sa structure* (Paris, 1906), quote from second edition (1914), p. 219; *The Aim and Structure of Physical Theory*, p. 145.

15. The value of the unknown resistance could then calculated from the reciprocal of the logarithm of the difference between successive extremum values. See discussion of this method in J. C. Maxwell, *Treatise on Electricity and Magnetism*, 3rd edn (Oxford, 1891), vol. 2, pp. 374–82. F. Kohlrausch (trans. T. H. Waller and H. R. Proctor), *An Introduction to Physical Measurements*, 3rd edn (from 7th German edition) (London, 1894), pp. 219–21; 308–9; 446–7.

16. P. Harman (ed.), *The Scientific Letters and Papers of James Clerk Maxwell*, two vols, vol. 2, (Cambridge: Cambridge University Press, 1995), pp. 165–75.

17. See Maxwell to Tait 10 December 1869, cited in Harman (ed.), *Letters and Papers of Maxwell*, p. 517.

18. Maxwell to Strutt 8 and 10 July 1871 in Harman (ed.), *Letters and Papers of Maxwell*, pp. 664–5. Maxwell's letter makes it clear that his advice drew upon information supplied by Thomson himself.

19. J. C. Maxwell 'On Colour Vision at Different Points of the Retina', *BAAS Reports*, 1870: 40–1; J. C. Maxwell, 'Note on a Singular Property of the Retina', *Proc Roy Soc Edinburgh*, 1872, 7: 605–7; Harman (ed.), *Letters and Papers of Maxwell*, pp. 552, 704.

20. I thank Andrew Warwick for discussion of material in his forthcoming volume on the likely readership of Maxwell's book as those studying for, or teaching in, the Cambridge mathematics tripos.

21. See Harman (ed.), *Letters and Papers of Maxwell*, for example p. 101. In 1857 Maxwell prepared for lectures to Aberdeen operatives on the eye by practising dissection on a cod's eye and bullock's eye. See Maxwell to his aunt Jane Cay, 27 February 1857 in Campbell and Garnett, *Life of Maxwell*, p. 264.

22. Maxwell, *Treatise*, vol. 2, pp. 96–7; 96.

23. *Ibid.*, pp. 99–100.

24. *Ibid.*, pp. 390–1. In an editorial note to this third edition, J.J. Thomson notes that he had been unable to reconstruct Maxwell's derivation of this equation and gives a more complex alternative instead.

25. Girton College was founded for women at Cambridge in 1869 and Newnham Hall originated at 74 Regent Street in October 1871. In spring 1872, the first three female undergraduates were carefully marshalled in from Girton to sit Cambridge tripos examinations apart from male students. P. Gould, 'Women and the Culture of University Physics in Late Nineteenth Century Cambridge', *British Journal for the History of Science* 1997, 30: 127–49, on p. 130.

26. The question 'Swing magnet, answer dearest, what's your final reading?' seems in this context to be a gendered comment on the volatile 'feminine' indecision of the mirror galvanometer. For another case of this see B. Hunt, 'Scientists, Engineers, and Wildman Whitehouse: Measurement and Credibility in early Cable Telegraphy', *British Journal for the History of Science*, 1996, 29: 155–69, especially on pp. 163–4.

27. M. Polanyi, *The Study of Man* (Chicago: University of Chicago Press, 1957), p. 25

28. C. Lawrence and S. Shapin (eds), *Science Incarnate: Historical Embodiments of Natural Knowledge* (Chicago: University of Chicago Press, 1998), pp. 6–7.

29. D. Ihde, *Technics and Praxis: A Philosophy of Technology* (Dodrecht: Reidel, 1979). Ihde does not address cases in which critical challenges are made to experimenters' claims to be using instruments in the 'embodied' mode (for example by suggesting self-delusional or disingenuous manipulation). See S. Schaffer, 'Experimenters' Techniques, Dyers' Hands, and the Electric Planetarium', *Isis*, 1997, 88: 456–83.

30. S. Schaffer, 'Glass works: Newton's Prisms and the Uses of Experiment', D. Gooding, T. Pinch and S. Schaffer (eds), *The Uses of Experiment: Studies in the Natural Sciences* (Cambridge: Cambridge University Press, 1989), pp. 67–104; M. Dörries, 'Balances, Spectroscopes, and the Reflexive Nature of Experiment', *Studies in History and Philosophy of Science*, 1994, 25: 1–36.

31. In a debate at the Institution of Civil Engineers in 1891, Chief Post Office electrician, W. H. Preece described the human eye as a 'remarkable instrument' for its ability to adapt rapidly to changes of light level. See J. Swinburne, 'Electrical Measuring Instruments', *Minutes of Proceedings of the Institution of Civil Engineers*, 1892, 110: 1–32, discussion pp. 33–64, quote on p. 55. For general discussion of the mechanical 'philosophy of the eye' in later nineteenth century British culture see Briggs, *Victorian Things*, Chapter 3.

32. S. Schaffer, 'Astronomers Mark Time: Discipline and the Personal Equation', *Science in Context*, 1988, 2: 115–45. To accommodate disparate results of the

dispersed international corps of astronomers, Airy used techniques of 'least squares' analysis from error theory, see G. B. Airy, *On the Algebraical and Numerical Theory of Errors of Observation* (London, 1861); Maxwell, *Treatise*, vol. 2, pp. 100–1; 128; Schaffer, 'Astronomers Mark Time'; S. Schaffer, 'Self-Evidence', *Critical Enquiry*, 1992, 18: 327–62; A. Soojung-Kim Pang, '"The Stars Should Henceforth Register Themselves": Astrophotography at the Early Lick Observatory', *British Journal for the History of Science*, 1997, 30: 177–202.

33. Maxwell, *Treatise*, vol. 2, pp. 102; 104; 106;112–13. Maxwell's advice sanctioned the practice of other British experimenters to record in great detail the qualitative parts of experimentation related in their publications, and thus mitigate against any need for detailed post hoc analyses of error. See G. Gooday, 'Instrumentation and Interpretation: Managing and Representing the Working Environments of Victorian Experimental Science' in B. Lightman (ed.) *Victorian Science in Context* (Chicago: Chicago University Press, 1997), pp. 409–37.

34. Maxwell, *Treatise*, vol. 2, pp. 376–7. This contrasts greatly with the common Germanic practice of multiple executions of a single measurement.

35. W. E. Ayrton and J. Perry, 'Modes of Measuring the Coefficients of Self and Mutual Induction', *Journal of the Society of Telegraph Engineers and Electricians*, 1887, 16: 391; 293–6; 394. For double adjustment see Maxwell, *Treatise*, vol. 2, pp. 397–8; the 1865 method is included on pp. 399–401

36. See C. W. Smith and M. N. Wise, *Energy and Empire: A Biographical Study of Lord Kelvin* (Cambridge: Cambridge University Press, 1989); Thompson, *Life of Lord Kelvin* for discussion of this.

37. H. R. Kempe, *Handbook of Electrical Testing*, 2nd edn (London, 1881), p. 33. I have not been able to trace any copies of the first edition (1876) of this book.

38. H. R. Kempe, 'Resistances and their Measurement. The Thomson Galvanometer', *The Telegraphic Journal and Electrical Review*, 1873–74, 2: 41–4, quote on p. 243. Reproduced in Kempe, *Handbook*, pp. 31–3.

39. H. R. Kempe, 'Resistances and their Measurement. XII', *The Telegraphic Journal and Electrical Review*, 1873–4, 2: 266–8. quote on p. 266.

40. R. H. Parsons, *The Early Days of the Power Station Industry* (Cambridge: Cambridge University Press, 1940).

41. J. Swinburne, [contribution to 50 year jubilee discsusion of Institution of Electrical Engineers] *Journal of the IEE*, 1922, 60: 422; J. E. H. Gordon, *Practical Treatise on Electricity and Magnetism*, 2 vols, (London, 1880). Mrs J. E. H. Gordon, *Decorative Electricity* (London, 1892), 2nd edn, pp. 161–2.

42. G. Gooday, 'The Morals of Energy Metering: Constructing and Deconstructing the Precision of the Electrical Engineer's Ammeter and Voltmeter',

M. N. Wise (ed.) *The Values of Precision* (Princeton: Princeton University Press, 1995), pp. 239–82.

43. J.Swinburne, 'Electrical Measuring Instruments', p. 2. Swinburne's point related to d.c generation, but in his discussion of alternate current equipment he offered no specific recommendations.

44. 'Amberley Road Electric Lighting Station', *The Engineer*, 1893, 75: 522–5.

45. Swinburne, 'Electrical Measuring Instruments', p. 2

46. For the importance of 'trust' in measurement see G. Gooday, *The Morals of Measurement* (Cambridge: Cambridge University Press, forthcoming).

47. Kempe, *Handbook*, pp. 54–5.

48. For Ayrton's familiarity with Thomson and the mirror galvanometer see, W. E. Ayrton, 'Kelvin in the Sixties', *Popular Science Monthly*, 1908, 27: 259–68, on pp. 265–7.

49. Gooday, 'The Morals of Metering'.

50. Swinburne, *Practical Electrical Measurement*, p. 47 et seq. For discussion of Bourdon pressure gauge see article in R. Bud and D. Warner (eds), *Instruments of Science* (New York: Garland Press, 1998). F. A. Freeth, 'James Swinburne, 1858–1958', *Biographical Memoirs of the Royal Society*, 1959, 5: 253–64.

51. Swinburne, 'Electrical Measuring Instruments', especially pp. 1–3, 6, 33, 42–3, 57. See K. Edgcumbe and F. Punga, 'Direct-reading Measuring Instruments for Switchboard Use', *Journal of the IEE*, 1904, 33: 620–93, especially p. 622.

52. Capt. H. R. Sankey, (late R.E.) and F. V. Andersen. 'Description of the Standard Volt- and Ampere-meter used at the Ferry Works, Thames Ditton', *Journal of the IEE*, 1891, 20: 516–90 (including discussion) quote on p. 589.

53. M. Deprez and J. D'Arsonval, 'Galvanomètre aperiodique', *Comtes Rendus*, 1882, 94: 1347–50, quote on p. 1347. M. Deprez , 'Sur un Galvanomètre à Indications Proportionelles aux Intensités', *La Lumiere Electrique*, 1884, 14: 401. Swinburne, *Practical Electrical Measurement*, pp. 29; 49–50.

54. Willans in discussion to Sankey and Andersen, 'Description', p. 574. For further criticism of the non-instantaneous reading of the dynamometer see J. E. H. Gordon, *A Practical Treatise on Electrical Lighting* (London, 1884), pp. 35–7; 44–7.

55. Sankey and Andersen, 'Description', p. 588. For 'very accurate' trials they took scale readings at regular intervals to obtain a mean value, and then checked this scale reading by calibrating with a standard resistance in 'legal ohms' and a Clark Cell: pp. 519–31; Willans in discussion to Sankey and Andersen. p. 575.

56. Swinburne in discussion with Sankey and Andersen, 'Description', p. 567. Trotter in discussion with Sankey and Andersen, 'Description', pp. 571–3. For more on Trotter's editorship see P. Strange, 'Two Electrical Periodicals: The Electrician and The Electrical Review 1880–1890', *IEE Proceedings*, 1985, 132A: 574–81, especially p. 579.
57. Sankey and Andersen, 'Description', pp. 517; 578; 589.

–8–

Bodies, Machines and Noise

Jon Agar

Prologue: Disordering Babbage

Let us follow the last days of Charles Babbage's body. It is a slow death. Shivering in his bed in Dorset Street, London, he is disturbed, yet again, by street-musicians. His son, Henry, recollected that Autumn of 1871:

> On the 16th the organ-grinders were particularly troublesome and before I went to sleep I wrote again to the Commissioner of Police, but the organs were playing all the same on 17th, both about midday and about 9 p.m., and in the afternoon there was a man inciting boys to make a row with an old tin pail . . . but no policeman in sight. At 8.45 p.m. there was again organ playing. On 18th organs playing again about midday . . . C.B. passed away about thirty-five minutes past 11 o'clock p.m.[1]

Seventeen hours later an autopsy identified an arterial disease that one later commentator says is 'now known to cause degeneration of the inner ear resulting in a hearing disorder'.[2] Babbage's brain is removed and pickled. Henry is sure that it is what is father would have wanted.[3] 'It will be of comparatively little value if not connected with his name and this you can use as freely as is necessary', wrote the son, 'his character is known by his deeds and his published works and the brain should be known as his, and disposed of in any manner which you consider most conducive to the advancement of human knowledge and the good of the human race.' (His character was also known, at least once, by phrenology: the practitioner, 'in perfect ignorance of this character having constructed a calculating machine' read Babbage's bumps in 1852 as indicating highest scores for 'number' and 'constructiveness'.)[4] The Hunterian Museum of Royal College of Surgeons commissioned a report on the state of the brain in 1905 from Sir Victor Horsley, which later appeared in the *Philosophical Transactions*.[5] While the remains of his body rests in Kensal Green cemetery, Charles Babbage's brain can still be seen in a jar in the Hunterian. His other 'thinking machines,' the Difference and Analytical Engines, ended up, in parts and unfulfilled plans, on the shelves of the Science Museum. Body and machines lay disordered and dismembered.

The story of how Babbage had struggled to complete his calculating machines is now a familiar one. We know he became increasingly bitter in his last decades, while his campaign against street musicians is usually told within this narrative frame to illustrate his cantankerous character, a distraction from his inventive projects.[6] But I want to explore a different theme, one that would understand the campaign against noise and the project to build machines as complementary.

Noise and Order

Most of the chapters in this book explore analogies between mechanical and bodily order. (See, for example, Noakes on the body of Florence Cook as an electrical inductor; Morus on other bodies as electrical apparatus; Musselman on governors; Ashworth on the factory and Watt's mind.) These kinds of arguments can be summed up diagrammatically:

$$\text{mechanical order} \leftrightarrow \text{bodily order}$$

Such arguments are plausible because both machines and bodies were considered to be organized, structured entities, inviting parallels between them. In this chapter I also examine the interrelation of bodies and machines, but proceed in a different manner. I am interested in knowing what can be known of the history of disorder. I will assume – and it is just an assumption – that disorder is an attribution by historical actors made only by appeal to order. For example, *The Rite of Spring* was regarded as noise by its first audience because it did not fit their preconceptions of musical order.[7] (What, after all, would a history of pure disorder look like?) Indeed the management of a complex world by casting some aspects out as disorderly (and worthless) has probably been essential to projects of building order.[8] If I was going to draw a diagram to represent my argument it would be as follows:

$$\text{order (e.g. bodies, machines)} \mid \text{disorder (e.g. bodies, machines)}$$

Where my attention is directed to where and why the line has been drawn between order and disorder by historical actors.

My case study of disorder is noise. In the spirit of Mary Douglas, noise can be understood as sound out of place – sound that has transgressed the boundary around what is orderly. As a subject it fits into my schema set out above, but the study of noise is also an ideal subject for a historian of bodies and machines. First, sounds and noise can both be the products of bodies and machines, and where the distinction was drawn between the two will tell us something about how historical actors delineated what was considered important to be ordered. Second, sound and noise are channels through which machines affect bodies. The historical literature on the sound/body nexus is, if you will excuse the pun, voluminous, although it dwindles in comparison with the emphasis elsewhere on visual culture. It ranges from musical instruments and the emotions to the radio and propaganda. Historians have had less to say on noise and the body.

For reasons of space, I limit my attention further. I will examine British campaigns against noise from the 1860s to the 1930s. In 1864 the first Bill passed through Westminster for the control of street noise, a cause enthusiastically championed by Charles Babbage – generating the mutual loathing that led to the 'tin pail' racket disturbing his deathbed. It is in this period, too, that noise became an issue of increasing concern because of heavy industry and industrialized warfare – or, more accurately, attitudes to industrial and military noise shifted. The campaigns against noise came to a head in the Anti-Noise League, founded in 1934 with the stated aim 'to promote the cause of quiet and to prevent interference with the amenities of life by avoidable noise' by means of propaganda, publication, legislation and research.[9] A magazine, *Quiet*, reached all fee-paying members.[10]

The League is interesting because prominent activists were drawn from at least three professions, each experts on the body – doctors, psychologists and engineers – yet what they were campaigning *against* was most often emanating from that exemplar of the modern, progressive world, the machine. The three professions brought different, and to some extent conflicting, traditions and model solutions to the problem of noise. But in all three, scientific research was to be brought to bear against the products of science. Indeed in 1937 the organization changed its name to the Noise Abatement Society, precisely because the new moniker was thought to be 'positive and constructive, for with it is associated a strong technical and experimental side'.[11] This chapter, therefore, should partly be seen as a contribution to a neglected history of what, for want of a better word, I will call 'conservative' science.

The actions of professionals do not explain the nerve struck by the Anti-Noise League. Doctors, psychologists and engineers, which I consider in turn, were mouthpieces of a movement that must then be accounted for in broader, contextual terms. Apparently trivial concerns about noise, I argue, should be understood in terms of a shifting interwar imagination of order and disorder.

Medicalizing Noise

Doctors viewed the problem of noise as being akin to other, older issues of public health. In both there were undertones of purification, a Christian inheritance. Preindustrial noise carried powerful religious overtones. Take, for example, the poem 'An answer to the Great Noise about Nothing: or a Noise about Something', written by a royalist, anti-Whig Scot in the first decade of the eighteenth century. 'When noise and clamour gets the upper hand. And right and wrong the crowd they will command. Then hypocrites they wear the Prize alone. And church is made a Monster of the Town.' 'We make no Noise,' the poet concluded, ''tis the Whigs that rais'd the Storm, And Yet pretend their manners to Reform.'[12] Nineteenth-century hymns made a 'joyful noise unto the Lord,' in which the undifferentiated character of the noise is made a religious good. Noise, *contentless within itself* but expressive in its act, was valorized because it conveyed simplicity and humility, akin to a childlike faith. Music, on the other hand, which had structure and *content within itself*, was far more problematic, as the range of attitudes of different churches testifies. Music moved the interior body, whereas noise was made external.

Noise could therefore have positive connotations, alongside neutral or negative ones. Indeed, the signature noise of the church – the church bells – could be viewed as producing order. Dan MacKenzie, a Glasgow MD, made the soundscape of the Sabbath into a joke about hierarchy:

> First the Auld Kirk starts off with a sound as if the 'clapper' were shaking lumps of rust out of the bell; then the United Free – two kirks two bells – chip in with a rich, not to say moneyed tone, followed by Episcopalian tinkles, E.U. jangles, the Auld Lichts, the Catholics, and so forth.[13]

However, jokes, as ever, have a serious purpose. MacKenzie wanted to silence the bells. 'Many of us', he reminded his readers, 'can remember how Irving was wont to make Mephistopheles writhe and twist in anguish when he heard the church bells chiming. Alas! some of the bells that break the Sabbath nowadays must be sources rather of pleasure than of pain to the devil . . .' MacKenzie's prognosis contained a vision that would give shape to the medical response to noise:

> In the future world – I do not mean the heavenly world – in this world in the future, I am sure that the inspector of nuisances will have among his duties the inspection or rather the audition of noises, including bells. Why "nuisances" should be legally restricted to noisome smells and should exclude noisome sounds, I do not know.

Just as doctors had led the public health movement to clean the city, so a parallel project was imagined: quietening the city in the name of public health. Furthermore, just as sewerage must be seen as a secular act of purification, washing away the dirt of the fallen industrial city, so we must note the seriousness of MacKenzie's proposal to silence positive religious noise.

The title of MacKenzie's book, *City of Din*, continued the joke. Published in 1916, it became one of the key texts circulated by the medical wing of the Anti-Noise

League. MacKenzie claimed the inheritance of a forebear, Dr Thomas Barr. Barr was surgeon to Glasgow Hospital of Diseases of the Ear and the Glasgow Royal Infirmary in the late nineteenth century, as well as a lecturer on aural surgery at Anderson's College in the city. His *Manual of Diseases of the Ear*, a student textbook, passed through many editions from 1884. In the origin stories of noise abatement, Barr has become the starting point cliché, a position which MacKenzie and the Anti-Noise League both helped cement.[14] Certainly Barr's work should be read as a late medical response to industrialization. In his practice he saw, examined and wrote about the damaged ears of Clyde ship-builders and Glasgow railwaymen. Boiler-makers, especially the 'holders-on' who held panels in place during riveting provided many cases of deafening. 'Confined by the walls of the boiler, the waves of sound are vastly intensified, and strike the tympanum with appalling force, while the vibrations from the iron pass directly through the bodies of the men to the delicate structures of the inner ear.'[15] Students learning from Barr would have no doubt that loud and continued noises led to permanent material effects in the inner ear, including deafness.[16] Also 'sudden and unexpected' noises, 'as when a cannon is fired close to the ear, or the piercing shriek of a railway whistle is suddenly heard, not infrequently originate disease of the ear.'[17] But we should note that Barr's work had very little effect: there was no contemporary movement to quieten the factory or shipyard. It was a retrospective move to claim him as an ancestor. And a clue to why is contained in the date of MacKenzie's tirade: the midst of the Great War, when sudden and unexpected noises were matched by the continuous background mayhem.

Organized anti-noise campaigns were born from the rupture of war. After lice, rats, and mud, it was a common topic in letters home from the front. MacKenzie did not need to remind his readers:

> We come now to the noises of modern war, beside which, in all conscience, all other earthly sounds, natural and artificial, are no more than the murmurs of a pigmy world. Of the frightful din of a modern battle it is impossible to convey even the faintest conception. There is no noise or combination of noises that even remotely approaches for loudness, for persistence, and for harmfulness both to hearing and to the brain. Many men who have had to endure its agonies have been rendered totally deaf; many others have been driven insane, their nervous system being hopelessly and permanently disorganised by its appalling intensity and persistence. A relative of my own, describing his own experiences, writes: 'The noise, especially during the two hours before the attack, was appalling. It was unceasing, heartrending, brain-rending. It was noise gone mad, out of all bounds, uncontrolled'.[18]

Expertise in industrial deafness was applicable in the conditions of industrialized warfare. The repetitive beat of the boiler maker was echoed by the sound of the machine gun. Machine gunners reported that 'though each individual shot may cause but a trifling report, nevertheless by the repetition of the explosions the sound makes up in duration what it lacks in intensity . . . the rattle of quick-firers is always more deafening than the individually louder but less frequently repeated discharge of heavy ordnance', and the extreme case of naval barrages was labelled by MacKenzie, without a trace this time of irony, 'probably one of the most destructive to hearing of all the sounds of civilisation'.[19] Doctors, with models of deafness that followed those of Barr or the London surgeon, Sir William Dalby, were mobilized to diagnose the deafened soldier. Judgments regarding the perm-anence of deafness had repercussions on discharge (from duty), or on accusations of malingering. Furthermore, as MacKenzie suggests, there was an incipient move towards considering psychological, besides physiological, effects – the hopeless and permanently disorganized nervous system and the protean subconscious, a move I discuss below.

During the war, doctors sought mainly to preserve the efficiency of the army through simple technological intervention. Proposals centred on the means to plug ears: prophylactics between body and machine noise. Cotton wool was rejected (not enough 'stopping power'), whereas hard rubber and cotton wool mixed with Vaseline both had adherents.[20] Dalby offered his 'plastic antiphone', but it proved too expensive to produce in adequate numbers. MacKenzie urged, successfully, a plasticine and cotton wool plug to the Admiralty and Home Office, although the Mallock-Armstrong Ear Defender made of ebonite was more often used. Gun silencers were mainly a German phenomena – they were used by the Turks at Gallipoli, a separate technological salient that met MacKenzie's approval: 'we ought to have guns which are silent firing shells which are noisy'.[21]

War prompted many doctors to consider deafness and noise, but the way they conceived the remedy was firmly based on the public health template, best exemplified by the role of the most prominent medic in the interwar anti-noise movement, Thomas Jeeves Horder – Lord Horder of Ashford from 1933. Born into a lower middle-class draper's family in Shaftesbury, Dorset, in 1871, his early education resembled that of H. G. Wells. Indeed, while taking a correspondence class in biology from a London offshoot of the University Correspondence College, he was briefly tutored by Wells who commented that the young man was not cut out for research. Horder responded by cultivating a gentlemanly posture; 'the artisan is quite capable of being a gentleman, or the converse, as is the aristocrat,' but, as Emerson had written, and Horder repeated approvingly, the distinction was that 'A gentleman makes no noise.'[22]

Whereas Wells turned radical, Horder dug himself deep into the establishment. First winning an entrance scholarship to London University and emerging with a first-class degree in physiology, Horder then qualified in medicine and by the end of the century was a London MD gaining hospital experience as a house physician to Dr Samuel Gee at St. Bartholomews, while also consulting at the Royal Northern Hospital. It was in a remarkable private practice that Horder began to establish his impeccable credentials, advising three prime ministers, and, crucially, three successive royals: the ailing Edward VII, his son (from 1923 until abdication), and, as Physician-in-Ordinary, George VI. Such elevation in turn drew Horder into public activities, as chair of several Royal Society of Medicine committees (including one investigating Joanna Southcott's box). He was President of the Eugenics Society, the National Society for the Prevention of Venereal Disease, and politically he was a leader in the Fellowship for Freedom in Medicine, campaigning against proposals for a national health service. Despite this he also found time to be President of the Birth Control Society and a leading light in the Cremation Society – from cradle to grave, Horder was against both.

On his death in 1955, the *British Medical Journal* could recall Horder as 'the most outstanding clinician of his time and the personality in British medicine best known to the general public . . . an interpreter of medicine to the public. He was "Harley Street" to the newspaper world'.[23] He was also, therefore, the perfect figurehead for the anti-noise movement. In speeches for the Anti-Noise League in the 1930s, Horder made the public health model explicit:

> In much the same way as there have arisen conglomerations of human dwellings, huddled together without design or plan, starving people of light and of air and spreading disease, so there has come upon us, as a result of increased motor-traffic, increased transport, aeroplanes and louder forms of amusement, a spate of uncontrolled noise for the suppression of which we must organise ourselves. It is necessary to be saved from the nerve-racking effects of noise as it is that we secure air and light and freedom from infectious diseases.[24]

Horder conceived of the effect of noise on the body as a process of enervation. While noise did not 'kill us as foul air and typhoid and diphtheria do', it did 'wear down the nervous system', which was the 'master stuff of our bodies' and it acted to 'stultify the spirit . . . the element in us which marks us off from the beasts'.[25] (For more on nerves and energy, see Morus, this volume.) The Anti-Noise League's nod towards 'air and light and freedom' connects it to the wider inter-war 'healthy minds and healthy bodies' movement that celebrated clean living and exercise in clean air. (Horder shared the sentiments: 'walking and hiking, outdoor games of all sorts . . . things that bring us once more into contact with mother earth, the sun, the wind and even the rain; all these make for health').[26] The League likewise inherited the late-nineteenth-century National Efficiency discourse of energy which had linked the individual to the health of the wider economy.[27] The Anti-Noise League was 'a constructive and a protective movement, for it aims at the conservation of nervous energy. It economises human effort'.

For Horder there were clear synergies between his work in the League and his promotion of eugenics, one of the few areas where he could countenance strong government intervention, or at least the co-ordination of departments towards 'achieving national fitness in a free people'.[28] In a *Nature* article, titled 'Old diseases and new', Horder expanded on the national consequences of conserving nervous energy:

> How long a man lives depends upon his ancestors and the state of the public hygiene. How *healthily* and how *happily* he lives depends upon himself. Therefore we welcome an attempt by the state to organise the national physique. Later, but I trust not too late, perhaps we might do something to organise the national mind; and so get back some of the *zest* for living that we seem to have lost.[29]

There was little point in improving immunity to disease if the individual did not have the energy to enjoy health. And if the individual lacked energy, so did the nation. Uncontrolled noise attacked the nervous system, enervating the body and disorganizing the mind. The Anti-Noise League was therefore, for Horder, also a national project for national order.

The parallels between the anti-noise and eugenics movements can also be seen in their constructions of targets. Eugenics divided the population into the genetically fit and the genetically unhealthy, with the latter – especially an unreformable 'residuum' – encouraged not to breed. The same split was imagined by Horder (he was discussing noise but the ambiguity was deliberate):

> In regard to every amenity there are two groups of persons recognisable. There is the group which is already endeavouring to foster the amenity . . . And there is the group which is anti-social, or even criminally-minded, on these as in all other matters affecting the community. The progress of society may be measured by the relative sizes of the two groups.[30]

The primary difference between how Horder conceived bad genes and noisy bodies lay in the role of the state. Perhaps eugenics was so important that government action was justified, or perhaps the satirical target presented by insisting on quiet was too large, but the Anti-Noise League decided to largely limit its campaign to appeals to individual reasonableness – individual, not political, moral reform: 'we believe that we shall do more eventually by securing intelligent, individual action than by policing people into a state of sullen quietness.' A pressure group composed of concerned free individuals was Horder's ideal of political organization, free of any hint of socialism yet with a role for strong leadership – it was the 'work of the expert', he told his readers in *The Listener*, 'to point out to us where we are wrong, to train us and put us on the right road'.[31]

Psychologizing Noise

Doctors were challenged for leadership of the anti-noise campaign by other experts. 'It is facts,' claimed Charles S. Myers in 1934, 'that the more intelligent section of the community demands about such a debated and debatable subject as the distracting, irritating and harmful effects of noise'.[32] His ally, F. C. Bartlett, professor of experimental psychology at the University of Cambridge, set out to ensure that it was facts provided by psychological experts that would shape the debate.

Bartlett presented two Heath Clark lectures to the National Institute of Industrial Psychology, subsequently published as *The Problem of Noise* in 1934. His analysis of cases was very different from Horder's theory of enervation. Three cases provided illustrations of his approach. In the first, a woman who lived with a 'physically rather weak, ineffective, unsatisfying' husband was upset by a 'newly married couple', described as 'young, magnificently vital, devoted', who move next door. She 'developed a fury of complaints . . . Complaints of what? Of the slamming of doors; nothing else.'[33] A second story featured an uncertain young man raging against convent bells. And in the third, 'an old lady, desperately poor, unbendingly independent. She will fend for herself till she is dead', but there were 'many things she would dearly like and cannot have. Her neighbours, not bad ones by any means, have many of these things.' The neighbours install a loudspeaker. 'The old lady hates and loathes the loud-speaker. She loses no chance of campaigning bitterly against "this disgraceful noise".'

For Horder the noise would have depressed individuals' nervous energy, leading to understandable and reasonable complaint. Bartlett's analysis was completely opposed. He argued that in all three cases noise was the 'burden of complaint that fundamentally has other and deeper causes as well'. Noise was a symptom of social malaise, manifesting psychological responses. Noise, because it was 'one of the things which, by its qualities, stands out prominently on almost any background' became merely the proximate cause. Anything else equally prominent might cause the same reaction. 'It is not too much to say', concluded Bartlett

> that whenever, in any community, a sweeping and passionate condemnation of noise is popular, there, within that community, are almost certainly a lot of people who are ill-adjusted, worried, attempting too much, or too little. Complaint against noise is a sign . . . of a deeper social distress.

Bartlett's social-psychological analysis of noise needs to be understood within the disciplinary and institutional dynamics of his time. Despite the plea to look to context, he and his peers conceded the phenomenon of noise-induced 'fatigue', for good disciplinary reason. Early twentieth-century psychology created lucrative room for itself in the workplace. Industrial psychology promised improvements through application of its expertise to problems of 'inefficiency'. Some illustrations of this interest is given by the inquiry that Sir David Munro, Secretary to the Industrial Health Research Board, directed to Richard F. Millard, general secretary of the Anti-Noise League. Research into noise, so far, had largely been confined to the laboratory, and 'enough is known, at present about the sort and level of noise that produces physical harm, also about the sort and level of noise that produces harmful distraction. It is the old story.'[34] The 'next step . . . should be out of the laboratory'. Noise should be added to the industrial psychologists' topics of expertise. However, care was required, and what was needed, argued Munro, was somebody

> on the look out for information about the frequency and objectives of complaints against noise – collecting opinions and following them up, and watching results, not in terms of measurable fatigue but in the increase of irritability and the growth of attitudes akin to neuroses. Noise, it seems, wants treating not as an individual problem, but as a public affair; I mean one wants to know whether the amount of social discord that is produced in this way is worth taking a lot of public notice of, or whether it is just the infrequent crank who sits up and howls about it.

While the psychologists remained unsure as to whether noise was indeed a significant public affair indicating deeper social discord, the fact that the anti-noise movement garnered considerable public interest and press coverage tempted them to bid for a slice of the pie. Munro himself ensured that the psychological perspective was kept before the public by assisting the Science Museum's Noise Abatement Exhibition of 1935, writing the 'Noise and industrial fatigue' chapter of the Exhibition handbook (and having the text checked and approved by Bartlett).

Engineering Noise

The psychological claim to expertise in solving problems of noise was, in turn, contested by physicists and engineers, who based their rival claim on the virtues of precise measurement using new standardized units. Unlike the psychologists they could – and did – claim a traditional corpus of research. In the nineteenth century poor acoustics were an acute political and commercial issue. Mass meetings, more often indoors than out, and large-scale symphonic, theatrical or operatic performances, increasingly depended on the control of noise. 'Reverberation', and its management, had been discussed in a British Association report by Reid in 1835. (The year in which expert advice was sought for the rebuilding of Parliament after the previous year's fire. Faraday offered the Royal Institution as a paragon of acoustics.)[35] Roger Smith, in his *Acoustics of Public Buildings* (1861) and John Tyndall, in evidence placed before a select committee of the House of Commons in 1868, proposed carpets, furnishings and low ceilings. The extent to which these interventions *did* resolve the political and commercial issue at stake, bearing in mind the quiet clarity that printed versions of speeches, say, provided as an alternative response, would repay historical study, perhaps taking a lead from Thompson's excellent histories of American acoustics.[36] What is certain is that acoustics increasingly became an increasingly important concern of scientists. The two-volume, *Theory of Sound* by James Clerk Maxwell's successor at the Cavendish Laboratory, John William Strutt, Lord Rayleigh, was published in 1877, a second edition appearing in 1896 containing a mathematical treatment of the absorption of sound by rigid porous surfaces (walls, ceilings and floors). Across the Atlantic, Professor W. C. Sabine at Harvard University investigated the relationship of architecture and acoustics, beginning with a lecture room of the Fogg Art Museum in 1895, publishing papers on the subject from 1900 to 1915. His main subject was decay – it is tempting but trite to link it to degeneration – measuring the seconds it took for intellectual speech to fade to silence.

Rayleigh's and Sabine's studies were continued at a novel British body, the National Physical Laboratory, established in 1900 as a muted response to German competition, but which would become one of the key loci of the anti-noise campaign. Under X-ray physicist George William Clarkson Kaye, and subsequently under Kaye's protégé and colleague Alfred Horace Davis, Sabine's sound-pulse photography technique was imported, and used to investigate sound waves reverberating within models of theatres and lecture halls.[37] It joined the older ripple-tank method of modelling acoustics, and a panoply of new instruments.[38]

The NPL was set up for two main purposes: as the centre of British metrology and as a laboratory for physical research. These made it the ideal location for British physicists and engineers to establish their claim to expertise in issues of noise through a strategy of defining and mobilizing standards. The 'bel', usually encountered in the smaller 'decibel', already existed as a logarithmic measurement of the intensity of sound. Physiologists, psychologists and physicists all agreed that in order to speak on the effect of sound on humans, a different measure was required. For example, Davis could uncontentiously note that 'sounds which have the same intensity . . . are not usually equally loud . . . Intensity is a matter of pressures, frequency, etc.; loudness is a question of the effect which these pressures have on the human ear.'[39] However Davis and Kaye moved to make the measurement of loudness the work of physicists and engineers, rather than psychologists. In 1933, by working through the Royal Society, the British Standards Institution, closely allied to the NPL, set up a committee under Kaye to produce a Glossary of Acoustical Terms and Definitions. Davis took the name of an existing measure (the German 'phon'), and made a crucial distinction 'for the first time between intensity and loudness measurements, the decibel being restricted to the former and the latter now being expressed in a new unit, the "Phon (B.S)".'[40] The Phon (B.S.) was defined as follows: taking a 'standard sound' of a 1000 c/s sound and an arbitrary 'zero of loudness' of 0.0002 dynes per square centimetre, the increase in loudness above this produced by an increase of one decibel was a phon. Davis popularized the phon in *Quiet* with an imaginary tour of London noise: from the oppressive 110 phons of a printing press room to the 30 phons of a 'quiet suburban garden in the evening'.[41]

However, hidden in the definition was still an embarrassing subjective judgement about loudness. So having used one aspect of the NPL's power to enforce standardization, Kaye and Davis deployed the techniques of another: instruments of measurement. First, Davis borrowed the approach of the German H. Barkhausen, and built 'subjective noise meters', in which one ear would receive a standard tone through a telephone earpiece, leaving the other to judge the noise source in question. But, Davis argued (firmly in the tradition identified by Galison and Daston as the strategy of 'mechanical objectivity')[42] 'it is very desirable to have a physical instrument giving on a meter, without suspicion of personal error or bias, readings in accord with the average aural judgement of the equivalent loudness of noise'.[43] The 'objective noise meter', designed and built at the NPL by Davis, was made in portable form. Now the physicist or engineer could take outside the laboratory what they hoped to be an unchallengeable instrumental source of expertise.[44] The Ministry of Transport was quickly persuaded to adopt it in its investigation, and proposed regulation, of traffic noise. Objective noise meters were manufactured by Standard Telephones and Cables Ltd and Metropolitan-Vickers.[45] Kaye put the matter starkly in an address to the British Association at Nottingham in 1937: 'phons are the psychological equivalents of decibels', but allowed physicists to pronounce on psychological terrain.[46]

Physicists and engineers were active members of the Anti-Noise League. Davis approved of the 'social tendency to control' and echoed the League's proposals in print: 'informed opinion is beginning to regard noise control as one of some moment', and as

> data for acceptable and existing noise levels in domestic and residential situations are accumulated, and the effects of various types of treatment measured and put on record, it will be easier to prescribe an adequate treatment . . . and less difficult for a person to prove that he is being subjected to noise so excessive as to be a nuisance.[47]

Kaye signed up to the League's worldview: 'the social evil of needless noise was "largely a pernicious by-product of an increasingly mechanised civilisation"'.[48] They were joined in the pages of *Quiet* by many others of their profession, such as Wing-Commander T. R. Cave-Browne-Cave, professor of engineering at University College, Southampton, and a member of the League's Council. What is remarkable is that in the scientists active in the League we have examples of physicists, engineers as well as doctors and other professionals, embracing a worldview that can fairly be labelled as anti-progressive, anti-modern and anti-technology.

The Appeal of the Anti-Noise League

The League could garner support because its concerns placed it on some of the key fault-lines of twentieth-century society. It was not alone in this position, and other organizations of a similar ilk shared attitudes, organizational style and members, for example the Campaign for the Preservation of Rural England, anti-litter movements and the societies for the preservation of ancient monuments.[49] The League joined up with the Our Dumb Friends' League and other animal welfare charities to oppose fireworks. These were popular 'conservative' projects, which spoke to peculiar, deep-seated, if sometimes inarticulate, inter-war worries. For brevity, I can only sketch the tensions that led to the League's wider resonance.

Natural versus Artificial

To what extent was noise a human creation? This question exercised MacKenzie in *City of Din*, and structured articles in the League's magazine, *Quiet*. MacKenzie was unequivocal: 'Unlike the world of men, the world of Nature is not noisy'.[50] While there were natural 'sounds', they were pleasant and therefore not noise. (This distinction was definitional for the author: 'In a word, noise is unpleasant. It is a painful sound.') Barking dogs ruffled the argument. First, he made light of the nuisance: 'My own dogs are lively, cheerful, protective, when they bark. Other people's dogs, however, may be, and generally are, even to a lover of dogs, noisy, ill-tempered, badly-brought up brutes.' However, such quicksands of relativism were escaped by an appeal to true nature. Was not barking an artificial sound? MacKenzie reported that he had heard that in the 'state of nature' dogs did not bark, 'If so, then it is domestication, coupled perhaps with artificial selection, that has given us the barking dog.'[51] MacKenzie extended the point to excuse cats, corn-crakes and babies.

Country versus City

For MacKenzie and the League, the moral distinction between nature and artifice mapped fairly squarely onto an opposition between country and city. There was of course nothing new in portraying the countryside as a haven of peace and quiet and the city as a place of clamour and turbulence. What was new in the interwar period was an erosion of barriers between urban and rural cultures, assisted by the construction of cinemas in small towns, the diffusion of the radio, and improved bus and train transport links.[52] In particular, the spread of automobile ownership to all classes widened access to the countryside and triggered ribbon developments of housing along roads. So, for example, Ainslie Darby and C.C. Hamilton's diatribe against noisy 'weekenders' and other city dwellers out-of-place, should be read, as Bartlett might have suggested, as indignation against social intrusion:

> Why is there hostility to the construction of arterial and by-pass roads in certain country districts? There appear to be three chief reasons. Firstly, the wide and straight arterial road cuts into natural features and inevitably spoils their harmony. Secondly, it opens a vein along which flows a stream of noisy traffic. This means that not only will the actual area of the road be spoilt but also a considerable strip of land on each side . . . In its wake come the hangers-on: petrol-pumps, advertisements, rural cottages turned tea-gardens and then the inevitable lines of villas.[53]

G. K. Chesterton was right to label this a complaint against a 'vulgarisation of the country' (a complaint he upheld). Note too that 'country' is ambiguous, Chesterton and others used it as shorthand for the nation, but the implication was there that the nation's true values lay in the countryside, in nature not in artifice.

If the countryside was the seat of virtue, the fallen city was a place of necessary individual reform. Individuals of the street were singled out – Babbage's organ-grinders were joined by other 'arch-noise makers': the road-mender, the 'street gramophonist', the 'street Scotsman (with bagpipes)', the 'muffin man (with bell)' or the 'news-boy with open mouth (bellowing)'.[54] The Anti-Noise League was a moral movement, its aim being correct, polite living in cities. For C. E. M. Joad, writing in *Quiet*, 'the first objection' might be 'the physical quality of the noise', but the second was the 'inconsiderateness of its makers'.[55] 'Civilisation is noise', declared MacKenzie, 'At least modern civilisation is. And the more it progresses the noisier it becomes.'[56] Thus Athens, Rome and Florence were not too noisy – he unfortunately doesn't state the grounds for believing this rather profound historical question – it 'has been left to scientific civilisation to fill the world with stridency. We have to pay for our comforts in racket.'

Old World versus New Technology and Tradition versus Progress

Here we can see two more key oppositions through which the League's rhetoric worked. Objects of ire were the new transport technologies: the motor car, the aeroplane and the motorcycle. The aeroplane was labelled by maverick MP A.P. Herbert a 'tyrannical invention', symbolic of an 'Age of Vulgarity and Noise'.[57]

'Aeroplanes clearly represent mechanical progress', state Darby and Hamilton. 'We shall not get much further in any part of our enquiry until the mechanical parrot stops shrieking "Progress!", "Progress!", "Progress!"' 'Sky Talkies', aerial advertising, the aeroplane combined with another novel technology, the loud-speaker, however unlikely it was that a slogan could be heard above the engine of a Gypsy Moth, was greeted with horror. Aeroplanes, of course, were no respecters of traditional land boundaries, and could equally fly over ancient monuments as over Brighton pleasure beaches. Likewise, transgression prompted fury over the motor-bike, with modern technology trespassing on ancient tracks. 'A motor-cycle "trial" on the Icknield Way is a sacrilege, it is the insolent affront of noise and speed to beauty and poetry. The motorist on the Icknield Way cannot under-stand the complaint against him because he finds no meaning in such words, but Vandals are as deficient of a sense as are the deaf and blind.'[58] Ironically, as Mat-less has shown, these words were being written precisely at the moment when the old straight tracks of Alfred Watkins were being invented and even celebrated as naturalizing precursors of the modern road network.[59]

Again there was a dilemma recognized and keenly felt by League members: the new technologies were providers of comfort and the 'benefits of civilisation', but upset pre-existing social boundaries - 'noise' was a symbol of bodies and machines out of place. Darby and Hamilton again: 'It is perhaps unfortunate that the magic of our new machines is so spectacular that it destroys our sense of proportion; moreover their novelty is deemed to put them outside existing laws and above new ones.' It could also be a generational issue. *Quiet* magazine reported with glee the off-the-cuff rant made by Walter Elliott, the Minister of Health, who was visiting Manchester to open a hospital. After dwelling on improvements in treatment of sepsis,

> he thought it quite probable that in the future our descendants would look back and wonder how we could be blind to the fact that every year we were reducing our resistant power until the nation and the whole of Western civilisation had got into a state of jitters. 'I sometimes wonder to myself what the younger generation will be like . . . I never see any of them who is happy – either a he or a she – without noise. If they cannot make noise themselves they hire a machine to make noise. They play the gramophone, not because they like to hear it but because they don't like silence'.[60]

Noisy vehicles were bad, but cars driven by 'upstarts' were far worse. Lord Horder's 'blackest' of bête noires was the 'sports car with the flamboyant exhaust . . . generally driven, I think, by a young gentleman in suede shoes with marcelled hair', who, and he adds a dubious medical opinion, 'is making up this way for what Dame Nature appears to have denied him otherways'.[61] Noisy machines were an affront to order, generational, traditional, social. However, within the engineering tradition, a technological solution was proposed to the problems of noise. A *Quiet* advert by the Celotex company was quite explicit: 'excessive noise is part of the price we have to pay for progress. It is not a price which we need continue to pay! The solution [Acousti-Celotex tiles], tried and tested, is ready.'[62] It was the engineers' response to noise, alongside aspects of the medical and psychological approaches, that survived the Second World War, not least because their instruments generated stable records useful in post-war bureaucratic regulation.[63] But their organization, the Anti-Noise League, was to see its appeal collapse.

Ironies of War Noise

In 1941 an editorial in the *Wembley Observer and Gazette* noted that the war was 'having a drastic effect upon individual views . . . Many things which we have regarded as essentials and of prime importance are now seen in their right perspective'. In particular, it was 'amusingly ironical to recall the formation of an anti-noise society', whose complaints now sounded 'incredibly puerile, if not comic, in comparison with our anti-aircraft barrage'.[64] Certainly as war approached, the League became the target of satire that hit home. *Punch* mercilessly ridiculed the League and its figurehead:

> Plans to deaden the sound of falling bombs in time of war have just been completed by the Anti-Noise League. Enormous quantities of cotton-wool will be stored at convenient points in the Metropolis and elsewhere and in a few days' time, members of the League, wearing felt-soled shoes will begin their task of calling from house to house to measure the ears of the general public . . . In addition straw will be laid down in the main thoroughfares during air raids to soften the noise of falling masonry. 'A people must guard itself against the danger of being deafened into surrender,' said Lord Horder to a class of cotton-wool instructors yesterday. He revealed that the Government have been quietly buying up aspirin tablets for the past six months in case of a widespread epidemic of air-raid headaches.[65]

In response the League tried to claim that their cause was *more*, not less, important. 'This war . . . is a war of attrition of nerves, especially the nerves of those living in towns and cities. As never before, it is necessary to conserve the nervous resources of individuals', as a *Quiet* editorial summarized in 1940.[66] But the impossibility of opposing the aeroplane was conceded by Lord Horder at the League's annual dinner in 1938: 'in the midst of our investigation of the problem of aircraft noise, the need for re-armament arose, and it was felt that the time was unsuitable to pursue the matter, as the League did not wish to take any step which might possibly interfere with the development of our air power, whether civil or military.'

If light satire made the League's wartime work difficult, there was no respite in the early years of peace from heavier critiques. George Orwell's *1984*, published in 1948, featured the terrifying Anti-Sex League, junior stormtroopers of joyless chastity. The name was clearly reminiscent of the Anti-Noise League, and Orwell was perhaps making the link between the eugenic enthusiasms of Lord Horder in the 1930s and the totalitarian world imagined from the mid-twentieth century. Horder, in his dislike of the state would have loathed Big Brother, but there was more than a hint of Orwellian themes in the doctor's popular writings. 'I have been regarded by a lot of critics as a visionary', Horder announced in *The Listener* in 1937, 'because I once conceived of the Ministry of Health as being . . . a Ministry of Happiness'.[67] It would have been a short walk in the administrative capital of Airstrip One from the Ministry of Happiness to the Ministry of Truth.

The biggest irony was that just as the public movement against noise wilted under ridicule, the engineering understanding of noise was recasting theories of what it was to be human. During the Second World War the performance of human operators as part of technological systems came under intense scientific scrutiny. The paradigm that emerged, through the work of Kenneth Craik on British radar but particularly that of the cyberneticists in the United States, provided a common language for discussing both bodies and machines, in terms of feedback and information.[68] Crucially, noise became redefined as *part of the system*, perhaps most clearly in Claude Shannon's information theory and George A. Miller's contributions to cognitive psychology that begin with his wartime stint at Harvard's Psycho-Acoustic Laboratory (PAL).[69] It is hard to over-state the influence of such research. PAL, writes Edwards, 'played a crucial role in the genesis of postwar information processing psychologies,' and thus to postwar conceptions of mind.[70] In this chapter, however, I only want to draw attention to two points. First, that the resources devoted to urgent defence science led to the shaping of theoretical and practical tools that defined noise as part of the system, not left as an uncontrollable outside phenomenon. Second, I think the ground was laid for such developments in the interwar response to noise of engineers and industrial psychologists. I have only discussed the British case, so I leave it as a suggestion.

Conclusion

Some see the present time as an heroic battle of 'Ideologies' – White against Red, Fascism against Communism, Privilege against Poverty.

Others see it proudly as the Age of 'Science', of Speed; of Electricity, of Internal Combustion and Steel.

Posterity may see it more simply as the Age of Vulgarity and Noise. History may record that the significant struggle lay between Impotent Man and Tyrannical Invention – especially the aeroplane.[71]

What would happen if we took A. P. Herbert's invitation seriously? How would history read if it was written, not from a foundation in rival ideologies, or as an unfolding story of modernity, but instead by beginning with categories such as noise? 'It is annoying that there is no stable borderline of what constitutes exactly a necessary or unnecessary noise', complained one contributor to *Quiet*.[72] It is this instability that makes noise a rewarding topic. I think the historian following Herbert's invitation would be led to examine where historical actors claimed disorder began, and in turn to their practical projects of building order in the world. Charles Babbage's complaints against noise increased in frequency as his powers waned and completion of such projects – the Difference and Analytical Engines in particular – receded.

Babbage helped launch the organized campaign against noise, leading to legislation. But, after the reaction to industrial 'noise gone mad' in the Great War, the campaign became a movement in the interwar years, with the formation of the Anti-Noise League. Three groups of professionals were prominent in the League's activities. Each was concerned with bodies. For doctors, such as Lord Horder and Dan MacKenzie, the anti-noise programme took a template from public health. A popular expression of this model was Peter Ritchie Calder's futuristic novel *The Birth of the Future*, in which he imagined a society in which noise would be as much a crime as smelly drains.[73] For Horder, noise was an indicator of the inefficient anti-social body, a drain on the nation's nervous energy. But for the psychologists, noise was analysed in social terms, a response to unarticulated conflicts. With the doctors and psychologists the attention to bodies is obvious, but physicist-engineers, too, must be viewed in this light. In general, human operators were increasingly understood in systemic terms, while sensitive precise instrumentation had to be considered in relation to the bodies near them, as the NPL staff active in the League knew well (see Gooday, this volume). One of the most interesting aspects of the League is that, paradoxically, scientists within it deployed their expertise against the products of modern science, in particular the new transgressive machines disrupting traditional social order. The worldview of 'conservative' science was very different from the left-wing progressive vision of the Haldanes, J. D. Bernal, P. M. S. Blackett, and so on, that historians are familiar with. Partly this is because 'conservative' science was not party-political but found expression in movements such as the Anti-Noise League and allied causes. (There was overlap, though: both could often agree on the importance of planning – order-building *par excellence*.)[74]

Note, however, that not all scientists involved with the League should be classed as 'conservative,' because, as I have shown, the attractions of the League were varied and deep-rooted in tensions in society. Almost certainly, similar oppositions could be found in other countries. I share Bartlett's analysis that as 'in almost every civilised country expert committees have been appointed to investigate what we can the "menace of noise"', and that a 'complaint against noise [was often] . . . a sign of deeper social distress,' then we should look comparatively for similarities in social distress afflicting interwar 'civilization'.[75]

Notes

1. Quoted in D. Swade, *The Cogwheel Brain: Charles Babbage and the Quest to Build the First Computer* (London: Little, Brown, 2000), p. 217.
2. Swade, *Cogwheel Brain*, p. 217. N. F. Babbage, 'Autopsy Report on the Body of Charles Babbage', *The Medical Journal of Australia*, 1991, 154: 758–9.
3. 'I have no objection; on the contrary I quite assent; to the idea of preserving the brain. In these things I have but one standard to guide me, viz my thoughts of what could be the judgement of my father and on this point I have no doubt. But my own ideas and those of my uncle Sir S. Ryan and his other relatives coincide entirely with those of my father. Please therefore do what you consider best with the brain.'

   Archive of the Museum of the Royal College of Surgeons. Letters Book 2, p. 94. Letter from Henry P. Babbage to Sir James [Paget], 19 October 1871.
4. British Library Add.37195, Babbage Correspondence, f.95. Leger to Babbage, 17 June 1852.
5. Sir V. Horsley, 'Description of the Brain of Mr Charles Babbage, FRS', *Philosophical Transactions of the Royal Society of London*, Series B, 1908, 200: 117–31.
6. C. Babbage, *Passages from the Life of a Philosopher*, ed. M. Campbell-Kelly (London: William Pickering, 1994), first published 1864.
7. M. Eksteins, *Rites of Spring: the Great War and the Birth of the Modern Age* (New York: Anchor Books, 1989), p. 52.
8. For an analysis of 'interference' in this light, see J. Agar, *Science and Spectacle: the Work of Jodrell Bank in Post-War British Culture* (Amsterdam: Harwood Academic Press, 1998).
9. 'The object of the Anti-Noise League is to promote the cause of quiet and to prevent interference with the amenities of life by avoidable noise:- (a) By propaganda and by the publication and circulation of literature or periodicals. (b) By securing the enforcement of the law relating to noise and by promoting and assisting legislative or administrative action directed to minimising of noise. (c) By supporting or carrying on research and encouraging invention and by acquiring and turning to account letters patent directed to minimising of

noise. (d) By maintaining a centre for obtaining and disseminating information. (e) By forming or assisting in the formation of other Associations having objects wholly or partly the same as the League.'

10. Joining the League had two rates, as a member for £1 1s 0d or as an associate for 5s. *Quiet* began in 1936.

11. 'Editorial notes', *Quiet*, January 1938, p. 3. The justification continued: '. . . The word "anti" in our former title tended to create the false impression that the League consisted merely of a group of people with a grievance.'

12. 'An answer to the Great Noise about Nothing: Or a Noise about Something', probably by Baring or Fyfe, 1705. The poem was in response to 'A Great Noise about Nothing: Or The Church's Danger. A Satyr', 1705, which attacked the 'False cry of Danger of the Church: 'Tis this deluding sound that fills our Ears'.

13. D. MacKenzie, *The City of Din: a Tirade against Noise* (London: Adlard and Son, Bartholomew Press, 1916).

14. See for example, M. Rodda, *Noise and Society* (Edinburgh: Oliver and Boyd, 1967).

15. Barr, quoted by MacKenzie, *City of Din*. Ship-building remained extremely noisy until the replacement of riveting with welding in British shipyards after the Second World War, see R.A. Buchanan, *Power of Machines*, p. 146.

16. T. Barr, *Manual of Diseases of the Ear, for the Use of Students and Practitioners of Medicine* (Glasgow, 1884), pp. 452–3.

17. Barr, *Diseases of the Ear*, p. 63. This was connected to inquiries into what appeared to be new industrial diseases, such as 'railway spine'. W. Schivelbusch, *The Railway Journey: the Industrialization and Perception of Time and Space* (Leamington Spa: Berg, 1986).

18. MacKenzie, *City of Din*, pp. 101–2.

19. MacKenzie, *City of Din*, p. 94.

20. A range prefigured by pre-war medics. 'It would be well if boiler-makers, gunners, and others who are exposed to great noise could be persuaded to use an india-rubber plug or other means for deadening sound. Cheatle has recently suggested "clay fibre," a plastic substance which can be moulded to fit the orifice of the ear. Dr. Legge suggests plastacine, used in school modelling, containing cotton wool fibre. The writer finds that this suits the purpose very well, and could be used also for keeping the water out of the ear while bathing. It is interesting to know that many gunners are in the habit of keeping something between their teeth during gun-fire, to ensure the mouth being open, which they say lessens the effects of the sound upon the ear.' T. Barr and J. Stoddart Barr, *Manual of the Diseases of the Ear*, 4th edn (Glasgow, 1909), p. 98.

21. MacKenzie, *City of Din*, p. 103.

22. Wellcome Archives, Lord Horder Papers, GP/31/B.4/4. Untitled memorandum (speech on Anti-Noise League), 1930s.

23. 'Lord Horder of Ashford GVCO, MD, DCL, FRCP', *British Medical Journal*, 20 August 1955.

24. Wellcome Archives, Lord Horder Papers, GP/31/B.4/4. Untitled memorandum (speech on Anti-Noise League), 1930s.

25. *Ibid*. See also the doctor Sir James Purves-Stewart, 'Noise and "nerves"', *Quiet*, April 1938, pp. 10–12, for a very similar account. George Beard had argued that 'noise' contributed to the neurasthenia, nervous exhaustion, which he took to be a peculiarly acute American problem. 'The chief and primary cause of this development and very rapid increase of nervousness is modern civilization, which is distinguished from the ancient by these five character-istics: steam-power, the periodical-press, the telegraph, the sciences, and the mental activity of women.' G. M. Beard, *American Nervousness: Its Causes and Consequences* (New York, 1881), p. vi, p. 106.

26. Lord Horder, 'Towards National Health', *The Listener*, 7 April 1937.

27. G. R. Searle, *The Quest for National Efficiency: a Study of British Politics and Political Thought, 1899–1914* (London: Basil Blackwell, 1971).

28. Wellcome Archives, Lord Horder Papers, GP/31/B.1/1. Speech to House of Lords, undated (probably 1937).

29. Lord Horder, 'Old Diseases and New', *Nature*, 3 April 1937. Horder's italics.

30. Wellcome Archives, Lord Horder Papers, GP/31/B.4/4. Untitled memorandum (speech on Anti-Noise League), 1930s.

31. Lord Horder, 'Towards National Health', *The Listener*, 7 April 1937.

32. Myers, preface to F. C. Bartlett, *The Problem of Noise* (Cambridge: Cambridge University Press, 1934).

33. Bartlett, *Noise*, p. 51.

34. Public Record Office (hereafter PRO) FD 1/4048. Munro to Millard, 20 May 1937.

35. A. H. Davis and G. W. C. Kaye, *The Acoustics of Buildings* (London: G. Bell & Sons, 1927), pp. 131–3. The RI remained a favourite example of architect-ural acoustics among British physicists. At Bragg's NPL there were wooden models, and sound-pulse analyses by Fleming.

36. For example, E. Thompson, 'Dead Rooms and Live Wires: Harvard, Holly-wood and the Deconstruction of Architectural Acoustics, 1900–1930', *Isis*, 1997, 88: 597–626.

37. Davis and Kaye, *Acoustics of Buildings*, pp. 50–5, includes two photographs of the apparatus.

38. Davis and Kaye discuss an analysis of the lecture hall of the British Institute of Radiology (the ex-chapel of the Russian Embassy, presumably vacated after the revolution) using NPL ripple-tanks. There is perhaps a connection

between Kaye's early expertise on X-rays and the Institute's invitation to investigation. Davis and Kaye, *Acoustics of Buildings*, pp. 135–7.

39. A. H. Davis, *Noise* (London: Watts and Co., 1937), p. 39.
40. 'Acoustical Terms: Note from British Standards Institution', *Quiet*, June 1936, p. 33.
41. A. H. Davis, 'Why London Noise Annoys', *Quiet*, January 1938, pp. 18–19. See also C. W. Glover, 'London Street Sounds', *Quiet*, October 1937, pp. 22–4. The Science Museum's Noise Abatement Exhibition also displayed a noise map of London.
42. L. Daston and P. L. Galison, 'The Image of Objectivity', *Representations*, 1992, 40: 81–128. Mechanical objectivity is the claim to objectivity through the reduction, or apparent removal, of human intervention. The ideal is measurement by self-registering machine.
43. Davis, *Noise*, p. 54.
44. See Davis, *Noise*, figure 8 for an illustration. Davis supposes it is a replacement for the human ear, but even he admits many problems. Unless it was 'carefully adjusted' the Portable Objective Meter gave too low readings for 'impulsive' or 'staccato' readings. But how was this judgment made? By appeal to necessary human experience. The objective meter did not really remove the human element from the measurement process, but acted as an effective rhetorical appeal to an ideal of objectivity.
45. Illustrations of both can be found in C.W. Glover, 'The Phon and the Decibel', *Quiet*, April 1938, pp. 24–6.
46. Kaye's talk was reported in 'Noise and the Nation', *Quiet*, October 1937, p. 9. By far the greatest number of publications on noise should be placed in this physics/engineering bracket. Bartlett calculated that in the five years before 1934, 60 per cent of accredited work dealt with measurement, 28 per cent was on physiological effects of noise stimuli and only 12 per cent was on psychological problems. Bartlett, *Noise*. McLachlan's book, despite its subtitle, was overwhelmingly from the physical perspective: N. W. McLachlan, *Noise: a Comprehensive Survey from Every Point of View* (London: Oxford University Press, 1935).
47. Davis, *Noise*, p. 131.
48. 'Noise and the Nation', *Quiet*, October 1937, p. 9.
49. For some of these connections, see: D. Matless, *Landscape and Englishness* (London: Reaktion Books, 1998).
50. MacKenzie, *City of Din*, p. 1.
51. MacKenzie, *City of Din*, p. 11. 'The fact is that in wide and spacious country parts the dog, even when he barks, is not a source of such serious or disturbing noise as he is in urban surroundings.'
52. Eksteins, *Rites of Spring*, p. 258.

53. A. Darby and C. C. Hamilton, *England, Ugliness and Noise* (Westminster: P. S. King and Son Ltd, 1930), pp. 16–17. For reaction to Cockneys in the countryside see Matless, *Landscape and Englishness*, p. 68.

54. 'Mr Punch and Ourselves', *Quiet*, December 1938, p. 14.

55. C. E. M. Joad, 'Sausages, Moral Reprobation and Noise', *Quiet*, March 1940, pp. 17–18.

56. MacKenzie, *City of Din*, p. 25.

57. A.P. Herbert, 'We're not Cranks, We're not Fusspots, We Just don't Like Noise', *Sunday Pictorial*, reprinted in *Quiet*, December 1938, p. 11.

58. Darby and Hamilton, *England*, p. 30.

59. Matless, *Landscape and Englishness*, pp. 82–3.

60. 'The Love of Noise', *Quiet*, April 1939, p. 5. *Quiet* was quoting the *Chester Chronicle* report of Elliott's visit to the Whitworth Park Hospital, Manchester. Davis reported that jazz music made the listener stronger but slower to react. Davis, *Noise*, p. 11.

61. Wellcome Archives, Lord Horder Papers, GP/31/B.2/24. Speech on work of League, undated (1939). See also Hamilton Fyfe, 'Thoughts on the Hooligan by Night', *Quiet*, April 1938, pp. 8–9 on those 'who make night hideous because they have not been taught and encouraged to produce pleasant noises and to enjoy harmony better than discord.' Fyfe notes that 'Rudeness of the kind we are considering is by no means confined to one class', for example what Arnold Bennett labelled the 'first-class passenger section of society' counted among them 'women who talk loudly in trains or on tops of omnibuses' with 'curt, assured voices'.

62. 'Progress without Noise', *Quiet*, Summer 1946 – Winter 1948, backpage.

63. A new Noise Abatement Society was launched in 1959 by John Connell, and lobbied for the Noise Abatement Act, 1960. The effectiveness of the Act depends on reliable stable records of noise.

64. 'Noises', *Wembley Observer and Gazette*, reprinted in *Quiet*, March 1941, pp. 21–2. C. H. Robinson, the aggrieved Honorary Secretary of the Noise Abatement League tried to respond that the stress of war made the League's work all the more important: 'I would ask him to try and imagine an Air Raid Warden, physically exhausted after a night of barrage and bombing, trying to recuperate his strength by much needed sleep during a peaceful spell next day and being prevented from doing so by rattling milk cans and barking dogs outside his bedroom window.'

65. 'Mr Punch and Ourselves', *Quiet*, December 1938, p. 14. *Punch* also carried a cartoon featuring four 'funereal' members of the League surrounded by 'arch-noise makers' of the street.

66. 'Editorial Notes', *Quiet*, March 1940, p. 4.

67. Horder, 'Towards National Health', *The Listener*, 7 April 1937.

68. P. Edwards, *The Closed World: Computers and the Politics of Discourse in Cold War America* (Cambridge, MA: MIT Press, 1996), especially pp. 175–207.
69. Edwards, *Closed World*, pp. 210–23.
70. Edwards, *Closed World*, p. 212.
71. A.P. Herbert, 'We're not Cranks, We're not Fusspots. We Just don't Like Noise', *Quiet*, December 1938, p. 11, reprinted from *Sunday Pictorial*.
72. R. Lygon, 'Modern Attitude to Unnecessary Noise', *Quiet*, Autumn 1936, p. 18
73. P. R. Calder, *The Birth of the Future* (London: Arthur Barker, 1934).
74. For example, E.A.A. Rowse, Principal of the Architecture Association's School of Planning and Research for National Development argued that 'the continuance [of noise] is made possible by our failure so to plan our environment, that things shall be in their right place', and he was an advocate of an 'ideal city plan' based on 'higher buildings'. E.A.A. Rowse, 'Escape from Noise Lies in Replanned Cities', *Quiet*, Spring 1937, pp. 15–17. Matless would call him a 'planner-preservationist'. Matless, *Landscape and Englishness*, p. 267.
75. Bartlett, *Noise*. Similar societies outside Britain were the Noise Abatement League (Melbourne, Australia), League for Less Noise (New York, United States), Noise Abatement Society (Auckland, New Zealand), La Société pur la Suppression du Bruit (Paris, France) and the Palestine Anti-Noise League (Tel-Aviv, Palestine).

Select Bibliography

Aarslett, H., *The Study of Language in England, 1780–1860* (Princeton, NJ: Princeton University Press, 1967).

Addams, R., 'An Account of a Peculiar Optical Phenomenon', *Philosophical Magazine,* 1834, 5: 373–4.

Agar, J., *Science and Spectacle: the Work of Jodrell Bank in Post-War British Culture* (Amsterdam: Harwood Academic Press, 1998).

Agassi, J., 'Sir John Herschel's Philosophy of Success', *Historical Studies in the Physical Sciences,* 1969, 1: 1–36.

Airy, G. B., *On the Algebraical and Numerical Theory of Errors of Observations* (London, 1861).

Airy, H., 'On a Distinct Form of Transient Hemiopsia', *Philosophical Transactions of the Royal Society of London,* 1870, 160: 247–64.

Aldini, J., *General Views on the Application of Galvanism to Medical Purposes; principally in cases of Suspended Animation* (London, 1819).

Allestree, R., *Eighteen Sermons* (London, 1669).

Althaus, J., *A Treatise on Medical Electricity, Theoretical and Practical* (London, 1859).

Altick, R., *The Shows of London* (Cambridge MA: Harvard University Press, 1978).

Armytage, W. H. G., *A Social History of Engineering* (London: Faber and Faber, 1976).

Ashworth, W. J., 'England and the Machinery of Reason 1780 to 1830', *Canadian Journal of History,* 2000, 35: 1–36.

Ashworth, W. J., 'Memory, Efficiency and Symbolic Analysis: Charles Babbage, John Herschel, and the Industrial Mind', *Isis,* 1996, 87: 629–53.

Ashworth, W. J., '"System of Terror": Samuel Bentham, Accountability and Dockyard Reform during the Napoleonic Wars', *Social History,* 1998, 1: 63–79.

Ayrton, W. E., 'Kelvin in the Sixties', *Popular Science Monthly,* 1908, 27: 259–68.

Ayrton, W. E. and J. Perry, 'Modes of Measuring the Coefficients of Self and Mutual Induction', *Journal of the Society of Telegraph Engineers and Electricians,* 1887, 16: 391; 293–6; 394.

Babbage, C., *A Word to the Wise* (London, 1833).

Babbage, C., *On the Economy of Machinery and Manufactures* (London, 1832).

Babbage, C., *Passages from the Life of a Philosopher,* ed. M. Campbell-Kelly (London: William Pickering, 1994).

Babbage, C., *The Exposition of 1851, or, Views of the Industry, the Science, and the Government, of England* (London, 1851).

Babbage, N. F., 'Autopsy Report on the Body of Charles Babbage', *The Medical Journal of Australia*, 1991, 154: 758–9.

Baldick, C., *In Frankenstein's Shadow: Myth, Monstrosity and Nineteenth-Century Writing* (Oxford: Oxford University Press, 1987).

Bann, S. (ed.), *Frankenstein, Creation and Monstrosity* (London: Reaktion Books, 1994).

Barlow, P., *A Treatise on the Manufactures and Machinery of Great Britain* (London, 1836).

Barlow, P., *The Encyclopaedia of Arts, Manufactures, and Machinery* (London, 1851).

Barr, T., *Manual of Diseases of the Ear, for the Use of Students and Practitioners of Medicine* (Glasgow, 1884).

Barr, T. and J. Stoddart Barr, *Manual of the Diseases of the Ear*, 4th edn, (Glasgow, 1909).

Barrett, W. F., 'Science and Spiritualism', *Light*, 1894, 13: 583–5.

Barrington, M. R. (ed.), *Crookes and the Spirit World* (London: Souvenir Press, 1972).

Barrow, L., *Independent Spirits: Spiritualism and the English Plebeians, 1850–1910* (London: Routledge & Kegan Paul, 1986).

Bartlett, F. C., *The Problem of Noise* (Cambridge: Cambridge University Press, 1934).

Beard, G. M., *American Nervousness: Its Causes and Consequences* (New York NY, 1881).

Beaune, J. –C., 'The Classical Age of Automata: An Impressionistic Survey from the Sixteenth to the Nineteenth Century', M. Feher, R. Naddaff and N. Tazi (eds), *Fragments for a History of the Human Body, Part One* (New York NY: Urzone Inc, 1989).

Beaver, H. (ed.), *The Science Fiction of Edgar Allan Poe* (Harmondsworth: Penguin Books, 1976).

Beer, G., *Open Fields: Science in Cultural Encounter* (Oxford: Clarendon Press, 1996).

Behagg, C., *Politics and Production in the Early Nineteenth Century* (London: Routledge, 1990).

Behagg, C., 'Secrecy, Ritual and Folk Violence: The Opacity of the Workplace in the First Half of the Nineteenth Century', R. D. Storch (ed.), *Popular Culture and Custom in Nineteenth-Century England* (London: Croom Helm, 1982).

Bell, C., *Idea of a New Anatomy of the Brain* (London, 1811).

Benschop, R. and D. Draaisma, 'In Pursuit of Precision: the Calibration of Minds and Machines in late nineteenth-century Psychology', *Annals of Science*, 2000, 57: 1–25.

Bentham, J., *Panopticon; or, The Inspection House: Containing the Idea of a new Principle of Construction Applicable to any sort of Establishment . . . in a Series of Letters Written in the Year 1787, from Crecheff in White Russia, to a Friend in England* (London, 1791).

Bentham, M. S., *The Life of Brigadier-General Sir Samuel Bentham* (London, 1862).

Bentham, S., *Services Rendered in the Civil Department of the Navy in Investigating and Bringing to Official Notice Abuses and Imperfections; and in Effecting Improvement in Relation to the System of Management* (London, 1813).

Berg, M., *The Age of Manufactures, 1700–1820: Industry, Innovation and Work in Britain*, 2nd edn (London: Faber and Faber, 1994)

Berg, M., *The Machinery Question and the Making of Political Economy 1815–1848* (Cambridge: Cambridge University Press, 1980).

Berg, M., 'Workers and Machinery in Eighteenth-Century England', J. Rule (ed.), *British Trade Unionism 1750–1850: The Formative Years* (London: Longman, 1988).

Blondel, C., 'Animal Electricity in Paris: From Initial Support to its Discredit and Eventual Rehabilitation', M. Bresadola and G. Pancaldi (eds), *Luigi Galvani International Workshop. Proceedings* (Bologna. Universita di Bologna, 1999).

Bloor, D., *Wittgenstein: A Social Theory of Knowledge* (London: Macmillan, 1983).

Bosher, R., *The Making of the Restoration Settlement* (London: Dacre Press, 1951).

Boyle, R., *The Early Essays and Ethics of Robert Boyle*, ed. J. Harwood, (Carbondale IL: Southern Illinois University Press, 1991).

Bradley, M., 'Engineers as Military Spies? French Engineers come to Britain, 1780–1790', *Annals of Science*, 1992, 49: 137–62.

Bradley, M. and F. Perrin, 'Charles Dupin's Study Visits to the British Isles, 1816–1824', *Technology and Culture*, 1991, 32: 47–68.

Brandon, R., *The Spiritualists: The Passion for the Occult in the Nineteenth and Twentieth Centuries* (London: Weidenfeld and Nicolson, 1983).

Braverman, H., *Labor and Monopoly Capital: The Degradation of Work in the Twentieth Century* (New York NY: Monthly Review Press, 1974).

Bresadola, M., 'Exploring Galvani's Room for Experiments', M. Bresadola and G. Pancaldi (eds), *Luigi Galvani International Workshop: Proceedings* (Bologna: Universita di Bologna, 1999).

Brewster, D., *Letters on Natural Magic, Addressed to Sir Walter Scott, Bart.* (London, 1832).

Briggs, A., *Victorian Things* (Harmondsworth: Penguin Books, 1990).

Brown, H. P., *The Comparative Danger to Life of Alternating and Continuous Electrical Currents* (New York NY, 1889).

Brown, T., *Lectures on the Philosophy of the Human Mind* (Hallowell, 1850).

Bud, R. and D.Warner (eds), *Instruments of Science* (New York NY: Garland Press, 1998).

Burke, J. G., 'Bursting Boilers and the Federal Power', M. Kranzberg and W. H. Davenport (eds), *Technology and Culture: An Anthology* (New York NY: New American Library, 1972).

[Burns, J.], 'A Scientific Séance – The Electrical Test for Mediumship', *Medium and Daybreak,* 1875, 6: 161–3.

Burns, J., 'How to Investigate Spiritual Phenomena', *Report on Spiritualism of the Committee of the London Dialectical Society* (London, 1873).

Buttmann, G., *The Shadow of the Telescope: A Biography of John Herschel*, trans. B. E. J. Pagel, (New York NY: Charles Scribner's Sons, 1970).

Bynum, W., 'The Anatomical Method, Natural Theology, and the Functions of the Brain' *Isis*, 1973, 64: 445–68.

Byrne, R., *Prisons and Punishments of London* (London: Grafton, 1992).

Calder, P. R., *The Birth of the Future* (London: Arthur Barker, 1934).

Campbell, L. and W. Garnett, *Life of James Clerk Maxwell* (London, 1882).

Carbutt, E., 'An Essay on the Signs of Ideas; or, the Means of Conveying to others a Knowledge of our Ideas', *Memoirs and Proceedings of the Manchester Literary and Philosophical Society*, 1819, 3: 241–70.

Carnot, L., *Essai sur les Machines en General*, 2nd edn (Dijon, 1786).

Carpenter, W. B., 'On the Influence of Suggestion in Modifying and Directing Muscular Movement, Independently of Volition [1852]', *Proceedings of the Royal Institution of Great Britain*, 1851–54, 1: 147–53.

Carpenter, W. B., *Principles of Mental Physiology; with their Applications to the Training and Discipline of the Mind, and the Study of its Morbid Conditions*, 4th edn (New York NY, 1877).

[Carpenter, W. B.], 'Spiritualism and its Latest Converts', *Quarterly Review*, 1871, 131: 301–53.

Carroll, B. E., *Spiritualism in Antebellum America* (Bloomington IN: Indiana University Press, 1997).

Castle, T., 'Phantasmagoria: Spectral Technology and the Metaphorics of Modern Reverie', *Critical Inquiry*, 1988, 15: 26–61.

Chapuis, A., and E. Droz, *Automata: A Historical and Technological Study* (Neuchâtel: Éditions du Griffon, 1958).

Charlesworth, A., 'From the Moral Economy of Devon to the Political Economy of Manchester, 1790–1812', *Social History*, 1993, 18: 205–17.

Charleton, W., *The Natural History of the Passions* (London, 1674).

Charleton, W., *Two Discourses. I. Concerning the Different Wits of Man: II. Concerning the Mysteries of the Vintners* (London, 1669).

Christie, I. R., *The Benthams in Russia, 1780–1791* (Oxford: Oxford University Press, 1993).

Christie, J. R. R., 'Laputa Revisited', J. R. R. Christie and S. Shuttleworth (eds), *Nature Transfigured: Science and Literature, 1700–1900* (Manchester: Manchester University Press, 1989).

Claeys, G., *Machinery, Money and the Millennium: From Moral Economy to Socialism, 1815–60* (Oxford: Oxford University Press, 1987).

Clarke, E. and L. S. Jacyna, *Nineteenth-Century Origins of Neuroscientific Concepts* (Berkeley and Los Angeles CA: University of California Press, 1987).

Clerke, A. M., *Modern Cosmogonies* (London, 1905).

Coats, A. W., 'Changing Attitudes to Labour in the Mid-Eighteenth Century', *Economic History Review*, 1958, 11: 35–51.

Cohen Rosenfield, L., *From Beast-Machine to Man-Machine: Animal Soul in French Letters from Descartes to La Mettrie* (New York NY: Octagon Books, 1968).

Collins, H., *Artificial Experts: Social Knowledge and Intelligent Machines* (Cambridge MA: MIT Press, 1990).

Collins, H., *Changing Order: Replication and Induction in Scientific Practice* (London: Sage Publications, 1985).

Collins, J., 'The Restoration Bishops and the Royal Supremacy' *Church History*, 1999, 68: 549–80.

Colvin, C. (ed.), *Maria Edgeworth: Letters from England 1813–1844* (Oxford: Oxford University Press, 1971).

Conan Doyle, A., 'The Los Amigos Fiasco', *Round the Red Lamp, being Facts and Fancies of Medical Life* (London, 1894).

Connor, R. D., *The Weights and Measures of England* (London: HMSO, 1987).

Connor, S., *Dumbstruck: A Cultural History of Ventriloquism* (Oxford: Oxford University Press, 2000).

Cooke, W. F., *Extracts from the Private Letters of the Late Sir William Fothergill Cooke, 1836–39, relating to the Invention and Development of the Electric Telegraph* (London, 1895).

Coon, D. J., 'Standardising the Subject: Experimental Psychologists, Introspection, and the Quest for a Technoscientific Ideal', *Technology and Culture*, 1993: 34: 753–83.

Cooper, C., 'The Portsmouth System of Manufacture', *Technology and Culture*, 1984, 25: 182–225.

Cossons, N., *The BP Book of Industrial Archaeology* (Newton Abbot: David and Charles, 1975).

Cranmore, R. T., 'On some Phænomena of Defective Vision', *Philosophical Magazine*, 1850, 36: 485–6.

Crary, J., *Suspensions of Perception: Attention, Spectacle and Modern Culture* (Cambridge MA: MIT Press, 1999).

Crookes, W., 'A Scientific Examination of Mrs. Fay's Mediumship', *Spiritualist*, 1875, 6: 126–8.

Crookes, W., 'Experimental Investigation of a New Force', *Quarterly Journal of Science*, 1871, 1: 339–49.

Crookes, W., 'Notes of an Enquiry in to the Phenomena Called Spiritual, During the Years 1870–73', *Quarterly Journal of Science*, 1874, 3: 77–97.

Crookes, W., 'On Repulsion resulting from Radiation – Part II', *Philosophical Transactions of the Royal Society of London*, 1875, 165: 519–47.

Crookes, W., *Psychic Force and Modern Spiritualism: A Reply to the 'Quarterly Review' and Other Critics* (London, 1871).

Crookes, W., 'Spiritualism Viewed by the Light of Modern Science', *Quarterly Journal of Science*, 1870, 7: 316–21.

Crookes, W., 'The Last of Katie King: The Photographing of Katie King by the Aid of the Electric Light', *Spiritualist*, 1874, 4: 270–1.

Crosland, N., *Apparitions: An Essay, Explanatory of Old Facts and a New Theory to which is Added Sketches and Adventures* (London, 1873).

Cullen, W., *Institutions of Medicine; Part 1, Physiology; for the Use of the Students in the University of Edinburgh*, 3rd edn (Edinburgh, 1785).

Cunningham, A. and N. Jardine (eds), *Romanticism and the Sciences* (Cambridge: Cambridge University Press, 1990).

Danziger, K., *Constructing the Subject: Historical Origins of Psychological Research* (Cambridge: Cambridge University Press, 1990).

Darby, A. and C. C. Hamilton, *England, Ugliness and Noise* (Westminster: P. S. King and Son Ltd, 1930).

Darnton, R., 'First Steps to a History of Reading', *The Kiss of Lamourette: Reflections on Cultural History* (New York NY: Norton, 1990).

Darnton, R., 'Philosophers Trim the Tree of Knowledge: The Epistemological Strategy of the *Encyclopédie*', *The Great Cat Massacre and other Episodes in French Cultural History* (Harmondsworth: Penguin Books, 1984).

Daston, L., 'British Responses to Psycho-physiology, 1860–1900', *Isis*, 1978, 69: 192–208.

Daston, L., 'Objectivity and the Escape from Perspective', *Social Studies of Science,* 1992, 22: 597–618.

Daston, L. and P. Galison, 'The Image of Objectivity', *Representations*, 1992, 90: 81–128.

Daunton, M. J., *Progress and Poverty: An Economic and Social History of Britain 1700–1850* (Oxford: Oxford University Press, 1995).

Davies, C. M., *Mystic London; Or, Phases of Occult Life in the Metropolis* (London, 1875).

Davis, A. H., *Noise* (London: Watts and Co., 1937).

Davis, A. H. and G. W. C. Kaye, *The Acoustics of Buildings* (London: G. Bell & Sons, 1927).

de Chadarevian, S., 'Graphical Method and Discipline: Self-Recording Instruments in Nineteenth-Century Physiology', *Studies in History and Philosophy of Science*, 1993, 24: 267–91.

de Vries, L., *Victorian Advertisements* (London: John Murray, 1968).

de Watteville, A., *Practical Introduction to Medical Electricity* (London, 1884).

Dear, P., 'A Mechanical Microcosm: Bodily Passions, Good Manners, and Cartesian Mechanism', C. Lawrence and S. Shapin (ed.), *Science Incarnate: Historical Embodiments of Natural Knowledge* (Chicago: University of Chicago Press, 1998).

Dekosky, R. K., 'William Crookes and the Quest for Absolute Vacuum in the 1870s', *Annals of Science*, 1983, 40: 1–18.

DeLacy, M. E., 'Grinding Men Good? Lancashire's Prisons at Mid-Century', V. Bailey (ed.), *Policing and Punishment in Nineteenth Century Britain* (London: Croom Helm, 1981).

Deprez, M. and J. D'Arsonval, 'Galvanomètre Aperiodique', *Comtes Rendus*, 1882, 94: 1347–50.

Descartes, R., *The Philosophical Writings of Rene Descartes*, trans. J. Cottingham, R. Stoothoff and D. Murdoch, (Cambridge: Cambridge University Press, 1985).

Desmond, A., *The Politics of Evolution* (Chicago IL: University of Chicago Press, 1989).

Dickinson, H. W., *Matthew Boulton*, (Cambridge: Cambridge University Press, 1936).

Dircks, H., *Scientific Studies: Or Practical in Contrast with Chimerical Pursuits; Exemplified in Two Popular Lectures* (London, 1869).

Dircks, H., *The Ghost! As Produced in the Spectre Drama, Popularly Illustrating the Marvellous Optical Illusions Obtained by the Apparatus Called the Dircksian Phantasmagoria: Being a Full Account of its History, Construction, and Various Adaptations* (London, 1863).

Dodd, G., *Days at the Factories and the Manufactory Industry of Great Britain Described* (London, 1843).

Dörries, M, 'Balances, Spectroscopes, and the Reflexive Nature of Experiment', *Studies in History and Philosophy of Science*, 1994, 25: 1–36.

Douglas, M., *Natural Symbols: Explorations in Cosmology* (London: Cresset Press, 1970).

Driver, F., 'Bodies in Space: Foucault's Account of Disciplinary Power', C. Jones and R. Porter (eds), *Reassessing Foucault: Power, Medicine and the Body* (London: Routledge, 1994).

Duhem, P, *La Theorie Physique: son Objet – sa Structure* (Paris, 1906).

Duhem, P., 'Some Reflections on the Subject of Experimental Physics', Roger Ariew and Peter Barker, (trans. and ed.) *Pierre Duhem: Essays in the History and Philosophy of Science* (Indianapolis IN: Hackett, 1996).

Duhem, P., *The Aim and Structure of Physical Theory*, trans. P. Wiener (Princeton NJ: Princeton University Press, 1954).

Dupin, C., *Two Excursions to the Ports of England, Scotland, and Ireland, in 1816, 1817, and 1818; with a description of the Breakwater at Plymouth, and of the Caledonian Canal* (London, 1819).

Eco, U., *The Search for the Perfect Language* (Oxford: Blackwell, 1995).

Edgcumbe, K. and F. Punga, 'Direct-reading Measuring Instruments for Switch-board Use', *Journal of the IEE*, 1904, 33: 620–93.

Edwards, P., *The Closed World: Computers and the Politics of Discourse in Cold War America* (Cambridge MA: MIT Press, 1996).

Eksteins, M., *Rites of Spring: the Great War and the Birth of the Modern Age* (New York NY: Anchor Books, 1989).

'Electrical Tests with Miss Cook when Entranced', *Spiritual Magazine*, 1874, 9 (New Series): 161–8.

Elias, N., *The Civilizing Process*, trans. E. Jephcott (Oxford: Blackwells Publishers, 1986).

Elliot, J., *Elements of the Branches of Natural Philosophy Connected with Medicine* (London, 1782).

Erb, W., *Handbook of Electro-therapeutics*, trans. L. Putzel (New York NY, 1883).

Fahie, J. J., *A History of Electric Telegraphy, to the Year 1837* (London, 1884).

Farrar, W. V., K. Farrar, and E. L. Scott, 'The Henrys of Manchester, part 2; Thomas Henry's sons: Thomas, Peter, and William', *Ambix*, 1974, 21: 179–207.

Featherstone, M., 'The Body in Consumer Culture', M. Featherstone, M. Hepworth and B. S. Turner (eds), *The Body: Social Process and Cultural Theory* (London: Sage Publications, 1991).

Ferguson, E. S., 'The Measurement of the "Man-Day"', *Scientific American*, October 1971.

Figlio, K. M., 'Theories of Perception and the Physiology of Mind in the late Eighteenth Century', *History of Science*, 1975, 13: 178.

Fleischman, R. and L. D.Parker, *What is Past is Prologue: Cost Accounting in the British Industrial Revolution, 1760–1850* (New York NY: Garland Press, 1997).

Fleischman, R. and T. Tyson, 'Cost Accounting During the Industrial Revolution: the Present State of Historical Knowledge', *Economic History Review*, 1993, 46: 503–17.

Flynn, C. H., 'Running out of Matter: the Body Exercised in Eighteenth-century Fiction', G. S. Rousseau and R. Porter (eds), *The Languages of Psyche: Mind and Body in Enlightenment Thought* (Berkeley and Los Angeles CA: University of California Press, 1987).

Foucault, M., *Discipline and Punish* (Harmondsworth: Penguin Books, 1977).

Frank Jr., R., 'Thomas Willis and His Circle: Brain and Mind in 17th-Century Medicine', G. S. Rousseau (ed.), *Languages of Psyche: Mind and Body in*

Enlightenment Thought (Berkeley and Los Angeles CA: University of California Press, 1990).

Freeth, F. A., 'James Swinburne, 1858–1958', *Biographical Memoirs of the Royal Society*, 1959, 5: 253–64.

French, R., *Antivivisection and Medical Science in Victorian Society* (Princeton NJ: Princeton University Press, 1975).

French, R. K., *Robert Whytt, the Soul, and Medicine* (London: Wellcome Institute, 1969).

Frost, T., *The Lives of the Conjurors* (London, 1876).

Galton, F., *Inquiries into Human Faculty and Its Development*, 2nd edn (London, 1892).

Galton, F., *Memories of My Life* (London, 1909).

Gamble, J., *An Essay on the Different Modes of Communication with Signals; containing an History of the Progressive Improvements in this Art, from the First Account of Beacons to the Most Approved Methods of Telegraphic Correspondence* (London, 1797).

Gatrell, V. A. C., *The Hanging Tree: Execution and the English People 1770–1868* (Oxford: Oxford University Press, 1996).

Gauld, A., *The Founders of Psychical Research* (New York NY: Schocken Books, 1968).

Gelbart, N., 'The Intellectual Development of Walter Charleton', *Ambix*, 1971, 18: 149–68.

Gillmor, C. S., *Coulomb and the Evolution of Physics and Engineering in Eighteenth Century France* (Princeton NJ: Princeton University Press, 1971).

Goethe, J. W. von, *Theory of Colours*, trans. Charles Eastlake, (Cambridge MA: MIT Press, 1970), first published 1840.

Gooday, G., 'Instrument as Embodied Theory', A Hessenbruch (ed.) *Reader's Guide to the History of Science*, (London: Fitzroy Dearborn, 2000).

Gooday, G., 'Instrumentation and Interpretation: Managing and Representing the Working Environments of Victorian Experimental Science', B. Lightman (ed.), *Victorian Science in Context* (Chicago IL: University of Chicago Press, 1997).

Gooday, G, '"Nature" in the Laboratory: Domestication and Discipline with the Microscope in Victorian Life Science', *British Journal for the History of Science*, 1991, 24: 307–41.

Gooday, G., 'Precision Measurement and the Genesis of Physics Teaching Laboratories in Victorian Britain', *British Journal for the History of Science*, 1990, 23: 23–51.

Gooday, G., 'Teaching Telegraphy and Electrotechnics in the Physics Laboratory: William Ayrton and the Creation of an Academic Space for Electrical Engineering, 1873–84', *History of Technology*, 1991, 13: 73–111.

Gooday, G., 'The Morals of Energy Metering: Constructing and Deconstructing the Precision of the Electrical Engineer's Ammeter and Voltmeter', M. N. Wise (ed.) *The Values of Precision* (Princeton NJ: Princeton University Press, 1995).

Gooday, G., *The Morals of Measurement* (forthcoming, Cambridge University Press).

Gooding, D., 'How do Scientists reach Agreement about Novel Observations?' *Studies in History and Philosophy of Science*, 1986, 17: 205–30.

Gordon, J. E. H., *A Practical Treatise on Electrical Lighting* (London, 1884).

Gordon, J. E. H., *Practical Treatise on Electricity and Magnetism* (London, 1880).

Gordon, Mrs J. E. H., *Decorative Electricity* (London, 1891).

Gould, P., 'Women and the Culture of University Physics in late Nineteenth Century Cambridge', *British Journal for the History of Science*, 1997, 30: 127–49.

Grattan-Guinness, I., 'Work for the Workers: Advances in Engineering Mechnaics and Instruction in France, 1800–1830', *Annals of Science*, 1984, 41: 1–34.

Green, I. M., *The Re-establishment of the Church of England, 1660–1663* (Oxford: Oxford University Press, 1978).

Green Musselman, E., 'Persistence of Sight: Problems of Idiosyncratic Vision and Knowledge in British Natural Philosophy, 1780'1860', unpublished PhD dissertation, Indiana University, 1999.

Gregory, O., *A Treatise of Mechanics, Theoretical, Practical, and Descriptive*, three vols, (London, 1806).

Gregory, O., *Mathematics for Practical Men: Being a Common-Place Book of Principles, Theorems, Rules and Tables, in Various Departments of Pure and Mixed Mathematics, with their Most Useful applications; Especially to the Pursuits of Surveyors, Architects, Mechanics, and Civil Engineers* (London, 1825).

Griffin, D., 'On an Unusual Affection of the Eye, in which Three Images were Produced', *Philosophical Magazine*, 1835, 6: 281–4.

Hahn, R., 'Laplace and the Vanishing Role of God in the Physical Universe', H. Woolf (ed.), *Analytic Spirit: Essays in the History of Science in Honor of Henry Guerlac* (Ithaca NY: Cornell University Press, 1981).

Haley, B., *The Healthy Body and Victorian Culture* (Cambridge MA: Harvard University Press, 1978).

Hall, T. H., *The Spiritualists: The Story of Florence Cook and William Crookes* (London: Gerald Duckworth and Co., 1962).

Hamilton, W. (ed.), *Collected Works of Dugald Stewart* (Edinburgh, 1877).

Hankins, T. L. and R. J. Silverman, *Instruments and the Imagination* (Princeton NJ: Princeton University Press, 1995).

Hanson, N. R., *Patterns of Discovery: an Inquiry into the Conceptual Foundations of Science* (Cambridge: Cambridge University Press, 1961).

Hardinge, E., 'Rules to be Observed for the Spirit Circle', *Human Nature*, 1868, 2: 49–52.

Hare, R., *Experimental Investigation of the Spirit Manifestations, Demonstrating the Existence of Spirits and their Communion with Mortals* (New York NY, 1855).

Harley, D., 'James Hart of Northampton and the Calvinist Critique of Priest-physicians: An Unpublished Polemic of the early 1620s', *Medical History*, 1998, 42: 362–86.

Harman, P. (ed.), *The Scientific Letters and Papers of James Clerk Maxwell* (Cambridge: Cambridge University Press, 1995).

Harris, J. R., *Industrial Espionage and Technological Transfer: Britain and France in the Eighteenth Century* (Aldershot: Ashgate Press, 1998).

Harris, J. R., 'Movements of Technology Between Britain and Europe in the Eighteenth Century', D. J. Jeremy (ed.), *International Technology Transfer: Europe, Japan and the USA, 1700–1914* (Aldershot: Elgar Press, 1991).

Harris, N., *Humbug: The Art of P. T. Barnum* (Boston MA: Little, Brown, 1973).

Harrison, P., 'Reading the Passions: the Fall, the Passions, and Dominion over Nature', S. Gaukroger (ed.), *The Soft Underbelly of Reason: The Passions in the Seventeenth Century* (London: Routledge, 1998).

Harrison, W. H., 'New Discoveries in Spiritualism', *Spiritualist*, 1879, 13: 186–91.

[Harrison, W. H.], 'Spirit Forms', *Spiritualist*, 1873, 3: 451–4.

[Harrison, W. H.], 'Stage Imitations of Spiritual Phenomena', *Spiritualist*, 1873, 3: 136–9.

Harrison, W. H., 'Weighing a Medium During the Production of Spiritual Manifestations', *Spiritualist*, 1878, 11: 210–16.

Hartley, D., *Observations on Man, his Frame, his Duty, and his Expectations* (London, 1749).

Harvey, D., *The Condition of Postmodernity: an Enquiry into the Origins of Cultural Change* (Oxford: Oxford University Press, 1989).

Harvey, D., *The Urban Experience* (Oxford: Oxford University Press, 1989).

Hase, W. M., *Description of the Patent Improved Tread Mill, for the Employment of Prisoners. Also of the Patent Portable Crank Machine, for Producing Labour of any Degree of Severity, In Solitary Confinement, For One, Two, or any Number of Prisoners: To Which is Added, The Description of the Gyrometer or Calculator, By R.B. Bate* (Norwich, 1824).

Heelan, P., *Space-perception and the Philosophy of Science* (Berkeley and Los Angeles CA: University of California Press, 1983).

Heidegger, M., *The Question Concerning Technology* (London: HarperCollins, 1977).

Heilbron, J., *Electricity in the Seventeenth and Eighteenth Centuries: A Study of Early Modern Physics* (Berkeley and Los Angeles CA: University of California Press, 1979).

Henriques, U., 'The Rise and Decline of the Separate System of Prison Discipline', *Past and Present*, 1972, 54: 61–93.

Henry, J., 'Occult Qualities and the Experimental Philosophy: Active Principles in Pre-Newtonian Matter Theory', *History of Science*, 1986, 24: 335–81.

Herschel, J., *A Preliminary Discourse on the Study of Natural Philosophy*, ed. J. Secord (Chicago IL: University of Chicago Press, 1987).

Herschel, J., *Familiar Lectures on Scientific Subjects* (London, 1867).

[Herschel, J.], 'Whewell on the Inductive Sciences', *Quarterly Review,* 1841, 68: 182.

Herschel, J. and C. Babbage, *Memoirs of the Analytical Society* (Cambridge, 1813).

Herschel, J. and J. South, 'Observations of the Apparent Distances and Positions of 380 Double and Triple Stars', *Philosophical Transactions of the Royal Society of London*, 1824, 114: 15.

Hessenbruch, A., 'Science as Public Sphere: X-Rays Between Spiritualism and Physics', C. Goschler (ed.), *Wissenschaft und Öffentlichkeit in Berlin, 1870– 1930* (Stuttgart: Franz Steiner, 2001).

Heyd, M., *'Be Sober and Reasonable': The Critique of Enthusiasm in the Seventeenth and Early Eighteenth Centuries* (Leiden: Brill, 1995).

Hills, R. L., *Power From Steam: A History of the Stationary Steam Engine* (Cambridge: Cambridge University Press, 1993).

Hilton, B., *The Age of Atonement. The Influence of Evangelicalism on Social and Economic Thought 1785–1865* (Oxford: Oxford University Press, 1987).

Hippisley, J. C., *Prison Labour: Correspondence and Communications Addressed to HM's Principal Secretary of State for the Home Department, Concerning the Introduction of Tread-Mills into Prisons* (London, 1823).

Hoagland, J. H., 'Charles Babbage – His Life and Works in the Historical Evolution of Management Concepts', unpublished PhD dissertation, Ohio University, 1954.

Hoff, H. E., 'Galvani and the Pre-Galvanian Electrophysiologists', *Annals of Science*, 1936, 1: 157–72.

Holland, H., *Chapters on Mental Physiology* (London, 1852).

Holmes, T. W., *The Semaphore: The Story of the Admiralty-to-Portsmouth Shutter Telegraph and Semaphore Lines 1796 to 1847* (Ilfracombe: Stockwell, 1983).

Home, R., 'Electricity and the Nervous Fluid', *Journal of the History of Biology*, 1970, 3: 235–51.

Hopwood, A. G., 'The Archaeology of Accounting Systems', *Accounting, Organisations and Society*, 1987, 12: 207–34.

Horn, J. and M. C. Jacob, 'Jean-Antoine Chaptal and the Cultural Roots of French Industrialization', *Technology and Culture*, 1998, 39: 671–98.

Horsley, Sir V., 'Description of the Brain of Mr Charles Babbage, FRS', *Philosophical Transactions of the Royal Society of London*, Series B, 1908, 200: 117–31.

Huggins, M. L. M., *Agnes Mary Clerke and Ellen Mary Clerke: An Appreciation* (private publication, 1907).

Hughes, H. M., 'Digest of One Hundred Cases of Chorea treated in the Hospital', *Guy's Hospital Reports*, 1846, 4: 360–94.

Hughes, J. T., *Thomas Willis, 1621–1675: His Life and Work* (London: Royal Society of Medicine, 1991).

Hughes, T. P., *Networks of Power: Electrification in Western Society* (Baltimore MD: Johns Hopkins University Press, 1983).

Hunt, B., 'Scientists, Engineers, and Wildman Whitehouse: Measurement and Credibility in early Cable Telegraphy', *British Journal for the History of Science*, 1996, 29: 155–69.

Hunt, B. J., 'The Ohm is where the Art is: British Telegraph Engineers and the Development of Electrical Standards', *Osiris*, 1994, 9: 48–63.

Hunter, L. C., *A History of Industrial Power in the United States 1780–1930*, three vols, (Charlottesville VA: University Press of Virginia 1985).

Hutton, R., *The Restoration: A Political and Religious History of England and Wales, 1658–1667* (Oxford: Oxford University Press, 1985).

Huxley, T. H., 'A Liberal Education, and Where to Find It', *Science and Education*, (New York NY, 1896).

Hyman, A., *Charles Babbage: Pioneer of the Computer* (Princeton, NJ: Princeton University Press, 1983).

Ignatieff, M., *A Just Measure of Pain: The Penitentiary in the Industrial Revolution 1750–1850* (Harmondsworth: Penguin Books, 1978).

Ihde, D., *Technics and Praxis: A Philosophy of Technology* (Dodrecht: Reidel, 1979).

Ihde, D., 'This is Not a "Text," or, do we "Read" Images', *Expanding Hermeneutics: Visualism in Science* (Evanston IL: Northwestern University Press, 1998).

Iliffe, R., 'Isaac Newton: Lucatello Professor of Mathematics', C. Lawrence and S. Shapin (ed.), *Science Incarnate: Historical Embodiments of Natural Knowledge* (Chicago IL: University of Chicago Press, 1998).

Iliffe, R., '"That Puzleing Problem": Isaac Newton and the Political Philosophy of Self' *Medical History*, 1995, 39: 433–58.

Inglis, B., *Science and Parascience: A History of the Paranormal, 1914–39* (London: Hodder & Stoughton, 1984).

Jackson, S., 'The Use of the Passions in Psychological Healing', *Journal of the History of Medicine and Allied Sciences*, 1990, 45: 150–75.

Jacob, M. C., *Scientific Culture and the Making of the Industrial West* (Oxford: Oxford University Press, 1997).

James, S., *Passion and Action: The Emotions in Seventeenth-century Philosophy* (Oxford: Oxford University Press, 1997).

James, S., 'Reason, the Passions and the Good Life', D. Garber and M. Ayers (eds), *The Cambridge History of Seventeenth-Century Philosophy* (Cambridge: Cambridge University Press, 1998).

James, S., 'The Passions in Metaphysics and the Theory of Action', D. Garber and M. Ayers (eds), *The Cambridge History of Seventeenth-Century Philosophy*, (Cambridge: Cambridge University Press, 1998).

Jenkins, L., *The Life of Francis Mansell, D.D. Principal of Jesus College, in Oxford* (London, 1854).

Jenness, G. A., *Maskelyne and Cooke, Egyptian Hall, London, 1873–1904* (Enfield: G. A. Jenness, 1967).

Johns, A., 'The Physiology of Reading and the Anatomy of Enthusiasm', O. P. Grell and A. Cunningham (eds), *Religio Medici: Medicine and Religion in Seventeenth-Century England* (Aldershot: Scolar Press, 1996)

Josephson, M., *Edison* (London: Eyre & Spottiswoode, 1961).

Keegan, J., *The Face of Battle* (London: Pimlico, 1991).

Kempe, H. R., *Handbook of Electrical Testing*, 2nd edn (London, 1881).

Kempe, H. R., 'Resistances and their Measurement. The Thomson Galvanometer', *The Telegraphic Journal and Electrical Review*, 1873–74, 2: 41–4.

Kieve, J., *The Electric Telegraph: A Social and Cultural History* (Plymouth: David and Charles, 1973).

Kipnis, N., 'Galvani and the Debate on Animal Electricity', *Annals of Science*, 1987, 44: 107–42.

Knox, K. C., 'Dephlogisticating the Bible: Natural Philosophy and Religious Controversy in late Georgian Cambridge', *History of Science*, 1996, 34: 167–200.

Kohlrausch, F., (trans. T. H. Waller and H. R. Proctor), *An Introduction to Physical Measurements*, 3rd edn (from 7th German edition) (London, 1894).

Kremer, R. L., *The Thermodynamics of Life and Experimental Physiology, 1770–1880* (New York NY: Garland Press, 1990).

Lawrence, C., 'Incommunicable Knowledge: Science, Technology and the Clinical Art in Britain 1850–1914', *Journal of Contemporary History*, 1985, 20: 503–20.

Lawrence, C., 'The Nervous System and Society in the Scottish Enlightenment', B. Barnes and S. Shapin (eds), *Natural Order: Historical Studies of Scientific Culture* (London: Sage, 1979).

Lawrence, C. and S. Shapin (eds), *Science Incarnate: Historical Embodiments of Natural Knowledge* (Chicago IL: University of Chicago Press, 1998).

Lenoir, T., 'Helmholtz and the Materialities of Communication', *Osiris*, 1994, 9: 185–207.

Lenoir, T., 'Models and Instruments in the Development of Electrophysiology, 1845–1912', *Historical Studies in the Physical Sciences*, 1986, 17: 1–54.

Lenoir, T., *The Strategy of Life: Teleology and Mechanics in Nineteenth Century German Biology* (Dordrecht: Reidel, 1982).

Lescaraboura, A. C., 'Edison's Views on Life and Death: An Interview with the Famous Inventor Regarding His Attempt to Communicate with the Next World', *Scientific American*, 1920, 123: 446; 458–60.

Levi, A., *French Moralists* (Oxford: Clarendon Press, 1964).

Littleton, A. C., *Accounting Evolution to 1900* (New York NY: Institute Publishing Co., 1966).

Locke, J., *An Essay Concerning Human Understanding*, ed. Peter H. Nidditch, (Oxford: Oxford University Press, 1975).

Loeb, L., 'Consumerism and Commercial Electrotherapy: The Medical Battery Company in Nineteenth-century London', *Journal of Victorian Culture*, 1999, 4: 252 75.

MacDonald, C. F., *The Infliction of the Death Penalty by Means of Electricity, Being a Report of Seven Cases* (New York NY, 1892).

Maceroni, F., 'An Account of some Remarkable Electrical Phenomena seen in the Mediterranean, with some Physiological Deductions', *Mechanics' Magazine*, 1831, 15: 93–6; 98–100.

MacKenzie, D., 'Marx and the Machine', *History of Technology*, 1984, 25: 473–502.

MacKenzie, D., *The City of Din: a Tirade against Noise* (London: Adlard and Son, Bartholomew Press, 1916).

Mackintosh, T. S., *The Electrical Theory of the Universe* (Manchester, 1838).

Martensen, R., "Habit of Reason': Anatomy and Anglicanism in Restoration England' *Bulletin of the History of Medicine*, 1992, 66: 511–35.

Martensen, R., 'The Circles of Willis: Physiology, Culture, and the Formation of the "Neurocentric" Body in England, 1640–1690', unpublished PhD dissertation, University of California, 1993.

Marvin, C., *When Old Technologies were New* (Oxford: Oxford University Press, 1988).

Marx, K., *Capital: A Critique of Political Economy*, vol. 1, (Harmondsworth: Penguin Books, 1990).

Maskelyne, N., *Modern Spiritualism: A Short Account of its Rise and Progress, with Exposures of So-called Media* (London, 1876).

Matless, D., *Landscape and Englishness* (London: Reaktion Books, 1998).

Maxwell, J. C., *Treatise on Electricity and Magnetism*, 3rd edn (Oxford, 1891).

Mayr, O., *Authority, Liberty and Automatic Machinery in Early Modern Europe* (Baltimore MD: Johns Hopkins University Press, 1986).

McConnell, A., *R. B. Bate of the Poultry 1782–1847: The Life and Times of a Scientific Instrument Maker* (London: Scientific Instrument Makers Society, 1993).

McKendrick, N., 'Josiah Wedgwood and Cost Accounting in the Industrial Revolution', *Journal of Economic History*, 1973, 45–67.

McLachlan, N. W., *Noise: a Comprehensive Survey from Every Point of View* (London: Oxford University Press, 1935).

McLuhan, M., *Understanding Media: The Extensions of Man* (New York NY: McGraw-Hill, 1964).

Medhurst, R. G. and K. M. Goldney, 'William Crookes and the Physical Phenomena of Mediumship', *Proceedings of the Society for Psychical Research*, 1964, 54: 25–156.

Meyer, A. and R. Hierons, 'On Thomas Willis's Concepts of Neurophysiology: Part I', *Medical History*, 1965, 9: 1–15.

Mindell, D., *War, Technology and Experience aboard the USS Monitor* (Baltimore MD: Johns Hopkins University Press, 2000).

Morrell, J and A. Thackray, *Gentlemen of Science: Early Years of the British Association for the Advancement of Science* (Oxford: Oxford University Press, 1981).

Morton, A. Q., 'Concepts of Power: Natural Philosophy and the Uses of Machines in Mid-Eighteenth-Century London', *British Journal for the History of Science*, 1995, 28: 63–78.

Morus, I. R., 'Correlation and Control: William Robert Grove and the Construction of a new Philosophy of Scientific Reform', *Studies in History and Philosophy of Science*, 1991, 22: 589–621.

Morus, I. R., 'Currents from the Underworld: Electricity and the Technology of Display in early Victorian England', *Isis*, 1993, 84: 50–69.

Morus, I. R., 'Different Experimental Lives: Michael Faraday and William Sturgeon', *History of Science*, 1992, 30: 1–28.

Morus, I. R., *Frankenstein's Children: Electricity, Exhibition and Experiment in Early Nineteenth-Century London* (Princeton NJ: Princeton University Press, 1998).

Morus, I. R., 'Manufacturing Nature: Science, Technology and Victorian Consumer Culture', *British Journal of the History of Science*, 1996, 29: 403–34.

Morus, I. R., 'Marketing the Machine: The Construction of Electrotherapeutics as Viable Medicine in early Victorian England', *Medical History*, 1992, 36: 34–52.

Morus, I. R., 'The Electric Ariel: Telegraphy and Commercial Culture in Victorian England', *Victorian Studies*, 1996, 39: 339–78.

Morus, I. R., 'The Measure of Man: Technologizing the Victorian Body', *History of Science*, 1999, 37: 249–82.

Morus, I. R., '"The Nervous System of Britain": Space, Time, and the Electric Telegraph in the Victorian Age', *British Journal for the History of Science*, 2000, 33: 455–75.

Müller, J., *Handbuch der Physiologie des Menschen für Vorlesungen*, two vols, (Koblenz, 1837–40).

Myers, F. W. H., *Human Personality and its Survival of Bodily Death*, 2 vols, (London, 1903).

Niebyl, P., 'The Non-Naturals', *Bulletin of the History of Medicine*, 1971, 45: 486–92.

Noakes, R. J., '"Cranks and Visionaries": Science, Spiritualism, and Transgression in Victorian Britain', unpublished PhD dissertation, University of Cambridge, 1998.

Noakes, R. J., 'Telegraphy is an Occult Art: Cromwell Fleetwood Varley and the Diffusion of Electricity to the Other World', *British Journal for the History of Science*, 1999, 32: 421–59.

Nye, D., *Electrifying America: Social Meanings of a New Technology* (Cambridge MA: MIT Press, 1990).

Olesko, K., *Physics as a Calling: Discipline and Practice in the Königsberg Seminar for Physics* (Ithaca NY: Cornell University Press, 1991).

Olson, R., *Scottish Philosophy and British Physics, 1750–1880: A Study in the Foundations of the Victorian Scientific Style* (Princeton NJ: Princeton University Press, 1975).

Oppenheim, J., *Shattered Nerves: Doctors, Patients and Depression in Victorian England* (Oxford: Oxford University Press, 1991).

Oppenheim, J., *The Other World: Spiritualism and Psychical Research in Britain, 1850–1914* (Cambridge: Cambridge University Press, 1985).

Owen, A., *The Darkened Room: Women, Power, and Spiritualism in Victorian England* (London: Virago, 1989).

Parsons, R. H., *The Early Days of the Power Station Industry* (Cambridge: Cambridge University Press, 1940).

Patrick, S., *A Friendly Debate between a Conformist and a Non-conformist* (London, 1669).

Pearson, K. (ed.), *The Life, Letters and Labours of Francis Galton*, three vols, (Cambridge: Cambridge University Press, 1914–30).

Pepper, J. H., *The True History of the Ghost; and all About Metempsychosis* (London, 1890).

Pera, M., *The Ambiguous Frog: The Galvani-Volta Controversy on Animal Electricity* (Princeton NJ: Princeton University Press, 1992).

Peterson, M. J., *The Medical Profession in mid-Victorian England* (Berkeley and Los Angeles CA: University of California Press, 1978).

Pinch, T. J., 'Towards an Analysis of Scientific Observation: The Externality and Evidential Significance of Observational Reports in Physics', *Social Studies of Science*, 1985, 15: 3–36.

Pocock, J. G. A., *Politics, Language and Time: Essays in Political Thought and History* (Chicago IL: University of Chicago Press, 1989).

Pocock, J. G. A., *The Machiavellian Moment: Florentine Political Thought and the Atlantic Republican Tradition* (Princeton NJ: Princeton University Press, 1975).

Pocock, J. G. A., *Virtue, Commerce, and History: Essays on Political Thought and History, Chiefly in the Eighteenth Century* (Cambridge: Cambridge University Press, 1985).

Podmore, F., *Modern Spiritualism: A History and Criticism*, two vols, (London, 1902).

Polanyi, M., *Personal Knowledge* (Chicago IL: University of Chicago Press, 1958).

Polanyi, M., *The Study of Man* (Chicago IL: University of Chicago Press, 1957).

Pollard, S., *The Genesis of Modern Management: A Study of the Industrial Revolution in Great Britain* (Cambridge: Cambridge University Press, 1965).

Porter, D., *Health, Civilization and the State* (London: Routledge, 1999).

Porter, R. and D. Porter, *In Sickness and in Health: The British Experience 1650– 1850* (London: Fourth Estate, 1988).

Porter, T. M., *The Rise of Statistical Thinking 1820–1900* (Princeton NJ: Princeton University Press, 1986).

Prescott, G. P., *History, Theory, and Practice of the Electric Telegraph* (Boston MA, 1860).

Prevost, J. –L. and F. Battelli, 'La Mort par les Courants Électriques', *Journal de Physiologie et de Pathologie Générale*, 1899, 3: 399–442.

Price, H., *Fifty Years of Psychical Research* (London: Longmans, Green, and Co., 1939).

Priestley, P., *Victorian Prison Lives: English Prison Biography 1830–1914* (London: Methuen, 1985).

Rabinbach, A., *The Human Motor: Energy, Fatigue and the Origins of Modernity* (Berkeley and Los Angeles CA: University of California Press, 1992).

Randall, A., *Before the Luddites: Custom, Community and Machinery in the English Woollen Industry, 1776–1809* (Cambridge: Cambridge University Press, 1991).

Randall, A., 'New Languages or Old? Labour, Capital and Discourse in the Industrial Revolution', *Social History*, 1990, 15: 195–216.

Randall, A., 'The Philosophy of Luddism: the Case of the West of England Woollen Workers, ca. 1790–1809', *Technology and Culture*, 1986, 27: 1–17.

Rather, L. J., 'The "Six Things Non-Natural": A Note on the Origins and Fate of a Doctrine and Phrase', *Clio Medica*, 1968, 3: 333–47.

Reingold, N. (ed.), *The Papers of Joseph Henry* vol. 1, (Washington DC: Smithsonian Institution Press, 1972).

'Report presented to the Class of the Exact Sciences of the Academy of Turin, 15th August 1802, in regard to the Galvanic Experiments made by C. Vassali-Eandi, Giulio, and Rossi, on the 10th and 14th of the same Month, on the Head and Trunk of three Men a short Time after their Decapitation', *Tilloch's Philosophical Magazine*, 1803, 15: 38–45.

Reynolds, E., *A Treatise of the Passions and Faculties of the Soule of Man* (London, 1640).

Richardson, B. W., 'On Research with the Large Induction Coil of the Royal Polytechnic Institution, with Special Reference to the Cause and Phenomena of Death by Lightning', *Medical Times and Gazette*, 1869, 38: 511–14; 595–9; 39: 183–6; 373–6.

Richardson, B. W., 'Researches on the Treatment of Suspended Animation', *British and Foreign Medico-Chirurgical Review*, 1863, 31: 478–505.

Richardson, R., *Death, Dissection and the Destitute* (Harmondsworth: Penguin Books, 1988).

Rider, R. E., 'Measure of Ideas, Rule of Language: Mathematics and Language in the 18th century', T. Frängsmyr, J. L. Heilbron, and R. E. Rider (eds), *The Quantifying Spirit in the Eighteenth Century* (Berkeley and Los Angeles CA: University of California Press, 1990).

Rockwell, A. D., *Rambling Recollections: An Autobiography* (New York NY: Paul B. Hooker, 1920).

Rodda, M., *Noise and Society* (Edinburgh: Oliver and Boyd, 1967).

Roget, P. M., 'Explanation of an Optical Deception in the Appearance of the Spokes of a Wheel seen through Vertical Apertures', *Philosophical Transactions of the Royal Society of London*, 1825, 115: 131–40.

Roll, E., *An Early Experiment in Industrial Organisation: Being a History of the Firm of Boulton and Watt, 1775–1805* (London: Frank Cass, 1968).

Rothermel, H., 'Images of the Sun: Warren De la Rue, George Biddell Airy and Celestial Photography', *British Journal for the History of Science*, 1993, 26: 137–69.

Roy, I. and D. Reinhart, 'Oxford and the Civil Wars', N. Tyacke (ed.), *The History of the University of Oxford*, vol. IV, (Oxford: Oxford University Press, 1997).

Rule, J., 'The Property of Skill in the Period of Manufacture', P. Joyce (ed.), *The Historical Meanings of Work* (Cambridge: Cambridge University Press, 1987).

Rules Proposed for the Government of Gaols, Houses of Correction, and Penitentiaries (London, 1820).

Rupke, N. (ed.), *Vivisection in Historical Perspective* (London: Routledge, 1990).

Russett, C. E., *Sexual Science: The Victorian Construction of Womanhood* (Cambridge MA: Harvard University Press 1989).

Ryley, J. B., *Physical and Nervous Exhaustion in Man. Its Etiology and Treatment by 'Electro-Kinetics'* (London, 1892).

Sabel, C. and J. Zeitlin, 'Historical Alternatives to Mass-production: Politics, Markets and Technology in Nineteenth-Century Industrialisation', *Past and Present*, 1985, 108:

Samuel, R., 'Workshop of the World: Steam Power and Hand Technology in mid-Victorian Britain', *History Workshop*, 1977, 3: 6–72.

Sankey, Capt. H. R. (late R.E.) and F. V. Andersen. 'Description of the Standard Volt- and Ampere-meter used at the Ferry Works, Thames Ditton', *Journal of the IEE*, 1891, 20: 516–90.

Sargent, E., *Planchette; or, the Despair of Science* (Boston MA, 1869).

Schaffer, S., 'Astronomers Mark Time: Discipline and the Personal Equation', *Science in Context*, 1988, 2: 115–45.

Schaffer, S., 'Babbage's Dancer and the Impresarios of Mechanism', F. Spufford and J. Uglow (eds), *Cultural Babbage: Technology, Time and Invention* (London: Faber and Faber, 1996).

Schaffer, S., 'Babbage's Intelligence: Calculating Engines and the Factory System', *Critical Inquiry*, 1994, 21: 203–27.

Schaffer, S., 'Deus et Machina: Human Nature and Eighteenth Century Automata', *La Lettre de la Maison Française*, 1997, 9: 30–58.

Schaffer, S., 'Enlightened Automata', W. Clark, J. Golinski and S. Schaffer (eds), *The Sciences in Enlightened Europe* (Chicago IL: University of Chicago Press, 1999).

Schaffer, S., 'Experimenters' Techniques, Dyer's Hands and the Electric Planetarium', *Isis*, 1997, 88: 456–83.

Schaffer, S., 'Godly Men and Mechanical Philosophers: Souls and Spirits in Restoration Natural Philosophy', *Science in Context*, 1987, 1: 55–86.

Schaffer, S., 'Glass works: Newton's Prisms and the Uses of Experiment', D. Gooding, T. Pinch and S. Schaffer (eds), *The Uses of Experiment: Studies in the Natural Sciences* (Cambridge: Cambridge University Press, 1989).

Schaffer, S., 'Late Victorian Metrology and its Instrumentation: A Manufactory of Ohms', R. Bud and S. Cozzens (eds), *Invisible Connections: Instruments, Institutions and Science* (Bellingham: SPIE Press, 1992).

Schaffer, S., 'Metrology, Metrication and Victorian Values', B. Lightman (ed.), *Victorian Science in Context* (Chicago IL: University of Chicago Press, 1997).

Schaffer, S., 'Natural Philosophy and Public Spectacle in the Eighteenth Century', *History of Science*, 1983, 21: 1–43.

Schaffer, S., 'Priestley and the Politics of Spirit', R. G. W. Anderson and C. Lawrence (eds), *Science, Medicine, and Dissent: Joseph Priestley (1733–1804)*, (London: Wellcome Trust/Science Museum, 1987).

Schaffer, S., 'Self-Evidence', *Critical Inquiry*, 1992, 18: 327–62.

Schivelbusch, W., *The Railway Journey: the Industrialization of Time and Space in the Nineteenth Century* (Berkeley and Los Angeles CA: University of California Press, 1986).

Schweber, S. S. (ed.), *Aspects of the Life and Thought of John Herschel* (New York NY: Arno, 1981).

Searle, G. R., *The Quest for National Efficiency: a Study of British Politics and Political Thought, 1899–1914* (London: Basil Blackwell, 1971).

Secord, A., 'Artisan Botany', N. Jardine, J. A. Secord and E.C. Spary (eds), *Cultures of Natural History* (Cambridge: Cambridge University Press, 1996).

Secord, A., 'Artisan Naturalists: Science as Popular Culture in Nineteenth-century England', unpublished PhD dissertation, University of London, forthcoming.

Secord, A., 'Science in the Pub: Artisan Botanists in early 19th-century Lancashire', *History of Science*, 1994, 32: 269–315.

Secord, J. A., 'Extraordinary Experiment: Electricity and the Creation of Life in Victorian England', D. Gooding, T. Pinch and S. Schaffer (eds), *The Uses of Experiment* (Cambridge: Cambridge University Press, 1989).

Semple, J. E., 'Jeremy Bentham's Panopticon Prison', unpublished PhD dissertation, London School of Economics and Political Science, 1990.

Senior, J., 'Rationalizing Electrotherapy in Neurology, 1860–1920', unpublished DPhil dissertation, Oxford University, 1994.

Senior, N. W., *An Outline of the Science of Political Economy* (London, 1836).

Shapin, S., 'Descartes the Doctor: Rationalism and its Therapies', *British Journal for the History of Science*, 2000, 33: 131–54.

Shapin, S. and S. Schaffer, *Leviathan and the Air Pump: Hobbes, Boyle, and the Experimental Life* (Princeton NJ: Princeton University Press, 1985).

Sharp, L., 'Walter Charleton's early Life, 1620–1659, and Relationship to Natural Philosophy in mid–17th Century England' *Annals of Science*, 1973, 30: 311–40.

[Sharples, E.], 'An Inquiry how far the Human Character is Formed by Education or External Circumstances', *The Isis* 1832, 1: 81–5.

[Sharples, E.], 'Fifth Discourse on the Bible', *The Isis*, 1932, 1: 241–7.

Shayt, D., 'Stairway to Redemption: America's Encounter with the British Tread Mill', *Technology and Culture*, 1989, 30: 908–38.

Shelley, M., *Frankenstein, or, the Modern Prometheus*, with an introduction by M. Butler (London: Pickering and Chatto, 1993).

Shortt, S. E. D., 'Physicians and Psychics: The Anglo-American Medical Response to Spiritualism, 1870–1890', *Journal of the History of Medicine*, 1984, 39: 339–55.

Showalter, E., *The Female Malady: Women, Madness and English Culture, 1830–1980* (London: Virago, 1987).

Sibum, O., 'Reworking the Mechanical Value of Heat: Instruments of Precision and Gestures of Accuracy in early Victorian England', *Studies in History and Philosophy of Science*, 1995, 26: 73–106.

Sleigh, C., 'Life, Death and Galvanism', *Studies in the History and Philosophy of the Biological and Biomedical Sciences*, 1998, 29: 219–48.

Smee, A., *Elements of Electro-Biology* (London, 1849).

Smith, C., *The Science of Energy: A Cultural History of Energy Physics in Victorian Britain* (London: Athlone Press, 1998).

Smith, C. and M. N. Wise, *Energy and Empire: A Biographical study of Lord Kelvin* (Cambridge: Cambridge University Press, 1989).

Smith, R., 'The Background of Physiological Psychology in Natural Philosophy', *History of Science*, 1973, 11: 75–123.

Snelders, H. A. M., 'Romanticism and Naturphilosophie and the Inorganic Natural Sciences 1797–1840: An Introductory Survey', *Studies in Romanticism*, 1970, 9: 193–215.

Soojung-Kim Pang, A., '"The Stars should henceforth Register Themselves": Astrophotography at the early Lick Observatory', *British Journal for the History of Science*, 1997, 30: 177–202.

Spencer, H., *The Works of Herbert Spencer* (Osnabruck, 1966).

Spurr, J., *The Restoration Church of England, 1646–1689* (New Haven CT: Yale University Press, 1991).

Standage, T., *The Victorian Internet* (London: Wiedenfeld & Nicolson, 1998).

Staubermann, K., 'Tying the Knot: Skill, Judgement, and Authority in the 1870s Leipzig Spiritistic Experiments', *British Journal for the History of Science*, 2001, 34: 67–80.

Stewart, D., 'Some Account of a Boy born Blind and Deaf, Collected from Authentic Sources of Information; with a few Remarks and Comments', *Transactions of the Royal Society of Edinburgh*, 1814, 7: 1–78.

Stewart, L., 'A Meaning for Machines: Modernity, Utility, and the Eighteenth-Century British Public', *The Journal of Modern History*, 1998, 70: 259–94.

Stewart, L., *The Rise of Public Science: Rhetoric, Technology, and Natural Philosophy in Newtonian Britain, 1660–1750* (Cambridge: Cambridge University Press, 1992).

Stone, W. H. and W. J. Kilner, 'On Measurement in the Medical Application of Electricity', *Journal of the Society of Telegraph Engineers and of Electricians*, 1882, 11: 107–28.

Strange, P., 'Two Electrical Periodicals: The Electrician and The Electrical Review 1880–1890', *IEE Proceedings*, 1985, 132A: 574–81.

Sturgeon, W., 'A General Outline of the Various Theories which have been Advanced for the Explanation of Terrestrial Magnetism', *Annals of Electricity*, 1836–37, 1: 117–23.

Swade, D., *The Cogwheel Brain: Charles Babbage and the Quest to Build the First Computer* (London: Little, Brown, 2000).

Swijtink, Z. G., 'The Objectification of Observation: Measurement and Statistical Methods in the Nineteenth Century', L. Krüger (ed.) *The Probabilistic Revolution*, two vols, (Cambridge MA: MIT Press, 1987).

Swinburne, J., 'Electrical Measuring Instruments', *Minutes of Proceedings of the Institution of Civil Engineers*, 1892, 110: 1–32.

Tait, P. G., *Lectures on Some Recent Advances in Physical Science; with a Special Lecture on Force*, 2nd edn (London, 1876).

Tann, J. (ed.), *The Selected Papers of Boulton and Watt* (London: Diploma, 1981).

Taylor, W. C., *Factories and the Factory System* (London, 1844).

Temkin, O., 'Basic Science, Medicine and the Romantic Era', *The Double Face of Janus and other Essays in the History of Medicine* (Baltimore MD: Johns Hopkins University Press, 1977).

Thackray, A., *John Dalton: Critical Assessments of His Life and Science* (Cambridge MA: Harvard University Press, 1972).

'The New Frankenstein', *Fraser's Magazine*, 1837, 17: 21–30.

Thompson, E., 'Dead Rooms and Live Wires: Harvard, Hollywood and the Deconstruction of Architectural Acoustics, 1900–1930', *Isis*, 1997, 88: 597–626.

Thompson, E. P., 'Time, Work-discipline and Industrial Capitalism', *Customs in Common* (Harmondsworth: Penguin Books, 1993).

Thompson, S. P., *Life of Lord Kelvin* (London, 1910).

Thurschwell, P., *Literature, Technology and Magical Thinking, 1880–1920* (Cambridge: Cambridge University Press, 2001).

Tibbits, H., *A Handbook of Medical and Surgical Electricity* (London, 1877).

Trumpler, M., 'From Tabletops to Triangles: Increasing Abstraction in the Depiction of Experiments in Animal Electricity from Galvani to Ritter', M. Bresadola and G. Pancaldi (eds), *Luigi Galvani International Workshop: Proceedings* (Bologna: Università di Bologna, 1999).

Tucker, J., 'Photography as Witness, Detective, and Impostor', B. Lightman (ed.), *Victorian Science in Context* (Chicago IL: University of Chicago Press, 1997).

Tyndall, J., *Faraday as a Discoverer* (London, 1868)

Ure, A., 'An Account of some Experiments made on the Body of a Criminal immediately after Execution, with Physiological and Practical Observations', *Quarterly Journal of Science*, 1819, 6: 283–94.

Ure, A., *The Philosophy of Manufactures* (London, 1835).

Uyeama, T., 'Capital, Profession and Medical Technology: The Electro-therapeutic Institutes and the Royal College of Physicians, 1888–1922', *Medical History*, 1997, 41: 150–81.

Varley, C., 'Evidence of Mr. Varley', *Report on Spiritualism of the Committee of the London Dialectical Society* (London: J. Burns, 1873).

Verne, J., *Around the World in Eighty Days* (Harmondsworth: Penguin Books, 1996), first published 1873.

Walker, W. C., 'Animal Electricity before Galvani', *Annals of Electricity*, 1937, 2: 84–113.

Warwick, A., 'Exercising the Student Body: Mathematics and Athleticism in Victorian Cambridge', C. Lawrence and S. Shapin (eds), *Science Incarnate: Historical Embodiments of Natural Knowledge* (Chicago IL: University of Chicago Press, 1998).

Warwick, K., *In the Mind of the Machine* (London: Arrow Books, 1998).

Wetzels, W., 'Johann Wilhelm Ritter: Romantic Physics in Germany', A. Cunningham and N. Jardine (eds), *Romanticism and the Sciences* (Cambridge: Cambridge University Press, 1990).

Whewell, W., *The Philosophy of the Inductive Sciences; Founded upon their History*, 2nd edn, two vols, (London, 1847).

Whytt, R., *Observations on the Nature, Causes and Cure of Those Diseases Which are Commonly Called Nervous, Hyperchondriac or Hysteric; to which are Prefixed some Remarks on the Sympathy of Nerves* (Edinburgh, 1764).

Wiener, J., *Radicalism and Freethought in Nineteenth-Century Britain: The Life of Richard Carlile* (Westport CT: Greenwood Press, 1983).

Wilks, S. and G. T. Bettany, *A Biographical Dictionary of Guy's Hospital* (London, 1892).

Williams, J. P., 'The Making of Victorian Psychical Research: An Intellectual Élite's Approach to the Spirit World', unpublished PhD dissertation, University of Cambridge, 1984.

Williams, L. P., (ed.), *The Selected Correspondence of Michael Faraday*, two vols, (Cambridge: Cambridge University Press, 1971).

Williams, R. B., *Accounting for Steam and Cotton: Two Eighteenth Century Case Studies* (New York NY: Garland Press, 1997).

Willis, T., *De Anima Brutorum Quae Hominis Vitalis ac Sensitiva est exercitationes duae* (Oxford, 1672).

Willis, T., *De Cerebri Anatome cui accessit Nervorum descriptio et usus* (London, 1664).

Willis, T., *Diatribae duae Medico–philosophicae* (London, 1659).

Willis, T., *Pathologiae Cerebri et Nervosi Generis Specimen* (London, 1668).

Willis, T., *Pharmaceutice Rationalis, pars secunda* (Oxford, 1675).

Wilson, D. B., *Kelvin and Stokes: A Comparative Study in Victorian Physics* (Bristol: Adam Hilger, 1987).

Wilson, G., *Electricity and the Electric Telegraph* (London, 1855).

Winter, A., *Mesmerized: Powers of Mind in Victorian Britain* (Chicago IL: University of Chicago Press, 1998).

Wise, M. N., 'Mediating Machines', *Science in Context*, 1988, 2: 79–92.

Wise, M. N. (ed.), *The Values of Precision* (Princeton NJ: Princeton University Press, 1995).

Wise, M. N. with C. Smith, 'Work and Waste: Political Economy and Natural Philosophy in Nineteenth Century Britain', *History of Science*, 1989, 27: 263–301; 391–449; 1990, 28: 221–61.

Wolfe, N. B., *Startling Facts in Modern Spiritualism*, 2nd edn (Chicago IL, 1875).

Worden, B., 'Cromwellian Oxford', N. Tyacke (ed.), The History of the University of Oxford, vol. IV, (Oxford: Oxford University Press, 1997).

Wright, T., *The Passions of the Minde in Generall* (London, 1630).

Wynne, B., 'Physics and Psychics: Science, Symbolic Action and Social Control in Late-Victorian England', B. Barnes and S. Shapin (eds), *Natural Order: Historical Studies of Scientific Culture* (London: Sage, 1979).

[Wynter, A.], 'The Electric Telegraph', *Quarterly Review*, 1854, 59: 118–64.

Yeo, R. R., 'Scientific Method and the Rhetoric of Science in Britain, 1830–1917', J. A. Schuster and R. R. Yeo (eds), *The Politics and Rhetoric of Scientific Method: Historical Studies* (Dordrecht: Reidel, 1986).

Index

Index

Index

Index

Smith, Willoughby, 177–179
Society for the Importance of Prison Discipline, 53
Society for Psychical Research, 129, 137, 139, 148, 154
soul, the, 5, 15–18, 24, 33
specialization, 40
Spencer, Herbert, 72
spirits, 125–128, 131, 137–138, 155
  animal spirits, 19–25, 32
spiritualism, 125–133 passim, 135, 137–143, 147–151, 154–155
standardization, 5, 56–57, 95, 102, 108, 115, 155, 206–208
  and commodification, 5, 108
Star Trek, 1
steam boilers, 68, 70
steam engines, 69–73 passim
Steavenson, William Edward, 105
Stewart, Balfour, 143, 145
Stewart, Larry, 39–40, 46
Stokes, George Gabriel, 106, 143, 145
Stone, William Henry, 105, 107
Strutt, William, 43
Sturgeon, William, 102
Swinburne, James, 179, 180, 182–189

Tatum, Edward, 111
telegraph, electric, 77, 79–80, 84, 102, 125
telegraph, optical, 77–80
telegraph networks, 5, 68, 72, 79, 83, 106, 176–183 passim, 188
Tennyson, Alfred Lord, 166, 172–173
Terminator, 1
theory ladenness, 168
thermodynamics, 68, 70
Thomson, William, 67, 72, 185
Tibbits, Herbert, 105

treadmill, prison, 6, 39, 50–54
  gyrometer, 52–53
Trevithick, Richard, 70
Trotter, Alexander, 186–188
Tyndall, John, 72, 140, 207

Ure, Andrew, 44, 69, 98–100, 102, 114

Varley, Cromwell, 126, 139, 147–149, 151, 154
Varley, Frederick, 151
Vassali-Eandi, Andrea, 95–96
Vaucanson, Jacques de, 94
Volckman, William, 130–131
Volta, Alessandro, 94–95

Wallace, Alfred Russel, 139
Watt, James, 42–43, 56, 71
Watteville, Armand de, 105, 107
Wedgwood, Josiah, 55–56
Weldon, Walter, 140
Wells, W. H., 202
Wheatstone, Charles, 77
Whewell, William, 74, 82
Whytt, Robert, 81
Williams, Perry, 154
Williams, Peter, 187
Williams, Robert B., 55
Williams, Thomas, 103
Willis, Thomas, 17–34 passim
  biographical details, 22–23
Winter, Alison, 137
working practices, 40–41, 56, 58
Wright, Thomas, 17
Wynter, Andrew, 106

Yeo, Richard, 83

Ziegler, Tillie, 109